AF559643

RESOURCES OF HEALTH CARE SYSTEM AND HOSPITAL ADMINISTRATION

HUMAN, FINANCE AND MATERIAL

RESOURCES OF HEALTH CARE SYSTEM AND HOSPITAL ADMINISTRATION

HUMAN, FINANCE AND MATERIAL

HEALTH CARE SYSTEM AND HOSPITAL ADMINISTRATION—2

DR. S.L. GOEL

Professor of Public Administration (Retd.),
Panjab University, Chandigarh
Editor, Indian Journal of Public Administration, IIPA, New Delhi
Former Member, UGC, Former Member Distance Education Council
Former Member All India Board of Management, AICTE
Member, Executive Council, IIPA, New Delhi.
Former Vice-President, IIPA, New Delhi.
Emeritus Fellow, University Grants Commission
Former Director, State Bank of India (Local Board) Chandigarh
Former Director, National Horticulture Board, Ministry of Agriculture,
Government of India, New Delhi.

DEEP & DEEP PUBLICATIONS PVT. LTD.

F-159, Rajouri Garden, New Delhi-110027

Resources of Health Care System and Hospital Administration
Human, Finance and Material
(Health Care System and Hospital Administration—2)

ISBN 978-81-8450-192-6

Typeset by S.S. COMPOSERS
3190, Mohindra Park, Shakur Basti, Delhi-110034.

Printed in India at MAYUR ENTERPRISES
WZ Plot No. 3, Gujjar Market, Tihar Village, New Delhi-110018.

Published by DEEP & DEEP PUBLICATIONS PVT. LTD.
F-159, Rajouri Garden, New Delhi-110027.
Phones: 25435369, 25440916
E-mail: ddpbooks@yahoo.co.in • ddpubs@gmail.com
Showroom:
2/13, Ansari Road, Daryaganj, New Delhi-110002 • Telefax: 23245122

Contents

Part C

MATERIAL

Preface

The United Nations Commission on Human Rights, which met in Geneva in December 1947, incorporated in the Charter of Human Rights the following article:

> "Everyone, without distinction as to economic and social conditions, has the right to the preservation of his health through the highest standards of food, clothing, housing and medical care which the resources of the State and community can provide. The responsibility of the State and community for the health and safety of its people can be fulfiled only by provision of adequate health and social measures."

Health Administration faces a great challenge and has an important role to play in improving the health status of the population. It must be a positive force providing good health services to all without discrimination. By its own work it must set an example. Its services have to be so devised that they may be within the reach of all alike. Improvement in health policy formulations and implementation of health programmes arising therefrom are crucial to our development and progress. We have to be conscious of the need to make health administration more efficient and socially responsive. We have to accept the challenges of those problems and overcome them. Health administration that does not respond to the demands of rapidly changing social and economic conditions will one day cease to be effective. Indeed, it has not only to respond but to anticipate problems in order to be effective. I have no doubt in my mind that the health administrators have the capacity to undertake such tasks. What is needed is determination and commitment. It can raise the level of consciousness to help develop health administrators who are sensitive to their environment, committed to socio-economic justice and trained to severe professionalism in administration.

"There is a need to vitalise health management. World Health Report 2000 has also endorsed this. Unfortunately, health system can also misuse their power and squander their potential. Poorly structured, badly led, inefficiently organised and inadequately funded health systems can do more harm than good. This report finds that many countries are fairing far short of their potential, and most making inadequate efforts in terms of responsiveness and fairness of financial contribution. There are serious shortcomings in the performance of one or more functions in virtually all countries.

These failings result in very large number of preventable deaths and disabilities in each country; in unnecessary suffering, in injustice and denial of basic rights of individual. The impact is most severe on the poor, who are driven deeper into poverty. The ultimate responsibility for the overall performance of a country's health system lies with government, which in turn should involve all sectors of society in its stewardship. The careful and responsible management of the well-being of the population is the very essence of good government. For every country it means establishing the best and fairest health system possible with available resources. The health of the people is always a national priority: government responsibility for it is continuous and permanent.

Ministry of health must therefore take on a large part of the stewardship of health systems, The World Health Report, 2000. "Health Systems, Improving Performance by WHO", has also felt the need of good management system.

Governments should be the "stewards" of their national resources, maintaining and improving them for the benefit of their populations. In health, this means being ultimately responsible for the careful management of their citizens' well-being. Stewardship in health is the very essence of good government. For every country it means establishing the best and fairest health system possible. The health of the people must always be a national priority: government's responsibility for it is continuous and permanent. Ministry of health must take on a large part of the stewardship of health systems.

A sound health manpower policy is the main requirement for the development of any functionally effective health care system. Most of the countries in the developing world have never formulated or implemented such a policy.

"The most crucial factor for the improvement of the world health situation.... Is undoubtedly the development of health manpower that is properly attuned to the health problems of the people and suitably trained to respond to health programme and service need."

We must find the method to achieve greater productivity, efficiency and cost-effectiveness in health manpower utilization. No society, especially the developing, can long justify investing years of education and training in individuals who later on perform rudimentary duties that could be achieved satisfactorily by people trained in half that time. The critical decisions in health manpower planning concern the kinds of personnel required, the type and adequacy of education and training and financial resources necessary to produce them, their relationship to each other in the health team, and where and how they would practice.

Eleventh Five Year Plan, 2007-2012, Vol. II observes that for development of Human Resources for Health, Plan will do as given below:

"Given the present scarcity of human resources, the next decade will posit newer opportunities and challenges for medical and health education. The country has to train an adequate number of health professionals with appropriate knowledge, skill, and attitude to meet the future health care needs of the people and the increasing disease burden. Additionally, there is the opportunity for India to become an important destination for health care services. Given the rising demand and growing need for expanding health services, systematic studies need to be launched for estimating requirements. In the Eleventh Five Year Plan, efforts will be made to develop an effective human resource MIS by involving concerned Ministries, Professional Councils, Technical Councils, UGC, Central and State Universities, Public Health Institutions, and knowledgeable individuals from Civil Society."

The developing countries give low priority in the allocation of resources to the health care of their people. The health expenditure to the total expenditure has been very low in India and South-East Asian countries, i.e. 1.6 per cent, in Indonesia, 2.1 per cent in India, 3.8 per cent while in Bangladesh. Mongolia has been spending 10 per cent for the health care of its people. There is a need to raise the health allocations to improve the quality of life. Dr. White has rightly said that, "Nothing can be done without the expenditure of money... Available financial resources set a maximum limit on administrative activity as a whole and on each of its separate parts."

A sound state of finance is of paramount importance to the political health of a nation. The soundness of public finance depends both upon the right policy and good organisation, but a great deal upon the latter. The scarcity of resources affect all aspects of the health delivery system. There is a need to step up the health allocations to the minimum of 10 per cent of the total budget. Secondly, there is mal-distribution of health resources. Most of the health budgets (about 80 per cent) are being spent only on a few people (20 per cent). This deprives the people living in rural areas and urban slums. The following are the problems:

(a) Disproportionate concentration of expenditure on health services in urban areas compared with expenditure in rural areas.
(b) Heavy concentration of expenditure on secondary and tertiary care services compared with expenditure on primary care services.
(c) Heavy concentration of expenditure on curatives services compared with expenditure on preventive services.

We can correct this imbalance through the innovative health policies developed in tune with the needs of the country rather than based on any foreign model.

The third serious problem in this area is of inefficient use of expenditure and non-utilisation of actual and potential resources judiciously and properly. In the developing countries, huge resources are being wasted because of the selection of inappropriate technology, inefficient management, and unsatisfactory control mechanisms.

"It is necessary that public revenue should be raised in an equitable manner and spent economically so that the tax-payers may get full value for his money."

The objects of financial control are to ensure: (i) that no wastage of resources occurs; (ii) that public money is not misused; and (iii) that intended results are obtained with the money spent. We can exploit the potential resources through careful planning and management. The traditional system of medicine can be of immense value to provide health care at a very low cost provided this is properly tapped by the designers of health services. It was reported in a UN Survey (1976) that, these adverse trends are despite the higher percentage of government expenditure being devoted to Health, compared with 1960s and the fact that ratio of population to the numbers of beds and of medical personnel have moved favourably. Essentially, the continuance of poor health standards is indicative of a less-than-optimal use of resources available.

Some aspects of this are the emphasis on curative, as opposed to preventive techniques as existing in the hospital systems and the inadequate development of indigenous medicine systems.

Materials are either not available or remain out of order. Material costs money, so we must keep our material properly. On the basis of our discussion and analysis the following suggestions are given in brief to revitalise the health care delivery system to meet the challenges and fulfil the basic health needs of the people:

(i) Need of will and determination on the part of the political elite to accept innovative measures to meet the population's health needs and priorities.

(ii) Identification and implementation of a clear and comprehensive, New National Health Policy.

(iii) Need of decentralised planning involving the participation of the target communities.

(iv) Mobilisation of existing and untapped resources—community, government (local and national), bilateral, multilateral and non-governmental to provide adequate health care for all.

(v) Establishment of appropriate administrative structures with necessary competence and capability and devolution of authority and responsibility for the implementation and development of the programme in a team spirit and a well-designed information system to help in planning, implementation and evaluation.

(vi) Manpower development for national health needs.

(vii) Strengthening existing rural establishment and graded extension of national administrative structures to provide adequate and accessible referral, supervisory, logistical and other supporting services to ensure the judicious use of health services.

(viii) More allocation of financial resources based on the principles of equitable distribution and maximum utility.

(ix) Encouraging integration and coordination.

(x) Reorientation of Medical Education to suit the needs of the community.

(xi) Designing health technology to suit the environment and making the best use of existing technology of traditional system of medicine.

(xii) Improving research and development capacity to solve health problems.

(xiii) Devising measures to promote the use of simple, standardised equipment and drugs, placing reliance on available local resources whenever possible to foster self-reliance.

In this volume "Health Care System and Hospital Administration: Resources: Human, Finance and Material", we have discussed the role of human, finance and materials in the promotion and development of health services. Part-A concentrates on the role of health and medical personnel in health development. It has been rightly said that human rather than capital is the key to development, This section has been divided into 7 chapters. Chapters 1 and 2 examine the role of health personnel including Nursing Personnel. Chapters 3 and 4 discuss the methods, importance and problems of Manpower Planning which include putting the right person at the right place, keeping them upto date through training as well as ensure induction in their service, for new personnel, we have discussed the process of induction to inject the newcomers in the team already existing. Chapter 5 discusses the methods of performance appraisal to know the strengths and weak points of health and medical personnel and take remedial action. Chapter 6 examines the role of career development and career planning through which both individual and health organization can be benefited. Chapter 7 examines the professional standards which are the live wire for health services. They are considered as second God which should be maintained by loyalty, integrity and dedication of health and medical personnel.

Part-B Finances examine the raising of financial resources allocation by the Union and State governments, planning commission, international agencies especially World Health Organisation and World Bank, user charges, health insurance, etc. However, the resources available to health are less as compared to the need. People have to spend a lot out of pocket expenses which make them to sell their houses, land, etc. Chapter 8 examines the allocation of finances by union and state governments as well as planning commission. The recent experiment of user charges has also been examined. Chapters 9 and 10 discuss the role of social and private insurance which are limited and have started picking up. These are prevalent in developed countries. Chapter 11 deals with a special scheme of Insurance created through Employees State Insurance Corporation under the Parliament Act of 1948. Last Chapter 12 discusses the methods of Performance and Zero-base Budgeting, Human Resource Accounting and Audit to optimize resources.

Part-C having 4 chapters examine the methods to make best use of materials, drugs, equipment and records. Chapter 13 examines materials management. Chapter 14 deals with Drugs Management. Drugs are essential for promoting good health. We have discussed the methods of storing and making right use of drugs. Chapter 15 discusses the managing of equipment. We generally find the equipment in Government hospitals not functioning properly and remain mostly out of order. Chapter 16 examines records management which is essential for maintaining the transactions of all sorts.

Thus, this volume examines critically the three most important inputs—Human, Financial and Material to promote Quality health care. The ultimate aim of resource management is to promote sustainable development and healthy environments. The concept of sustainable development encompasses economic, ecological and social parameters. The economic approach focuses on generating maximum income/economic growth while maintaining the stock of assets or capital. The ecological view stresses the stability of biological and physical systems and their protection and management for posterity. The social concept is people-oriented and seeks to maintain the stability of social and cultural systems leading to human capital formation, correspondingly, sustainable development has economic growth, human development and resource management as its central goals.

The World Summit on Sustainable Development held in Johannesburg in 2002, reaffirmed the importance of Investment in people as the key to sustainable development and highlighted the central place of health within that agenda. At this summit, improving people's health was accepted not just as an outcome of sustainable development but as a powerful means through which it can be achieved. The major outcomes of the World Summit were a plan of implementation and a political declaration. The plan of implementation includes new agreements as well as a reaffirmation of past commitments, many of which have still to be acted on by governments. To provide a focus for the World Summit, the United Nations Secretary-General proposed that delegates should concentrate on five sectoral issues: water, energy, health, agriculture and biodiversity. The health agenda, as it emerged from the negotiations, addresses a variety of issues that intersect health, environment and development. These can be categorized into two key areas: health care and disease control and environmental health and lifestyle issues. All these can be taken care of to a great extent through Good Governance of health.

What is needed is to lay emphasis on emerging and thrust areas to keep the medical science knowledge and delivery of health services as per the needs of the people. It is hoped that this book on "Health Care System and Hospital Administration—Resources: Human, Finance and Material" would make a modest contribution to the knowledge and existing literature on this expanding field. Besides, this would help the academicians, national health officials, public health administrators, medical research workers and the policy-makers and planners in the proper understanding of health care delivery system. I will consider my labour well rewarded if the findings of the study are translated to provide decent health care to the millions of people living in rural areas, urban slums and tribal areas. Comments and suggestions from the readers would always be welcome.

Chandigarh S.L. GOEL

Part A

HUMAN

Human Resource for Health and Medical Services Delivery System

INTRODUCTION

Health services require large members of well-trained qualified professionals and workers, with a variety of skills and appropriate knowledge, and attitude to improve the health of the people, and to reduce suffering due to ill-health. It is necessary to have formal and informal educational centres to train persons in adequate numbers and of the requisite quality.

When one tries to analyse the current value system among the health and medical personnel one notices that most of our cultural values are gradually degenerating. Our character has been devalued faster than our rupees. The worse that has happened is that we have started rationalizing and justifying our degraded value system on one or the other pretext. Therefore, there is a indispensable and urgent need for introspection to revive our value system to old glory so that medical personnel can provide decent health care.

Among the three components required for developmental tasks—men, money and material (M3)—it is more the men (or the human elements) than any other factor which determines the quantity and quality of the performance and output. After all, even the contribution of money and material to performance depends substantially upon their manipulation by the men in an organization. Walter R. Sharp has aptly remarked, "Good administration is a composite of effective organization, adequate material facilities and qualified personnel—Even poorly devised machinery may be made to work if it is manned with well trained, intelligent, imaginative and devoted staff. On the other hand, the best planned organization may produce unsatisfactory results if it is operated by medicre or disgruntled people."[1]

CHART 1.1

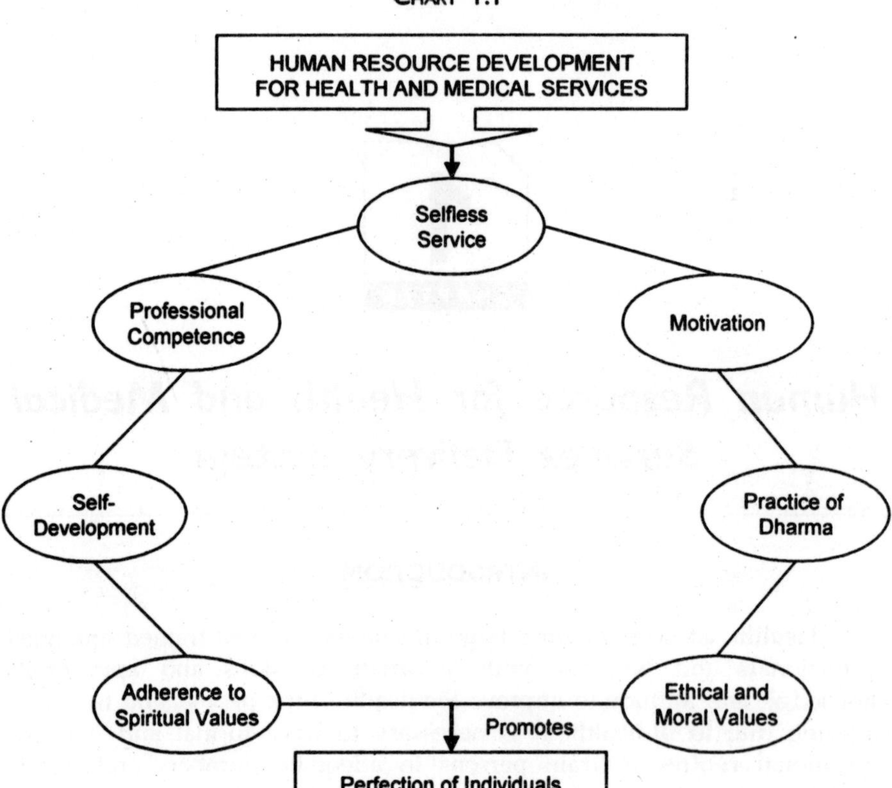

The biggest challenge to the health-care education institution is not just technical, managerial or financial development, but quality human resources development, which includes:

1. formation of young health professionals and supportive staff who are responsive to social, technical, scientific and management abilities to work effectively in a comprehensive health system;
2. development of a faculty team, consisting of not just good teachers but learners-oriented facilitators an educational process, who are also good role models with social vision,

commitment to ethical norms and values; and inspirers of people and community-oriented vocations through precept and example; and

3. development of a supportive team of staff who will complement the faculty in the educational institutions, laboratories, out-patients, wards and other specialized clinics, field practice areas and community health centres with needed skills and motivation.[2]

Human excellence depends upon the will power of human beings which is basic to excellent personality development. Will is the motive power, driving force and takes human beings at a higher plane. Will power strengthens spirituality and character. Human excellence, to become mature needs time and thus patience is required for maturing. Impatience only wastes our vital energy and impairs our will power.

The modern physician must also be a soul, which strives to attain a moral ideal and to establish equanimity with fellow souls. He should have intense urge to search for a light in the ignorance and the darkness of this world. While treating patients our action must blend with their pysiological processes. We should learn to respect their personal rhythm, unique composition and socio-economic individuality. Indeed individuality is fundamental in man. It stamps its mark on the whole of body and consciousness. A blend of mental, structural and humoral individualistic gives us our uniqueness."[3]

Steven Hla Myint, Dean of Medicine, University of Surrey, UK Scientific Advisor, European Centre for Disease Control delivered the VIIth Convocation of Sri S.A. Khan Ramachandra Medical College and Research Institute (Deemed University), Porur, Chennai on 23rd February 2006, he said, "A 21st century health care practitioner requires not only the technical skills of diagnosis and treatment but also relational skills of communication, team-working, developing themselves and others and general management. They will also need to be equipped to be flexible, adaptable and ready to encompass a climate of more frequent change." (Excerpts).

From the top to the bottom, from the centre to the periphery and in-between, it is the men that make the machinery of administration work. Bacon, philosopher and administrator, has rightly said, "It is vain for princes to take counsel concerning matters if they take no counsel likewise concerning persons, for all matters are as dead images; and the life of the execution of the affairs lies in the good choice of person." Therefore, the first and foremost task is to pay attention to the administration of personnel, if we expect the effective performance of such organisations.

Personnel Administration is becoming complex in modern times. While it is often possible to see the organisations of a simple machine either in the form of plans or as an actual object, an administrative organisation is essentially invisible, even assembling the entire staff in a single room would reveal little about the patterns of their relationships over time which is the essence of organisation.

Today, there is great alienation between the goals of the health organisations and the personnel working in them resulting in inefficiency, tensions, conflicts and low morale. Personnel in any organisation have abundant potential, energy and capacity. Why, then, is the management ineffective in utilising this energy? Since the 1960s many Committees and Commissions appointed at the Union and State levels either to advise exclusively on Personnel Administration in totality or segments of Personnel Administration have mentioned that the Personnel System needs overhauling to cope with the existing and changing functions of the Government. Such thinking is visible not only in the developing countries but also in the developed countries. Most of the thought revolves round the need of the revision of the basic concepts of personnel policy, modernisation of administrative practices, reform of recruitment methods, modification of the structure and emoluments of the staff, greater delegation of authority and responsibility in selected areas of Personnel Management from the office of Personnel to other departments and offices and structural changes in that office. There is also a lack of clearly defined administrative norms, which need examination, review and analysis. There has been a large number of such Commissions of inquiry into public services in both developed and developing countries.

Now let us define personnel administration. Personnel administration is that branch of Public Administration which can help an organization in the management of personnel resources with the use of well thought out principles, practices and rationalised techniques in selecting, retaining, and developing personnel for the fulfilment of organizational objectives systematically and scientifically. It is the art and science of planning, organizing, implementing and evaluating the personnel resources in any organisation to ensure their best use for the achievement of the objective, goals and targets of an organisation.

As shown in the Chart 1.1, Personnel Administration is the art and science of policy-making, planning, decision-making, organising, directing, controlling and motivating human resources for securing, maintaining, developing, integrating, involving and compensating as well as enriching human environment for the blooming of human skills and capacities in an organisation, to secure organisational and social objectives as well as employees' satisfaction. Under a good personnel system, the personnel in an organisation would direct action towards a common goal in a cooperative and coordinated fashion.

Personnel Administration is systematized, specialised knowledge and techniques which can help the organisations in administering their personnel for optimum performance. It is becoming complex day-by-day. Until and unless, we understand all the implications of such an administration, we may not be able to reap the potential benefits of the personnel engaged in an organisation. A large number of training Institutes have sprung up in all the countries at all levels to impart the raining in the art of personnel administration. All the organizations have set-up personnel departments to administer and manage their personnel efficiency. Thus, personnel administration is a definite art which can be learnt und practiced to produce pre-designed output. It is an art that can help to direct and guide the efforts of those involved in the Implementation of policies of an organisation efficiently and systematically.

SIGNIFICANCE

The quality of the health institutions run by Government would be dependent to a great extent upon the quality of the health personnel engaged in their operation. Personnel move the machinery. To quote Mrs. Indira Gandhi: "If Government has to do more for the people, its employees must play a more dynamic and more creative role as the instrument for implementing government policies and prorammes."[4] The progress of development would also depend upon the personnel in an organisation.

The health Professionals are a product of medical education. The primary objective of medical education is to support the health development of the nation; it should be, Community-oriented, unfortunately the medical education system till date has been hospital-based, specialization-oriented and dependent on sophisticated investigatory procedures. The curriculum is over crowded with factual information and this inhibits a student from developing creative and critical thinking to solve problems. The Edinburgh Declaration (1988) States, 'the aim of medical education is to produce health professionals who will promote the health of all people'. Further, it states that scientific research continues to bring rich rewards, but man needs more than science alone, and it is the health needs of the human race as a whole and of the whole person that medical education must affirm. The declaration also emphasizes in shifting the training from passive to active learning. The existing medical education system does not follow the spirit of Edingurgh declaration. Health professional education is presently centered on tertiary care units, whereas it should necessarily be based on a priority of primary, secondary and tertiary care with the largest component being primary healthcare. Our medical colleges are sequestrated from the community and the present system of medical education is not need-based.

Physicians worldwide are trained in the academic niche of tertiary hospitals, where day-to-day discussions revolve around the obscure mechanisms of rare diseases, state-of-the-art diagnostic tools and sophisticated, high-tech medical interventions. Despite strong indications that the requirement is more of training in primary care and more investment in the critical public health issues, precious time is spent on investigation of diseases, which afflict a tiny proportion of the humanity. Graduates from the present medical colleges feel that all this learning is wasted in a primary or secondary care hospital, which in fact is the backbone of our healthcare delivery system. Healthcare providers are not mere professionals with technical knowledge to solve health problems but are accountable to the society. Medical education and Healthcare delivery should be linked. At present these are two systems going parallel, often not complimenting each other. We have a product for the purpose he is needed. Medical education should be linked to all levels of healthcare—primary, secondary and tertiary.[5]

Personnel constitute an Integral part of the organisation. It is with their requisite skills, aptitude, integrity and organising capacity that they can build the image of their organisations as effective institutions in the nation-building process. Dr. Rajendra Prasad said at the concluding session of the Constituent Assembly:

Whatever the Constitution mayor may not provide. the welfare of the country will depend upon the way in which the country is administered. That will depend upon the men who administer it... it requires men of strong character, men of vision, men who will not, sacrifice the interests of the country at large for the sake of smaller groups, and areas and who rise above the prejudices which are born of these differences.[6]

There is a general tendency in the organisations to lay emphasis on materials and financial management to the utter neglect of the personnel. What are the consequences! It is observed that the process of development takes longer, sometimes even fails. Why! The main reason for this is that we are not attending to the administration of personnel earnestly and forget that they are the real agents of development and ultimately the beneficiaries of the process of development. Persons, properly selected and given the job of their choice, produce excellent results otherwise they are a liability on the organisation.

A truly exciting future—a brave new world is waiting for you out there. I have no doubt that you will not only be a part of all these. but also significantly contribute to the progress and development of our profession hopefully in this country rather than abroad. As you pursue a successful career be it in practice or in academia, I hope and pray that you will not loose sight of the tact that medicine is as much. If not more, of an art as it is a science—an art that we are privileged to practice for the betterment of the human condition. Inherent in this philosophy is the imperative need to look beyond the immediacy of the disease on hand to all those factors—social, economical and environmental that impact on health.[7]

OBJECTIVES

The health personnel are appointed in a health system to achieve its goals. The primary objective of personnel administration, therefore, is to ensure the effective utilization of human resources in the, achievement of organisational goals. The personnel administration departments should design and establish an organisational structure and an effective working relationship among all the members of an organisation by division of organisational tasks into jobs, defining clearly the responsibility and authority for each job and its relation with other jobs/personnel in the organisation. The personnel administration must create a soothing environment for the personnel to secure their integration so that they may feel a sense of involvement, commitment and loyalty to the organisation. Such an atmosphere would automatically discard the frictional situations leading to personal jealousies and rivalries, prejudices and idiosyncrasies, Personality conflicts, cliques and factions, favouritism and nepotism.

Health personnel administration implies proper planning for work. Selection, placement and training of employees so selected and distribution and assignment of work among them. It includes the supervision, conduct and discipline, motivation, communication and welfare, grievance settlement, terms of employment, etc. It also deals with all other auxiliary functions starting from recruitment and ending with retirement. Personnel administration functions are comprehensive and over the entire work career of the employees *vis-a-vis* the organisation. This function is universal and is useful for all organisations whether government, industry, hospital or universities.

"All the functions performed by the health services must be oriented to rebuild their country, transform its health system, instill in people an ambition for higher standards of life and arouse in them the will und determination to work for such standards. The ambition of greatest man of our times, Mahatma Gandhi, was to wipe out every tear from every eye. The work of the health service will not be complete until this noble objective is achieved, i.e. decent health care to all. In a broader sense, the Government through its health system should ensure happiness to the people (as given in sruti)."

"All human beings may enjoy happiness and bliss. All should be free from troubles. All should promote the welfare of others. No one should suffer from any visible cause which can be prevented by human efforts."

Thus, it is of great importance for state and district level health functionaries, to manage health personnel efficiently to optimize the health services for the benefit of the people and the nation. Management can help them in the following ways:

(a) Detection

Detection is to find out or discover something, e.g. what is happening or what is wrong. We can include such techniques here as input-output analysis, attitude survey, production study, activity sampling, critical path examination, break-even analysis, etc.

(b) Evaluation

Evaluation is a measure or estimate of the value of an item. We can include such techniques here as job evaluation, work measurement, work estimation, performance, appraisal, cost benefit analysis, etc.

(c) Improvement

Improvement is better performance, and includes such techniques a management by objectives, method study, value analysis, etc.

(d) Optimization

To optimize performance, we can use such techniques as linear programming, operations research, etc.

(e) Specification

To specify a desired value or situation or action, we can use such techniques as strategic planning, office and plan layout, designing, etc.

(f) Control

Here we can include such techniques as cost control, credit control, labour control, budget control, etc.

(g) Communication

To communicate information, we can use techniques such as visual aids, suggestion schemes, report writing, communication theory, information theory, management information, etc.

(h) Demonstration

To demonstrate something would include such techniques as programmed learning, job instruction, management development and training, etc.

We are in a hurry; we wish to achieve most; we cannot afford the luxury of wasting our resources for experimentation. What is, therefore, needed is a proper identification of opportunities, setting out of priority areas and accordingly, continually devising technology and techniques appropriate to set-up our value system and to our environment. Let us strive to usher systems/technologies/techniques that are compatible. The call is, therefore, to stress on the know why rather than just on the 'know-how' of techniques and technology. This can materialise only when we bear in mind the following motto:

The Right Technique/Technology
At The Right Place
At The Right Time
At The Right Cost
With The Right Methods/Means

There is a real need to reform the current personnel policies in Government, semi-government, Private, co-operative organizations through intellectual and idealistic approach. The day-to-day personnel administration is the responsibility of the personnel departmènt, but, the major policy decisions in the form of rules or regulations would require the approval of the chief executive. Most of the personnel in an organisation agree that the personnel administration is passing through a crisis caused by the antiquated procedures backed by unwillingness and incapacity to introduce the desired reforms.

The performance of the personnel functions by the personnel department is limited in practice because of the following drawbacks:

(a) Inadequate understanding and appreciation of the basic and the essential problems of personnel management;
(b) No future personnel planning resulting in the absence of timely corrective measures;
(c) Lack of control and supervision over the personnel especially of the field personnel;
(d) Lack of effective decentralisation to substantive departments resulting in delays and confusion;
(e) Absentee of effective participation of the employees resulting in a gulf between the management and the staff;
(f) Lack of a manual setting out all the rules and regulations clearly and fully in a single document;
(g) Lack of effective communication between the staff and management; and
(h) lack of personnel standards of performance which should be realistic, appropriate and flexible. Besides, these should be stated with sufficient clarity to allow measurement of achievements and rationale in the sense that it is based on acceptable criteria related to performance and to the degree of responsibility.

The need to have a competent, motivated and a sustainable health workforce in ensuring an efficient and effective health system is essential. The important of HRH development cannot be undermined at any cost. Health workforce has a pivotal role in effective, efficient and sustainable delivery of health services.

Therefore, there is a need to design properly structured personnel departments or personnel staffed by competent personnel.

CRITICAL ANALYSIS

We have all kinds of health personnel, i.e. super-specialists, MBBS doctors, Nurses, LHV, ANMS, Multipurpose workers, radiologists, Laboratory technicians, etc. As a result of opening up of large institutions in health sector, we are getting adequate number of these medical and technical personnel available to meet the growing medical and health needs of the people. However based on facts, discussions with experts and medical personnel, we give here facts and suggestions to make medical personnel serve the society.

1. Students getting admission through huge amount of capitation fee demoralize them from the beginning of their career

Large number of students pay heavy amounts ranging from 35 lakhs onwards to get admission to medical and health institutions. In such a situation, how can we impart to them the values of selfless services, an essential ingredient of medical profession.

Swami Chinmayanand beautifully warns those who want to serve others as it is a demanding exercise on the part of individuals. To quote: "Missionary work is subtler than art, more demanding than science, more precise than literature, more adventurous than space-walking. Therefore, we must exhaustively and thoroughly prepare ourselves before we enter our fields of action, to serve others, to lead and guide the seeker. All discordant and undesirable elements in our life must be eliminated. The sovereign remedy for all ailments in us is found nowhere else but just within ourselves. The great secret of true success, of true happiness, then, is this; the man who asks for no return, the perfectly unselfish man, is the most successful. It seems to be a paradox. Do we not know that every man who is unselfish in life gets cheated, gets hurt? Apparently, Yes, "Christ was unselfish, and yet he was crucified." True, but we know that his unselfishness is the reason, the cause of a great victory—the crowning of millions upon millions of lives with the blessings of true success."[8]

It is also suggested that the Government must ban all these evil practices so that minds of would be medical persons may not be polluted and his thinking is not perverted. Hence, these private institutions to provide medical education would make doctors as commercial commodity.

2. Low quality of medical personnel engaged for imparting Medical Education

Medical colleges, nursing colleges, etc. are being set-up in the private sector as well. These colleges appoint second-rate or retired faculty members to impart medical education. How can be expect quality medical personnel coming out of these institutions who have neither the quantity nor quality medical faculty.

3. Doctors need be responsive to their patients

They should serve them from their heart. They must possess the following qualities in order to be effective and efficient medical persons:

(i) Openness in the sense of having wide contact with the people administered;

(ii) A sense of justice, fair play and impartiality in dealing with men and matters;

(iii) Sensitivity and responsiveness to the usages, feelings and aspirations of the people;

(iv) Securing the honour and dignity of the people however humble he or she might be;

(v) Humility and simplicity in the persons manning the administration machinery and their easy accessibility;
(vi) Creating and sustaining an atmosphere conducive to development, growth and social change; and
(vii) Honesty and integrity in thought and action.

4. Medical Education should promote perfection and character-building among medical and technical students

Dr. M. Lakshmi Kumari rightly stresses in her Foreward to "Yoga in Education", Vol. I, that the aim of all education, undoubtedly, is the attainment of human excellence and perfection, not just in any field of knowledge or activity but life in totality. Education should be the means to fashion excellent characters out of the very ordinary human raw material. This means culturing of the qualities of head and heart in a way congenial to the growth and development of oneself and others around him. In practical life, this has to be translated as qualities of truthfulness, righteous living, purity in personal life, self-confidence, integration of body, mind and intellect, love and compassion towards all living beings and surrender to Almighty. These are steps leading to the unfoldment of perfection already in man. Such a truly educated and cultured man alone can meet the challenges, internal and external, in a positive way, converting them into opportunities, helping in his ultimate evolution. Pursued further, one's entire thought, behaviour and life itself would come to express the spiritual oneness of the creation and this would be the manifestation also of the divinity inherent in man. A truly educated man, like a true scientist, satisfied with nothing but the one truth, has to be necessarily spiritual as well.

Swami Vivekananda stressed on man-making, character-building education. To quote him, "education is not the amount of information that is put into your brain and runs riot there undigested all your life. We must have life-building, man-making, character-making assimilation of ideals. We want education by which character is formed, strength of mind is increased, the intellect is expanded, by which one can stand on one's feet. What we want is Western science coupled with Vedanta, Brahmacharya as the guiding motto and also *shraddha* and faith in one's own life." Education is the panacea for all the ills affecting us individually, socially and nationally.[9]

5. Medical personnel are considered as second God on this earth. They must work with commitment

Swami Chinmayananda says, "The highest and noblest type of an individual working in the world is known as the "man of achievement" (Yogi). Such men work, neither for the sake of wages, nor for success; they are not after mere sensual pleasures, nor do they aspire to reform the world; they dedicatedly perform their obligatory duties finding peace and fulfilment in their very activity. Their fulfilment consists in doing their duties to the best of their ability without claiming any rights and they are totally unmindful of whether the society commends or condemns their actions.

To one who is not ready to act in a Spirit of dedication (Yajna) there is no real gain in this world, nor does he discover his happiness and fulfilments in this life. The secret of happiness and success is to act diligently in thé Yajna spirit. The responsibility of the future entirely rests on the shoulders of the day's youth. They may learn the art of hardening their mental faulty from the Geeta, the art of reorganizing themselves to work in the Yajna Spirit.

FUNCTIONS OF MEDICAL PERSONNEL

1. Excellence

It has been sent that the persons engaged in work think only of their salary and the health system and not the patents and their resulting into exploitation. A true HRD programme should emphasize that work is its own reward and the medical person should be discouraged to follow wrong practices.

We should go on efficiently doing our duty without attachment. Doing work without attachment man attains the Supreme, i.e. excellence.

Renunciation of attachment involves renunciation of desire as well; for it is from attachment that desire springs up (2/62). Desire will cease when renunciation is followed. It is, therefore, that renunciation of the desired for fruit has not been separately mentioned.

Health and Medical Personal who become attached to senses, they cannot achieve excellence. They become slaves of their senses. They should work without having any personal interest as it causes diversion leading to blockage of mind. Neither think yourself as actor, because no actor can manage to do anything. Conduct whatever is your duty, and remain at your ease with having done your part.

2. Dedication and Devotion

Medical personnel must work with dedication and sincerity as they are dealing with human lives. Today, in medical personnel, we daily read in press and see in TV the carelessness, negligence and negative attitude towards their medical profession. How can they serve the patients and provide decent health care? There is a need to make the medical professionals in employment through HRD to understand the purification of motives which can propel them to work sincerely, earnestly and with purity. This will lay the solid foundation of an excellent organization.

Health and Medical personal must create work culture and not psychofancy. Work culture is at the lowest ebbs. Bata K. Dey in his Article, Work Culture in India: Achievements and Failure rightly says that culture is not something which can be imported or transplanted; it must grow from within; it grows, and it does, in fertile soil and congenial climate. Gap in capital equipment or technology can be filled by import. You can even buy mana, but not dedication commitment, culture. How to create that is a million dollar question. An expensive answer to such a costly question is that, work culture tends to be congruous with, and is an extension of, the societal, indeed national culture. And the latter, at the moment, is the elusive commodity, despite this country's ancient civilization and old culture. The search is on. And we shall succeed.

Murtaza Mithani, Chairman and Managing Director of Wintech Group in his article, The High Road, in *The Tribune*, dated June 28, 2000 expect his employees to be committed to their work. As the head of an organization, expect my employees to be innovative, competitive and flexible. They should possess total commitment, be actively involved in every day work, and have no hastiness while interacting. He wants his team to be able to work in synergy with various departments. Failure and challenge should be treated as a steppingstone to success. Think big, create your own space and help yourself.

3. Competence in Work and Knowledge

Knowledge is powerful and without this medical professionals cannot discharge their duties. In this context, it may be of interest to note that without the expert trainers and desirous trainees, there can be no knowledge. Knowledge depends both on the teacher and taught.

Men should act according to *buddhi* or understanding. If we are victims of our impulses, our life is as aimless and devoid of intelligence as that of the animals. If we do not interfere, attachments and aversions will determine our acts. So long as we act in certain ways because we like them and abstain from other because we dislike them, we will be bound by our actions. But if we overcome these impulses and act from a sense of duty, we are not victims of the play of prakrti. The exercise of human freedom is conditioned and not cancelled by the necessities of nature.[10] There is no purifier as great as Knowledge, as knowledge is power, he who has attained purity of heart through a prolonged practice of Karmayoga automatically sees the light to Truth in the self in course of time.

4. Sincerity and devotion in Actions

Whatever result a doctor intends to achieve he may succeed in realizing it according to his visualization and aspiration, provided he pursues his end with a steadfastness of will. In executing an action that is clearly discerned to be the right one, the adequate course must be pursued with the steadfast will without hesitation or procrastination.

Swami Jagadatmananda in his book, "Learn to Live", Vol. I, rightly says:

> Instability and indecision mark the state of mind which is not subject to any discipline. The energies of an undisciplined mind are scattered in many directions and are wasted. A person with an unsteady mind cannot achieve any thing worthwhile. By doing all work, big or small,

with concentration and methodically, one gathers the ability to work with efficiency and ease.[11]

5. Love and Affection to Patients Suffering from Diseases

Health Administration is manned by and meant for people. We must attend to their problems with love and affection which would in return give strength and bliss.

Happiness on earth and bliss above are certainly the fruits of living the life of love. The changeless abode of the soul is reached by the path of love. Those that are devoid of love are just the skeleton covered with skin. The journey of this world is delightful to one, who after the removal of his errors and dispersion of the cloud of his ignorance, has come to the knowledge of truth.

6. Self-Introspection

Health and medical personnel must do self introspection which can help them in making their personality strong and they can serve their patients efficiently. We are to take care of ourselves—that much we can do—and give up attending to others; for a time. Let us perfect the means; the end will take care of itself. For the world can be good and pure, only if our lives are good and pure. It is an effect, and we are the means. Therefore, let us purify ourselves. Let us make ourselves perfect.

7. Good Character

Health and medical professionals must possess good character as service to patients who are already in trouble is the real reward to them. All good character traits have a common denominator of social courage, usefulness, common sense besides self-acceptance and self-confidence. Men of character may not be popular, but they are respected and followed. They are true leaders of men and times. They will fight but not quarrel, differ but will not oppose or criticize, will be firm but not rigid, dogmatic, appreciate without flattery, cooperate without surrendering, self-confident but not self-important, cooperate, compromise and reconcile on non-essentials but put up a valiant, relentless fight for basic principles, act and never react.

Will power and patience are basic to personality development. Both provide fibre and tone to it. Will is the motive power, driving force and patience is the period over which this force works to develop character.

All human endeavours achievements require minimum necessary time to mature and fulfil. Impatience only wastes vital energy, tires, confuses, sickness and impairs our will power. Our personality does not register on others if we are impatient with them who can benefit or be friend you without your giving him time.

To make health and medical personnel effective and efficient human excellence is the only need of the 21st century as all other programmes depend upon it. We should devise ways and means to rejuvenate human excellence which can change the world culture and make this earth worth-living a life of quality and excellence.

Yajurveda has beautifully put as:

O man
Do not be afraid of performing
Your marital duties
With courage and conviction
Follow the path of Dharma
Endowed with strength,
Honour and Valour
May you obey
Your god assigned duties
And be happy.

CONCLUSION

Thus the success of medical profession depends upon the attitude, qualification, commitment and dedication among medical personnel. They can serve the people with smiling face. They should not make the profession as a business but a service.

You are poised on the threshold of a world of opportunities. Some of you will choose to be scientists, discoverers and inventors; some will opt for teaching; but most of you, I am sure, will prosper in professional practice. Whichever fields you may choose, or find yourself in, I wish you a glorious future. But please do remember always that our fellow human beings—their health, happiness and meaningful life—are the ultimate reason for our existence. Treat them with care, compassion and empathy. Treat them as we would like to be treated. Nothing more is required; nothing less is acceptable. Go out and conquer the world by winning the hearts and minds of the people through professional competence, dedicated service and humane treatment.[10]

In a nutshell, we may keep the following commandments in mind:

- Timely, prompt service
- Minimum red tape and forms to fill
- Courteous Behaivour
- Minimum waiting time
- Good Ethical values
- Minimum visits to multiple offices
- Minimization of arbitrariness
- Prompt information on delays, waiting times, etc.
- Prompt information on status of application
- Prompt disposal of cases.

Notes and References

1. Walter R. Sharp, Field Administration in United Nations System, London, 1961, p. 19.
2. Karnataka Towards Equity, Quality and Integrity in Health, Final Report, Govt. of Karnataka, April 2001, p. 246.
3. Mahendra Bhandari, Holistic Medicine and a Complete Human Physician, *University News*, 44(80), Feb. 20-26, 2006, p. 18.
4. Presidential Address by Mrs Indira Gandhi delivered on October 22, 1971 at the Annual Meeting of IIPA, New Delhi.
5. A. Rajeshekaran, "Radical Changes Required in Medical Education", *University News*, 44(23), June 5, 2006, p. 15.
6. Quoted in H.R. Khanna: Making India's Constitution, Lucknow, Eastern Book Company, 1981, p. vi.
7. K. Mohandas, Director, "Preservation and Promotion of Health", *University News*, Aug. 14-20, 2006, p. 20.
8. Complete Works of Swami Vivekananda, Vol. III, p. 237
9. *Ibid.*, Vol. II, p. 3.
10. *Ibid.*, p. 225.
11. K. Mohandas, Director, "Preservation and Promotion of Health", *University News*, 44 (33), Aug. 14, 2006, p. 20.

Nursing Services and Health

Nursing Human Resource is as important as that of a medical personnel, i.e. Doctors, Nurses are the backbone of the hospital. Hospital where sick people are suffering, becomes a source of happiness with Nurses in white dresses moving around.

The Institution of nurses is the backbone of the organization that provides health services to the community at large. Nursing is a vocation, implying dedication to the service of suffering mankind and a missionary services to be rendered at any hour of the day and night as the need arises. It is a demanding and exacting profession. The ideal relations of a doctor, patient; nurse and the medicine are the four pillars upon which a cure must rest.

Nursing in its broadest sense. may be defined as the provision of nursing care to individuals, families or communities in connection with the restoration or preservation of health. and comprising the nursing component or the organised health care and preventive services. Such care may be provided by personnel ranging from the nursing aid to the professional nurse and nurse-midwife. The National League for Nursing has adopted the following principles for nursing care:

Nursing care encompasses health promotion, the care and prevention or disability and rehabilitation, and involves teaching, counselling and emotional support as well as the care or illness. Nursing care is an integral part of total health care and is planned and administered in combination with related medical education and welfare services. Nursing personnel respect the individuality, dignity and rights of every person regardless of race, colour, creed, national origin, social or economic status.[1]

The following is a statement taken from the Code of Ethics as Applied to Nursing published by the International Council of Nurses:

Nurses minister to the sick, assume responsibility for creating a physical, social and spiritual environment which will be conducive to recovery and stress the prevention of illness and promotion of health by teaching and example. They render health service to the individual, the family and the community and coordinate their services with members of other health profession.

The words and expectation appear to vary a great deal, and, as with many other professional groups, the nurses' role is a shifting one. A unique function of the nurse has been identified as "........ to assist the individual, sick or well, in the performance of those activities contributing to health or its recovery (or to peaceful death that he would perform unaided if he had the necessary strength, will of knowledge. And to do this in such a way as to help him gain independence as rapidly as possible."[2]

From these definitions, we infer that nursing is to nurse the patients or to serve the patients. It is the duty of the nurse to ensure the healing touch of sympathy for the patients. In view of these, Florence Nightingale felt a nurse should be chaste, sober, honest, truthful, trustworthy, punctual, quiet cheerful and kind.

Nursing was born out of great struggle and hardship. The lady with the Lamp Florence Nightingale withstood tremendous amount of pressure and brought not only acceptance but also recognition to the noble profession. In 1857 the Indian Mutiny turned Miss Nightingales interest to the health of the Army in India. It was for this purpose the Royal Commisison was appointed in 1859. In 1868 a sanitary department was established. In March 1888 ten qualified British nurses arrived in India to look after the British Army in India. In 1905 during the British rule in India, missionary nurses arrived as members of Missionary Medical Association. This was the very start of formalized nursing service in India. Gradually, the increasing need of adequately trained nurses led to creation of South India Examining Board in 1911 and the North India Examining Board in 1912. It was the mission hospital Nursing leaders who laid the foundation of systematic Nursing education in India. However, the mid-India Board of Examination was started in 1934. But this was not regulated for registration.[3] The Central Government granted an approval to the Bhore Committee's (1946) recommendations by starting two colleges of Nursing in Delhi (1946) and Vellore (1947). This provided university degree level course. With the efforts of Prof. S. Radhakrishanan, Nursing education in the country was integrated into the system of higher education. The following courses of various levels for nursing education are offered in various educational institutions established in various parts of the country:

1. Auxilliary Nurse Mid-Wives (ANM)
2. General Nursing and Mid-Wives (GNM)
3. Diploma in Nurisng Education and Administration (DNE)
4. Bachelor of Nursing (B.Sc.-N)
5. Post Basic Bachelor in Nursing (PB B.Sc.-N)
6. Mater of Nursing (M.Sc.-N)

National Health Policy, 2002 states that in the interest of patients care, the policy emphasizes the need for an improvement in the ratio of nurses *vis-à-vis* doctors/beds. In order to discharge their responsibility as model providers of health services, the public health delivery centres need to make a beginning by increasing the number of nursing personnel. The Policy anticipates that with the increasing aspiration for improved health care amongst the citizens, private health facilities will also improve their ratio of nursing personnel *vis-à-vis* doctors/beds.

The policy lays emphasis on improving the skill-level of nurses, and on increasing the ratio of degree-holding nurses *vis-à-vis* diploma-holding nurses. NHP-2002 recognizes a need for the Central Government to subsidize the setting up, and the running of training facilities for nurses on a decentralized basis. Also, the Policy recognizes the need for establishing training courses for super-speciality nurses required for tertiary care institutions.

The nursing profession is crucial to the functioning of hospitals as they are directly involved with the patients and their relatives. That is why nurses are considered by the society as sisters. A nurse must combine scientific and technical knowledge along with communication, observation and clinical skills. In addition, she must possess personal qualities like sympathy, perseverance and skill of interpersonal relations. Other essential attributes are: compassion, passion, integrity, tolerance of ambiguity, willingness to play with ideas, knowledge and inquiry, committed to viewing the social world from the viewpoints of people being studied, valuing of detail, willingness to inject something of themselves into the CARE process and hence into the outcomes. This combination makes nursing a challenging as well as a fascinating occupation. The nursing profession gives a sense of satisfaction that comes from knowing that you have made a difference in another person's life. This satisfaction is priceless and serves as a source of inspiration to the nurses to do their best.

Nurses may work in a variety of settings ranging from large institutional settings to patient homes. The hospital, nursing homes, and extended care facilities employ most of the nurses. A new dimension of nursing is public health nursing employed in primary health services, which is the pillar of sound health infrastructure. The type of work nurses does vary greatly depending on where they work. The medical and surgical wards involve the care and assessment of patients with diseases, injuries, and those who are waiting for or recovering from operations. Nurses on these wards should have from four to five. Patients to care for each day depending on the facility. The broad range of medical problems and the frequent use of nursing skills make this a good unit for new nurses to begin their careers. However, in Indian set-up a nurse may have to care many more patients that may affect quality of care. The intensive care/critical care unit should involve the care of no more than three seriously ill patients, since this unit involves special skills and more intense assessment. These nurses are supposed to attend further training to attain critical care skills.

There are different specialties in nursing services for which they are trained in nursing colleges. Pediatric nurses care for children aged twelve and under. Some of the larger hospitals have special newborn units that involve the care of newborns and include their parents in that care. Maternity (also called obstetrical or 08) nurses assist mothers through the childbirth process. They teach mothers and families to care.for their infants. They also do some of the prenatal (before birth) testing to make sure the unborn baby is healthy. Psychiatric nurses care for patients with emotional problems and thought disorders. This occupation requires patience and the ability to understand and accept the patient's thoughts and feelings. Emergency care nurses care for patients in life-threatening situations. They must be able to evaluate which patients need immediate care and which ones can wait. The nurse in this unit must be able to assess patients and make decisions quickly. Community health nursing is another dimension, where nurses are to take care of the community through primary health care.

Nurses are constantly using their knowledge, energy and skills to make a difference in the lives of patients, giving an immense satisfaction. Every day they come across a new opportunity for teaching and/or learning something new. Working as a nurse is never boring. Being a Nurse is a career by which they can feel satisfied spiritually, emotionally and financially. A special person with qualities such as empathy, compassion, intelligence and above all patience should only decide to become a nurse. During nursing career they will encounter many wonderful and terrible experiences from a death to a birth. It is a paradox of sweet and sour. Nurses must have the ability to manage emotions during these extreme times and be able to perform with confidence and accuracy. A true nurse will assume the role of patient advocate; at times she will be the only voice they have.

As per the Xth Plan of Govt. of India, around 7.37 lakh nurses have been registered in the various state nursing councils in the country; it is estimated that only about 40% are in active service. About 1.5 lakh nurses are employed in the government sector. Out of the 654 general nursing-midwives training schools in the country, private/voluntary/missionary institutions run 465. Around 20,000 trained nurses become available in the country annually. The current capacity being just adequate to fill the vacancies in the government sector. There is a growing demand of the specialized nurses, which has to be met.

What is required is: (a) To set-up excellent nursing institutions attached to post-graduate medical institutions wherein all facilities are available. (b) The faculty of nursing must be given U.G.C. grades and the positions of professors must be created to improve teaching; and skills. (c) The head of the nursing institution should be given the authority and powers so that she is able to work efficiently and not have to look up towards higher ups for small things. (d) A lot of innovation through projects and Ph.D. guidance is required. (e) Research which is very hollow at present, needs upgradation. (f) Nurses may be trained in clinical work so that they can take up independent positions for minor and repetitive ailments. (g) B.Sc. nurses with 5 years' experience may be admitted to MBBS against 5% reserve seats. (h) There must be refresher courses to update their knowledge.

However, being a nurse is no bed of roses. Working in an emergency room is hectic. Often there are no lulls. A hall full of ailing, irritable people that have over-flowed from the waiting room greet you at the beginning of each shift. Every frantic minute of the day is spent racing from one task to the next. Nurses have to learn to deal with a hysterical mother whose child has a fever while nurses are titrating drugs and monitoring a patient who has just suffered a heart attack. This type of work environment takes a toll on them, physically, mentally and emotionally. It also takes a toll on their family when they come home too tired and are miserable to play with their children. Or when they have to work weekends and holidays, or during the school play. Also, one of the most stressful things is to know that a mistake could hurt their patient or cost them their life. Even when your work is flawless, there is always the threat of a lawsuit. Nursing is suffering. Often doctors view them not as equals, but as helpers. Their knowledge and skills are highly overlooked. Another problem facing nursing is themselves. Too often are nurses unfriendly and unwilling to assist one another that they make their jobs even less pleasant. Nurses are pushed to take out aggression and hostility amongst themselves because they do not do so with patients or physicians.

CATEGORIES OF NURSES AND THEIR EDUCATION

There are a large number of categories of nursing personnel depending upon the duration and purpose of training and the level of general education. Let us discuss these categories briefly:

1. Auxiliary Nurse Midwives

This category of nurses are trained to function as multi-purpose workers in rural areas. Their functions are: care of the sick, home visits, treatment of minor ailments, maternal and child health care, family planning follow-up, nutritional education, etc. The entrance qualification for training to such category is Middle Standard and the age between 18-30 years. The duration of the training is two years and includes shorter and simpler courses in nursing and midwifery. Students are provided stipends and free accommodation.

2. Lady Health Visitors' Course

This is of one and a half year's duration. This is a modified Auxiliary Nurse-Midwives Course with more emphasis on maternal and child health. The minimum entrance qualification is matriculation.

CHART 2.1

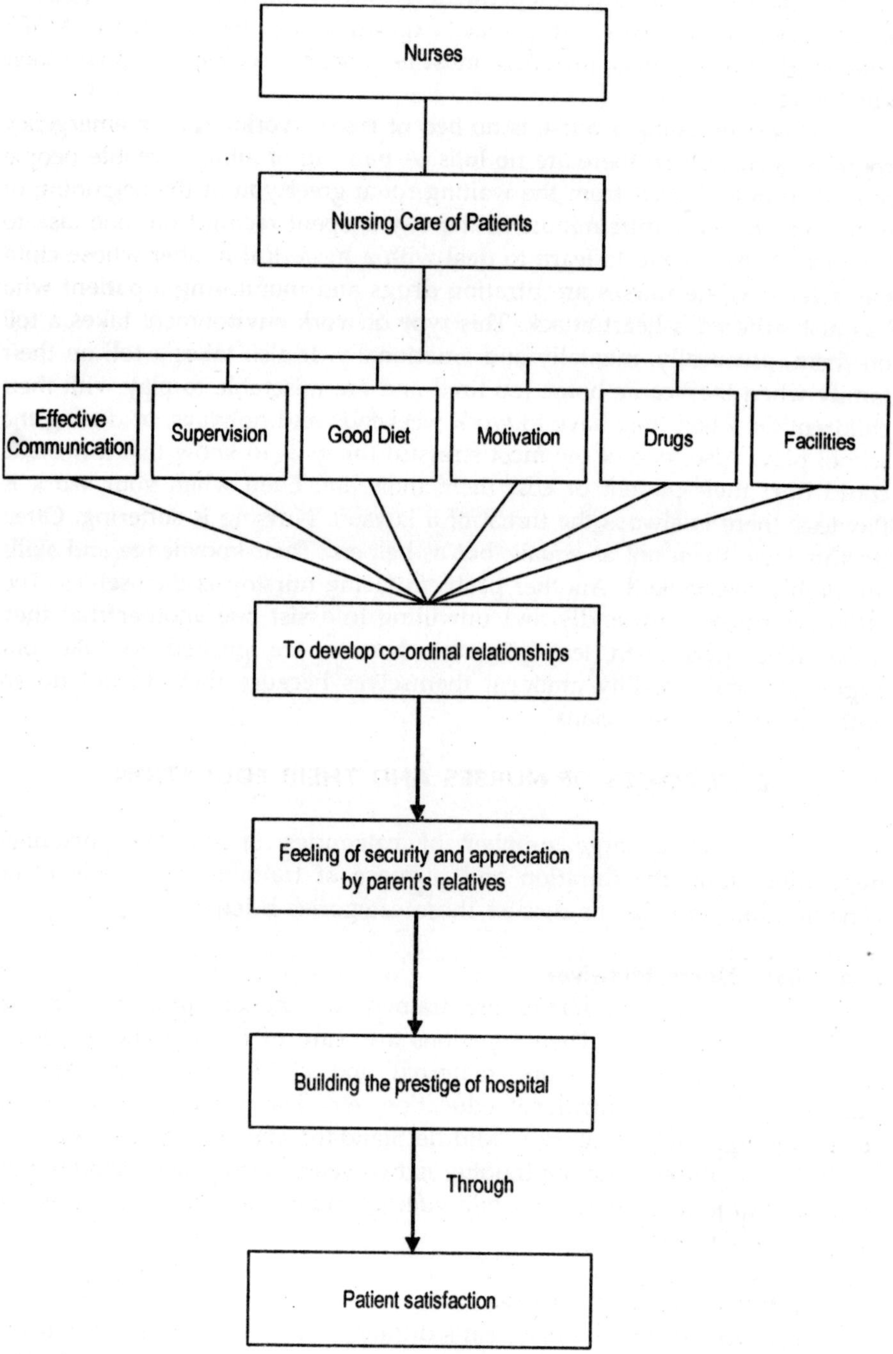

Nurses

↓

Nursing Care of Patients

↓

Effective Communication	Supervision	Good Diet	Motivation	Drugs	Facilities

↓

To develop co-ordinal relationships

↓

Feeling of security and appreciation by parent's relatives

↓

Building the prestige of hospital

↓ Through

Patient satisfaction

3. General Nursing and Midwifery

Minimum education is matriculation with 45 per cent aggregate marks, having science subjects. Duration is 3 years. They are trained to function efficiently both in hospitals and in the community. It is also called "A" Grade Nursing Course.

4. B.Sc. Nursing Degree Course

This is a University Programme in General Nursing and Midwifery of 4 years' duration. Educational requirements are higher secondary or intermediate with science subjects. Degree programmes are conducted in colleges of nursing in our country at Delhi, Bombay, Bangalore, Chandigarh.

5. Post-Certificate B.Sc. Degree Course

This course is conducted for diploma-holders in seven colleges of nursing in India. Duration of this course is two years.

6. Masters of Doctorate in Nursing

Master is of 2 years' duration and is conducted at Delhi, Bangalore, Chandigarh and Bombay. Doctorate is a 3 year course.

7. Specialised Course

A large number of specialised courses are conducted for diploma-holders. They are:

(a) Ward Sister's Course for efficient management in the wards
(b) Public Health Nursing is for better community health services
(c) Tutor's Course
(d) Administration in Nursing
(e) Operation Theatre Training
(f) Pediatric Nursing
(g) Psychiatric Nursing
(h) Orthopedic Nursing

These are essential for efficient functioning of specialized departments.

8. Nurse Technician

This category includes Senior Dressers, Assistant Nurses and Community Nurses. More than one but fewer than three years of nursing education and training is required with a minimum of nine years of general education.

9. Nursing Aides

This category at present includes servants, messengers or other personnel actually performing certain nursing functions. Although aides must be literate, formal training is not generally required, since they are trained on the job to assist in patient care.

On examining critically, we find that it is illogical to classify all the personnel engaged in the assistance of health care as 'Nursing Personnel'. We must restrict the classification of nursing personnel to the nurses formally trained to do the job. We may give different names to the personnel helping the nurses. This would enhance the status of nursing personnel and would focus our attention on a definite category of personnel. The numerous categories of nurses diffuse functions and responsibilities. Dr. Gunaratne, the former Regional Director of the South-East Asia Regional Office of WHO observed that Sri Lanka had experienced some faculties because of the numerous categories of nursing personnel, including staff nurses (who underwent three years' training), emergency nurses (with only three to six months' training), assistant nurses, nursing aides and ward attendants. The Government intended to have only two categories of personnel staff nurse (a fully qualified nurse) and ward labourer (who would have nothing to do with patient care). The same is the problem in many countries. There is a need of rational classification of nursing personnel so that their duties may be clearly demarcated.[4]

In order to provide incentive and motivation to nursing personnel, five per cent of the seats in the proposed short-duration course of medical education may be reserved for the nursing personnel who fulfil the minimum qualifications and have set good standards of service. This would also attract good candidates to this profession. Let us explain the duties of Important Nursing Personal.

Staff Nurse

Job Summary

Staff Nurse is a first-level professional nurse who provides direct patient care to one patient or a group of patients assigned to her/him during duty shift. She/he Assists in ward management and supervision She/he is directly responsible toward supervisor.

Direct Patient Care

- Admits and discharges the patient.
- Maintains personal hygiene and comforts of the patient.
- Attends to the nutritional needs of the patient, prepare invalid's diet and feeds helpless patients.
- Maintains clean and safe environment for the patients.
- Implements and maintains ward policies and routines.
- Co-ordinates patient care with various health team members.
- Follows doctor's rounds.
- Performs technical tasks, e.g., administration of medication

assisting doctors in various medical procedures, preparation articles and the patient for medical or nursing procedure recording vital signs, tube feeding, giving enema, bowel wash dressing, stomach wash, eye and ear-care, collection sending of specimens, pre and post-operative care, Assists administration of transfusion. Perineal care, breast care, etc.

- Helps doctors in diagnosis and treatment.
- Maintains intake and output chart.
- Observes change in patient's condition and records, takes necessary action and reports to the concerned authority.
- Imparts health education to the patient and his/her families.
- Accompanies very ill-patients sent to other departments transferred to other institutions.

Ward Management

- Hands over and takes over the patient and ward equipment supply.
- Keeps the ward neat and tidy.
- Maintains safety of the ward equipments.
- Prepares and checks ward supplies.
- Assists Ward Supervisor/Sister in ward management and officiates in her/his absence. Assists in taking inventories.
- Maintains ward record as assigned to her/him by the sister incharge.

Nursing Sister/Supervisor

Job Summary

Nursing Supervisor is accountable for the nursing care management of a ward or a unit assigned to her/him. She is responsible to the Nursing Superintendent/Assistant Nursing Superintendent for her ward management. She takes full charge of the ward and assigns work for various categories of nursing and non-nursing personnel working with her. She is responsible for safety and comfort of the patients in her ward. In a teaching hospital she is expected to ensure good learning fields.

Direct-Patient Core

- Ensures proper admission, discharge of her patients.
- Plans nursing care and makes patients' assignment as per their nursing needs.
- Assists in the direct care of the patient as and when required.
- She/he sees that total health needs of her/his patients are met.
- Ensures safety, comfort and good personal hygiene of her/his patient.

- Assist in planning and administration of therapeutic diet to her patient.
- Sees that helpless patients are regularly fed as per direction.
- Sees that proper observation records of the patients are made.
- and necessary information imparted to the concerned authorities.
- Takes nursing rounds with staff and students.
- Makes rounds with doctors. Assists him in diagnosis and treatment of the patients.
- Implements doctors' instructions concerning patient treatment.
- Assists patient and his/her relative to adjust in the hospital and its routine.
- Co-ordinates patient care with other departments.

Supervision and Administration

- Ensures safe and clean environment for the ward.
- Makes duty and work assignments.
- Indents Ward store and keeps necessary records.
- Does regular inventory checking of her/his ward.
- Makes list for condemnation of articles and submits it to all concerned.
- Assists in making ward requirements.
- Establishes and reinforces ward standards prescribed in the procedures and manuals of the ward and the hospital and policies that are in force.
- Acts as liaison officer between ward staff and hospital administration.
- Maintains good public relations in her/his ward.
- Sees that ward statistics are regularly submitted.
- Maintains discipline among the ward workers, e.g., Staff Nurses, students and domestic staff.
- Deals appropriately with any adverse situation that has occurred in the ward and reports to the concerned authorities.
- Reports about any medico-legal cases in the ward.
- Writes and submits confidential reports of the staff.
- Sees that students get desired learning experience in the ward.

Educational Function

- Organises orientation programmes for new staff.

INDIAN NURSING YEAR BOOK: 1983

- Organises formal and informal ward teaching, conducts bedside clinics and demonstrations.

- Conducts ward conferences/meetings.
- Gives incidental teaching to patients, relatives, Staff Nurses, students and the domestic staff.
- Guides in formulation of Nursing care studies, and Nursing care pans, etc.
- Evaluates the students' performance and submits reports to the school authorities.
- Helps in medical and nursing research.
- Encourages staff development programme in her/his ward.

Assistant Nursing Superintendent

Job Summary

She/he is responsible for developing and supervising Nursing Services of a department of a floor consisting of two or more wards or units managed by the ward supervisors. These Units may be In-patient wards, Out-patient Departments/Clinics, Operation Theatres, Obstetric units, central supply departments, etc. She/he is responsible to the Nursing Superintendent and Deputy Nursing Superintendent.

Patient Care and Ward Management

- Organises and plans nursing care activities of the department or floor according to hospital policies and service needs.
- Plans staffing pattern and the other necessary requirements of his/her department.
- Compiles and submits nursing statistics to the concerned authorities.
- Conducts and attends to departmental and intra-departmental meetings/conferences from time to time. Makes regular rounds of her/his department.
- Sees to the safety and general cleanliness of the department.
- Look into general comforts of the patient and his/her relatives.
- Receives report from the night Superintendent of her/his department.
- Evaluates nature and quantum of care required in each unit/ward.
- Makes rotation plan for the Nursing staff under her/his jurisdiction.
- Plans ward management with the ward/unit supervisor of each ward/unit.
- Reinforces the principle of good ward management in each ward.
- Helps ward/unit supervisors to procure their ward unit supplies.

- Supervises the proper use and care of the equipments and supplies in the department.
- Acts as a Public Relations Officer of the unit and deals with problems faced by the ward supervisor, if any, especially with the Class IV employees and patient's attendants.
- Keeps the Nursing Superintendent/Deputy Nursing Superintendent's office informed of the needs of the nursing units/wards under her/him and of any special problem/problems.

Educational Functions

- Arranges classes and clinical training of nursing students in the department, related to the specialty experience.
- Implements the teaching programme and clinical experience of the students with the help of doctors and Ward Sisters.
- Does counselling guidance of staff and students.
- Arranges and conducts staff development programmes of her/his department.
- Assists in planning for and participation in the training of auxiliary personnel.
- Writes the confidential reports of her this supervisors.

General

- Escorts the Nursing Superintendent/Deputy Nursing Superintendent and special visitors in the department.
- Participates in various professional activities, e.g. staff education, staff meetings, etc.
- Acts as a liaison officer between the Nursing Department and higher hospital authorities.
- Carries out any other duties delegated by the Nursing Superintendent/Deputy Nursing Superintendent.

Deputy Nursing Superintendent

Job Summary

Responsible to the Nursing Superintendent as assistant to her/him in the Nursing Service administration of the Hospital. She/he is independent incharge of Nursing Service Department of a less than 400-bedded hospital.

Nursing Service

- Officiates in the absence of Nursing Superintendent.
- Participates in the formulation of Nursing Services, philosophies, objectives and policies.

- Assists in the recruitment of Nursing Staff and Students' selection.
- Makes master duty roster of the Nursing Staff.
- Helps in allocating Nursing personnel to various Nursing Services Departments.
- Keeps records and reports of the Nursing Services.
- Assists in planning and organizing the new units in the hospital, e.g. I.C.U., C.SD, etc.
- Maintains confidential report and records of the Nursing staff.
- Takes regular hospital rounds.
- Supervises care given in various departments.
- Serves on several hospital committees, e.g., purchase to committee, Class IV employees committee, etc.
- Interprets the policies and procedures of the hospital care to subordinate staff and others.
- Acts as a liaison officer between the Nursing Superintendent and die Nursing staff of the hospital.
- Receives night reports from the night Supervisor. Maintains the attendance and leave register for nurses.
- Assist in the supervision of Nurses' Home, Nurses' Hostel.
- Conducts regular physical verification of hospital stock.
- Initiates condemnation of old worn-out articles and procurement of new articles.
- Attends to emergency calls in rotation concerning hospital or hostel problems.

Educational Functions

- Assists in planning and implementing of staff development programmes.
- Ensures clinical experience facilities for student nurses in various clinical areas of he hospital.
- Guides and counsels Nursing staff.
- Arranges orientation programmes for new Nursing staff.
- Maintains discipline among nursing personnel.
- Organises experience programmes for post-graduate students from different hospitals.

General Duties

- Escorts special visitors, Nursing Superintendent, Medical Superintendent for hospital rounds.
- Arranges and participates in professional and social functions of the staff public relations.
- Maintains good public relations.
- Carries out other duties assigned to her by the Nursing Superintendent.

Nursing Superintendent

Job Summary

Nursing Superintendent is responsible to the Medical Superintendent, in a hospital having 400 or above bed strength. She is accountable for the safe and efficient running of the various Nursing departments in the hospital. She is assisted in carrying out her duties, by the Deputy Nursing Superintendent/Assistant Nursing Superintendent, Ward Supervisors and Clerical, linen room and domestic staff.

Nursing Service

- Participates in the formulation of the philosophy of the hospital in general and those specific to the nursing service.
- Determines goals, aims, objectives and policies of the Nursing Services.
- Implements hospital policies and rules through various Nursing Units.
- Decides and recommends personnel and material requirement for running various Nursing Service departments of the hospital.
- Interviews and recruits Nursing staff.
- Assists in student selection and recruitment of other auxiliary staff whose duties are related to Nursing.
- Ensures the safe and efficient care rendered in the various Nursing departments of the hospital.
- Makes regular hospital rounds in hospitals and wards.
- Checks if standard of care is maintained and patients are nursed in clean, orderly and safe environment.
- Takes hospital rounds with Medical Superintendent.
- Selects and secures proper equipment needed for the hospital or nursing home.
- Looks after the welfare of the patients, their relatives and the Nursing Staff.
- Prepares budgets for the Nursing Services Departments.
- Functions as a member of the condemnation board for linen and other hospital equipments.
- Prepares duty roster, plans staff leave, and disburses salaries.
- Gives counselling and guidance to the subordinate staff.
- Maintains discipline among Nurses and other auxiliary staff.
- Enforces implementation of the hospital rules, regulations and policies conferences.
- Investigates complaints and takes necessary steps.
- Evaluates confidential staff reports and recommends for promotion or higher studies.

- Plans staff development programmes and arranges for in-service education and orientation programmes, etc.
- Inspects hospital kitchen and dietary services of the hospital.
- Arranges students' clinical experience and Council examinations.
- Initiates and participates in Nursing Research.
- General and Office Duties.
- Attends to the general correspondence.
- Maintains necessary records concerning the Nursing Staff, students, confidential reports and health records, etc.
- Submits annual reports of the Nursing Service departments to
- Medical Superintendent, Indian Nursing Council and Nurses' Registration Council.
- Participates in professional and community activities.

SCHOOLS OF NURSING

Clinical Instruction

Supervision and teaching of students in the Clinical and Public health field—

- Planning and supervision of Clinical teaching schedule including assignment of patients.
- Supervision and guidance of patient care activities carried out by students.
- Assisting in evaluating students' progress.
- Maintaining records related to Clinical experience and teaching.
- Guidance of students.
- Helping students with extra-curricular activities.
- Assisting in conduct of practical examinations.
- Any other duty assigned.

Tutor

- Teaching Nursing subjects.
- Supervision of students in clinical field.
- Arrangement for external lectures.
- Assists in planning and implementation of specific courses.
- Participation in clinical teaching.
- Participation in the School's Committee work.
- Conducting tests (theory and practical).
- Helping students with extra-curricular activities.
- Guidance and counselling of students.
- Maintenance of class-room equipment, supplies and teaching aids.
- Evaluating students' assignments.
- Preparing teaching material under guidance of senior teachers.
- Any other duty assigned.

Senior Tutor

- Responsible for planning and implementation of teaching programmes.
- Teaching subjects in the curriculum.
- Over-all supervision of Clinical teaching programme of subject in hospital/Public Health field.
- Assisting in the administration of the School of Nursing.
- Supervision and guidance of junior teaching staff including in-service education of teacher.
- Supervision of students' health, welfare and security.
- Assisting in the selection of students and admission.
- Assisting in examination, tests (sessionals and terminals).
- Supervision of living conditions of students in the hostel.
- Preparation of reports on students' progress.
- Assisting in maintenance of School records.
- Participation in student guidance activities.
- Guiding students' extra-curricular programmes.
- Assisting the Principal Tutor in the general administration of the school.
- Assisting the Principal Tutor in the procurement of School supplies and equipments.
- Assisting in the Library.
- Planning, implementation and evaluation of specific courses.
- Officiating as Principal Tutor in her/his absence.

Principal Tutor

- General administration of a School of Nursing.
- Administration and overall supervision of teaching programmes.
- Supervision and guidance of teaching staff including organization of in-service education of staff.
- Responsibility for organizing work-load of staff including teaching assignments.
- Supervision of students' welfare, health and security.
- Guidance and counselling of students.
- Administrative arrangements for students' clinical experience and teaching in hospital and Public Health field.
- Recruitment of students and staff.
- Responsibility for conduct of examinations.
- Supervision of living conditions of students in hostel.
- Maintenance of permanent School records.
- Preparation of reports (School reports, progress reports).
- Review and revision of policies, rules, regulations, philosophy of the School.

- Performing Public Relations duties for the School.
- Procurement of School equipments, supplies, stationery.
- Preparation of budgetary proposals
- Supervision of hostel and office staff.
- Participation in the School's committee work.
- Participation in professional activities.
- Supervision of library services.
- Planning for development of the school.

PUBLIC HEALTH COMMUNITY NURSING ORGANIZATION

Auxiliary Nurse-Midwife/Female Health Worker

Under the Multipurpose Workers' scheme, a Health Worker (Female) is expected to cover a population of 5000. At present, however, she covers a population of 10000 of which about 4000 are in her intensive area and the remaining are in the twilight area. In the intensive area, she is responsible for all the activities listed. She carries out the following functions:

Assisting in conducting MCH and Family Planning Clinics; surveying the area and maintaining contact with the local Dais; supervising the work of local Dais, especially in conducting delivery cases, and assisting in the training of minor ailments, ante-natal care, intra-natal care, post-natal care: Family Planning follow-up, Nutrition education; maintaining records of daily work; assisting in the registration of deaths and births and other vital events occurring in her, area, assisting in the immunization programmes; associated with the school health programme; providing Primary Medical care, treatment of minor ailments; first-aid in emergencies and referring of cases; any other duties assigned to her by LHN/PHN/Medical Officers.

Male Health Workers

- Under the Multipurpose Workers' scheme, a health worker (male) is expected to cover a population of 5000 wherein he is to carry out the responsibilities assigned to him. He will have different sets of responsibilities of MCH, Family Planning, immunization and nutrition in the intensive and twilight area of the health worker (female).
- Making a visit to each family once a month.
- To identify and notify communicable diseases like Malaria, T.B, etc.
- Educate public about identification, prevention and control of diseases.
- To maintain contact with and educate people about environmental sanitation. To carry out immunization and Family Planning Programmes.

- To carry out nutrition programmes and identifying cases of malnutrition and helping in their treatment.
- To record vital events and maintain records and statistics. To provide treatment for minor ailments and emergencies.

Lady Health Visitor

Lady Health Visitors are directly responsible for the preventive, promotive, curative and rehabilitative health care carried out in the health centres, maternity homes, hospitals and in the community. Each Health Visitor is responsible for the care of 40,000 populations in the community. She is responsible to the Medical Officer incharge of the center. She independently runs the family planning and maternity centres, maternity home, maternity section of the P.H.C. and Anganwaries in I.C.D.S. projects.

Area of Work

Clinics, fields, maternity homes and hospitals, family planning camps, Emergency duties in flood and epidemic area.

Clinic

Organises ante-natal and post-natal clinics, well baby and family planning clinics; runs full-time clinic with the help of ANMs, Dais, Family Planning social workers, etc. Principal motivator for achieving net Family Planning targets; independently runs 20-bedded or more maternity home; assists doctors in the insertion of I.U.D. and other emergencies; responsible for error of audit, condemnation, etc.

Field Duties

Making regular home visits; arranging educational programmes, raising total health care planning and implementing community health education programmes; arranging seminars, group meetings, etc.

Public Health Nurse Junior

Assists senior PHN in carrying out her responsibilities.

Public Health Nurse (Senior)

- Provides health care (preventive, promotive, and curative/ rehabilitative) to all individuals, families and community in any field that she is appointed.
- Trains, supervises and guides the health workers in the delivery of health care services to the community.
- Plans health and family welfare programmes along with Health Workers.
- Carries out supervisory home visits in the area covered by the health workers.
- Coordinates the work of male and female health workers and other personnel.

- Arranges educational programmes for the community.
- Assists in conducting medical examination of the school children. Reports any anomaly to the concerned specialist.
- Does follow-up and maintains records of the school health care programmes.

Public Health Nurse Supervisor

- Public Health Nurse is responsible to Chief Public Health Nurse/Medical Officer for the provision, supervision and improvement of community health care within the assigned area. She carries out preventive, promotive, curative and rehabilitative care.
- Assists in determining the philosophy and objectives of the community health programme.
- Gives leadership in planning total health care to all individual; families and community in any field that she is appointed.
- Assists in the development of standards of health care in assigned area in harmony with the accepted philosophy, objectives, aims and health policies.
- Assist in the preparation of a budget for the Community Health Department and Administers the approved budget for the department.
- Major responsibility in guidance and supervision PHN/LHV/ ANM/students who are under her care.
- Organizes educational programmes for the Community members including school children, mother and other interested groups in her area.
- Ensures that the workers under her maintain proper records and achieve their targets of work.

Chief/District Public Health Nurse

Provide health services to the Community according to the policies of the department in the area of preventive, promotive, curative and rehabilitative care.

Determines the philosophy and objectives of the Community Health Department of the assigned area; gives leadership in organizing and implementing the various health schemes; provides effective Supervision and guidance to the members of the health team (community workers); plans, implements and evaluates training programmes at the P.H.C. for various categories of health team; recommends appointments, transfers and promotions of her staff; effectively discharges the responsibilities as administrator and manager of P.H.C.; carries work in the P.H.C. area; contributes to research planned by other health services; Plans and implements community education programmes.

UNION MINISTRY OF HEALTH AND FAMILY WELFARE

Nursing Officer

- Assists Nursing Advisor in all matters of Nursing.
- Relieving Nursing Advisor as and when required.
- International Assistance-UNICEF equipment and supplies and vehicles for all training institutions of Nurses/ANMs.
- Organising and conducting Refresher Courses on an all-India basis, e.g., Nursing Superintendents, Tutors, Principals, Public Health Clinical areas.
- Representing on Committees, give advice and teaching as and when required specially in the area of Public Health Nursing.

Deputy Nursing Advisor (Department of Family Welfare)

Training of various categories of Nursing personnel in Family Planning on an all-India; periodical assessment of the needs of Nursing personnel working in the Family Planning in terms of quantity and quality advising State Government on ways and means of meeting the situation; advising the Government of India in term of policy-making as regards Nursing training. Any other responsibilities assigned.

Nursing Advisor (D.G.H.S.)

- Nursing Advisor being the Head of the Nursing Services in the country is responsible for advising the Government of Indian on all matters concerning Nursing Service, Nursing Education and specialization in Nursing, etc.
- She/he guides, supervises, and co-ordinates Nursing Service and Nursing Education in the States.
- She/he plans total Nursing manpower requirements of the country in the area of Nursing Service, Nursing Education and Continuing Education, etc., in co-operation and co-ordination with State Government units and voluntary agencies.
- Responsible for developing the national and international projects concerning Nursing in India.

She is a programme officer for Nursing Section in the office of the D.G.H.S., which involves components of all the National Health programmes.

Maintains liaison with all professional bodies concerned with improving the standard of Nursing Service and Nursing education in the country.

Changing Concept to Meet Present Needs

There has been a change today in the concept of nursing care. In the words of the WHO Expert Committee on nursing, "Minor modifications of existing nursing systems will be inadequate to meet new situations and demands in a rapidly changing society nursing must break with some of its traditions as well as alter existing stereo-types.[5]

The current trend is to involve the nurse in the planning, implementation and evaluation of health programmes rather than simply expecting from her a subservient role in patient care. This requires a great change in the contents and methodology of nursing education. The present nursing education does not encourage research. The nursing journals contain articles of descriptive nature. There is a need to encourage research among the post-graduate nursing students and the faculty members to prepare them for senior positions in the health care delivery system. In a report of an international seminar on Research in Nursing. Brotherston has summarised the position thus: Whereas the ability and opportunity to carry out research must be limited to a minority in any profession, an urgent and understanding sense of the need for research should be part of the mental equipment of every member of any profession worthy of the name.

He further adds that there is a need for the profession to cultivate research-mindedness which he defines as readiness to look analytically at the events or working methods, a willingness to encourage scientific study or experimentation and an ability to accept the proven conclusions and act accordingly.[6] Research is a fundamental function of a profession which is necessary to ensure its growth and progress. The professional competence of nursing personnel also greatly depends on the availability of research reports based on basic as well as applied researches. A recent book on Essentials of Nursing Research by Notter says that "Research is serious business. It should not be entered into lightly, but neither should it be feared." Nursing research in India still remains neglected. In order to keep the nursing service up-to-date it is necessary to organise programmes of in-service education and training for all nursing personnel as a means of improving the quality of patient care. The contents of these programmes may be carefully scrutinized. At present, wherever such programmes are being carried out, they are few and lack in seriousness and purpose.

The literature available for the study and research in nursing services and administration is in the context of the developed world and is written by the writers and their professional associations from the developed world. This situation needs to be improved by rejuvenating the nursing professional associations to inculcate professional standards among their members and produce stimulating literature in the context of the needs of their countries. Dr. Chitt (Thailand) while speaking in the Regional Committee meeting of the WHO suggested that steps should be taken to stimulate the establishment and development of professional nursing associations. The essential part to be played by them in the overall growth of the profession has not been fully appreciated even by the nurses themselves.[7] Besides, the nursing associations can help in building professional standards for the professional growth of their members.

According to Gardner:

> Standards are contagious. They spread throughout an organisation, a group, or a society. If an organisation or group cherishes high standards, the behaviour of the individual who enters it is inevitably influenced.[8]

The future of the nursing profession is in the hands of its members who must strive for creativity, academic excellence and the pursuit of a lofty standard in their professional activities.

CRITICAL APPRAISAL OF NURSING EDUCATION

The quality of nursing education needs immediate change so that qualitative nursing care can be assured. The following facts and suggestions can be taken into consideration to improve the situation:

I. Classification of Nurses Need Review

There should be two categories of nursing personnel-Graduate Nurse and an Auxiliary Nurse/Midwife. The nursing aides may not be included while classifying or defining nursing services.

2. Strict and Higher Entrance Qualifications to Attract Better Quality of Nurses to the Profession

The entrance qualifications should be higher secondary with science. At present, there is no admission policy, i.e. a fixed criteria for admission to nursing schools. It was learnt from direct interviews of some nurses that "merit is no criteria to get admission in a nursing school. Those who have political and other pressures get admitted leaving the best available candidates." It is suggested that nursing schools and colleges should declare their admission policy to ensure fairness, impartiality and proper selection. This would go a long way in improving the nursing profession.

3. Continuous and Well Planned Nursing Education

All nursing education should be continuous and not terminal. Besides, the in-service training programmes may be arranged to keep them abreast of the latest development. The nursing leaders do not appreciate the need for higher education among nurses as they think that nurses are to carry out only routine and mechanical duties which as already mentioned in the earlier part of this chapter is quite short-sighted and wrong. A nursing superintendent of a big hospital informed the present author that the nurses did not need higher education as they were responsible only for elementary activities like bed-making, spongebath noting the temperature, pulse-rate, respiration, etc. The doctors in a hospital hold the same view about the status of nurses. Mrs Narinder Nagpal, Secretary, Trained Nurses Association of India. in her article 'Noble Profession in. Neglect' in *The*

Tribune (Nov. 15, 1979) had rightly mentioned: "The nursing profession is treated as an auxiliary to the medical profession. We have been telling the medical men that they should leave the nursing profession to the nurses. But, so far we have not met with success." This is the reason why most of the nursing superintendents and hospital authorities are not in favour of deputing their nursing personnel for higher education. Some nurses even seem to feel that they are not allowed to improve their qualifications so that they may not become more qualified than the existing nursing leaders thereby posing a professional threat. It is strange to find that most of the nurses have improved their general qualifications through correspondence courses or by appearing in examinations in a private capacity. Many of them have completed the university degree courses while some of them have passed M.A. examinations from first rate universities. It is suggested that correspondence courses in B.Sc. Nursing may be instituted by some universities to ensure professional growth of nurses otherwise they would be misutilising their energy for improving general qualifications.

4. Status of Nursing Institutions should be Autonomous and not under Medical Personnel

Nursing schools and colleges should be independent institutions. There may be arrangement for formal and informal coordination between the hospital and the nursing institutions. This would save the exploitation of nursing student-perhaps relieve them from excessive clinical work and thus neglects of their studies. Miss Simone Liegois, Secretary, International Committee of Catholic Nurses, New Delhi, has rightly mentioned that the shortage of nurses led to the use of student nurses for services much to the detriment of theoretical instructions. This problem needed to be studied in order to raise the quality of basic training. Besides, nursing schools should adopt some hospitals to enlighten and develop the existing nursing personnel with the latest developments in the field of nursing education and administration. The nursing personnel in the hospital should be encouraged to study in the library so that they keep themselves aware of the latest developments.

5. Developing Quality Nursing Faculty

The nursing teachers of right quality and caliber should be prepared. Some research degree may be instituted. This would encourage research among the nursing educators. Their conditions of service must be the same as of Lecturers in a college. Besides, the time devoted by them in the nursing institutions is about 9 hours which is too much. This leaves no time for research and library reading. They must be encouraged to do independent work by reducing their duty hours. Most of the nurse educators interviewed by the writers were unaware of the system of health care prevailing in the country. They were only equipped in the paper they were teaching. It is suggested that an independent paper on "Health Care Administration" may be started to inform them of all the developments in this sector from the international to the local levels. Whenever a new post-graduate course in a particular medical speciality is started for doctors-a course for nurses and other workers should also be started simultaneously to prepare a team and provide effective services to the patients. The school and college subjects may include 'Nursing' as one of the papers which can create interest among the students to pursue this profession.[9]

6. Status of Nursing Faculty is too Low: Need of Upgradation

The dearth of nurses especially really well qualified and the unsatisfactory standards of education are because of the poor status of nursing as a career. Besides, the teachers of nursing institutions are not at par with their counterparts in schools and colleges. Professor P.K. Devi has suggested that: "In order to improve the image of nursing, the profession has to consider three aspects. First, the independent way in which nursing benefits humanity by taking crucial decisions at critical times where timely action by nurse-in-charge has led to saving of life, e.g., easily diagnosis by fatal complications like pulmonary embolism, collapse, hyperpyrexia, etc. Secondly, administrators must recognise the place of nursing in the medical team and nurses must prepare themselves to take their due place and accept this challenge. Thirdly, economic rewards must be commensurate with the nature of their responsibilities. Employment conditions must not be laid down unilaterally, nursing personnel must have a voice in determining how best and efficiently their services can be utilised.[10]

7. Need of Introducing Administration as a Component of Curriculum

There is a need of introducing principles of management and administration of health care in the curriculum of B.Sc. and M.Sc. Nursing. At present, the principles of administration are taught without making them understand their application in the provision of health care. It is suggested that an independent paper on 'Health Care Administration' may be started at B.Sc. and M.Sc. levels.

8. Need of Expansion of Nursing Institutions

There is a need to open more colleges/schools for imparting nursing education. The delegates at the Third All India Nursing Education Conference held at Chandigarh from 14 to 16 November 1979, strongly demanded a sizable increase in the number of seats in nursing colleges to tackle the growing need for nursing personnel in the country. The conference also urged that the nursing education curricula may be improved so that nurses are able to manage minor ailments on their own.

Indian Nursing Council

We may mention here briefly the role of the Nursing Council. It is a statutory body constituted under the Indian Nursing Council Act, 1947. The Council is responsible for regulation and maintenance of a uniform standard of training for nurses, midwives, auxiliary-nurse-midwives and health visitors. The Council prescribes syllabus and regulations for various nursing courses. In every meeting, the council discusses the issues pertaining to education and training of nursing personnel. There is a need of developing Nursing profession at par with other medical personnel. For this Nursing Council of India should make earnest efforts.

Nursing Associations

Besides there are Nursing Associations at the union level and in all the states. These Associations are engaged in routine activities and are not taking active steps to improve the status of the profession. They should publish material based on research in their journals which can influence policy-makers to look into the demands of the Nursing Profession.

Development of Nursing Education Services

The Rajkumari Amrit Kaur College of Nursing, New Delhi, a subordinate organization of the Ministry of Health and Family Welfare was established in 1946 with the object of developing and demonstrating model programmes in Nursing Education. The college works in close association with health centres, hospitals, medical centres and allied agencies for teaching undergraduates, post-graduates and also for continuing education of Nursing Personnel. The college provides advisory and consultative services on nursing education matters to the States, Union Territories and some developing countries.

Let us mention the role of a Leading Institution in Nursing Education:

Development of Nursing Services

In order to improve the quality of Nursing Services, the following activities are being implemented under the scheme of Development of Nursing Services:

- (i) Training of Nurses.
- (ii) Strengthening of existing schools/colleges of Nursing.
- (iii) Upgadation of schools of Nursing attached to Medical Colleges into Colleges of Nursing by providing one time non-recurring assistance of Rs. 1.50 crores to states.
- (iv) Providing recurring assistance to schools of Nursing which were opened during IXth plan with assistance under the scheme of Development of Nursing Services.
- (v) Establishment of College of Nursing at JIPMER, Pondicherry.
- (vi) Strengthening of RAK College of Nursing as "Centre of excellence."
- (vii) Upgradation of Schools of Nursing into Colleges of Nursing attached to Dr. R.M.L. Hospital, S.J. Hospital and Lady Hardinge Medical College, New Delhi.
- (viii) Construction of Delhi Nurses Colony.[10]

The Rajkumari Amrit Kaur College of Nursing, New Delhi, a subordinate organization of the Ministry of Health and Family Welfare was established in 1946 with the object of developing and demonstrating model programmes in Nursing Education. The College works in close association with health centres, hospitals, medical centres and allied agencies for teaching undergraduates, post-graduates and also for continuing education of Nursing personnel. The college provides advisory and consultative services on nursing education matters to the States, Union Territories and some developing countries. A provision of Rs. 85 lakhs in Plan and Rs. 285.00 lakhs under Non Plan has been made for the College in the budget for the year 2005-06.

Nursing education has always been an important part of education system due to its prime utility in the upkeep of human health. It is clear from the above that there is an acute shortage of nursing staff not only in India but also in other developed countries like USA and UK. It has been seen that almost all students passed out diploma/degree courses are getting jobs either in sufficient which has resulted a wide gap in demand and supply in nursing profession. It has become absolutely necessary that the Government of India should come forward to introduce courses in nursing education in large number in universities so that the gap of supply and demand is met. The kind of higher education a university in a developing country provides to its students today, will play a vital role in determining the shape of social, economic, political and industrial development of the country in the times ahead. The task of the educational institutions today is not only to enable to students to attain excellence in knowledge but also to contribute directly to national development. The goal of university education has a dual character: firstly the pursuit of knowledge and the attainment of excellence in different disciplines, which makes the university community conscious of its obligations to the community at large of which it is an important segment. As the report of Education Commission (1964-66) so aptly points out, the University education should have emphasis on internal transformation so as to relate it to the life, needs and aspirations of the nation. Promotion of nursing education in India will not only help in meeting the requirements of our country in the health care system but also helps in generating huge foreign currency by supplying of manpower in large number to other countries. The policy requires planned efforts to find an appropriate role and place for nursing education in overall health care delivery system.[11]

CRITICAL APPRAISAL

1. Status of Nursing Personnel is low: Need of Upgradation—Nurses in teaching and health services are not provided good salary. A lecturer in Nursing gets lower pay then a lecturer in a college or university. How can we expect quality from them. It is high time that to attract talented persons, grades and their promotion must be improved.

2. Curriculum is outdated—The curriculum of all categories of Nurses is very old and needs changes to accommodate new development.
3. Faculty needs improvements—Faculty is teaching the same material over the years. There must be some colleges where refresher courses can be arranged for them like Academic Staff College of University Grants Commission or these Academic Staff Colleges must be used to impart refresher courses.
4. Some health and hospital work may be decentralized to Nursing so that they get confidence and doctors can concentrate on critical patient.
5. Nursing Research must be promoted so that we may introduce innovations in Nursing profession.
6. Nurses must be taught as how to win the confidence of patients, doctors and their colleges.
7. A nursing commission may be appointed which can go into all the problems of Nursing especially Nursing Education.
8 Nursing colleges in the private sector do not impart good quality education as they make them work more in hospital to avoid expenditure on qualified nurses. There is a need of strict supervision.

Role of South-East Asia Regional Office in Nursing Education in the Region

Nursing and midwifery

The numerous challenges in field of nursing and midwifery being faced by member countries of the South East Asia Region are to be addressed through: the global framework for nursing and midwifery services 2006-10; World Health Assembly resolution WHA 59.27 on strengthening of nursing and midwifery; resolution WHA 59.23 on the rapid scaling up of production of public health workforce and the Regional Committee resolution SEA/RC59/R6 on health workforce in South-East Asia. In addition, Member countries are being encouraged to develop the nursing and midwifery workforce database to monitor the gaps in the workforce. an inter country meeting on networking Of nursing and midwifery education institutions for nursing and midwifery development was organized in July 2006 as part of multi-country activities. Issues of quality of education (especially of teachers), nursing curriculum and the need for adequate infrastructure were discussed. On the recommendations of the meeting, a South-East Asia nursing and midwifery education institution network (SEANMEIN) was established to serve as a forum for sharing information and resources, as well as for capacity building of nursing and midwifery educational institutions. The first meeting of the network was organized in Chandigarh, India in May 2007. The focus was on three Critical areas:

(a) Scaling up the quality of Nursing and midwifery production;
(b) Midwifery education; and
(c) Community Nursing education.

The results of the study Regarding inclusion of HIV/AID in the pre-Service nursing and midwifery teaching curriculum were also discussed at the meeting.

A network plan was developed to improve nursing and midwifery education, services and research. The Regional Office will continue to advocate for a midwifery framework and to strengthen midwifery teaching and capacity building of existing midwives. Also planned are a training course on community nursing and a regional conference on revisiting the community-based health workforce in order to strengthen capacity at the community level.

Capacity building of nurses and midwives in response to health problems and MDG No.5 has been continuously emphasized by WHO. In addition to fellowships, the Regional Office supported the implementation of the third and fourth training-of-trainers courses on nursing management in HIV/AIDS prevention, care and support, organized in November 2006 and May 2007, respectively, by the three WHO collaborating centres for nursing and midwifery development in Thailand.

Furthermore, the following training/short courses were also organized:

(i) training of trainers on development of an education module on midwifery teaching, Chiang Mai, Thailand;
(ii) training of nursing and midwifery management trainers on malaria prevention and care, Chittagong, Bangladesh; and
(iii) a short training course on community-oriented nursing education in Bangkok and Khon Kaen, Thailand.

The following other activities were undertaken in Member-countries of the Region:

- Strengthening the functions of the nursing council in Bangladesh;
- Mobilization of funds for conducting the third training course for post-bachelors degree students of nursing in Bhutan;
- Revision of the nursing curriculum and training on accreditation of nursing services for DPR Korea;
- Strengthening the teaching faculty of the Ph..D programme in nursing in India;
- Review of nursing regulations in Maldives;
- Development of accreditation guidelines and strengthening of skilled birth attendants in Nepal;

- Advice on the ladder programme in Nursing, and the election of the nursing council board members in Sri Lanka; and
- Financial support to the nurses' association of Timor Leste.

Member-countries are being encouraged To develop and implement policies and National strategic plans for health workforce Development. Efforts are being made to ensure that nursing and midwifery work-force policy and planning form integral parts of the human resources for health (HRH) plan to build an adequate, competent and motivated nursing and midwifery workforce.

Most countries of the SEA Region are faced with similar challenges in nursing and midwifery, including shortages of qualified nurses and midwives, migration of qualified nurses, low quality of nursing and midwifery, education and service, inadequate in-service training programmes for capacity building to respond to health problems and lack of effective regulations. Members-countries are being encouraged to scale up training of nurses and midwives with an emphasis on retention and recruitment, as well as quality of education and educators.[12]

Nurses voicing their commitments potentials, and good intentions will no longer suffice. Are nurses prepared to challenge the present system of education in order to effectively work towards the goal of health for all, or are they merely going to pursue the status quo? The greatest number of health workers are nurses; but what are they doing about primary health care? They, above are other health workers, have been prepared to be closer to people—but are they close to all people?

What can nurses do to really have an impact on acheving health for all? A lot of new things will have to be done:

New ways of thinking
New attitudes about health
New ways of doing things
New ways of working
New relationship formed
New priorities
New functions
New ways of teaching and learning

Once the nursing community begins to apply the new thinking and becomes actively engrossed in the new way of doing things, partnership with communities will be visibly strengthened and the goal of health for all can be more realistically pursued. Education for nurses based on the concept of primary health care is an essential means of achievements this goal.[13]

Nurses around the world will continue to be an important link in the health care chain. A prime motivator in this regard is the International Council of Nurses, which is working through its 114 national nurses' associations to strengthen nursing forces worldwide. And to give nurses adequate support and recognition in all countries. WHO has created a Global Adivsory Group on Nursing and Midwifery charged with finding "Innovative and practical options to ensure the optimal contributions of nursing for the health of all people in the worth.[14]

We cannot ensure quality nursery care until and unless nurses are selected on merit, given right education and training. The recognition of the institution is done by Nursing Council of India and University of healthy. Chitleen K. Sethi in his article in *The Tribune* dated Dec. 7, 2007 clearly defines that the Akali-BJP government in the state apparently believes that two wrongs make a right. After having allowed seven unapproved nursing colleges in the state to run the B.Sc. (Nursing) course, the government has now allowed several unapproved nursing colleges to offer the post-basic B.Sc. (Nursing) Course. None of these institutes are either affiliated to the Baba Farid University of Health Sciences or have the approval of the Indian Nursing Council (INC) to run these courses.

To add to this, "generosity", the state government has also done away with the entrance test, normally held for admission to the post-basic B.Sc. course and allowed individual colleges to admit students on their own. This is a diversion from the procedure for centralized admission. The INC website lists only 10 institute in Punjab that have been approved by the council to offer the post basic B.Sc. (Nursing) course. Added to these now are the eight unapproved colleges allowed by the government to admit students to the course. The government has like it did for the B.Sc. course earlier, bypassed the INC and the university and unilaterally determined the number of seats these colleges can offer. These eight colleges are the Mata Sahib Kaur College of Nursing, Mohali, Baba Ke Educational Trust, Moga, Baba Farid Educational and Medical Research Society, Kotkapura, Gian Sagar College of Nurisng, Banur, National Institute of Nuring, Sangrur, Bharat Institute of Nursing, Jallandhar, Sunrise Educational Society, Tarn Taran, and Kular Medical Educational and Research Society, Ludhiana. All these colleges have been granted 60 seats each for the post-basic B.Sc. (Nursing) course. Three of them are already the beneficiaries of the government's largesse in permission for the B.Sc. (Nursing) course. All these measures would dilute quality nursing care.

CONCLUSION

Nursing is an integral part of the health system. Nursing can promote good health. We were not attending earlier about their conditions of service. Time has come when we must improve their status through good conditions of service as well as through job enrichment and job enlargement.

Thus, an adequate and sound salary structure together with healthy working conditions is the *sine qua non* for the organizational efficiency and effectiveness. Otherwise, as the Administrative Reforms Commission aptly observes, the lack of those conditions has been: "one of the major factors for strikes, agitations, inter-service tensions and rivalries, indifferent attitude to work, poor performance, frustration and low morale of the employees." In other words, the aim of health care systems should be to create and maintain such conditions whereby an employee feels like giving his best, gets satisfaction out of his job and is suitably rewarded. Besides the conditions of service, the personnel management may look after the following aspects of nursing personnel:

(a) to treat the nurses as key personnel and as partners along with the other members of health care and medical team;
(b) to help the nursing personnel reach self-actualisation and thereby help release their creative energy for the promotion of health;
(c) to create facilities for continuous growth, development and training of nursing personnel to make them fit for higher jobs;
(d) to ensure adequate working arrangements and maximum participation in management and decision-making of the health system by nursing personnel;
(e) to provide institutional safeguards for redressal of their grievance especially to bring their emoluments at par with other professionals and improve their working conditions;
(f) setting good professional standards by senior nursing personnel;
(g) development of unity, energy, initiative and loyally among nursing personnel;
(h) to promote their creativity, insight and loyalty; and
(i) to improve the nurse-patient ratio from 1:12 to 1:3.

Notes and References

1. National League for Nursing, What People can Expect of Modern Nursing Service, New York, 1959.
2. Henderson, Virginia (1969), Basic Principles of Nursing Care, Geneva, International Council of Nurses, p. 4.
3. Manju Chhugani, "Status of Nursing Education in India", *University News*, 45 (11), March 11, 2007.
4. WHO, SEA/RC//19/2, p. 96.
5. WHO, Technical Report Series, 1966, NO. 347, p. 7.
6. Brotherston, J.H., Research Mindedness and the Health Profession, quoted in International Council of Nurses, Learning to Investigate Nursing Problems, London, 1960, p. 24.
7. WHO, SEA/RC/21/2, p. 111.
8. Garnder, John W. Excellence, New York, 1961, Harper and Brothers, p. 74.
9. WHO, SEA/RC/21/2, p. 111.
10. The First All India Nursing Education Conference, Chandigarh, April 19-24, 1971, Proceedings of the Conference, p. 26.

11. Annual Report, Ministry of Health and Family Welfare, GOI, New Delhi, 2006-07, p. 18.
12. Manju Chhugani, Status of Nursing Education in India, *University News*, March 12, 2007, pp. 11-12.
13. Amelia Mangay Maglacas, "The Challenge for Nursing Education", *World Health*, June 1985, p. 21.
14. The Work of WHO, in the South-East Asia Region, Report of Regional Director, WHO, June 2007, pp. 70-73.

APPENDIX 2.1

SUMMARY OF RECOMMENDATIONS OF SHETTY COMMITTEE

Nursing Training

1. Recruitment of additional students, and the necessary staff for supervision and teaching, in the existing training centres as a first step towards increasing the number of nursing personnel.

2. Creation of posts for nursing staff in institutions and in the public health field to absorb the additional number of nurses who will be trained.

3. The appointment of auxiliary nurses and midwives to supplement the nursing service in hospitals or wards which are not used for training nurses. Establishment of training centres in District Headquarter's hospitals for auxiliary nurses and midwives.

4. Improvement in conditions of training of nurses. Priority to be given to:

(a) provision of adequate living accommodation;
(b) proper facilities for practical work, and adequate training for sister tutors and ward sisters;
(c) proper care of student's health;
(d) raising of educational standards wherever possible; and
(e) shorter working hours.

5. Better publicity to the potentialities of nursing as a career.

6. Special consideration to be given to personality and home background when recruiting students, providing that they meet other minimum requirements. Selection Committee to be constituted of Medical and Nursing Superintendents and Sister Tutor.

7. Ordinarily, married women, unless widowed or separated from their husbands, not to be admitted for training. Students not to be allowed to marry during training period.

8. Minimum requirements for admission to training schools to be in accordance with the regulations of the Indian Nursing Council.

9. Medium of instruction to be decided on by each State. Individual training centres should also have discretion to decide this question.

10. Setting up a system of counseling for students, an experienced sister being assigned to a group of students for this purpose.

11. Students to be required to be resident during training.

12. Stipend and allowances adequate for messing, uniforms and laundry expenses.

13. Students may be required to execute a bond for two years

Appendix 2.2

RECOMMENDATIONS OF MUDALIAR COMMITTEE (1959-61)

1. There should be three grades of nurses, viz. the basic nurse with four years of training. the auxiliary nurse midwife with two years of training and the nurse with a degree qualification.

2. Candidates admitted to the general nursing course should have the minimum qualification of matriculation or equivalent; and the candidates for the degree course should have passed the higher secondary or pre-university examination.

3. In view of the need for securing a larger number of recruits for the nursing profession the age of admission can be relaxed to 16 in suitable cases as a transitional measure particularly in States where there are difficulties in recruiting candidates at the age of 17.

4. The medium of instruction should preferably be English for the general nursing course, while the degree course should be taught only in English.

5. Nurse pupils should not be over-burdened with the routine duties in hospitals, but more attention should be given to training and practical experience. They should not be subjected to too many spells of night duty in hospitals.

6. A large number of hospitals in the country can be utilised for Nursing Schools. District headquarters' hospitals with a bed strength of 75 to 100 should also be utilised for this purpose.

7. The minimum number of admissions to the course should be 12.

8. Student nurses should be provided free furnished accommodation in hostels, free board, free supply of uniforms, laundry arrangements, free books, free medical services, medical check-up twice a year and suitable recreational facilities. The stipend during training should be a minimum of Rs. 35 increasing by Rs. 10 every year.

9. There should be a Nursing Advisory Committee in each school for advising on admissions and welfare of the trainees.

10. Each nursing school should have its own separate budget.

11. The training of auxiliary nurse midwives should be continued and extended, because it will be necessary for a long time to come to have a second line of trained personnel to meet the needs of the country.

12. The number of auxiliary nurse midwives to be trained should be phased in such a way that there will be one auxiliary nurse midwife for 50,000 population by the end of 15 years.

13. The time is come when fresh thinking on the type of training at present given to health visitors should be done. There should, instead, be a public health nurse with a basic nursing qualification and one year's further training particularly in domiciliary care and other public health aspects of community work.

.Appendix 2.3

INC RECOMMENDATION FOR STAFFING PATTERN

Staffing in Hospital

1. Nursing Supenntendent-1 (for minimum of 150 beds)
2. Deputy Nursing Superintendent-1
3. Assistant Nursing Superintendent-2

(for every additional 50 beds one more Assistant Nursing Superintendent)

Nursing Staff for Wards Special Units and Out-Patient Department

	Staff Nurse	*Sister*	*Deptt. Sr ANS*
Medical Ward	1:3	1:25 each shift	1 for 3-4 wards
Surgical Ward	1:3	1:25 each shift	1 for 3-4 wards
Orthopaedic Ward	1:3	1:25 each shift	1 for 3-4 wards
Paediatric Ward	1:3	1:25 each shift	1 for 3-4 wards
Gynaecology Ward	1:3	1:25 each shift	1 for 3-4 wards
Maternity Ward (induding newborns)	1:3	1:25 each shift	1 for 3-4 wards
Intensive Care Unit	1:1 (24 hrs.)	1 each shift	1 each shift.
Coronary Care Unit	1:1 (24 hrs.)	1 each shift	1 Department
Nephrology	1:1 (24 hrs.)	1 each shift	Sister/ANS for 3-4 units clubbed together
Nephrology and Neuro Surgery	1:1 (24 hrs.)	1 each shift	
Special Wards, Eye, ENT, etc.	1:1 (24 hrs)	1 each shift	
Operation Theatre	3 for 24 hrs	1 each shift	Per table 1 Departmental Sister/ANS for 4-5 Operation theatres
Casualty and Emergency	2-3 S.N.	1 each shift	1 Departmental sisters Depending ANS for Emergency on the No. of beds Casualty, etc.

Out-Patient-Based on Actual Observation

(a) Minor Operation theatre	1 staff nurse for every 13 patients
(b) Injection Room	1 staff nurse for every 86 patients
(c) Surgical	1 staff nurse for every 120 patients
(d) Medical	1 staff nurse for every 140 patients
(e) Gynaecology	1 staff nurse for every 35 patients
(f) Paediatric	1 staff nurse for every 85 patients
(g) Orthopaedic	1 staff nurse for every 120 patients
(h) Dental	1 staff nurse for every 120 patients
(i) ENT	1 staff nurse for every 120 patients
(j) Eye	1 staff nurse for every 186 patients
(k) Skin	1 staff nurse for every 120 patients

Health Manpower Planning

Manpower planning is the keystone in the arch of personnel management.

> "Good Management provides the surplus which on investment nourish the processes of industrialization and modernization of society. Good administration furnishes the infrastructure and modernization of society. Good administration furnishes the infrastructure for services which secure the order, stability and social development. Carefully recruited and periodically trained or re-trained top-personnel are needed for both spheres of operation. How to regulate the affairs of the nation so as to maximize the efficiency of both is the supreme challenge to political leadership. Only by meeting it successfully can a democratic polity, survive in the non-too-long run."
>
> —*Dr. C.D. Deshmukh*

A. GENESIS AND NEED

The health problems inspite of researches are increasing rapidly. To plan for more effectiveness in improving the health and well-being of the people would require a probing analysis of what has worked well and what has fallen short, as well as a careful assessment of future options available. It is not only that patterns of disease and threats to health are changing, but the modes of response are being increasingly determined by larger societal forces—political, economic, cultural—functioning at global, national and local levels.

Despite the importance given to health manpower development in the country by the Health Committees, National Health Policy and successive Five Year Plans, this has remained as one of the weakest areas and has turned out to be a 'liability' rather than an 'asset' in the health care delivery services in the country. Over the years, lack of appropriate manpower planning, *adhoc* and short-sighted policy measures, weak organizational control mechanisms and over emphasis on rapid expansion seem to have conspired together to create a situation in which despite availability of huge health manpower and health infrastructure, the quality of health services and expected outputs are confronted with a rapid declining trend.

A developing economy needs high-level technical manpower as urgently as it needs capital. A crucial factor in improving the coverage and quality of health services is the availability of adequate number of health personnel with task-oriented training. Ninth Plan has been very critical of Health Manpower Planning. To quote the Plan:

The outcome and impact of any health programme depends on the competencies and skills of the personnel who implement it. Both in the State and in the Central sector, over 75% of the funds provided are spent to meet the salary of the employees. Personnel costs form a major portion of investment in health service delivery in voluntary and private sector. Unlike health service planning, health manpower planning in India has not received adequate attention. There has been very little attempt to assess the requirement in manpower and to match health manpower production with requirement. While the production of physicians and specialists has been more than the estimated requirement, dental and para-professional manpower production has lagged far behind the present and projected needs. The curricula have not kept pace with the changing health are requirements of the population or skills and attitudes required for implementation of health and family welfare programmes. Continuous updating of skills and knowledge have not been made an essential mandatory requisite for all practicing health professionals. There are regional disparities both in quantity and quality of available health care professionals. These factors constitute a major Impediment to effective implementation of the health and family welfare programmes.

Accordingly the Ninth Plan enunciated the following objectives:

1. to establish an Education Commission of Health Sciences with the assigned responsibility of planning and producing health manpower that is appropriate in quantity to the present and projected needs of the health system;
2. to strengthen the educational process for all categories of health Professionals at all levels so that health are professionals possess necessary .knowledge and have appropriate skills. Health programme orientation and people orientation; and
3. to ensure continuing knowledge and skill up gradation of all health care providers through continuing Education Programmes with emphasis on multi-professional problem-solving learning strategies.

World Health Organization Regional Office for South-East Asia, New Delhi, in its declaration on Health Development in the South-East Asia Region in the 21st Century mentioned the following foremost challenge.

Our Foremost Challenges:

- Closing the gaps and inequities in health in our societies.
- Creating conditions that promotes health and self-reliance.
- Ensuring basic health services to all, especially the poor, women and other vulnerable groups.
- Upholding and enforcing health ethics.
- Placing health at the centre of development.

Manpower Planning must follow the Health Public Policy

- *Create conditions to support health*: We will advocate and encourage advocacy for healthy public policies including population policies, and for empowering people with knowledge and skills to improve their own health. Health promotion will be intensified. Forces promoting unhealthy life styles will be counteracted.
- *Ensure quality health programmes for children and families*: Children and families will continue to receive quality health care, including physical and mental health. Special provision needs to be made for children in difficult circumstances, such as those who are physically and mentally disabled, victims of natural and man-made disasters, orphans and children of parents suffering from HIV and AIDS.
- *Strengthen existing partnerships and forge new ones for health development at all levels*: Determinants of ill-health cover multi-sectoral concerns such as lack of education, environmental degradation, economic reversals and poverty. Efforts will be made for interaction between health planning, policies and actions with other sectors and these sectors will be urged to include health concerns in their agendas.
- *Prevent health hazards that may result from development*: Development projects, such as construction of dams and irrigation schemes, can bring in their wake malaria and other vector-borne diseases. Similarly, unplanned urbanization leading to proliferation of slums causes many health problems. The time has come to make those responsible for creating a fertile ground for the spread of disease also accountable. In formulating strategies to accelerate growth and development, we will insist that all parties, public and private, recognize and prevent the health hazards they are likely to create, from the very inception of their enterprises

- *Ensure adequate nutrition*: Malnutrition attributable to dietary deficiencies and faulty dietary habits is correctable. We will promote nutrition education and ensure implementation of a healthy public policy on fair price distribution of quality food.
- *Advocate intensively for health*: We shall advocate as widely as possible that health is central to development and that sustained development is important for health. We will ensure that health is placed high on the political agenda of governments and on the social agenda of people.
- *Uphold and enforce health ethics*: We realize that with new scientific and technological advancements in tertiary health care, the poor and underprivileged in countries with large populations run the risk of exploitation, as evident in trading in human organs for transplantation We shall remain vigilant towards the ethical issues involved, and protect these sections of the community from such exploitation

Other Actions

- *Ensure quality and social relevance of education and training for health personnel*: In order to realize the new vision of health it is essential to bring about appropriate reforms in the education and training programmes of health personnel, including continuing professional development. We shall strive for a cost-effective mix of human resources for health.
- *Strengthen epidemiological surveillance and health Information*: Unforeseen outbreaks and epidemics, such as HIV/AIDS, have strained our resources and diverted attention from current commitments. To enhance our capacity for vigilance within and among countries, particularly at our borders, we will assist one another in developing epidemiological surveillance and will exchange information critical to health. We will strive to collect reliable and disaggregated data so that the true burden of disease and disability can be reflected.
- *Strengthen health care for the elderly*: The elderly represent a growing proportion of our Region's population. Their health problems, often chronic and disabling, require both medical and psychosocial care. We will accord greater attention to geriatric care, particularly as joint families give way to nuclear families.
- *Develop regional self-reliance*: We will increase the capacity of each country and of the Region to be more creative and innovative in developing health and medical sciences, medical technology and health care services. Such regional self-reliance calls for regional solidarity and inter-country cooperation. Support for research and development in the Region, with particular attention to quality assurance, affordability and accessibility will be enhanced.[1]

Manpower planning is a technique of correcting imbalances between the manpower demand and manpower supply in the economy. Such imbalances can create either the problem of unemployment or shortage. Both situations are dangerous and suicidal for the socio-economic development of a country. Thus, it is necessary to plan the long-term growth and development of highly skilled manpower to avoid the evil consequences. Manpower planning is not only concerned with balancing of demand and supply of different categories of manpower, but also with overall development and utilization of manpower resources in a country. Prof Harbison has rightly remarked in this connection that in the broadest terms, manpower policy should be concerned with development, maintenance and utilization of actual or potential members of the labour force including those who are fully and productively employed as well as those who experience difficulty in getting work. The development of manpower is the process of man's acquiring the skills, knowledge and capacities of work—the maintenance of manpower is the process of preservation and continuous renewal of man's capacities for work. The utilization of manpower is the process of matching men and work in accordance with their level of development."[2]

Manpower planning has not received due attention in the health sector in spite of its expansion and diversification. The development of human resources has an importance that can only be overlooked at the cost of survival. An important prerequisite for improving the health situation in any country is undoubtedly the availability of different categories of manpower suitably trained to fulfil the health programmes and to respond to the established and emerging needs of the people. Effective health manpower planning is a vital national responsibility because on it largely depends the success of all other health activities. Let us now define Health Manpower Planning.

MEANING AND DEFINITION OF HEALTH MANPOWER PLANNING

According to Dev Ray, "A health manpower plan is meant to ensure that the right number and quality of manpower are available to staff the health facilities as the needs expand, so as to keep up with current and future demands of services from the people."[3]

According to Tamas Fulop, Director of the Health Manpower Development Division, WHO, the objective of a health manpower should be: "to concentrate all national efforts so as to satisfy the health services composed of balanced teams of health personnel; that is to ensure that all health activities are undertaken at the most peripheral level of the health services as is practicable, by workers most suitably trained to carry out these activities. Their emphasis should be put on the most 'suitably' trained as opposed to the most 'highly' trained since the latter term might entail confusing the most sophisticated and most costly with the optimal."[4]

According to John Bland, information expert at Geneva, health manpower planning is: "a process of estimating the quality and type of knowledge, skill and attitudes of a health system. The object of the exercise is not merely to promote health in the wide sense, but to provide the appropriately trained staff who will, as far as possible, treat diseases, prevent their onset and meet community's demand for services."[5]

The WHO Chronicle states:

> "Manpower Planning is concerned with organizing, in systematic fashion, the goals, objectives, priorities and activities of manpower development in order to ensure that the right number of staff with the appropriate skills are provided at the right time to meet the requirements of the work to be done."[6]

There should be only one yardstick to judge the effectiveness of manpower planning, namely, continuous improvement of the health status and the quality of life of the population with the least trouble to those who supply the services and the maximum satisfaction to those who receive it. We have to achieve all this with the minimum cost and maximum efficiency.

Thus, manpower planning is the keystone in the arch of personnel management. Manpower planning, looked at from the statistical point of view, is a process of information collection, analysis and projection to determine the likely effect of existing or proposed manpower policies on the manpower system under study and to present, and advise upon possible course of action to overcome present or future problems. This process is designed to help management to match manpower supply to requirements in accordance with the health polices of the country. Manpower planning can help the organisation in the development of uniformity and consistency: designing tools of personnel appraisal and developing the standards to avoid the impact of pressure. This would lead to effective and sound decision-making relating to personnel in an organization.

NEED FOR MANPOWER PLANNING

Human resources planning is necessary for all organizations for the following reasons:

(i) To carry on its work, each organization need personnel with the necessary qualifications, skills, ethos, knowledge, work experience and aptitude for work. These are provided through effective planning.

(ii) There is a constant need for replacing such personnel. Since a large number of persons who have grown old, or who retire, die or become incapacitated because of physical or mental ailments, have to be replaced.

(iii) In order to meet the needs of expansion programmes, human resources planning is unavoidable.

(iv) To meet the challenge of a new and changing technology and new techniques, existing employees needs to be trained or new look injected in an organization.

(v) Manpower planning is also needed in order to identify areas of surplus personnel or areas in which there is a shortage of personnel.

INGREDIENTS OF HEALTH MANPOWER PLANNING (Chart 3.1)

Health manpower planning must take into consideration all the factors which are considered by manpower planning units in other sector of development. Besides, health manpower planning units have to make a note of many other factor which are peculiar to this sector alone. In the present situation, most of the factors are ignored resulting in defective personnel policies and decisions. Let us now discuss all the factors which must be taken into consideration by the personnel responsible for Health Manpower Planning.

(I) Long 'Lead Time' between the Need and Supply of the Health Manpower

Manpower consists nor only of people but also of knowledge, skills and attitudes acquired through education and formal training. The difficulty arises from the long 'lead time' required to bring about such education and training. It takes about 7 year after the college education to prepare an under-graduate physician in India. It has been rightly said that:

> "For a profession such as medicine, even a ten-year planning period is insufficient. Decision made in year one can begin to affect supply only by year eight or nine."[7]

The same is true of other categories of health personnel. There is a need to re-examine the curriculum of medical education at the under-graduate level. Is it necessary to teach everything? Can we reduce the duration of training without endangering the quality in terms of needs and performance? All these decisions must be taken to prepare an effective Health Manpower Plan. Dr. Dowling of WHO in an interview to World Health suggested: "To prune down and adapt the curriculum to the needs of the population; that curriculum will be very different from those which apply in a wealthy industrialised country. But it is easy for those responsible for health services in a developing country to assume that such different education and training will produce a second-class doctor. We on the contrary believe that it will produce a first-class doctor."[8] Such re-examination of curriculum is required for all types of courses.

CHART 3.1

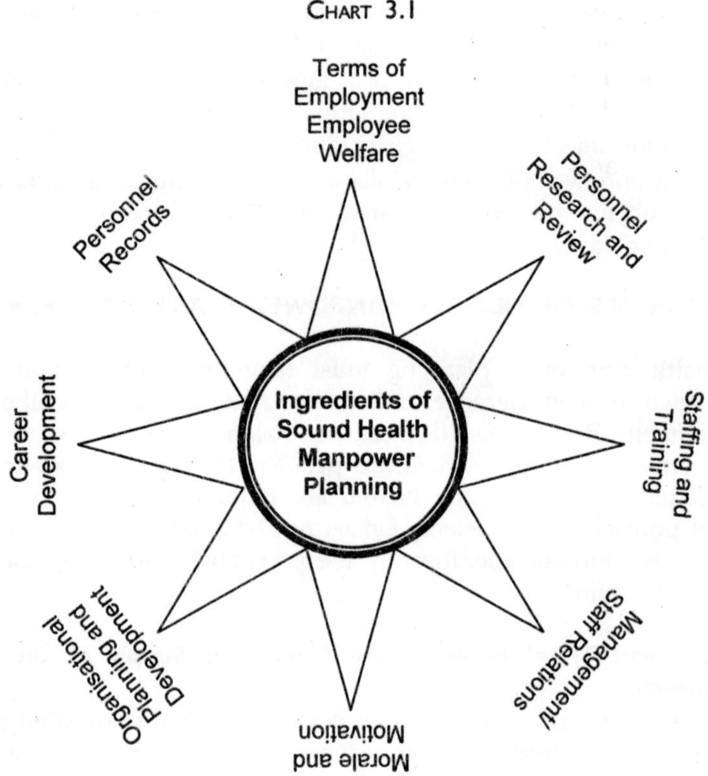

(2) High Cost of Training Health Personnel

The largest element in the budget of health services is cost of training and retention of staff. Data from various sources indicate that the expenditure on the establishment of health personnel in many countries ranges between 60-70 per cent of the cost of delivering health services. The cost of educating a physician ranges between US $ 50.000 and US $ 80,000 depending upon the socio-economic conditions in the country and the level of specialisation of the physician. In India, it is estimated that the cost of training an under-graduate doctor is Rs. 500,000. We need today a large number of health personnel to provide health care services to seventy per cent of the rural people. The number of medical doctors for every 10,000 inhabitants of the world in 1970 was only 7.9 for the developed countries, the ratio was 14.7. In Africa and Asia this ratio was 0.7 and 1.00 respectively.[9] It appears that the coverage in the developing countries is very poor. The same situation prevails with regard to nurses, dentists, pharmacists, etc.

For the first time in recorded history, it is today possible to reduce the ravages of crippling diseases by a systematic application of the increasing knowledge of bio-medical sciences to the health problems of the world community. But without a significant increase in the number of physicians and other health workers in the coming years. It is unlikely that the people of the world will achieve that degree of freedom from disease that optimal care can now provide. Leroy E. Burney (USA), President of the 11th World Health Assembly, 1958 rightly said:

> "A paramount responsibility of the World Health Community is To reduce the lag between the discovery of new knowledge and its application."[10]

The education and training of health staff holds for all member-states a universality of interest in that it is basic to their total health endeavors. But, the basic question which must be kept in mind by health manpower planning officers is the cost and utility of training physicians and specialists.

(3) Comparative Cost of Training and Retaining Health Workers for Primary Health Care

How to decide about the possible mixes of different sorts of health Workers? We may decide the mix which can train and retain the manpower of cover the whole of the country and be within the financial limits of the country.

There is a need of innovation in the concept of health manpower planning to make it relevant to present and future community health needs. The new innovations may take into consideration the following:

(a) Training and utilisation of more auxiliary and primary health worker and their supervisors.
(b) Training of health personnel should not be only hospital and Disease-oriented but should be preventive and promotive. It should help the health personnel to develop an effective link with the health of the community.
(c) Education of physicians may be made relevant to the needs of the society.
(d) Education must prepare health professionals for their leadership role in a Community development.
(e) The specialists must concentrate only on secondary and tertiary care and should not devote their time and waste the resources in promoting primary health care. More services can be made available if some of the health workers, trained for certain simple routine tasks, can release the professional personnel and enable them to concentrate on activities which require a higher level of competence.

Thus, the health manpower planners will have to decide about the proper mix between the different categories of health personnel to provide health care to the community.

> "These changes should result in a sound health manpower system which will plan. develop and manage/utilise efficiently the right 'mix' of health personnel within well-conceived health and other services, which will continuously monitor whether they all are functioning properly and which will adjust the planning and 'production' system on the basis of such monitoring, so as to achieve a full health coverage for the entire population in the coming decades."[11]

(4) Migration of Physicians and Nurses

It was estimated in 1991 that there were at least 140,000 physicians and 135,000 nurses working outside their country of birth, citizenship or training. The most affected countries in this regard are India and the Phillipines, each with over 10.000 physicians abroad. Other countries suffering heavy losses are Ireland, Iran, Pakistan, Bangladesh and the Republic of Korea with over 3,000 physicians abroad. Brain drain from one country is another country's brain gain. What is the impact of this migration on the health manpower planning machinery in a developing country?

> "The Policy implications, for both donor and recipient countries alike, are quite clear: reform the professional system so that the right skills in the right proportions are produced; create the right local institutions to train the needed secondary and tertiary levels of health manpower; send abroad only those students for whom specialized training at home cannot be provided and whose specialities will be directly applicable on their return. Such reforms can be effected only on the basis of well-calculated policies and plans for producing and utilising health manpower within the context of the health services requirements."[12]

Besides, the health manpower planning units should discourage the migration through: (a) fostering of national loyalties and ideals of service; (b) opening of new avenues to retain qualified and competent personnel; (c) strict legislation to stop migration; (d) raising the status of technical personnel; and (e) strict legislation to serve in the country while granting fellowship to study abroad.

In this way, the developing countries can save a lot of money spent on the education and training of health personnel serving overseas. Besides, the retention of those persons in these countries would improve their health system.

(5) Individuals with differing Skills may not be easily Substituted

The field of health is highly specialised. It is not possible to substitute any health expert in an other's place. They are to be substituted only by the personnel of the same specialisation. Sometimes, if happens that in a hospital two physicians are provided but no surgeon. One cannot substitute the other. This becomes very serious in the case of teaching-*cum*-research institutions. The manpower planning units must attend to this difficulty and avoid overgrowth or undergrowth in any branch of specialization.

(6) Team Work

Most of the health workers are working in isolation, i.e. their activities are not coordinated resulting in lower output of services. The health workers should form part of health manpower planning system. According to Antonio Ordonez-Plaja:

> "Team work requires, among other things, that the members have an image of their learn-mates which coincides as precisely us possible with reality. In addition, each member must have a self-image which adjusts to reality as much as possible and thus coincides with the image the other members have of him."[13]

Team work would develop common practices and shared experiences. This would also raise the morale of the health personnel working at the grass-root level. Dr. Daneil Aahault, head of the team of Development Unit, WHO, has rightly said:

> "Backed up by health service officials working at a higher level. conscious of belonging to a group and not being in isolation, the local health team will find its prestige and its credibility strengthened. It will find it easier to win the confidence of the local population, and that confidence in turn will facilitate the development of services that are better adapted to the needs."[14]

(7) Coordination among the Public, Private and Voluntary Health Sectors

Health services are being provided through public, private and voluntary agencies. It is very difficult to control the personnel policies of the private and voluntary sectors. Private sector is helping a great deal in the promotion of health. The health manpower planning unit must take into consideration the personnel of all the sectors and not concentrate only on the public sector.

(8) Feed-back System

Feed-back is important to remove the defects of health manpower planning. In developing countries, there is no machinery to develop the health manpower plans on scientific lines resulting in the malutilisation of scarce technical resources. This can be avoided if there is a proper feed-back machinery to evaluate the manpower planning system.

(9) New Patterns and a Variety of Approaches

The concept of health manpower planning is still in its infancy. The health departments in the developing countries pay little attention to this aspects. We will have to find new structures, new patterns and a variety of approaches to develop health manpower planning suiting the requirements of the developing countries. We must encourage applied researches to find the solutions to the problems of health manpower development. The association of social scientists interested in health care administration would be a step in the right direction. Besides these peculiar features, there are certain other ingredients which may be kept in mind while developing plans for manpower development. Most important of them are mentioned below (refer to Chart 3.1, "Ingredients of Sound Manpower Planning"):

(a) Finding and selecting the right caliber and number of people required to perform the operations of the organisation involved.
(b) Adequate briefing of new employees to the organisation and the job.
(c) Fair, sound and effective terms of employment.
(d) Provision of incentives.
(e) Establishment and maintenance of personnel inventories based on periodic appraisals of the productivity, methods, qualifications and potential of employees.
(f) Well-organised and specific training.
(g) Continuing personnel research.
(h) Management and staff relations based on mutual confidence and respect.

B. DEVELOPMENT OF HEALTH MANPOWER PLANS

Health manpower planning is a coordination of three main elements of the health manpower development process—Planning, Production and Management of health manpower. This process needs to be linked with health planning and socio-economic planning. The planners must consider the manpower planning process as a part and parcel of the process of Socio-economic planning undertaken by a country, otherwise desirable results may not be possible in human resource development. According to the Indian Planning Commission.

> "Manpower Planning is an integral part of the economic plans formulated by the Central and State Governments and their agencies, and, within their own specific fields by industrial association representing different activities or interests as well as by individual undertakings and institutions, both public and private."[15]

Let us discuss the important steps in this process. (See Chart 3.2)

CHART 3.2

Inter-Relationship in Health Services and Manpower Development

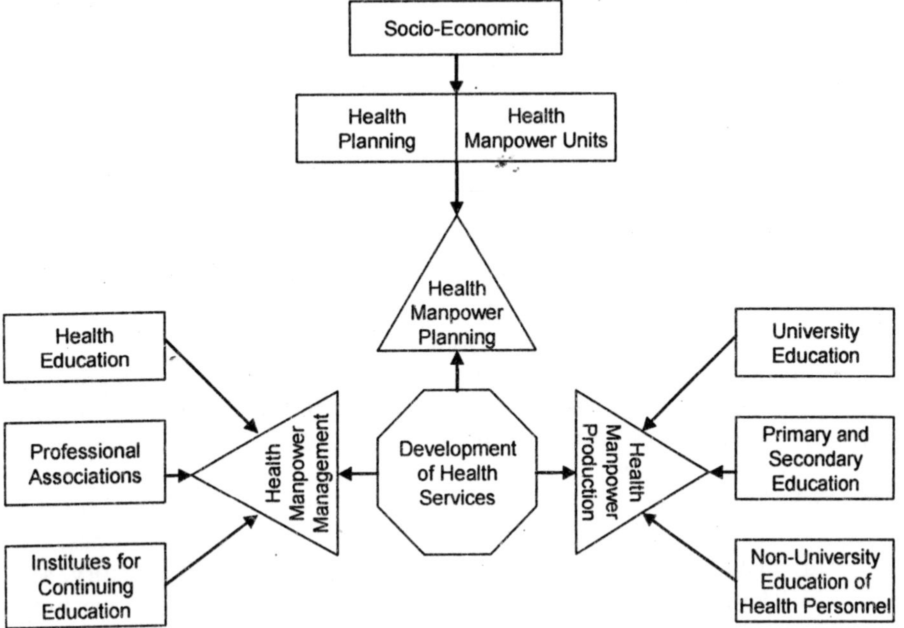

(I) Linking Health Manpower Plan with the Health Policy and Plan

The first important step to develop health manpower plan is to link it to the health policy and plan of the country, It may also be kept in mind that health manpower planning cannot be divorced from the national socio-economic and health plans. Health manpower planning should be an integral part of the health planning and it should endeavour to achieve the objectives, goals, and targets of health planning, otherwise this would be an exercise in futility. It is necessary to develop a continuous understanding between the health manpower planners and training institutions so that the curriculum for the health personnel may be appropriately planned. In this way the curriculum would be based on reality of needs and not on false prestige. The Director General of WHO stated in his address to the Fourth Rehovoth Conference:

> "The success of all plan depends, in the last analysis, on the availability of people competent to carry them out. There is a shortage of trained persons everywhere and at all levels. But no educational system can be effective unless its purposes are defined. The members of the health team must be trained specifically for tasks which they are destined to perform, taking Into account the circumstances under which they will work. These tasks can only be defined in accordance

with a plan in which the nature of the services to be provided is defined, priorities are allotted, and the staff needed to provide these services determined both in numbers and in terms of the training required for the duties envisaged. The training provided must then be tailored to meet these needs."[16]

(2) Assessment of the Health Manpower Situation

At the time manpower planning exercise, we may collect the following data, which would serve as the base for the future projections. The information so collected should cover the following:

(a) The System-public, private and voluntary, through which health services are delivered: the medical care services provided to individuals and families; all types of health care system—Allopathic, Ayurvedic, Homeopathic, etc.

(b) The organisation of health services, i.e. the types of categories of services the number, size and geographical distribution of each category of service; agency or institution; the programmes of each category.

(c) The structure of the health manpower system of the country; Type of health personnel categories within different types.

(d) The health manpower available according to each category, sex, level of training, type of functions (administrative, teaching, direct care, etc.). Information may also be obtained on the migration of trained personnel.

(e) The deployment of health manpower, i.e. staffing patterns.

(f) The adequacy of education and training, i.e. the extent to which health personnel in each category have been prepared for the functions they are performing and the number and kind of in-service training programmes available.

(g) The utilisation of health personnel, i.e. how far health personnel are utilising their time for providing health/medical services.

(h) The number of vacant positions existing in the services.

(i) The health manpower policies of employing institutions, since such policies affect not only current recruitment but also future health manpower. Information may be obtained on policies relating to such matters as hours of work, age of retirement, salaries and benefits, recruitment and appointment, the creation of new positions, career possibilities.

(j) For education and training programme in training institutions. information is needed on the following admission requirements; number of students passed for the last five years; total number of students in training, by class; student attribution rate; number of students that could be admitted to each class for each year with current facilities of teachers; number and kinds of full-time and part-time teaching staff; facilities used for part-time clinical practice; students' maintenance and other operational costs and adequacy of the buildings and equipment.

(k) Potential health manpower supply-information on this factor is necessary for realistic planning of the number, types, levels, location and output of different education and training programmes. For example, a recent study entitled "Stock of high-level manpower allopathic graduates" was carried out by the Institute of Applied Manpower Research which was published in May 1979. The study indicates the stock of doctors and their supply during the Fifth Five Year Plan period. Such studies must be carried out for all categories of personnel.

Let us mention briefly the current scene in India as analysed by Ninth Five Year Plan (Refer Table 3.1)

The current stock of medical, denial, nursing and para-professionals in the country and the number of training institutions for each category are given in Table 3.1 During the Ninth Plan, no new medical colleges were to be opened and there was no proposal for any expansion in the admission capacity of existing institutions as there are adequate number of doctors in the country. Already, over two-third of the doctors are undergoing post-graduate training. Hence, there was no need for any addition 10 existing number of seats in various post-graduate institutions, except for identified specialities with unmet manpower needs.

There is an acute shortage of dental manpower in the country. There is need to ensure that adequate number of dental professionals of appropriate quality is trained. The dental colleges are unevenly distributed in the country. As many as 41 out of 96 dental colleges are in one state. 'The quality of dental education needs to be reviewed and appropriate remedial measures instituted.

Nursing education and nursing services have been given a high priority in order 10 bridge the large gap between requirement and availability of nurses and ensure quality of nursing training. These efforts were being continued during the Ninth Plan. In addition, efforts are being made to meet the increasing demand for nurses with specialised training in speciality and sub-speciality areas—intensive, medical and surgical care in hospitals and for public health nurses in health care system.

Many programmes are faltering because of lack of critical para-professional manpower. Over the last three decades, there has been an increasing requirement of several categories of para-medical persons such as male multipurpose worker, laboratory technicians, radiographers. Their availability and requirement vary from State to State and from time to time. Till the Eighth Plan the medical colleges, dental colleges and nursing training institutions have been the major training institutions for para-professional. During the Eighth Plan the Open University system and the vocational training courses at 10+2 stream have provided two additional mechanisms for education and training of para-medical manpower. During

TABLE 3.1

Health Manpower Position

Category	*Existing No.*	*Training Instts. No.*	*Admission Capacity*
Medical Graduates	474270	160	15000
Dental Surgeons	19525	67	1300
Nurses (a) General	512595	487	20400
Nurses (b) ANMS/FHW	229304	494	12377
Health Workers			
Lab. Technicians	23617	97	2193
Dental Mechanics	1903	18	50
Dental Hygienists	6800	17	65
Physiotheraphists	6800	4	174
Occupational Therapists	800	4	75
X-Ray Technicians	4872	33	410
Phartracists	175000	290	16555
Ophthalmic Assistant	4390	7	134

Sources: (1) Working Group Report on Medical Education, 1996.
(2) Steering Committee Report on Development of Human Resources for Health, 1996, Ninth Five Year Plan.

the Ninth Plan the State manpower cells were to assess the changing requirements for para-professionals, preferably at the district level and take necessary steps to meet the requirement through all available training channels. The Universities of Health Sciences (UHS) would ensure that appropriate curricula are evolved and followed. The State Governments would make necessary amendments in recruitment rules for these posts so that those who qualify through vocational courses and open university system become eligible for the jobs in Government, voluntary and private sectors. The feasibility of introducing pre-vocational courses at the 9th and 10th standards was to be explored.

(3) Classification and Interpretation of Information (Health Situation)

The information collected must be classified or arranged so as to facilitate analysis in terms of percentages. Proportions, ratios, etc., as such analysis can provide information regarding the number of health personnel per given unit of population or the ratio of one type of health personnel to another, i.e. ratio of nurses to physicians, etc. and mortality and morbidity in the various areas of the country in relation to the health manpower.

(4) Up-dating of Information

Devising a means for keeping manpower information up-to-date is an important part of health manpower planning.

(5) Developing Professional Standards or Norms

They may be defines as; Uniform units of measurement. Prevailing practices or average levels of attainment; or goals or descriptions of the desired state of affairs.

Health Manpower standards are those by which the quality and quantity of the work performed by health personnel may be measured, as such, they provide a basis for the development of alternatives, to be realistic, health, manpower standards must be developed in the light of all the available knowledge concerning health manpower and health situation and in conformity with the needs and limitations of the country concerned. All planning includes a standard-setting component in the development of service models and of the staffing patterns used to determine total programme requirements. A standard should satisfy the following basic criteria: it should be realistic, i.e. its achievement within the period designated in the plan must be possible; it should be provisional, i.e. must be subject to evaluation and revision as the situation changes and as new knowledge and experience are required; it should be appropriate, i.e. relevant to the type of service or programme for which it is being developed; it must be flexible, i.e. it should provide guidelines rather than set rigid limits; it should be stated with sufficient clarity to allow measurement of achievements.

Determination of Priorities and Alternatives Concerning the Health Sector and Health Manpower

Priorities and alternatives should be seen in the light of:

(a) financial constraints;
(b) the health manpower functions, activities, and tasks to be performed and the level of knowledge and skill required for their performance,
(c) the proper mix of health personnel which can provide health care of the people; and
(d) kind of people to be covered; etc.

On the basis of these considerations, priority of health care may be worked out and priority of health manpower may be decided accordingly. Health manpower plans should also decide the knowledge. Skills, attitudes and the area and level of competence required for each category of personnel.

Supply of Health Personnel (making arrangement for the preparation of health personnel)

The mismatch between demand and supply of different categories of health manpower has led to tremendous disequilibrium. While in certain staff categories like Doctors and ANMs, over production has resulted in unemployed, in many staff categories among paramedical manpower such as Nurses, MPW (male), we have a large number of vacancies. In the

CHART 3.3

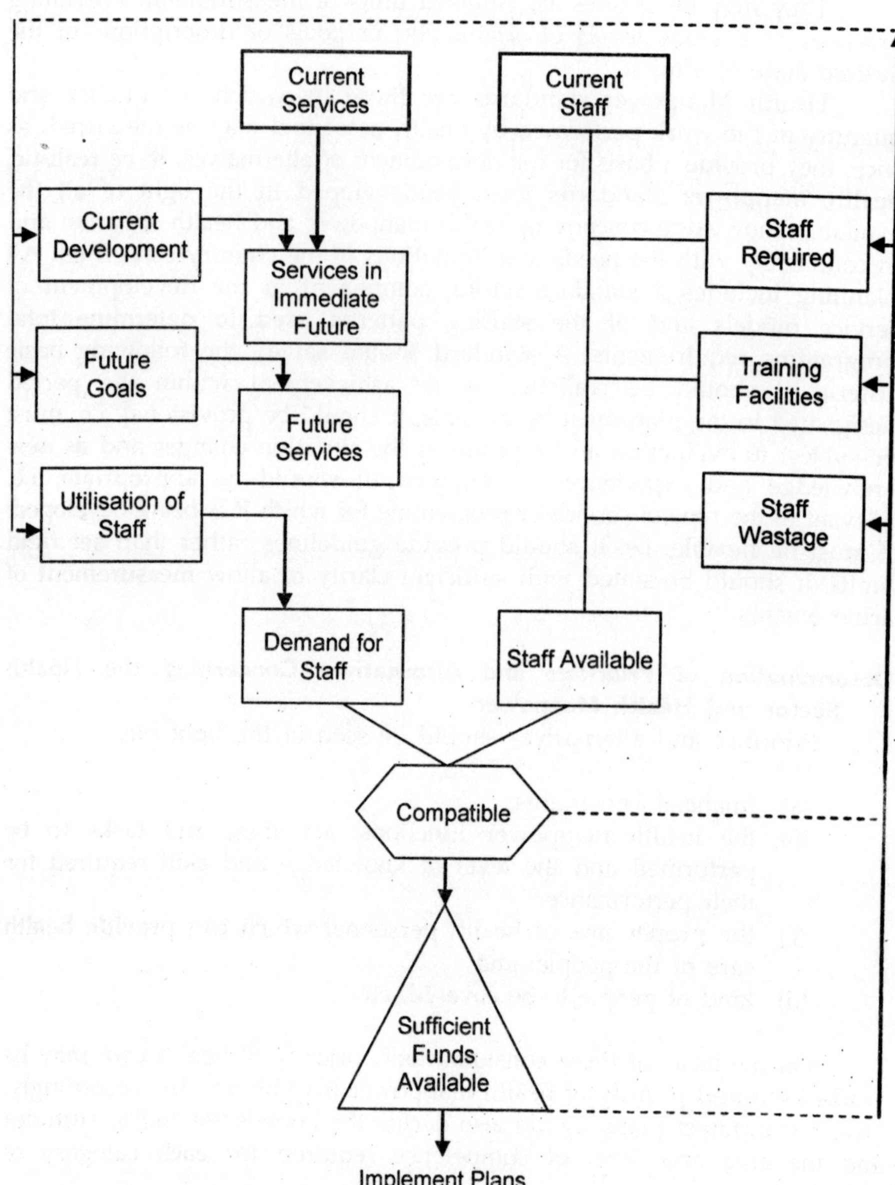

absence of appropriate education and training institutions, the shift from vertical programmes to multipurpose work has aggravated the situation further for proper orientation and training to paramedical staff, ISM practitioners and CHGs in different states. It is essential to undertake a through review of the current health manpower situation in the country and design long-term policy on health manpower development at different levels keeping in view the organizational requirements norms for job evaluation of the staff and goals of health care services. Further for ensuring effective health manpower development, the recruitment, promotion and other human resource development policies for different categories of staff need streamlining and immediate follow-up actions to avoid bureaucratic delays and frustration among the staff. In view of the large and complex character of health service system in the country guided by multiple intra and inter-sectoral variables, it would be useful to demarcate the organizational and functional boundaries of the system as well as develop appropriate indicators and information system for ensuring the role clarity, job functions and effective decision making by staff at different levels.

The health manpower planners may work in close cooperation with The training Institutions so as to produce health personnel in adequate Numbers and of desired quality. We must try to make training relevant. To the needs of health services. The training institutions could impart Useful and Innovative knowledge to solve the current and future Problems. According to Simon Kuznets,

> "The greatest factor in growth of output per capita is the increasing stock of tested, useful knowledge."[17] The training institutions should make the trainees consider ways and means of adapting Western technology to suit local conditions. Five points emerged from the technical discussion of World Health Assembly (1970) which need the attention of the national health Administration for obtaining health personnel best suited to local needs and resources.
>
> These are:
>
> (a) close cooperation between those responsible for the provision of health services to the public and those responsible for the education of the required health personnel;
> (b) reasonable distribution of functions between various members of the health professions and their auxiliaries, with attention to team work;
> (c) effecting change in the education programme, both as to the types of personnel 10 be trained and as to the content of their training;
> (d) continuous education of all health personnel, both to refresh and to advance their basic knowledge, including pedagogic services for teaching staff; and
> (e) continuous study of the inter-relationships, between education and services and also of the performance of each of these two constituents through systematic evaluation and operational research—with a view to introducing such changes whenever indicated.[18]

Manpower Utilization

Manpower utilization is concerned with the efficient use of the existing manpower resources. At present, we have large number of personnel in various organizations without much work for them, resulting in useless expenditure and indiscipline.

There are two methods for assessing manpower utilization. The first one is the manning ratio which is based on the relationship between the number of the employed in an organization and a specified measure of productivity. The second method is work study.

One of the serious drawbacks in health personnel planning is that it does not attend to the optimum utilisation of the capacity of personnel. Many studies round that the physicians in hospitals at the district and local levels are utilizing only 21% of their duty time for the benefit of the patients. The health manpower planning should attend to this aspects.

(6) Research Studies

It is important to carry out research to measure the utility of health manpower planning. The studies can be in the form of case studies. On the basis of these studies, future changes can be advised. The Government of India set-up an Institute of Applied Manpower Research in 1962. It is an autonomous institute devoted to research in the field of manpower planning. During the period of it; existence, the institute has conducted a number of useful and stimulating studies pertaining to manpower utilisation, forecasting demand and supply of various categories of manpower and coordinating the training and educational facilities with the manpower requirements of our plans. Besides, the department of Personnel and Administrative Reforms also helps in the formulation of the basic policies and programmes in matters relating to manpower and employment.

In carrying out health manpower studies, the following points should be kept in mind:

(1) Manpower is an input to health services and should be related to all other inputs, such as technology, facilities (including equipment and supplies), and organisation of services.
(2) Utilisation of personnel is a factor which should be given due consideration when assessing shortages of personnel.
(3) Poor utilisation of personnel could be due to defective organisation of services or to deficiencies in their training.
(4) Closer collaboration between health and teaching institutions would be to the advantage of both and should be encouraged.
(5) Manpower studies should be related to health plans.
(6) Planning additional training that may be required for better utilization of existing personnel.
(7) Adoption of training programmes for health personnel, including medical men, to give them a rural bias, in view of the fact that nearly 80% of the population in the developing countries lives in rural areas.[19]

It has been rightly mentioned by Dr. Gunaratne that "the process of health manpower development, so crucial for the organisation and implementation of health care services, is afflicted with a number of ills, most of which although preventable, tend to perpetuate themselves in the absence of coordinated mechanism."[20]

Dr. Dev Ray feels that there are many causes of the lack of proper health manpower planning, He specifically mentions the following:[21]

(a) failure to consider the political framework;
(b) lack of coordination between the services and training institutions;
(c) fragmentation of health services among multiple administration and agencies;
(d) uncoordinated use of resources—manpower, materials and money;
(e) organizational rigidity;
(f) Lack of appreciation of planning and what it entails; and
(g) Lack of involvement of the planners in the implementation of their plans.

Health planning with special reference to Health manpower planning when undertaken in un appropriate manner, will provide the blueprint for the kind action which will usher in a new order of health care to the benefit of society at large. There is a need of un effective machinery for ensuring the integrated development of the proper manpower needed for the delivery of health care services,

All the countries in the South-East Asia Regional are endeavoring to plan their health manpower requirements to suit the needs of their countries. The developing countries have concentrated in the past in modeling their costly health structures on western models, This model failed to meet the needs of 80 per cent people living in rural areas. The developing countries have realised this mistake and are now busy

In modifying their health manpower plans, The Regional Director of WHO in his Annual Report 1977-78, has struck a note of optimism and Stated that:

> "The beneficial effects of these innovative efforts can now be seen in the development programmes for training medical assistants in Bangladesh, experimental physicians in Thailand, community physicians in Nepal, the compulsory internship of medical graduates in rural health centres in India, the training of traditional mid-wives in Bangladesh, the increasing use of village volunteers in Bangladesh, Thailand, Nepal, India and Sri Lanka and the employment of practitioners of traditional systems of medicine to support primary health care, after appropriate training, in Nepal, Sri Lanka and India. These are all encouraging trends. Much more efforts need to be made,

however, to produce the necessary health manpower with training relevant 10 the needs of health services that are being developed In the entire region."[22]

South-East Asia Regional Office in its Declaration suggests the need of Health. Sector Reform to make Implementation on Health Planning a ready:

- Accord highest priority to alleviate the burdens of disease, disability, premature death and suffering afflicting our people, especially the poor. The burden of disease is of greater magnitude in this region than in any other. We call for urgent policy, budget and programmatic initiatives.
- Ensure universal access to quality health care: We will initiate reforms of the health sector (needed to respond to the broader concept of health and contemporary core values) to ensure the new role of government in relation to health which emphasizes, policy formulation, facilitation, regulation and coordination functions, in addition to the traditional provider role. This includes strengthening the infrastructure, equitable financing, decentralized decision-making and governance, promoting private sector panicipation and improving emergency preparedness and response.
- Invest in women's health and development to eliminate gender discrimination and disparities: In this we recognize the inextricable link between women's health and the development process and the vital contribution women make to family and community life. Gender issues will be brought into the mainstream of development.
- Encourage application of scientific knowledge and technology: Science is an essential feature of health development and requires strong links with policy-makers. We will strive to ensure that both the generation and the application of scientific knowledge and technology are relevant and appropriate to the needs of the community.
- Mobilize financial resources for health and promote their effective and efficient use: We will advocate for increased allocation of funds for health development and ensure their optimal utilization. Indeed, voices must rise from society as a whole, insisting that adequate resources are made available for basic health care.
- Involve communities as active partners in health development: We recognize that communities are essential resources for health development. They must be actively involved in planning, implementing and monitoring policies and programmes for health.

- Propagate and preserve medicinal plants: We will ensure that in the conservation of biological diversity, the great wealth of medicinal plants in our Region is preserved and their extinction or exploitation for mere commercial gain prevented. The scope for intercountry cooperation in this area is great. We urge other countries to transfer technical know-how on favourable terms to the developing countries.
- Promote traditional medicine: Our Region has a rich heritage of indigenous systems of medicine. We will strive to integrate these into the mainstream of health care, promoting traditional systems that provide relief, are scientifically proven to be safe, and are easily available, accessible and affordable.

C. RECOMMENDATIONS AND CONCLUSIONS

What are the lessons to be learnt from our experience with manpower planning? Based on our analysis we suggest the following measures for effective manpower planning:

(i) Eliminate haphazard growth of health personnel; there should be adequate manpower planning, so that there is logical forecasting of the manpower needs at least ten years in advance. It should be related to the health plans and health policy.

(ii) It is essential that the health organisations should have a declared and well accepted personnel policy. It should reflect the total personnel system rather than tackling the sub-systems on piecemeal basis. Manpower planning like health planning, is a continuous cyclical process with constant reviews and adjustments being made to ensure that the health service goals and manpower demands are matched by an appropriate supply of staff.

(iii) This declared personnel policy must be developed by a staffing section at headquarters or comparable level. It would be quite desirable if the academic guidance may be sought from NIHFW and the universities.

(iv) The staffing section must be under the charge of a duly qualified and trained personnel officer. It is often forgotten that manpower planners, as well as health planners must acquire special skills, not only through experience but also by learning the principles and theories.

(v) Manpower planning should be based on a proper-mix of different categories of health workers. This proper-mix should be determined by the health policy and the socio-economic status of the country. They must have special aptitude and motivations if they are to be effective.

(vi) While formulating the personnel policy, internal as well as external sources may be explored. To supplement the internal data. The administration must collect information from external sources, e.g. associations/unions of employees.

(vii) There is a need of proper classification of health personnel so that their duties and responsibilities may be clearly demarcated. The ambiguity in this sphere results in confusion.

(viii) Manpower planning should ensure optimum utilisation of the capacity of the existing personnel.

(ix) There is a need to provide proper motivation which can help the employees for the maximum optimisation of goods and services. This would require judicious decentralisation. Delegation, job enlargement and proper system of performance appraisal.

(x) Health manpower planning should be relevant to the existing disease pattern.

(xi) Manpower planners must be involved in implementing their plans. The separation between planning and implementation must be broken down if plans are to be successfully converted into reality.

(xii) Health manpower planning should not concentrate on the personnel und training resources of the public sector only but also take into account the private sector and voluntary sector.

(xiii) The entire efforts in the field of health manpower development should be directed towards making the manpower relevant to the needs of the health services which should also be reoriented to provide wider coverage to the rural people and the under-served urban poor.

(xiv) Training programmes for health manpower should be formulated to make them need-based, task-oriented and relevant to specific situations where the trainees will work and apply their skills.

(xv) More emphasis should be laid on the training and utilisation of auxiliary und primary health workers rather than on the classical 'categoreis' of health workers (doctors, nurses, etc.). Health manpower planning should therefore be considered as an endless process producing successive approximation and not simply as an event ending up with a report.

Ensuring quality and bringing in accountability in health care providers is of utmost importance. In recent years, there has been increasing public concern over these issues because of both increasing awareness of the population and mushrooming growth of institutions providing health care, especially in the private sector. The Consumer Protection Act provides one mechanism for redressal of grievances pertaining to quality of care. Some states have attempted to provide a legal framework for the functioning of private health care institutions on the lines of Bombay Nursing Home Registration Act, 1949. Until now these legislative measures have not been effectively implemented mainly because of lack of objective criteria for defining quality of care and the possible impact of such regulations on cost of care. The cumulative experience generated thus far will be utilised to evolve norms for quality and cost of health care and ensure accountability in a uniform standardised manner.

An important operational objective for the 21st century is, therefore, to improve personnel systems, develop manpower planning in health services, and expand the opportunity for education and training of personnel to achieve developmental goals as it is the human capacities which transform the passive natural resources into active agents of production. Most developing countries confront the immense task of reforming their system of personnel administration so that they will assist rather than hinder development programmes. Thus, the most important task is the development of sound personnel planning and improvement of the policy-making and implementation capabilities of personnel units in health care administration.

Ninth Plan priorities for Human Resources Development for Health include:

- Creation of a district data base on requirement, demand and availability for health manpower in the Government, Private and voluntary sectors.
- Periodic updating of information on.
- Requirement of different categories of health manpower.
- Availability of health manpower.
- Health manpower production based on the needs.
- Improvement in quality of under-graduate/post-graduate education.
- Efforts to promote appropriate health manpower distribution.
- Continuing medical education for skill upgradation and appropriate people and programme orientation.
- Continuing multi-professional education for promoting team work and inter-sectoral co-ordination.

Manpower planning should therefore be considered as an endless process producing successive approximations and not simply as an event ending up with a report. An important operation objective is, therefore, to improve personnel systems, develop manpower planning and expand the opportunity for education and training of personnel to achieve development goals, as it is the human capacities which transform the passive natural resources into active agents of production. Most developing countries confront the immense task of reforming their system of personnel administration so that they will assist rather than hinder development programmes. Thus, the most important task is the development of sound manpower planning and improvement of the policy-making and implementation capabilities of personnel units.

NOTES AND REFERENCES

1. Health Development in the South-East Asia Region in the 21st Century, WHO, New Delhi, pp. 7-8.
2. R.A. Gordon, (ed): Towards a Manpower Policy, New York, 1967, pp 136-38.
3. Dev Ray, "Manpower Planning" in *World Health,* April. 1979, p. 24.
4. Tamas Fulop, "Who will care for Health", in *World Health,* April, 1977, p. 4.
5. John Bland, Basic Skills in *World Health,* July, 1976, p 19.
6. WHO, *WHO Chronicle,* 30, 447-S4, (1976).
7. Hall, T.L., Health Manpower in Peru: A Case Study in Planning, Baltimore, Johns Hopkins, 1969, p 7
8. Three specialists from the Health Manpower Development Division at WHO Headquarters in Geneva—Dr. M.A.C Dowling, Dr. J.J. Duilbert and Dr. F.M Karz talks to World Health about the training of Health Personnel Meet, World Needs in World Health, "New Schools for Old", April, 1977, pp 12-15
9. Dr. Alfonso, Mejia and Helena Pizurki, "The Brain Drain", in *World Health,* April, 1977, p. 6.
10. WHO, *WHO Chronicle,* Vol. 22. No.7, 1968, p. 295.
11. Tamas Fulop, *op. cit.,* p. 4.
12. Alfonso Mejia and Helena Pizurki, *op. cit.,* p. 11.
13. Antonia Ordonez—Plaja, "Teamwork at Ministry Level," in *Team Word for World Health* (ed.) *op. cit.,* p. 170.
14. Dr. Daniel Flahault, "Vital Team Work," in *World Health,* April 1977, p. 18.
15. Ghosh, P., Personnel Administration in India, Sudha Publications (P) Ltd., Delhi, 1975, p. 100.
16. Candau, M.G. (1967), "Knowledge, the Bridge to Achievement," *WHO Chronicle,* 21, 505-09.
17. Simon Kuznets, *op. cit.,* p 126.
18. WHO (1970), Background documents of the Technical Discussions of the Twenty-third World Health Assembly, Geneva. A/23ffechnical Discussions/I.
19. WHO, SEARO, SFA/RC 21/pp. 52-53.
20. Gunaratee, *op. cit,* p. 146.
21. Dr. Dev Ray, *op. cit.,* p. 28.
22. WHO, SEARO, Annual Report of Regional Director, 1977-78, p. xiii.

Personnel Training, Executive Development and Induction

I. TRAINING AIMS AT PURPOSEFUL DEVELOPMENT OF HUMAN CAPITAL

Annual Report of the Ministry of Health and Family Welfare, 2006-07 suggests that availability of Quantitative services to the community depends largely upon the efficacy with which health functionaries discharge their responsibilities which in turn would depend mainly upon their education and training.

> "It was generally accepted that professional training in the field of public administration was a necessity. Many countries which had introduced training schemes with an emphasis on an up-to-date approach to the day-to-day problems had achieved impressive improvements in efficiency. It is true that sending an official on a training course meant a loss of working time that had to be balanced, against the gain from increased efficiency on return to work. Experience around the world had shown that the long-term benefits of carefully planned training far outweighted the short-term loss."
>
> —*Mr. Nicol, Executive Director, UNITAR*

Ninth Five Year Plan has rightly mentioned that one of the important reasons for the sub-optimal performance of health care institutions is the poor quality and inappropriateness of the education and training of health care providers resulting in a lack of problem-solving competencies and skills during the Ninth Plan period. Appropriate changes in syllabi, curricula, teaching methods and assessment system will be made through various professional councils to improve the under-graduate and post-graduate training so that the medical and dental graduates as well as allied health professionals acquire necessary technical knowledge and managerial skills to solve health problems and implement ongoing major national health and family welfare programmes within the existing constraints.

One of the key factors in the efforts of the health system to accomplish its health goals is to enhance its professional and administrative capability for development at all levels of a health system, which is very much a part of the development process. Our experience during the last five decades has demonstrated that the health plans have not been satisfactorily implemented because of inadequate professional/ administrative performance. The reasons for the low level of administrative performance include organisational defects, lack of coordination, complex and cumbersome administrative and financial procedures. These defects and deficiencies need to be corrected in order to bring about a sharp reduction in the administrative obstacles to health development and to bridge the gap between aspirations and performance. Simultaneously, the level of competence of health personnel directly involved in the execution of development plans can be raised by training them in modern concepts and techniques of administration and management and their field of specialization. This category of personnel at the senior or intermediate levels, comprising both technocrats and generalists, is constantly called upon to discharge increasingly heavy administrative and managerial responsibilities. In order to equip such personnel with the required expertise, skill, methodology and aptitude, there is a definite need to train them. Training is: (a) an action process, (b) by which capabilities of the personnel can be improved, (c) to meet the organisational needs in terms of their knowledge, skills and attitudes required in performing organizational tasks and functions, and (d) within relatively short period of time.

Training is the well articulated effort to promote competence in the health services by imparting professional knowledge, by broadening of vision and adoption of correct patterns of behaviour among the health personnel with regard to their existing functional responsibilities. It also enables the employees to equip themselves for senior professional and administrative positions in future.

OBJECTIVES OF TRAINING

The objective of the training is to provide an individual with the knowledge of the environment or ecology under which he is to function; the knowledge of administrative management to achieve optimum performance, cultivation of necessary attitude and professional competence.

T.V. Rao in his article on "Human Resources Development" in *Business India*, January 13-26, 1986 has rightly mentioned that:

"Human Resource Development aims at creating mechanisms and processes in organizations to continuously develop the qualities of employees so that they can perform their present jobs well, become better equipped to perform the future roles of the changing organizations may demand and thus contribute to organization vitality and growth." Let us discuss the role of training:

(a) Environmental or Ecological Understanding

An employee must understand the legal framework under which he is to operate. He must be provided with the basic knowledge of social sciences to understand the intricacies of social environment, With the knowledge of social sciences, he can react with the environment favourably. A.R. Tyagi has justified it from three different points:

(i) Administration is a human process largely depending upon first hand experience drawn from the actual administrative situation in all its facets and on weighing each problem from every angle.
(ii) The role of public servant in a welfare state is that of a social scientist in action. In order to be able to act properly and effectively, he must have scientific acumen which he can develop only by systematic and sustained education in theory and practice of social science.
(iii) The need for a basic training in the fundamentals of social science becomes all the more necessary in the context of our public recruitment being based on lower age limit; which limits the entry of advanced research students of the public service.[1]

(b) Improving Administrative Capability

There is a great need to enhance the administrative capability of public services so that they can achieve the objectives of the government in the shortest possible time. Administrative capability is an important means of converting or processing programme inputs into outputs such as goods and services. Kantz says: "Administrative capability for development involves the ability to mobilize, allocate and combine the actions that are technically needed to achieve development objectives.[2] It is felt that experimentation is a costly and slow process. As such, we need to learn from the experience of others and use their results to help achieve our goals. In this context, Ernest Dale and L.C. Michelon observe that, "Today's manager lives in a world of rapid change, yet the rate of change increase in the years ahead. Unless he can keep up with this change, he is likely to find himself obsolete—perhaps unpromotable or even unemployable."[3]

(c) Cultivating Genuine Attitudes

Administration is manned by and meant for human beings. Administration is the art of conducting human affairs. Training must also aim to cultivate a new attitude and behaviour in human personality. In the public service, this is more important than the other two objectives. Marshall suggests the development of the following ingredients to promote right and rational attitudes:[4]

(i) development of rational thinking.
(ii) development of objective thinking,
(iii) development of social understanding,
(iv) development of aesthetic responsiveness,
(v) development of practical abilities, and
(vi) development and placement of memory in action.

(d) Professional Competence

Health experts can be trained in the latest development in their field of specialisation at the institutes of National importance.

TRAINING CONTENTS (See Chart 4.1)

The training courses generally include the following aspects:

(a) Job Aspects

Knowledge of the job, that has to be supervised, planning procedures, work analysis, methods of work, organisation and co-ordination and cost analysis of the services.

(b) Human Aspects

Skills to improve motivation to increase the productivity of the personnel working in the organisation.

(c) Organisational Aspects (See Chart 4.1)

The knowledge of the organisation, the use of records, communication skills, etc.

DESIGNING TRAINING PROGRAMMES

Training is an investment. It can give dividends only if it is properly designed, Designing a useful training programme require a systematic, thorough and critical enquiry into the organisational needs *vis-à-vis* the training design. All agree that training is useful but differ regarding the rationale and philosophy of the training programme. There are some who believe that training is an essential part of a sound personnel policy and that the organisations should, if they have not already done so, make arrangements for a systematic and continuing training programme, covering general orientation, in service refresher and development training. Such views do not help in deciding exactly what ground the training should cover. There are others who think that training is meant to remedy the deficiency of recruitment. It is very difficult to reach un operational definition of training. The inference from the foregoing is that a training programme should be prepared with three levels in view:

1. the real level of existing knowledge,

CHART 4.1

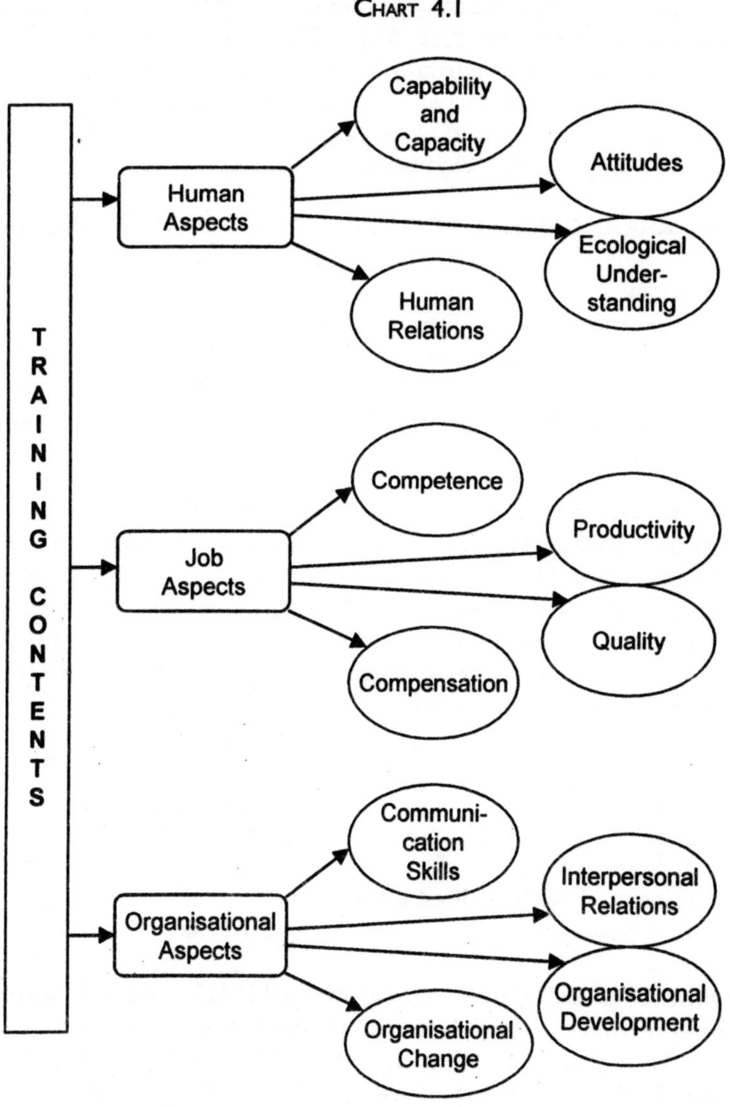

2. the level of knowledge which should normally be required at the time of recruitment, and
3. the level of knowledge desirable in order to obtain the maximum return.

A training programme should, therefore, be in two distinct parts: a remedial progamme designed to bring the trainee up to the normal recruitment level: a programme defined by a difference between levels (1) and (2). A normal training programme should correspond to difference between the recruitment levels (2) and (3). The contents of a training programme should correspond to the various directions in which it is desired to improve upon the base level. The training bridges the gap between self-motivated behaviour and needed requirements of task. These may include the following: refresher training, advanced theoretical training in a branch of the specialized field of knowledge, development of professional knowledge and background knowledge.

TRAINING ARRANGEMENT FOR HEALTH AND FAMILY WELFARE

Personnel In India

There is no organized training arrangements for medical and health personnel in India. However, there is one apex institution to provide in-service training that is National Institute of Health and Family Welfare, New Delhi. At the state level, we have 'Health and Family Welfare Training Centres':

Health and Family Welfare Training Centres (HFWTCs)

Health and Family Welfare Training Centres are established in the country with the objective of giving in-service training to health personnel. These training centres are set-up: with 100% financial assistance from the Central Government. There are 47 HFWTCs in the country at present.

The category of health personnel given in service training at HFWTC and the period of training is as below:

Medical Officer	2 weeks
Health Assistants	2 weeks
(Male and Female) Health Workers	2 weeks
Block Extension Educators	2 weeks
Key Trainers of ANM school and MPW (M) basic schools	2 weeks

In addition to the above training. the HFWTCs take up in-service training under various vertical National Programmes as well. From 1982, HFWTCs are giving basic training to MPWs (M) also. The HFWTCs are funded under 100% Central Assistance from the Family Welfare Budget.

Department of Family Welfare had recognized the crucial role of training of health personnel in providing effective and efficient health care to the rural community from the very beginning of the Five Year Plans. The pre-service and in-service training for different categories of health personnel are imparted through the following schemes activities:

TRAINING OF ASHA UNDER NRHM

The Government of India in April 2005 has launched the NRHM to improve access of people, especially the poor women and children to quality primary health care services. Accredited Social Health Activist

(ASHA) is a major strategic intervention under the mission for the 10 high focus States namely, Uttar Pradesh, Uttaranchal, Bihar, Jharkhand, Madhya Pradesh, Chhattisgarh, Orissa, Rajasthan, Assam and Jammu and Kashmir.

ASHA is envisaged as a trained women community health volunteer who will reinforce community action for universal immunization, safe delivery, new born care, prevention of water borne and communicate disease, improved nutrition and promotion of household toilets. She will inform, interact, mobitize and facilitate improved access to preventive and promotive health care and also provide basic curative care through her drug kits. She wilt assist in formulation of village health plan by the village health and sanitation committee. ASHA will also promote awareness and usage of ISM. There will be one ASHA per 1000 population. In tribal, hilly, desert areas, their norm could be relaxed to one ASHA per habitation, depending on work load, etc.

ASHA must be primarily a woman resident of the village -married/ widow/divorced, literate with formal education up to class VIIIth with and preferably in the age group of 25 to 45 years. This may be relaxed only if no suitable person with this qualification is available. It is envisaged that selection and training process of ASHA will be given due attention by the concerned State to ensure that at least 40 per cent of the envisaged ASHAs in the State are selected and given induction training in the first year as per the norms given in the guidelines.

ASHAs are to be selected by the community, from among the residents within the community. She is to work in close coordination with AWW and ANM and these will be integrating in their roles with use of common resource facilities like AWW centres, etc.

Capacity building of ASHA is critical in enhancing her effectiveness and this has been seen as a continuous process. The induction training of ASHA would be completed in 23 days spread in five rounds over a period of 12 months to be followed by periodic re-training for about two days once every alternate month. For the training of ASHA, training modules based on thematic approach have been developed. Four modules have already been disseminated to the states. The States can change as per their local needs. The States have translated the training modules in the local language for use in the training of ASHAs. The States training teams of the 10 States attended the orientation programme for ASHA training at NIHFW in September 2005. The States have constituted the District Training teams and Block Training teams for training of ASHA. The Block Training teams are providing training to ASHAs.

ASHA scheme which was initially introduced for only 10 high focus states under NRHM, has been extended to NE states and tribal areas of other states. A total of 1963 ASHAs are proposed to be selected by NE states (other than Assam), out of which 11,200 ASHAs are to be selected during the year 2006-07. Whereas in rest of the country states Governments may opt for link Workers (similar as ASHA) in their Project Implementation Plan (PIP) under RCH.II.

BASIC TRAINING OF ANM/LHV

ANMs/lHVs play a vital role in MCH and Family Welfare Service in the rural areas. It is therefore, essential that the proper training to be given to them so that quality services be provided to the rural population.

For this purpose Department of Family Welfare provides financial assistance under the scheme, to the states, to run 336 ANM/Multipurpose Health Worker (Female) schools with an admission capacity of approximately 13,000 and 42 promotional. training schools for LHV Health Assistant (Female) with an admission capacity of 2600.

These training institutions are imparting pre- service training to prepare required number of ANMs and LHVs to man the Sub-centres, Primary Health Centres, Community Health Centres, Rural Family Welfare Centres and Health posts in the country. The duration of training programme of ANM is one and half years and minimum admission requirement for this course is 10th pass. Senior ANM with five years of experience is given six months promotional training to become LHV Health Assistant (Female). Health Assistant (Female) provides supportive supervision and technical guidance to the ANMs in sub-centres. Curricula of these training courses are provided by the Indian Nursing Council.

The staffing pattern of the school for which financial assistance is provided by the Department of Family Welfare, varies according to the annual admission capacity of the school. The financial pattern of assistance has been revised w.e.f. 7.2.2001. Other approved costs besides salary to staff are stipend to trainees, contingency and rent as follows:

BASIC TRAINING FOR MULTI-PURPOSE HEALTH WORKER (MALE)

The Basic Training of Multi-Purpose Health Worker (Male) scheme was approved during 6th Five-Year Plan and taken up since 1984, as a 100% Centrally Sponsored Scheme. This pre-service training is provided through Health and Family Welfare Training Centres and also through basic training schools of Multi-purpose Health Workers (Male). The training is of one-year duration and on successful completion of the training, the Male Health Workers is posted at the sub-centre along with an ANM/ Health Workers (Female)

Item	*Norm (In Rupees)*
1. Salary and allowances of Staff	As per state government
2. Stipend for trainees	500 per month/trainee
3. Contingency	10,000 per annuam/school
4. Rent	60,000 per annum school

The Financial Assistance are as follows:

Item	*Norm*
Rent (for basic schools)	Rs. 10,000 month
Rent for Hostel (for basic Schools)	Rs. 250 month per candidates
Stipend	Rs. 300 month/candidate
Educational Aids and Training Material	Rs. 15,000 per annum
Transportation (for hiring bus)	Rs. 30,000 per annum
Contingency	Rs. 50,000 per annum

Source: Annual Report, Health and Family Planning Ministry, 2006-07, p. 123.

Strengthening of Basic Training Schools

The main objective of the scheme "Strengthening of Basic Training School" is physical strengthening of the ANM/LHV training schools for making these schools workable/suitable, which have gone into dilapidated condition on account of no investment made to these infrastructures and were established more than 20 years back. The provision under the scheme is maximum of Rs. 21.5 lakhs per ANM/LHV school for following activities. The releases will however depend on the actual requirement based on the estimates of the repair/up-gradation of work for the buildings as well as other teaching materials.

During the year 2005-06, Rs. 203.86 lakh have been released to 4 states Mizoram, Tamil Nadu, Nagaland and Orissa) for strengthening of 13 ANM Training Schools under the scheme and during 2006-07 so far Rs. 104. lakh have been released to 2 states (Goa and Kerela) for strengthening of 6 ANM Training Schools. This scheme is launched in 10th Plan period with plan period allocation of 10 crores.

REPRODUCTIVE AND CHILD HEALTH TRAINING PROGRAMME

RCH Training Programme envisages in-service training of Family welfare service providers. During the phase one of RCH Training Programme approach was centralized and all the states were asked to carry out certain type of training. Funds for the training at States were released to NIHFW from Ministry of Health and Family Welfare and in turn NIHFW used to release the same to states (through SCOVAs) as per their Comprehensive Training Plan.

National Institute of Health and Family Welfare (NIHFW) was appointed by the Government of India in December 1997 as the National Nodal Agency to coordinate various training activities under the Reproductive and Child Health (RCH) programme (Phase-I). In RCH Phase II, for in-service training of Family welfare service providers, a decentralized approach has been adopted. States have been asked to submit their requirements for various Programme interventions in Project

Implementation Plan (PIP) including training requirements and funds are released to states from Ministry of Health and Family Welfare from a single point.

National Institute of Health and. Family Welfare (NIHFW) has also been appointed as Nodal Institute with support of 20 Collaborating training Institutes (CTIs) for training under NRHM and under RCH-I Phase II. NIHFW has been made responsible of organizing some centrally steered training programme and monitoring the NRHM/RCH training activities through out the country with the help of Collaborating Training Institutions (CTIs). The details of activities undertaken at NIHFW are as under:

Skill Development Training

(i) Integrated Skill Development Training (IST) for Health Personnel Integrated Skill Development

Training for different categories of service providers including MO(PHC), ANM, LHV, HW(M), HA(M) and Staff Nurse under RCH Programme is continuing at district level in various States and UTs. During 2006-07 (till 15.11.06), a total of 201 MOs, 357 ANMs, 105 LHVs, 413 HWs(M), 176 HSs(M) and 223 Staff Nurses were trained.

(ii) Specialized Clinical Skill Training

Specialized Skill Training of MOs in Minilap sterilization and MTP as well as a team of Gynecologist/Surgeons, Staff Nurse and OT Technician for Laparoscopic sterilization and ANM for IUCD insertion is continuing in all the states. The objective is to ensure that there is adequate number of trained manpower to provide good quality of services for prevention and management of unwanted pregnancy. During the year 219 persons have been trained in various specialized clinical skill training programmes.

Achievement in Various Types of Training

Details regarding the total number of persons trained since beginning of the programme under each of the above training activities reported upto 15/11/06 are given in the consolidated table below:

Gender Training

This is a UNFPA assisted programme. Main Objective of the Programme is Local capacity enhancement of trainers in training institutions at National, State and District level in some identified states. The training would enable the faculty to incorporate in all their training programmes analysis of service data to identify gender bias in utilization of services and other gender related issues concerns and suggest corrective health related actions as appropriate to the concerned programme. It is envisaged that the incorporation of such gender issues would be done in an integrated fashion and woven in all the sessions and not taken as separate issue. Progress of Training is as under:

Types of Training	Progress from 01-04-06 upto 15.11.06	Cumulative Progress to 15.11.06
Master Trainers' Training	—	150
Training of Trainers	—	5998
Integrated skill Development Training	1475	239148
Specialised Clinical Skill Training	219	44949
Specialised Management Training—Dist. Level	—	2030
Specialised Management Training—State Level	—	152
Specialized Communication Trg. (DMEIO)	—	628
Specialised Communication Trg. (BEL)	—	4730
Immunization Strengthening Project	—	1786
Gender Training	171	1212
ASHA	1498858	1498958
SBA	518	733
NRHM	55	55

1. Training for Master Trainers at NIHFW

Two Master trainer's training course were conducted at NIHFW, New Delhi. 42 persons have been trained from various identified state collaboration training institution.

2. Training of Trainers at SIHFWs

A total of 1170 persons were trained by various CTIs till 15.11.06 under TOT. The objective of the training programme was to enable the participants to mainstream gender issues in various aspects of Health and Family Welfare Programme to improve the quality of services. TOTs is being conducted in several states for mainstreaming gender issues. A total budget of Rs. 70.00 lacs has been approved by MOHFW.

3. Release of funds as on 15.11.06

- Total funds received from MOHFW Rs. 68. 50 lacs
- Total funds released/Refunds Rs. 33.90 lacs
- Total SOEs received Rs. 30.09 lacs

Professional Development Course (PDC)

The Professional Development Course in Management, Public Health and Health Sector Reforms for District Medical officer is supported by European Commission and it has been made pre-requisite for their promotion to CMO/Civil Surgeon. Realising the relevance and importance, the course now is being rolled out in the entire country with the help of 13 identified training institutions (besides NIHFW) to train with the span of 2-3 years nearly 1800 district level medical officers, who are in the service bracket of 12-16 years. The NIHFW has been designated as the National Nodal Training Institute by the Ministry of Health and Family Welfare. During the year 2006, 166 district level Medical Officers have been trained and total of 613 Persons were trained till 31st October 2006 out of the courses are as under:

List of institutes selected for rolling out of the courses are as under:

Sl. No.	*Name and Address*
1.	National Institute of Health and Family Welfare, Munirca, New Delhi
2.	State Institute of Health and Family Welfare, Bhubaneshwar
3.	Shree Chitra Tirunal Institute of Medical Science and Technology/ Medical College PO Thiruvananthapuram, Kerala
4.	Public Health Institute, Poonamallie, Tamil Nadu
5.	Indian Institute of Public Administration, New Delhi
6.	Indian Institute of Health Management and Resources, Jaipur
7.	All India Institute of Hygiene and Public Health, Calcutta
8.	State Institute of Health and Family Welfare, Shimla
9.	IIHFW, Hyderabad (Andhra Pradesh)
10.	Sanjay Gandhi, P.I.M.S., Lucknow
11.	State Intitute of Health and Family Welfare, Ahmedabad
12.	Public Health Institute, Nagpur
13.	RHFWTC, Indore, M.P.
14.	State Institute of Health and Family Welfare, Panchkula, Punjab

Source: Annual Report, Ministry of Health and Family Planning, 2006-07, p. 125.

In AYUSH, training is given at the following place:

1. National Institute of Ayurveda (NIA), Jaipur
2. National Institute of Siddha (NIS), Chennai
3. National Institute of Homoeopathy, Kolkata
4. National Institute of Naturopathy, Pune
5. National Institute of Unani Medicine, Bangalore
6. Institute of Post-Graduate Teaching and Research in Ayurveda, Jamnagar
7. Rashtriya Ayurved Vidyapeeth, New Delhi
8. Morarji Desai National Institute of Yoga, New Delhi

Besides, there are training arrangements for Nurses. Multipurpose workers, Health Assistants, Health Guides, Dais, etc.

The institutes of National Importance like PGI, AIIMS, etc. provide training in various specializations. However, there are no good training arrangements for administrative training for senior health functionaries in administrative positions.

CRITICAL APPRAISAL

1. Neglect of Training Aspect

One of cardinal principles of manpower planning and career development is that the health organisation should classify the various categories of jobs and assess developmental needs in order to provide the need-based training (with reference to jobs that have to be performed, the knowledge and skills requiréd for the performance of the jobs and the gaps in the knowledge and skills of the personnel responsible for the job) to the individuals to increase their operational efficiency for the current and future needs.

In fact, training programmes are in a very neglected condition. Only those officials/officers who have close links with the decision-making authorities and those who have already undergone a number of training courses in different fields are sponsored by the organisations.

In this respect, the training institutions are also to be blamed because the tartar do not adhere to the required level of qualification/experience at the time of accepting the nominations of trainees.

Thus, the dilemma of training in India is that those who deserve to be trained cannot be spared and those who can be spared do not always deserve the training. Hence, it is suggested that only those officials/officers who fulfil the requisite qualifications/experience, have aptitude for training and are senior enough in the line, should be deputed and a well designed roster system should also be devised for need-based training programmes.

It has also been observed that training programmes are not linked to the work of the incumbents. Instances are not lacking of persons trained for a particular purpose being used for something else. On the other hand, such employees have been given one training after another, and often one training course is unrelated to another.

2. Costly Exercise

The training, if properly designed, is an investment which would yield rich dividends. There is a need to design economical methods. The training should not be a formality but purposeful and linked with career development.

3. Lack of Training Manual

Written information is by far the most economical as it can be used by a large number of persons without using official time. No system of the professional training can be run on sound and economical lines unless standard textbooks are prepared and annotated bibliographies are kept updated for use by trainees.

4. Negligible Expenditure on Training

It has been observed that the Government has not been making adequate provision of funds for the training programmes. Besides, training resources are not distributed on any rational or equitable basis. There is an urgent need for earmarking at least I per cent funds out of the total expenditure on staff establishment for the development of training programmes by the Government.

5. More Emphasis on Theory

Most of the training institutions impart only theoretical training. Training must be relevant to the practical situations and must make the executives deal efficiently with concrete and practical situations. To quote Koontz O'Donell, "Training is one side of a coin, which is the teaching of theory and the demonstration of techniques; the other is the actual practice of management, wherein managers are developed. Nowhere is situational, or contingency, management more obvious than in applying training to practice.[5]

6. Lack of Physical Amenities

It is recognized that the suitable location, building and other necessary facilities are essential conditions for a proper training centre. It was mentioned that "Most of the training institutions have no proper campus, and are ill-equipped."[6] We firmly agree with the view of Sri Livingstone that, "Even in education, man remains a social animal. No doubt, the lamp of wisdom can burn in solitary shrines and even in dismal lecture halls, but for the many it will not brightly, if at all, unless fanned by that social corporate life which both educates and makes education attmctive."[7]

7. Lack of Qualified Teachers for Training

The success of training programmes depends to a large extent on the trainers. Investment in a teacher is a gain to the hundreds whom he trains in turn. But most of the trainers have bookish knowledge.

They are not fully alive to the style of working in the health system. As a result, lack of duly qualified educators is also one of the handicaps in making the training progmmmes effective. In the words of Prof. Laidlaw, "You could not teach surgery to medical students out of a Textbook, only a surgeon with long experience can teach others to be surgeons."[8] Hence, training centres must have expert teachers. There is also a need that experts in various fields from the leading training institutions in the country and abroad are invited to conduct workshops and conferences on the latest developments, which can further sharpen the minds of trainers.

8. Concentration of Training Courses at Headquarters

At present, most of the training arrangements exist for the staff at headquarters. Special efforts must be made by the agencies of the health to arrange for the training of the staff in the field areas. We can make use of distance education in the training of health personnel. Even an open university for health personnel may be set-up to provide refresher courses.

9. Conclusion

In India, the Union and State Governments have made a good headway in deputing their health personnel for the various training programmes. But on its critical examination we find that the training programmes have not been qualitatively developed to meet their diversified and emerging needs in different fields. Some of the issues and suggested remedies are discussed below

All jobs in health administration, whether high or low, involve an element of skill and if they are to perform at optimum efficiency, such skills have to be methodically and systematically cultivated. It is high time that a few lessons are drawn by the management from the experience gained so far and necessary steps, as suggested above, are taken to design the training facilities. A well designed training programme can be a real weapon to accommodate the philosophy and tools of organizational change to achieve optimum performance.

Ninth Plan has suggested the need of continuing medical education for health (CME) professionals.

"In the context of the rapidly evolving technology, demographic transition, changing lifestyles and disease patterns it is imperative that the process of continuing education is internalised throughout the working career of all health professionals so that their knowledge and skills are updated. Currently, in-service training courses in various institutions, thematic CME programmes conducted by National Academy of Medical Sciences, National Board of Examinations, and various professional bodies and associations have played a major role in CME. All these programmes will be expanded and intensified during the Ninth Plan. In addition, Open Universities will play a major role in periodically updating the skills and knowledge of various categories of health personnel. The Open University mechanism can efficiently and cost effectively provide specific training programmes where there is a major component of didactic learning, e.g. epidemiology, hospital administration and health management. It is also likely to be one of the most effective, efficient and cost-effective method of CME involving practitioners in Government, private and voluntary sectors and hence requires increased utilisation.

During the Ninth Plan, a major programme of multi-professional and inter-professional education will be initiated for training the members of health care delivery team, so as to enable them to accomplish group tasks in providing health care in the community. At the national level there will be training of the trainers in newer technologies, national programmes on emerging diseases and their management. At the state level, there will be a similar training of personnel with special reference to the State's requirement. At the district level two types of training programmes have to be undertaken:

(1) the multi-professional health team training in delivery of integrated health and family welfare service at the primary health care level; and

(2) the training of the multi-professional team for the delivery of evolving programmes, e.g. the delivery of RCH care programme.

In addition, there will be training of the health professionals working in the government, voluntary and the private sectors together as to learn to tackle the identified health problems in the district. Inter-sectoral training of personnel from related sectors e.g., nutrition, agriculture, water resource management and environment sanitation will be undertaken as and when necessary.

Operational Strategy

1. Attempt to create a district data base on health manpower belonging to various categories including ISM & H practitioners working for Government voluntary and private sectors. Based on the availability, need and demand appropriate policy and programme initiatives for manpower development to be made at State/district level.
2. Improvement in quality of pre-service and in-service training for medical and paramedical personnel.
3. Periodic updating of knowledge/skill for all categories of health manpower throughout their working careers so that they are able to provide appropriate quality of health care. In addition to available training programmes increasing use to be made of the distance learning.

B. INDUCTION AND BRIEFING

The importance of the induction process is indeed very high as the employees once adjusted to the philosophy of the organisation are going to be permanent assets. A brief survey of the new recruits in various health organizations by the author has revealed that this activity is generally neglected and very little interest is exhibited by employing agencies. New recruits are mostly left to their own fate. They make their own friends and relationships resulting in ad hoc induction. Private Nursing/hospital organizations attend to this function more seriously. In many cases, it was mentioned, the new recruits fall a prey to the bad elements in the organisation resulting in liabilities. In some cases, the new recruits leave job. All these problems can be solved and proper relationships between the individual (new recruit) and the organization can be developed through proper induction and briefing. The aim of induction and orientation is to help the new employees and the organization to become acquainted with, and accommodate, each other.

Briefing/induction may be defined as a systematic organizational effort to minimise problems facing newly recruited personnel so that they can concentrate on the work of the organisation whole heartedly while

CHART 4.2

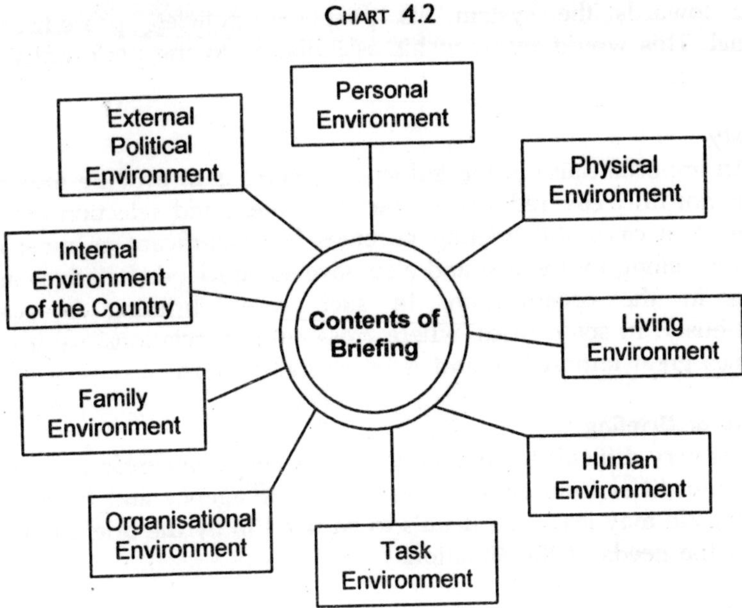

realizing personal satisfaction. An organization can select talented persons, but until these individuals become attuned to the philosophy of the organization, they cannot be expected to give their best efforts to the attainment of the goals of the organization. This process helps the new recruits in meeting their need for security status. Information and direction in both position and organizational environment, briefing and induction process should entail the following:

Information

The new incumbent must be informed about his duties and responsibilities *vis-a-vis* the organization and *vice versa*. Besides, he may be furnished all information to clear his doubts so that he can function intelligently.

Assistance

All assistance in understanding the goals of the organization or in developing attitudes and skill should be provided to ease adjustment.

Acceptance

To generate good will and co-operation among his colleagues, the newcomer should be properly introduced. This will make him feel at ease in the new environment.

Assimilation

The new incumbent should be encouraged to develop a positive attitude towards the system, its purposes, policies, procedures and personnel. This would result in his assimilation to the philosophy of the organization.

Continuity

An important aim in the induction process is to provide information that was not fully covered during the recruitment and selection processes.

In most cases the briefing becomes less significant as most of the employees belong to the area and also have some friends/relatives already working in the organization. In such cases, briefing is achieved unconsciously. In some cases, where cross cultural relations are involved, it assumes great importance and is of central concern.

Contents of Briefing

It is very difficult to enumerate exhaustively the contents of briefing. these would differ from area to area; agency to agency and from persons to person, We may leave the details to be filled in by the briefing agencies to reflect the needs of the situation.

Conclusion

There is a need to improve the process of briefing to make it useful and reliable. This activity may need more money and time but it is worth it. This would yield dividends.

EVALUATION OF TRAINING PROGRAMMES

With rapid developments in technology and changing nature of today's business, the role lining has assumed increased importance. The amount spent by organizations on formal training is estimated to be 60 billion in the United States alone. Hence, business is demanding not accountability but also greater articulation of how training programs benefit organization.[9] Evaluating training programs is a very difficult task and several issues need to considered, which include employee development, performance improvement and employee.

This paper begins with a description of the different approaches to evaluate training programs. This is followed by the issues in evaluating training programs and a critical analysis on the relevant literature related to this topic.

Evaluating Training Programs

Organization conduct evaluation programs for three specific reasons:[10]

- To justify the existence of the training department and how it contributes to the organizational goals and objectives.
- To evaluate the cost effectiveness of value of training programs.

- To gain information on employee needs and ongoing requirements to improve future training programs.

There are many approaches to evaluating training programs but the most popular was published by Donald Krikpatrick. His model has 4 levels of evaluating training programs.

Reaction

Evaluation on this level measures the reaction of the participants. This is also known as "Happiness Sheet or Smile Sheet" evaluation. Measuring reaction is important as it gives be feedback, which could be incorporated in future programs to improve organization performance. Though this is used in many countries, it is extensively used in countries in the Asian region and in the Middle-East.

Learning

Learning can be defined as the extent to which participants change attitudes, improve knowledge, and improve their skills as a result of attending the program (Krikpatrick, 1998). Performance tests are an important mechanism to evaluate training at this level.

Behaviour

Behaviour is the change in the participant as a result of the training program. Evaluating behaviour is difficult because trainees cannot change their behaviour unless they have an opportunity to do so. Surveys and periodical questionnaires are a good way of evaluating changes in behaviour. Companies in the US with particular reference to Anderson Consulting and IBM are using the behavioural approach extensively in evaluating their training programs with particular reference to measuring the soft skills (Abernathy, 1999).[11]

Result

Evaluating results is the most difficult and cumbersome of the evaluation procedure. The final results include increased production, decreased costs, which might be the reason for having these training programs (Krikpatrick, 1998). Evaluating results is a difficult task because trainers find it difficult to measure the results and compare them with the cost of the program. This is especially true when measuring soft skills, as they are difficult to quantify. Apart from Krikpatricks's 4 stage evaluation model, there are several other theories of evaluation. Evaluating training programs through Return on Investment (ROI) is another approach to measure the value of training investments in financial terms. With the integration of the European Union, companies are using financial techniques to evaluate the value of training programs (O'Connor, 1992).[12] Robert S. Kaplan and David Nortem however argue that financial measures are inadequate for guiding the evaluating organizations (Abernathy, 1999).

Jack Phillips, founder of P.R.O. (Performance Resource Organization) feels that though it is easy to measure hard data, measuring soft data is subjective and more difficult to transfer of monetary values (Wholey, 1999).[13]

ISSUES IN EVALUATING TRAINING PROGRAMMES

Though companies spend lots of time planning and implementing training programmes, evaluating training programmes is a low priority area in most organizations. The attitude of the organization influences the quality of evaluation considerably. The more insecure people feel in a particular situation, the greater the anxiety that becomes associated with evaluation. Employee trainers should treat evaluation as opportunity to prove the business impact of training, instead of looking at it as a threat (Nelson and Dailey, 1999).[14]

Another issue is the design of a suitable evaluation programme. Training in many ways is an intangible asset and the measurement of soft skills can prove to be a difficult task for an organization. Even today "smile sheets" are the most popular form of evaluating training programs even though they are at level of the evaluation process, many organizations are thinking further blat have not been successful due to lack of evaluation knowledge and also because of lack of pressure from management (Krikpatrick, 1998).[15]

With the growing tendency of organizations to resort to flatter structures, managers cannot spend a lot of time and effort on evaluating programs as they have other responsibilities too. Evaluation also becomes a problem when there is more than one stake holder. There is another issue as to who should be evaluating the programmes in these circumstances.

An indepth analysis of the vast literature on evaluating training programmes, one comes to an understanding that even though companies spend thousands of dollars on training programmes, there is little effort to measure its effectiveness. Managers at higher levels are worried only about profits, stock prices and other areas of concern for top management. They pay little attention to training programmes unless they hear something negative about it (O'Connor, 1992). With the importance of training programmes increasing significantly, it has become easier to convince top management about the benefits of training. Hence organizations today believe in investing more money in training than on detailed evaluation. These include having training programmes in exotic locations with all the available luxuries, instead of focussing on delivering a high quality training programme. There is also a tendency among trainers to conduct costly research projects to determine the value and effect of training. This makes the process of evaluation tedious, cumbersome and hence, ineffective.

Though it is difficult to put a dollar value on the effect of training programmes, through continuous evaluation, companies can actually measure the returns on training programmes. Companies like General Electric have used evaluation to improve the effectiveness of their training programmes. A good approach could be to get line managers involved in evaluation so that it is more interactive and participative. Also evaluation should be conducted on an ongoing basis rather than being one time affair.

CONCLUSION

Training programmes are an integral part of most organizations across the globe. To maintain competitive advantage, it has become imperative for companies to provide ongoing training and development to its employees. As a result of huge amounts being spent on training programmes, evaluating training programmes has gained increased importance. Positive evaluation ensures that organizations conduct training programmes that improve performance standards of both the employee and organization. Evaluators should conduct a thorough study of the organization before designing an evaluation programme and should strive to keep evaluation as simple as possible.

NOTES AND REFERENCES

1. A.R. Tyagi, "Administrative Training: A Theoretical Postulate", *International Review of Administrative Science*, Vol. XL, No. 2, 1974, p. 157.
2. M. Kantz Saul, Methodological Note on Appraising Administrative Capability for Development, UN Publication (Sales No. E69-11 4.2), p. 8.
3. Ernest Dale and L.D. Michelon, Modern Management Techniques, Penguin Books, 1974, p. 6.
4. Hames L. Marshell, Development Teaching, New York: 1949, pp. 190-306.
5. Koontz and O'Donnell, A System and Contingency, Analysis of Managerial Functions. Sixth Edition. McGraw-Hill, London, 1976, p. 520.
6. GOI: Report of the Informal Expert Group on Co-operative Education, *Training and Research*, p 28.
7. Quoted in the Report of Study Team on Co-operative Training, *op. cit.*, p. 64.
8. A.F. Laidlaw, "Extension Work in the Co-operative Movement", The Central Committee for Co-operative Reserve Bank of India, 1958, p. 32.
9. L.N. Long (1999), ROI: Capturing of Big Picture (Industry trend or event), *Technical Training*, Vol. 1016, p. 31.
10. D.Krikpatrick (1998), Thinking Outside the Evaluation Box, *Training and Development*, Vol. 53, p. 18.
11. D.J. Abernathy (1999), Thinking Outside the Evaluation Box, *Training and Development*, Vol. 53.
12. R.O. Connor (1992), New Approaches for Europe, 93, *Personnel Journal*, Vol. 71, n. 5, p. 96(6).
13. S.J. (1990), Performance Based Management, *Public Productivity and Management Review*, San Fransico.
14. B. Nelson and P. Dailey (1999), Four steps of evaluating recognition programmes, *Workforce Journal*.
15. D. Krikpatrick (1996), Great Ideas Revisited: Evaluation of Employees Training Programmes, *Training and Development*, Vol. 50, n. 1, p. 54(6).

Performance Appraisal

"Performance appraisal is the process of evaluating the performance and qualifications of the employees in terms of requirements of the job for which he is employed for purposes of administration including placement, selection for promotion, providing financial rewards and other actions which require differential treatment among the members of a group as distinguished from actions affecting all members equally."

—*Heigel*

Performance appraisal is the most neglected area in the health services. Appraisal is not done on the basis of quantity and quality of health services provided but on extraneous considerations. A multi-purpose health worker who is very good at his work may get average rating while another very poor at work may get excellent because of personal reasons or compulsions.

Performance appraisal is the problems of measuring quantitatively and qualitatively an employee's past or present performance against the background of his expected role performance, the background of his work environment and about his future potential for an organization. Performance appraisal facilitates the development of an organizational climate of mutuality, openness and collaboration and helps towards achievement of individual as well as organizational goals. To quote Heigel. "Performance and qualifications of the employees in terms of the requirements of the job for which he is employed, for purposes of administration including placement, selection for promotion. Providing financial rewards and other actions which require differential treatment among the members of a group as distinguished from actions affecting all members equally."[1] The primary purpose of performance appraisal is to help each medical person handle his current job better.[2] It is the principal medium through which human talent in organizations may be most effectively utilized.

It must be kept in mind that performance appraisal is a continuous activity. Many scholars use different terminology, e.g., Megginson[3] prefers to use the term "Employee appraisal" while Cunning,[4] prefers to use the term "staff assessment." If managers accept that one of their responsibilities is to ensure the development of their subordinates and to improve their job performance, they should also accept that appraisal of job performance is essential to the process.

The performance of health and medical personnel is unsatisfactory but their appraisal reports are good. It appears that the reporting officer and the person who is being assessed have joined hands to do all types of corrupt practices not only relating to finances but also absenteeism, non-punctuality, indulging in private practice, etc. The author has personally seen a great deal of inefficiency in health area but their reports are excellent. We must devise new system of appraisal.

Supervision is a compound word and its two parts are 'super' and 'vision' which means overseeing. In a hierarchical organization no one can claim to work without proper supervision. Generally, each officer is given certain powers and responsibilities and is supposed to be responsible to the officer above him for proper execution of the decisions and use of delegated powers. Moreover, for proper functioning of an organisation it is very essential that there should be proper coordination and link among different parts and organs of an organisation. It is also to be ensured that departments of an organisation do exactly the same work which is expected of them. In common parlance, by supervision we mean direction accompanied by authority. In a broad sense we mean superintendence and overseeing. Margaret Williamson has defined supervision as "a process by which workers are helped by a designated staff member to learn according to their needs, to make the best use of their knowledge and skills and to improve their abilities so that they do their jobs more effectively and with increasing satisfaction to themselves and the agency."

John D. Millett rightly observe, "Supervision is more than a process, it is a spirit which animates the relationship between levels of organisation and which induces maximum administrative accomplishment. or when unsuccessful generates administrative paralysis." Effective management is concerned to realise the first and to avoid the second.

Nigro has identified the following aspects of the supervisor's job:

(i) To satisfy the employees' desire for recognition.
(ii) To keep them informed.
(iii) To allow subordinates to make as many independent decisions as possible.
(iv) To avoid invading the specialist's bailiwick.
(v) To keep the door open for conference and consultations with subordinates.

(vi) To accept the probability of being unpopular with at least a few subordinates.
(vii) To avoid over-optimism.
(viii) To assure the proper interpretation and execution of orders.
(ix) To abolish useless regulations.
(x) To recognise that assistants will sometimes be more intelligent than oneself.
(xi) To make no promises that cannot be fulfiled.
(xii) To expect loyalty and give it too.
(xiii) To avoid discrimination even in favour of a friend.
(xiv) To resist undue pressure and fight for the interests of subordinates.

A. CRITERIA OF PERFORMANCE APPRAISAL

1. The employees should be made aware of the performance in terms of goals, targets, behaviour, etc., expected of them. A personal equation between the evaluator and the evaluate has to be developed to achieve mutual understanding of the criteria of evaluation. Evaluators themselves are not discharging their duties. How can they write adverse remarks against any medical personnel. Evaluator should be evaluated about himself as well as the persons whom he has evaluated.
2. The employees should be encouraged to express themselves freely on the performance reports. However, no leniency should be shown if they are not satisfying the patients
3. It is believed throughout the organization that the appraisal system itself is job-related, performance-based, uniform and non-variable, fair, just and equitable; there is a general belief in the organization that appraisers are honest, rational and objective in their approach, judgement and behavioural orientations. It has been seen in health department that performance appraisal is a mockery. Doctors and para medical staff do not bother for their work and are not serious. The fault lies with the appraiser who wants to be lenient and join them in making the health services worse. Some of them even have the knowledge of the health work they are doing. The health department must set quantitative standards which can be measured.
4. Supervisor responsible for performance appraisal should be well trained in the art and science of performance appraisal to ensure uniformity, consistency and reliability. The ultimate success of evaluation rests with the evaluator, it does not depend on any system however perfect a support it may ensure.
5. Performance appraisal reports should be examined meticulously before taking any positive or negative action. It is a sad state of affairs that no body looks after these reports thoroughly and

wants to please their subordinates resulting into the tendency of increasing discipline and spoiling the tone of health organizations.

6. To promote intra- and inter-departmental consistency and uniformity, line and staff coordination should be ensured.
7. There should be provision for appeals of appraisals to ensure confidence of the employees and their associations/unions.

1. Objectives

Objectives can be discussed under four heads (Refer Chart.5.1)

CHART 5.1

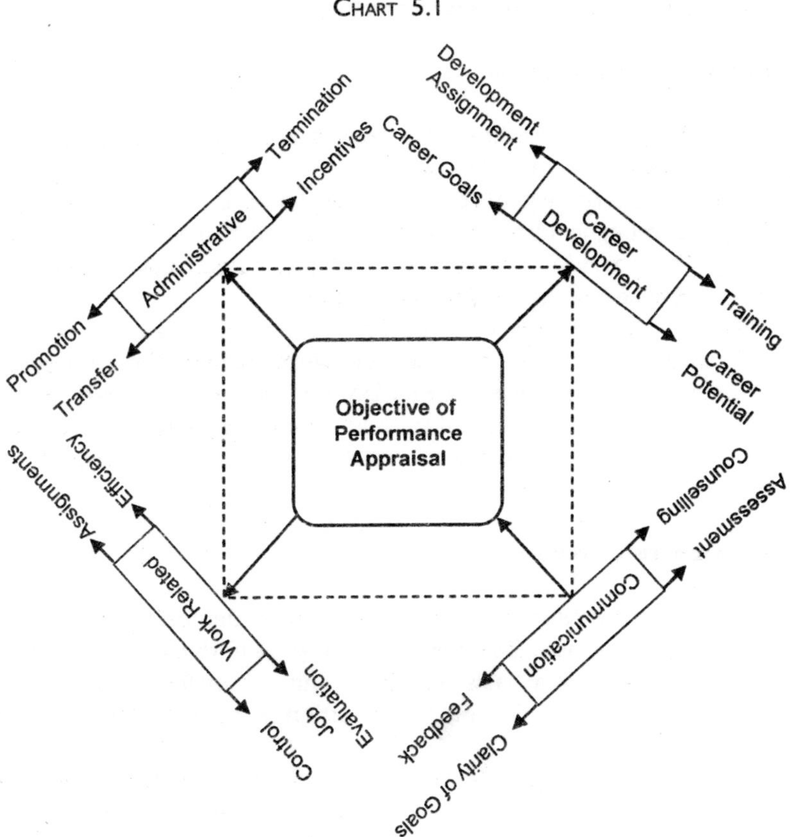

(a) Work-related Objectives

(1) To provide a control for health work done; whether they are performing duties efficiently towards patients;
(2) To improve efficiency so that patients feel satisfied.
(3) To help in assigning work and plan future work assignment; and
(4) To carry our job evaluation.

(b) Career Development Objectives

(1) To identify strong and weak points and encourage finding remedies for weak points through training;
(2) To determine career potential;
(3) To plan developmental (promotional or lateral) assignments; and
(4) To plan career goals.

Performance Evaluation can identify strong and weak points of the persons working in health system and take appropriate action to make them do excellent work through corrective action.

(c) Objectives of Communication

(1) To provide feedback on performance, i.e. what is the quantity and quality of work done.
(2) To clearly establish goals, i.e. what is expected of the staff member in terms of performance and future work assignments;
(3) To provide counselling and job satisfaction through open discussion on performance; and
(4) To let employees assess where they stand within the organization in terms of their performance. The employees in a Government health organization take easy as they think that they will get their salary and promotion whether they work or not. This tendency must be curbed through good communication.

(d) Administrative Objectives

(1) To serve as a basis for promotion or demotion;
(2) To serve as a basis for allocating incentives;
(3) To serve as a basis for determining transfers; and
(4) To serve as a basis for termination in case of reduction of staff.

If appraisal system is to achieve the four major objectives outlined above, appraisal content should include work-related components and career-related components appraisal forms should provide an action on each of these appraisal forms should stimulate communication of appraisal content. follow-up action is required after appraisals to ensure that appraisal results are taken into account in administrative decision-making; and finally, appraisal system should be evaluated from time lo time lo determine if the four major objectives are being achieved.

2. Methods of Performance Appraisal

There are two types of methods:

Traditional Methods

There are a number of systems for measuring the performance of employees:

(1) Graphic Scale
(2) Ranking
(3) Forced Distribution Methods
(4) Critical Incident Methods
(5) Forced Choice Rating Methods.
(6) Group Appraisal
(7) Nomination
(8) Work Sample Test
(9) Result-oriented Performance Appraisal system
(10) Confidential Reports.

We shall discuss here only ACR as it is mostly used in health institutions.

B. ANNUAL CONFIDENTIAL REPORTS

In Government Health Departments in India. performance appraisal is done through annual confidential reports. A very casual attitude is found among raters while filling confidential reports of the employees working under them. Confidential reports combine different techniques of rating discussed earlier.

The confidential report is written for a unit of one year and relates to the performance ability and character of the person during that year. The most important factor on which the success of confidential reports depends is objectivity. The essential feature of the methods of preparation and communication of confidential reports of officers under the administration control of the health department are:

(1) Annual confidential remarks are recorded with a view to judging the performance and efficiency of health functionaries.
(2) The object of maintenance of character reports is to put health functionaries on proper line by pointing out the defects.
(3) Adverse entries should be communicated to him in time to enable him to rectify the defect.
(4) From December 4, 1946, till April 20, 1966, both remediable and irremediable defects were being communicated. From 1966 defects touching integrity and morality are not being communicated.
(5) The confidential character roll recorded by reporting officers is to be countersigned by superior authorities in certain cases, as indicated in the letter.

(6) The countersigning authority may take a view different from that of the reporting officer in which case the view of the former will prevail.
(7) Until the countersigning authority gives his remarks, the character roll is not complete and is not to be acted upon.
(8) Time schedules have been prescribed in each case for recording remarks at different levels and to submit them to the government for maintenance of confidential character roll.
(9) Representation against adverse remarks will not ordinarily be entertained as the very purpose of such communication is to enable the officer to know his failings to rectify them and the officer should profit by it. The communication should not be taken as a matter of argument to enter into controversy.
(10) In rare cases, however, where the remark is on specific facts or is obviously the result of a mistake on the part of the reporting officer, representation exists.
(11) The views of the superior officers on the representation must reach the government within two months of the date of filing of such representations and the representation is to be disposed of by the government within three months from the date of receipt of the same.

Confidential reports have a far reaching influence on the career of employees since their future prospects depend on such reports and, therefore, these should be handled scientifically. It need not be emphasized that the remarks such as "good", "very good", "satisfactory", "fair", etc. cannot be construed to have been made with exactitude because each one of these different objectives carries with itself different shades of meaning having a great subjective content therein.

Inspite of all the efforts made to make performance appraisal as objective and useful as possible, there are many inherent weaknesses and drawbacks to the entire system of performance appraisal—

(a) There is high degree of subjectivity in the writing of the performance appraisal reports for all employees at all levels.
(b) The high turnover in transfers ensures that employees especially if they are due for promotion have to "chase" the concerned reporting reviewing and accepting authorities to ensure that their appraisal report is written on time.
(c) Invariably, in most of departments, the appraisal reports are never written on time. The time lag handicaps the reporting and reviewing authority from being able to accurately remember the performance of the employee during the period of assessment.
(d) For those categories of employees who are transferred frequently in a year, it becomes very difficult to assess the performance as a whole.

(e) It is difficult for secretariat employees especially from assistant level upwards to that of under secretary, to write anything meaningful in their annual confidential reports in the columns against targets and achievements. It is not possible to prescribe any target for officials or officers who are entrusted with one desk work.

(f) The overall assessment of an employee to be made by the accepting authority in terms of 'satisfactory', 'good', 'very good', 'outstanding', is highly subjective. The interpretation of the above description for assessing the employees performance would differ from each officer making the assessment and also from department to department. In departments where the output of work can be easily quantified and judged, it may be easier to be more objective, but in departments dealing purely with policy matters, it is difficult to be a very objective.

(g) Only adverse remarks are communicated to the employee and in the present system, this is also not done on time by many of the departments.

(h) All information about the annual confidential reports of the employees must be computerized and include whether there are any missing annual confidential reports or if in a particular year one of the levels of reporting in the annual confidential report is incomplete.

In order to improve the performance appraisal system, the following is recommended:

- There should be a different format of ACR for different employees.
- Apart from the adverse comments, a copy of every year's completely written ACR must also be given to the employee. This would enable the employee to know how his/her performance is judged not to make any improvements if required for the next year.
- As is done for the Armed Forces and Central Police Organizations, a grading system on a 10 point or a 7 point scale to assess the individual traits and attributes could be introduced as part of the ACR for health employees.
- All levels of officers who have to write ACRs must be given proper training in how to write an ACR objectively especially health personnel.
- Counselling may be introduced to those employees who get repeated adverse remarks. Such health employees must be observed thoroughly.
- Action should also be taken against those health officers who delay in writing the ACRs where they are either reporting, reviewing or accepting authorities.

- ACRs, which are to be approved by the concerned health minister sometimes, are delayed for several months. A time frame be fixed for approval of the ACRs by the concerned ministers.

Confidential reports have a far reaching influence on the career of employees, since there future prospects depend on such reports and therefore, these should be handled scientifically. It need not be emphasized that the remarks such as "good", "very good", "satisfactory", "fair", etc. cannot be construed to have been made with exactitude, because each one of these different objectives carriers with itself different shades of meaning having a great subjective content therein.

A. and G. Prageetha Raju in their article, "Assessment of Confidential Report Method as a performance appraisal systems—A Study of Managerial and Non-Managerial Responses" in the *Journal of Ford School of Management* rightly states that if training is provided meticulously at regular intervals, both for appraisers and appraises, the conceptual clarity improves and ensures that the appraisal systems acceptable in the organization. In such training there is exchange of ideas and experiences and there are stimulated role plays which ensure better understanding of Performance Appraisal systems."[5]

Critical Evaluation

1. Performance is not evaluated in terms of its impact on organizational objectives, goals and targets. It, however, gives more attention to the personality of an individual rather than what he is expected to do, or what results he has achieved. No care is taken about his contribution to health department.
2. Appraisal tools lack reliability, validity, and are mostly subjective and that is why ratings and raters are subject to organizational influence. Raters display biases.
3. Most health administrators do not possess knowledge of the art and science of performance appraisal, resulting in different assessments of the same employee by different administrators.
4. Results of appraisals are not utilized to correct the behaviour of the employees rated low to assist individual development. There is also no scope for counselling the employees rated low through performance appraisal. Counselling the employee on his past performance with a view to influencing his behaviour in future is the prime objective of the counsellor.
5. The existing performance appraisal techniques hamper effective communication between appraiser and appraised. Personnel are not taken in confidence and they lack understanding of the criteria upon which their performance is appraised. This increases the psychological distance between them.

6. Performance appraisal is not done on the basis of achievements but on the basis of usefulness of the employees to the appraising authority. Those who can be personally useful to him get higher ratings than those who have really achieved results. This increases the distance and distrust between the appraising authority and other so-called less loyal subordinates.

Modern Method (MBO Approach)

According to Odiorne, result-oriented appraisals or MBO is "a system wherein the superior and the subordinate managers of an organization jointly define their common goals, define each individual's major areas of responsibility in terms of results expected of him and use these measures as guides for operating the unit and assessing the contribution of each of its members." The main steps in the process are:

(1) Determination of the key result of the organization;
(2) Performance improvement guide for all positions;
(3) Appraiser and appraised records observations;
(4) Performance progress review conference;
(5) Individual development programme; and
(6) Post-development programme review conference.

Performance appraisal must be done scientifically and continuously sort out problems in the initial stage otherwise, it becomes difficult to change when the habits become stiff.

CONCLUSION

An effective Performance Appraisal system is a continuous activity beginning with goal setting, having periodic reviews and ending with the traditional year end evaluation. This is supposed to increase the overall effective functioning of an Organization. However, performance appraisal is still perceived as a fault finding exercise done year after year by the superiors. On the whole, performance appraisal is ineffective and encourages timidity and servitude. The final grading of an employee depends more on personal loyalty than on performance. Final grading is made as a personalized decision. Besides, appraisal is done seriously. Confidential reports are generally completed barely a few minutes before the submission indicating that the supervisors take this actively casually.

Raheim Bakshe in the *Daily Tribune* dated 6.11.2007 clearly observes that some clerks of the PGI, posted at the OPD counters and at other public dealing points, behave rudely and don't cooperate with patients. Similarly, nurses also behave badly with the indoor patients. Poor and illiterate patients at the PGI should be attended/guided politely and if they do not understand once, nurses/clerks should not hesitate to explain the things again.

Such things should be checked sincerely. In my opinion, feedback on hospitality and behaviour of the staff should be taken from the patients while discharging them and measures should be adopted to put things in place. Training should be imparted to the staff in public dealing. Action against complaints and suggestions should be taken immediately. Employee's ACR's should have mention of their behaviour. Medical superintendent/deputy medical superintendent should check the staff regularly. A suggestion box should be installed near the enquiry office.

In government, however, the appraisal system has been reduced to a purely control mechanism to discipline the appraisal system and is held as a stick over their heads rather than as an instrument for improving the organization as well as the individuals. It is for this reason that the appraisal system has been named as "Annual Confidential Report" or "Confidential Character Role." The two obvious characteristics of performance appraisal in Government organization are secrecy and fairness. Whereas secrecy emanates out of the strict hierarchical structures of the government and its impersonal character, the fairness of the system has been in question for a very long time. Subjective attitudes, personal bias and out-dated value system have pointed out as the main faults of the appraisal system in Government.[6]

Finally, it is necessary to discuss how such responsibility can be made more meaningful:

- The employee should be made aware of the organizations expectations and its norms for evaluation.
- The employee should have the right to express himself on any unfair practices in rating. Such provision for hearing should be built into the appraisal system evaluation and potential evaluation should be clearly distinguished for the benefit of the employee.
- Each superior, (all though to the top manager) should in turn, be evaluated frating his subordinates. This would ensure more responsible evaluation.
- Organizations should be aware of the difficulties in an desirability of differentiating amongst those lying between extremes of very good and very poor. If no use is being made of such distinction. Public Administration becomes a development-oriented evaluation approach.

Performance Appraisal should be based on surveys of patients as our ultimate objective is to provide decent health care services. What is the use of a medical person who is otherwise good but avoids patients.

Since you are required to write annual confidential reports, you should put in a little extra time and effort needed to make the system work well and serve as a motivator for your staff. Below are some guidelines for carrying out a good performance appraisal based on the annual confidential reports:

Step 1. Provide feedback to subordinates throughout the year so that your evaluation does not come as a surprise. The subordinate should have already heard everything that appears in the confidential report.

Step 2. Review the subordinate's file before filling out the confidential report. Pay attention to previous reports

Step 3. Meet with the subordinate to review his performance once you have filled up the report. Give him advance notice of the meeting, so he has time to reflect on his performance during the past year. Allow ample time for the meeting, including time for preparing a plan for Improvement

Step 4. Begin the meeting with favourable comments. Strive for a relaxed, friendly meeting. Do not hurry Encourage the subordinate to explain his point of view and to ask questions.

Step 5. Be positive. Discuss the subordinate's performance objectively, but try to give two or three favourable comments for every criticism. Follow-up criticism immediately with suggestions for Improvement. Compare the subordinates performance to his job description Never compare one staff member with other staff members.

Step 6. Discuss strengths and weaknesses. Suggest ways that the subordinate can use his strengths to overcome his weaknesses. Decide with the subordinate which problems might have been caused by the subordinate himself, which by the supervisor, and which by the job situation. For example, the supervisor might not be giving clear instructions or the subordinate might be frustrated by lack of equipment, or lack of cooperation from other staff, or by a heavy workload. Pinpoint the cause of the problems. Be careful not to place all the blame for poor performance on someone else, and therefore beyond the control of this subordinate. Each staff member must do the best with the resources available to him

Step 7. Plan Improvements Decide on a plan for Improving performance in the next year Make the plan realistic, yet challenging Consider the subordinate's strengths and areas In need of Improvement. Write the plan down after both of you agree on it.

Step 8. Set dates for review of progress in carrying out the performance. Improvement plan. The review dates might be every three months. End the meeting on a positive note Impress the subordinate with the opportunities he has to improve his performance. Assure him that you will do your part to help him.

Step 9. Follow-up on progress. Meet on the dates agreed upon during the meeting to review the performance. Improvement plan. Provide support and motivation on a continuing basis to the subordinate, as he strives to improve his performance.[7]

NOTES AND REFERENCES

1. Heigel, The Encyclopedia of Management, New York, Reinhold Publishing Corporation, 1973, p. 654.
2. V.K. Rowland, Evaluating and Improving Managerial Performance, New York, McGraw Hill, 1970, p. 210.

3. L.C. Megginson, Personnel—A Behavioural Approach to Administration, Homewood, Illinois, Richard D. Irwin. Inc. 1967.
4. M.W. Cunning, The Theory and Practice of Personnel Management, London, William Heineman Ltd., 1972.
5. A. Suryanarana and G. Prageetha Raju, "Assessment of Confidential Report Methods as a Performance Appraisal System—A Study of Managerial and Non-Managerial Responses", in the *Journal of Ford School of Management*, Vol. XVI, Nos. 1 and 2, January-June 1998, p. 41.
6. K.C. Sharma, Harinder Singh and Bata K. Dey, in Management in Government (eds.) B.C. Mathur, *et. al.* New Delhi, 1979, Ministry of Information and Broadcasting, p. 276.
7. NIHFW: Management Training Module for Medical Officer, New Delhi, 1987, pp. 209-10.

Career Development and Career Planning

"Career Planning is an important instrument for motivation and development of health personnel in any public health or hospital organization, if the concept of career planning is properly understood at all levels, it can then be used to the maximum advantage of both the patients/ public and the health organization. For making the career plan work as an effective instrument, two important aspects have to be accepted. First, a commitment on the part of the health supervisor that his men and their growth is his primarily responsibility and that his success should be judged in terms of men's career he has helped to build by his contribution and assistance. Secondly, the health management as a whole should be committed to help the health employee attain their full potential by training, job rotation and acceptance and involvement of health management at various levels. Thus, personnel policies are to be tailored to fit and needs of the health organization and medical personnel so that motivation is kept in a dynamic form." —S.K. Bhatia and Nirmal Singh

A career system is one in which a hierarchically organized group includes posts at different levels, e.g. medical officer to Director of Health Services or from multipurpose Health worker to Health Assistant. The whole professional life of the medical officer under this system is utilized profitably from one level to another. In the Contract or position system, the health person is recruited for a particular job which he will occupy throughout his stay in the health organization. The recent trend in personnel administration is to favour the career system. Many Commissions in different countries favoured the adoption of the career system. No health service can hope to survive long if it fails to compensate adequately through reasonable career prospects, those of its staff who have served it for long periods conscientiously and with dedication. The career system is a guarantee of efficiency and integrity and a shield against patronage and political pressure.

In the developed and developing countries, there is a feeling that their health and medical Personnel System do not fulfil the requirements for setting foot in the 21st Century. The Volcker Commission appointed by the Bush administration under the Chairmanship of Paul Volcker presented its report in 1989. The introduction to the Volcker Commission's report stated:

"Commission members saw three main threats to the health of the Public Service—Public attitudes, Political leadership and internal-management systems. These threats were seen as eroding the ability of the health system to function effectively and at the same time demands on health systems were growing. This was done to draw a National Public Service for the year 2000."

Similarly, J.L. Monion in his Article "Career Public Service in Canada: Reflections and Predictions" in *International Review of Administrative Sciences* mentions these objectives.

To Foster and encourage a public service that:

- is professional, highly qualified, non-partisan and imbued with a mission of service to the public;
- recognizes its employees as assets to be valued and developed;
- places as much authority as possible in the hands of first line employees and managers; and
- provides scope for different organizational forms to meet different needs, but in the context of a single public service.

We need to develop such futuristic plans for career development in all health organizations in India to make the optimal use of health personnel.

MEANING OF CAREER DEVELOPMENT

Career Planning refers to planned and systematized efforts of organizations to chalk out the work of health personnel in such a way as to optimise their efforts for excellence in their health work. The basic approach is to plan the future rather than leave the individual health employees to chance.

Career development means to provide all conditions conducive to the development of the health persons once recruited in the health organization so that they can occupy higher positions in the organization and ultimately occupy the top echelons in the health system. In essence, a career system may comprise the careful selection of able young men with the requisite qualifications and the necessary attributes of character and motivation. Such persons may be carefully trained later on in those aspects of the health organisations which cannot be acquired beforehand and their attitudes continually tested by assigning them a variety of tasks during a period of probation after which a candidate may be retained on a career basis or released. Moreover, forward planning of their assignments may be made to ensure the maximum utilization and proper development of their aptitudes. Constant in service training courses may be provided to keep them abreast of the latest developments and to prevent them from becoming stagnant. This may be followed by an open system of promotion, permitting the ablest officers to serve at the highest posts whether at headquarters or in the field. The career status should not prevent the management from releasing persons who prove ineffective or who lose their effectiveness.

Career Development and career planning will ensure that health personnel will:

- Work with mass organizations to identify health-related problems and advise on means of overcoming them;
- Organize, manage and administer the health services so as to ensure maximum coordination of the available services and to achieve optimum coverage, efficiency and effectiveness;
- Plan the health services;
- Ensure the coordination of inter-sectoral health-related activities;
- Develop and/or strengthen the system for the collection, analysis and interpretation of information necessary for health planning and management, including monitoring and evaluation at all levels; and
- Participate in the planning and operation of training progarmmes for professional and other cadres of health staff.

Above all, the training stresses the importance of the health worker as an agent of change. Through discussion, persuasion, and mobilisation, he or she must bring about a commitment to primary health care on the part of professional health workers, members of other key sectors, and the mass organizations involved.

In order to impart the knowledge and develop the skills needed to carry out these functions, the course emphasizes the concept of "learning by doing." The first part of the course consists of theoretical training in planning, epidemiology, management, and communication, interspread with two months of practical field work, with emphasis on designing surveys involving the community and on the identification of priority problems.

During the following year, the students become acting health managers and are expected to carry out in practice what they have learned.

B. STEPS FOR CAREER DEVELOPMENT

(a) Selection, on the basis of promise or potential for growth as well as on the basis of the capacity to meet the changing needs and challenges of new functions in an health organization;

(b) Training, to assist the person in timely preparation for changing work requirements, through the acquisition. improvement and adaptation of knowledge and skills, in order both to further health organizational goals and to promote individual growth and job satisfaction;

(c) Mobility, to assist a flexible deployment of personnel resources according to need, as well as to promote the self-actualisation of individual staff and to enhance their value to the organization through their progressive exposure to different facets of its work;

(d) Promotion by merit, to stimulate, assist and to reward high quality performances and individual growth;

(e) The establishment and implementation of a unified staff policy embracing staff from both field and headquarters; and

(f) The implementation of a policy of systematic rotation of staff within units to provide training and experience of all kinds, and at various levels.

I. Benefits of Career Development to the Individual

(a) It helps the health worker to discover his/her own talents, needs and motives related to work (through performance appraisal, career counselling and planned work assignments and training);

(b) It helps fulfil the individual's need to know what his/her position and future in the organization will be (by providing realistic information and feedback related to career expectations);

(c) It provides a sense of affiliation with the organization and a feeling that the organization is interested in the staff member's development;

(d) It provides a greater opportunity for the individual to obtain the optimal return for his/her personal investment (contribution of talents, time, energy, etc.) in the organization;

(e) It provides the individual with a greater awareness of his/her work environment and hence promotes more intelligent decision-making with respect to careers and avoids frustration caused by lack of career information;

(f) It helps fulfil the individual's need to retain a sense of control over his/her personal destiny in the increasingly complex and impersonalized modern industrial society;

(g) It provides greater opportunities for change in the working environment that would otherwise have lead to boredom;

(h) It is conducive to job satisfaction by providing assignments most suited to the individual's needs and talents; and

(i) It leads to optimal personal development by developing abilities and aptitudes to the full.

2. Benefits of Career Development to the Organisation

(a) It helps to increase efficiency/productivity in jobs, and in turn, effectiveness in meeting the health organization's objectives (through greater creativity, motivation and contribution of the staff);

(b) It helps reduce the turnover of high potential staff and absenteeism;

(c) It facilitates staff mobility by planning assignments well enough in advance to avoid some of the obstacles which arise when staff are required to move at short notice;

(d) It provides greater assurance of an adequate supply of qualified personnel for future openings in managerial, health, medical and other key positions;

(e) It promotes continuity of health organizational knowledge to depends in more upon internal personnel resources;

(f) It helps reduce the pressure on job classification and other personnel systems resulting from frustrated careers;

(g) It provides an added input in programme planning by offering more data on the capabilities of the work force which in turn permits a better judgement to be made of whether or in what manner proposed programme objectives can be accomplished;

(h) It prevents organizational chaos by helping to provide a more regulated, ordered and objective procedure for upward mobility of staff members;

(i) It promotes the optimal utilization of human resources both at present, by preventing instances of mismatched staff members (those having suitable qualification for jobs other than those in which they are presently placed) and in the future by permitting longer-term planning of the development of the staff member's usefulness to the organization; and

(j) It contributes significantly to the reduction of costs.

A survey of the views and comments of most of the personnel responsible for the formulation of personnel policy and personal discussion with others reveal that career development should be an integral part of the personnel policy whether a staff member is offered long-term or short-term appointment.

PLANNING FOR A CAREER DEVELOPMENT PROGRAMME

Planning for career development is not a simple affair. It is dependent upon a number of personnel factors which are essential for the fruition of this concept. Besides, it is not a single time dimension activity but a cyclical phenomenon entailing continuous attempts. What is happening in most of the health organizations is that this concept is given only lip service and theoretical importance. If the organizations and specialty of their personnel departments want to get the best out of their employees, they must plan the career development programmes. In their organizations. Planning effectively is one of the most complex and difficult Intellectual activities in which man can engage. Not to do it well is not sin, but to settle for doing it less than well is. There is no planned development to make the best use of the capacity of Individual staff members through selective assignments, or through planning in advance for new recruits and the existing personnel. This needs to be strengthened to get the best out of the employee's performance. Some important components required to plan the programme profitably benefiting the organization and the personnel are given below. (Refer Chart 6.1)

FIG 6.1

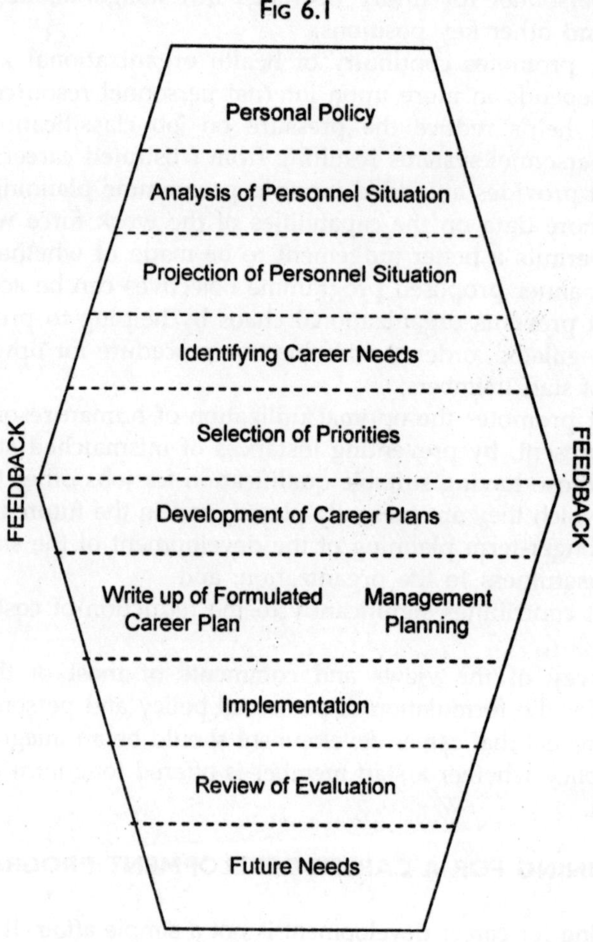

(I) Analysis of Personnel Situation

This relates to time from which career planning is to be done. It is nothing but relates to time from which career planning is to be done. It is nothing but setting up a base line to help the planners to make projections for the planning period and to help in the evaluation of plans. Generally, the following would be required to analyse the present career situation:

(a) *Number of health employees*—their age distribution, qualifications, specializations, etc.
(b) *Structure*—broad as well as detailed and the qualifications for each grade.
(c) Personnel needs of the organization category-wise.
(d) Span of control within the organization.
(e) Headquarters and field staff.
(f) Facilities for training within and outside the organization.

(2) Projection of the Personnel Situation

This can be done on the basis of assumptions which can predict what is likely to happen at the end of the career development plan.

(3) Identification of Career Needs

On the basis of the data collected, we identify the scope and limitations of career development needs. This should be supplemented with discussions between individuals and the personnel responsible for personnel administration.

(4) Selection of Priorities

It may be very difficult to meet all the needs of the health employees and the organizations for career development immediately. Therefore, there is need to select the pressing and urgent problems. There are a number of factors (economic, technical. financial, political, administrative, etc.) which must be taken into consideration while laying down the priorities. This can be decided with the help of techniques like cost-benefit analysis, cost-effectiveness, organizational anaylsis work measurement, method study, etc.

(5) Development of Career Plans

A development plan must be described in terms of:

(a) What is to be attained?;
(b) The extent to which it is to be attained;
(c) The employees involved;
(d) The departments/divisions or units in which the proposed programme will operate; and
(e) The length of time required for achieving the goals. In this context, it is suggested that the organization should:
    (i) Introduce systematic policies and programmes of staff training and career development, such policies and programmes to cover, *inter alia*, development of definite training plans, including in-service training, for all categories of staff, to enable them to:

(a) improve their level of skill and knowledge;
(b) gain wider experience;
(c) assume higher responsibilities; and
(d) encourage the cultural and individual development of every staff member;
 (ii) establish and effectively implement a system of study leave;
 (iii) develop the experience of the staff by encouraging rotation;
 (iv) take positive steps to encourage career development. such as:
(a) providing adequate and appropriate training opportunities;
(b) giving priority in the filling of vacancies in the following order for;
 (i) promotion from within the organization;
 (ii) transfer from within the organization; and
 (iii) outside recruitment;
(c) removing artificial barriers to promotion;
(d) establishing, wherever appropriate, a register of headquarters staff and field staff for promotion on merit-*cum*-seniority basis;
(e) realistically assessing the duties and responsibilities of posts with a view to ensuring their correct classification; and
(f) ensuring full participation by representatives designated by the staff in all matters relating to training, promotion, reclassification of posts, recruitment, etc.

Career plans must identify the hierarchy of objectives, i.e. ultimate, intermediate and immediate. Intermediate objectives may be further divided into effort objectives and performance objectives (targets).

(6) Write-up of Formulated Plan

After deciding the priorities, goals and objectives, the next major step is to prepare a write-up of the career plan. This may contain a schedule (time sequence for the plan to be implemented) and procedures (a set of rules for implementing the plan) and other details so that evaluation becomes easy and meaningful.

(7) Managerial Planning (Monitoring) of Career Plans

Managerial planning can help in ensuring the scheduled operations of career development plans through the advance fixing of targets to be achieved in short periods of time. We can compare constantly the achievement targets with the targets planned. If there is a gap between the two, we can locate the reasons and take remedial action. Managerial planning helps to verify whether the performance is according to the time schedule.

(8) Implementation of Career Plans

Plan implementation is an integral part of the planning process. It requires co-operation, co-ordination and commitment at all levels of the implementing machinery starting from the upper echelons in administration to all individuals in the organization. Implementation must be watched properly and timely action should be taken to improve administrative, technical, financial or personal inadequacies so as to enhance performance.

(9) Review and Evaluation

Evaluation is a built-in device to measure the effectiveness of planning. Evaluation measures the degree to which objectives and targets are fulfiled and also the quality of the result obtained. It measures the productivity of available resources in achieving clearly defined objectives. The benefits from career development plans to the individuals and the organization are reviewed.

(10) Future Needs

After evaluation, we must again start with the first stage, i.e. reassessing career needs, aspirations and opportunities. The results of evaluation make possible reallocation of priorities and resources on the basis of completed results and the changing needs of the organization and of the individuals.

CONCLUSIONS AND RECOMMENDATIONS

1. Career service and career development are different. Career service presupposes permanent appointment and later on movement upward, through promotion. Career development, though linked with career service, can be used to plan both career and non-career staff; the emphasis should be to get the best out of the work of an employee even on a short duration.
2. Career development in its proper perspective should be viewed as being beneficial for both the organization and the staff member. The success of this programme should be measured in terms of the extent to which the needs of both the staff member and the organization are integrated.
3. There is a need to plan the career development programme effectively, including all employees both individually and collectively.
4. Planning for career development is not a one time dimension activity but is continuous and cyclical in nature.
5. Career development is not an isolated activity, but must be inter-linked properly with other aspects of the personnel policy and organizational objectives.
6. Career development should not be restricted to the development of the upper and middle levels of administrative echelons but should cover all personnel who should be encouraged to develop their careers as far as feasible.

7. Career development should be voluntary. It should not be forced on unwilling employees. Investment in such disgruntled employees would yield no dividends. Career development needs to be promoted or encouraged but not forced.
8. There is a need to develop plans for career development for the 21st century, so that we can avoid a large number of problems in future.

Career development and career planning would ensure the achievement of congruence of goals of decent health care to the people as well as satisfaction of health personnel. All this should be achieved spontaneously, voluntarily and systematically. Health System can multiply the benefits through career development and career planning. Health personnel working in a system based on career development can do miracles and provide excellent health services to the people. and raise the status and prestige of the health system.

FUTURE PERSPECTIVES IN THE NEW MILLENNIUM

In the new millennium, the Governments and the Private sector have to attend to career development and career planning to ensure optimum utilization of potential capacity of health infrastructure and facilities. The conference of Chief Secretaries held on November 20, 1996 admitted that the public administration and the civil services at all levels are passing through difficult times in terms of eroded credibility and effectiveness of the civil service, growing public perception of an unholy nexus between certain elements among politicians and civil servants and criminals (as elaborated in the Vohra Committee Report), and increasing criticism of the low level of honesty, transparency and accessibility to the political and bureaucratic elements in charge of administration.[1]

To quote Bata K. Dey, "Career Management" is a neglected, poor cousin of many other more glamorous activities of civil bureaucracy—more talked about less practiced, more tears shed for not doing anything than lifting even the little finger for doing something. The result is that in civil services in this country, there is neither 'career' nor 'management'. The 'main-line bureaucracy' is blissfully unconcerned about the significance of career planning, development and management of people, who populate the government, content with a self-satisfying thought that time, that is efflux of time, will take care of all the bureaucratic oddities as well as functional insufficiencies that may creep in and crop up because of lack of good and effective management of career of most categories of public personnel. A further reason for this absent-mindedness is perhaps the facile assumption at higher rungs of the hierarchy that everything about the employees in running rather smoothly, along right lines, without any additional interventionist need, and careers should be left alone to themselves. The fact of the matter is that it is too costly to leave careers to the tyranny of time.

In bureaucratic terms, the consequence of no-planning in this regard or adhocry in crisis-responsive attitude may be a discontented work force, loss of motivation, withdrawn efforts, manpower-turnover, sub-optional productivity and origanisational goal-derailment."[2]

Department of Administrative Reforms and Public Grievances (AR & PG) was set-up in 1970, following ARC's recommendations, on the model of Britain's Civil Service Department, created, in turn, on the basis of Fulton Report of 1968, which dwelt on this vital question of career management in some depth and detail, The AR and PG Department has spearheaded certain civil service reforms like Rightsizing, e-governance, review of administrative laws, and Total Quality Management in government, etc. However, it needs to play a pioneering role in inducing scientific career development and management practices in government.[3]

Health Organizations have becomes a liability to the government. Neither the doctors and para-medical staff nor patients are satisfied. Therefore, there is need of career development and planning among health personnel so that they can serve the people efficiently and health resources can be economized and used optimally.

Notes and References

1. Bata K. Key, Career Management, in *IJPA*, July-Sept. 1997, pp. 579-80.
2. Ibid., p. 593.
3. Ministry of Personnel Public Grievances, New Delhi, (Document for an effective and Responsive Government), 1997.

Professional Standards

The ingredients of professional standards are:

(a) Administrative Ethics
(b) Impartiality
(c) Political Neutrality
(d) Integrity
(e) Administrative Ethics

Administrative ethics is the study of those administrative standards on the basis of which a particular action is judged to be right or wrong, moral or immoral, good or bad. The practice of these ethical standards in the health services is basic to the preservation and promotion of public health and in pursuing good and right conduct. In spite of the enactment of laws, rules and regulations to ensure impartiality, honesty and devotion among the health services, there still remains a vast area of administrative discretion which cannot be controlled by formal laws, procedures and methods. In such areas "no supervision from above", says Ono Krichheimer, "can be as effective to automatic control on the minds of those possessing it and creating standards of efficiency as well as honesty. Any deviation from the common standards under such circumstances is likely to be discovered sooner or later and rooted out."[1] In the words of M.C. Canny, in all such areas "they must answer to their own consciences, to their own senses of dignity and pride, to the opinions of their fellowmen and above all, to their devotion. to their own honest effort to define the total welfare and to serve it."[2]

The group of health personnel must be imbued with the ideal of service. It was rightly held by Gamer that "No society can reach heights of greatness unless in all fields critical to its growth and creativity there is an ample supply of dedicated men and women."[3]

The ideals of ethics enshrined in the valuable scriptures of all religions must be imbibed by health administrators at all levels to make administration worthwhile. Swami Vivekananda has put beautifully the ideals of service which must be practised by health and medical personnel with interest and dedication.

"It is a great privilege
For all of us to be allowed
To do anything for the world
In helping the world
We really help ourselves."

Prof. J.S. Neki has rightly said in the context of health personnel:

To help, to heal, to reconstruct. to comfort—and all along the line to act with compassion—all these bear testimony to the moral consciousness of the doctor. Whatever the new strains imposed upon medical ethics. this structure will survive and continue to guide doctors In their professional conduct. Legal and juridical obligations, they have, of necessity, to fulfil. But these are not genuine ethics. Genuine ethics has to be ingrained into character and does not have to depend upon external controls.[4]

Bertram M. Gross, an eminent Professor of Urban Affairs, Hunter College. City University of New York, has remarked:

One of the most important characteristics of a genuine profession in addition to a recognized body of knowledge or skill and some organized provision for training. recruitment or certification is a code of ethics. Professional codes of ethics recognise the special power that may be exercised by someone with expert skill and knowledge. They are designed to protect clients against the abuse of such power by the professional-whether he be a doctor who penetrates bodily secrets of clients or a lawyer who learns the details of their private affairs.[5]

There is a need to develop both human and modern technology to improve efficiency. However, priority should be given to human. Organizations are usually more sensitive to possibilities offered to them by the achievements of modern technology than to the refinements of human behaviour as revealed by the sciences of sociology and psychology. On the other hand, the lessons drawn from, experience show that technical innovations deriving from the engineering sciences encountered considerable resistance unless supported by corresponding changes in human attitudes and behaviour.

In an era of rapid change, the improvement of management in its human aspect had become a critical issue. It is important to make full use of the findings of social sciences which endeavour to be Instrumental in giving guidance regarding the behaviour of individuals and groups in varying circumstances. Organization should, therefore. be conceived as complex socio-technical systems whose management requires both technical skills and insight into the motives of human behaviour.[6]

It is widely agreed that manipulation and lack of ethics produce strong negative side effects and reduce organizational effectiveness. With this Important value commitment, the organizations may shift their styles and ultimate from direction, control and surveillance to providing help, support and instruction. Mutuality and collaboration between the leaders and the led, self-control and mutual support are essential for creating a dynamic organization. Let the newcomers strive to set-up organized society with social democracy and high human values setting up ideal societal or public management institutions and if such timely warnings are not accepted, social upsurges are bound to develop in a mild or a violent form.[7]

Our health and medical personnel have become materialistic and many cases have come to light where doctors have removed kidneys from some patients without the knowledge of patients, to be sold to rich persons to make money. Organ transplant has become a roaring business and such incidents happenings everyday require the need of administrative ethics.

A. ESSENTIALS TO ENSURE THE PRACTICE OF PROFESSIONAL AND ADMINISTRATIVE ETHICS

I. Faith and Determination

The most important factor for the success of any health organization is its leadership. Health services must develop ethical standards which help them perform best. Standards are contagious. They spread throughout an organization, a group, or a society. If an organization or group cherishes high standards, the behaviour of the health functionary who enters it is inevitably influenced. They should not develop an excessive sense of self-importance or arrogance. As has been said in the Gita: "We should pursue the path of excellence without fear or favour and work ceaselessly to achieve the objectives," Senator Paul Douglas's remarks quoted below should be imbibed by the health services.

It is fortunate that there are in government a large number of men and women who lead devoted lives of public service. They work extremely hard for far less pay than they could get in private industry. They never sellout the public interest but instead defend it with great difficulties. They do all this. moreover, without receiving appreciable praise. They are generally either little known or actually ignored by the public. Sometimes, they are bitterly attacked by interests which are seeking to obtain unfair privileges or which are swayed by unfounded prejudices. These men and women are indeed unsung heroes, who deserve far more recognition than they receive.[8]

Their internal conscience help them to maintain equanimity and peace which result in their happiness and growth. The future of the health services is in the hands of its members who must strive for creativity, academic excellence, and the pursuit of excellence of service in their professional activities. In this way, it would be possible to create a climate of creativity and optimum performance. Such a situation would have a chain effect. "Good organization building has to create around it a bracing

CHART 7.1

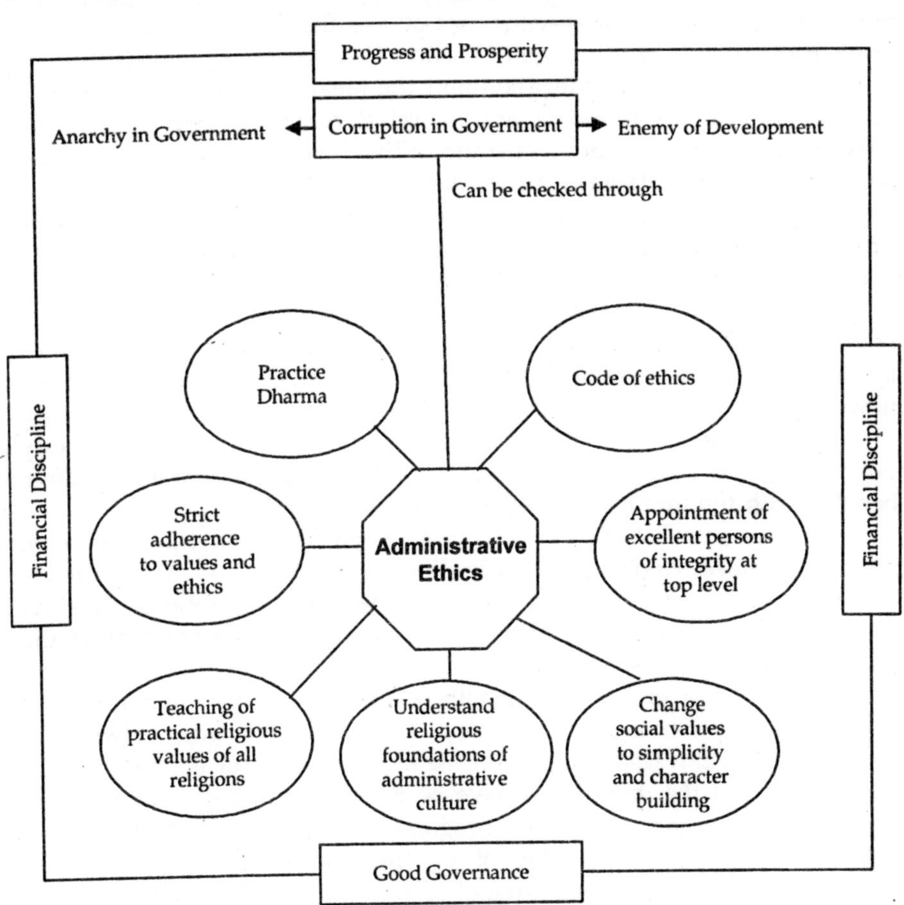

atmosphere. A prideful tradition of integrity, excellence and fellowship. Human beings breathe an ethos around them almost unconsciously. and these traditions make for that ethos."[9] In the present times, money has become the moving force for health and medical personnel.

An attitude of dedication to the set goals of health organization should be an indispensable trait of the top health leaders. This is their primary source of self-confidence to operate and function effectively and efficiently, and in turn transfer the same to the public. It is not just performing development linked administrative duties; it is taking action and encouraging people to take the action required to bring about structural change and growth in health sector. This needs to be supplemented by their belief in the organizational goals. This is what is expected from the top health functionaries at state and district levels.

2. Infusing Ethics into Politics

The country is passing through a terrible crisis. The aggravation of material greed has, as a reaction, set ablaze the fire of corruption at all levels especially among the political elite. Through the dominant influence of the present material civilization and the ideal of enjoyment fostered by it, even the basic framework and moral fibre of the country has been affected by an internal demoralization. This has become more serious in health services. People have lost confidence in medical person. There is no limit to the fraud and hypocrisy and moral degradation that are being practiced in, the name of politics. Arvind Bhandari in his Article "Tradiness over Lok Par" in *The Tribune,* dated October 13, 1982, has rightly said that the truism is that character which like liquid, flows from top to bottom and that. Therefore, attainment of even the limited objective of lessening the malaise requires an attack on it at the highest echelons of power. [10]

Prem Bhatia, Editor-in-Chief of *The Tribune* stated that today's political scene is influenced by short cuts, i.e. the urge to reap the maximum benefits with the minimum of efforts. He commented:

A large number of politicians had chosen the shortest path to power. They had bribed, cajoled and bullied their way to the top. The patronage of office was used by them to consolidate their positions This had inevitably led to the spread of the short-cut system in spheres other than politics.[11]

Most of the problems in health administration are emanating from political corruption and interference. The credibility gap between the political and health leadership is on the increase. Most of the commissions. committees and the daily press have been emphasizing the gravity of the situation. No organization can progress until and unless its political leaders are above board. One of the founding fathers of the Indian Constitution, Mr. H.V. Kamath, regretted that the total devaluation of moral values and ethical ideals in public life and administration today has given rise to the present day rat race for position, power and pelf by any means more by crook than by hook. The political elite must demonstrate integrity and instil faith among their subordinates about their fairness and impartiality. Faith is a contagious disease and once it is developed. it would bend the various levels of the administration into a cohesive structure. All the decisions in such an organization are affected by the whims of political elite rather than the needs of the organization. Thus. there is a need to train the political elite to encourage them to pursue ethical ways so that they fulfil the pledges made to the people to lead a good clean life.

3. Practice of Ethics

Words, written or spoken. are of no use unless put into action. The emphasis should be more on performance rather than paper planning. The health personnel must exhibit integrity, patience, Impartially. honesty and fortitude in their public dealings to gain public confidence and participation and to avoid any action which is in contravention of public welfare. Merit should be sole criterion while taking decisions. They should strive for excellence and encourage others to move to excellence. They should eliminate all frauds which endanger the prestige of the health organisation. Khalil Gibran has rightly said that:

Believing is a fine thing, but placing those beliefs into execution is a test of strength. Many are those who talk like the roar of the sea, but their lives are shallow and stagnant, like the rotting marshes. Many are those who lift their heads above the mountain tops. but their spirit remains dormant to the obscurity of the carvens.[12]

The Tribune editorial rightly commented that:

Man's future was in his own hands and assisted by science he should be trusted to shape it to his own liking. The disappearance of this belief has left our minds a waste-land, empty of hope, lacking in ideals, devoid of aspirations. In a word, sceptism, apathy and disillusion go wider and but deeper than they have ever done before. [13]

Thus, the future of this budding developing democracy depends upon the attitude of its elite. There is no substitute for good ethical values which will be reflected in better performance.

4. Ethical Commitment to Ideals

No health organization can develop until and unless the health personnel working in these organizations are ethically committed to achieving its ideals. Commitment is the syndrome of attitudes, understanding and feeling that identify the team-dedicated participation.

Jawaharlal Nehru, while addressing the Fourth Annual General Body meeting of the Indian Institute of Public Administration, said:

In a period of dynamic growth, however, we want health and medical persons who are not, if I may use the word without any disrespect, merely head clerks but people with minds, people with vision. People with desire to achieve, who have some initiative for doing a job and who can think how to do it. But the person who is to be completely neutral is a head clerk and no more. He would do his work efficiently as a head clerk, no doubt, but nothing more. Can a person be neutral. I ask you, about basic things which we stand for, our state stands for, our plans stand for, e.g., a socialist pattern of society. [14] A certain degree of informed zeal and identification with tasks entrusted to a functionary with a view to ensure higher levels of performance are the hallmark of excellence in public service. In the words of Jawaharlal Nehru:

No administration, I suppose, or anyone else for the matter of that, can really do first class work without a sense of function, without some measures of a crusading spirit; I am doing this, I have to achieve this, as a part of a great movement in a big cause. That gives a sense of function, not the sense of the individual. narrow approach of doing a job in an office for a salary or wage, something connected with your life's outlook or anything, perhaps being interested, as people inevitably are, on one's personal preferment in that particular work.[15]

The Prime Minister, Mrs. Indira Gandhi, addressing the officer-trainees at the Lal Bahadur Shastri National Academy of Administration, stressed the need for them to equip and acquaint themselves as instruments of a national unit. She observed: You have to get out of the exclusive or elitist attitude and Atmosphere. You have to be prepared to assist and not obstruct change. You have to rise above narrow loyalities of caste, of province and Think of the good of the country as a whole. You have to think of refusing to promote sectional interest and always put any loyalty or any interest in the perspective of what is good for India as a whole, you have to develop to professional competence and conscience and you have to know that you can never stop learning. Thus, all organizations, can function and achieve excellence provided all its members strive ethically to pursue the goals of the organization earnestly, sincerely, heartedly and with dedication.

5. Effective Involvement of the Public

Many well intentioned and technically sound programmes aimed at solving problems have been frustrated by lack of popular acceptance and community participation. It has been observed that such programmes are either not actively associated or passively ignored because they do not belong to the population they are designed to help; they are rather seen by the population as imposed external programmes that belong to the government and consequently deserve and require little. if any, of the population's attention, action or other response.

Public relations is the establishment of a climate of understanding. It means Interpreting the programme of health organization to the Public and *vice-versa*. The purpose of public relations is not only to Supply information, but also to encourage an understanding and co-operation between the citizens and the public servants. It is the duty of every member of the organization to maintain good public relations.

There is a great deal of alienation between the people and the organization. This has undermined the legitimacy, effectiveness and credibility of the public administration in our country. We need to promote harmony and mutual trust among the people and public administration. The objectives of public relations should be to increase prestige and good will and protect the life of the organization by safeguarding it against unwanted attacks as well as to remove the genuine complaints and grievances of the people.

To improve understanding between the citizens and the personnel, public relations need to be developed in an effective manner to create favourable community opinion towards public services. This would create confidence in the minds of the people about the competence, fairness, honesty, impartiality and sincerity of the public services.

There should be good relations between people and medical and health personnel's, doctors and para-medical staff have been appointed for the people.

6. Need for Character Building

Professional morality is a part and parcel of the general morality of the community. Dr. Finer said, 'The ethics of every profession will be found, on close analysis, to be not much higher and not much lower than the general decency of the nation as a whole. Their nature, at best, is powerfully moulded by the level of the surrounding and prevailing civilization'.[16]

The success of any government depends upon the effective collaboration of its citizens. All the books of civics would emphasize civic consciousness for the progress of the country. This is possible only if our educational system and mass-media are reoriented to character building among the people. People's character is the ultimate source which can supply kinetic energy for modernization and development. Swami Vivekananda rightly says:

The national ideals of India are renunciation and service; intensify her in those channels, and the rest will take care of itself. He further adds:

What the world wants is character.

7. Study and Practice of True Religion

There is need for infusing the ideology of positive religion among health services through encouraging the study and propagation of the true ideals of religion, i.e. ideals of truth, service and sacrifice. This can be supplemented through circulation of the extracts from the lives of great men who practised the principles of true religion in their lives and are the living embodiment of true religion. This will cement the different sections of the people into cohesive unity and remove all differences based on caste, colour, creed and sex and lead to emotional integration. Mahatma Gandhi has rightly said, "No man can live without religion" and further says, 'There are some who in the egotism of their reason declare that they have nothing to do with religion. But that is like a man saying that he breathes. but that he has no nose." Again he says, "My devotion to truth has drawn me into the field of politics, and I can say without the slightest hesitation, and yet in all humility that those who say that religion has nothing to do with politics do not know what religion means." It is obvious that he was using in a sense probably moral and ethical more than any other different from that of the critics of religion. According to Prof. John Dewey, "any activity pursued on behalf of an ideal end against obstacles, and in spite of threats of personal loss, because of conviction of its general and enduring value, is religious in quality." Nehru admits that true religion means the inner craving and spiritual growth of human beings. A truly religious man seeks truth at all costs with single-minded sincerity and is prepared to make any sacrifice for it. There is a need to encourage the study and practice of true religion. Thus, we can say that mechanical efficiency is not enough. What we need to develop is the human approach. As Graham Wallas says: "In the case of government officers, most of those who have had dealings with them would say that they need to be humanized. The official should be man, should be known as a man and should be expected to behave as a man."[17] The most important religion of health and medical personnel is to serve their patients with dedication and sincerely.

B. IMPARTIALITY

The prestige and reputation of the health services depend to a great extent upon the ethos, attitudes and perception of its members. An allied requirement of promoting impartiality is the necessity of developing and maintaining a national outlook. It involves on the part of the health services a willingness to try to understand and be tolerant of different points of view, different cultural patterns, and different work habits. It also entails willingness to work without prejudice or bias with persons of all regions, religions and cultures. It involves conduct of the highest type and exercise of judgement and restraint in all expressions of view whether public or private; any expressions which could be construed as biased or intolerant, particularly in respect of regional interests or political issues with which the organization is confronted, must be scrupulously avoided.

We can thus conclude by saying that loyalty and impartiality require a positive attitude, i.e. to act with dedication divorced from emotions and prejudices. The Roman Emperor, Marcus Aurelius wrote about his duties in memorable words which are quoted below and must be imbibed by civil servants in the present day.

Do what comes to hand with correct and natural dignity and with humanity, independence and justice, and allow your mind freedom from all other considerations.

C. NEUTRALITY

Political neutrality is an essential ingredient of civil service in a democratic set-up for integrity and efficiency in administration. It means that the health service should give free and frank advice to the government impartially and without any political consideration. It also means the implementation of the decisions of the government by the health and medical services faithfully whether such decisions were in consonance with their advice or not.

The administrators should manifest complete commitment to the goals of their organisations and maintain the necessary non-partisanship and impartiality in taking decisions in individual cases to prevent discrimination merely on grounds of political affiliation. Recently, there has been great tussle between the health minister (GOI) and the Director All India Institute of Medical Sciences. Even the courts had to intervene in this tussle. This has lowered the prestige of AMMS.

D. INTEGRITY

The dictionary defines 'integrity' as soundness of moral principle; the character of uncorrupted virtue; uprightness, honesty, sincerity. The First and Second Five Year Plans have attached the highest priority to integrity in administration. This is more required in social services like health and education.

Deviation from moral standards or lack of integrity takes various shapes in the form of corruption, patronage (based on communalism, sectarianism, nepotism and favouritism), and influence, black-marketing, profiteering and similar other malpractices commonly associated with administration, politics or business or industry are not all that is meant by corruption. But lack of integrity includes all these things. In general terms, lack of integrity means corruption. Scholars, administrators and politicians agree that the main factor responsible for the shortfalls in the implementation of development plans to ensure nation-building and modernization is the prevalence of corruption in administration on a large scale.

Corruption will flourish until the general mass of the people resist it with determination and strength. Most of all, the elimination of corruption requires widespread and steadfast opposition to it, coupled with the courage to act against it. There can be no doubt that the people of India can gel rid of corruption.

There is a need to change social values to ensure social discipline. in order to promote a society based on Social Service. To quote S.C. Dubey, "The vitiated social ethos stands in need of a transformation so that society may undergo a major shift from the ethic of power and self-gratification to the ethic of service and self-imposed authority. There is growing corrupt practice in health administration which need be checked to provide decent health care.

CONCLUSION

Ethics is the moving spirit of a welfare state. All the problems emanating today in a family or a society or Government are the product of ignoring ethics for selfish motives. Ethical government may appear to be harsh for temporary period but this is the only alternative for a permanent beneficial government. "One could argue that ethical behaviour should in itself be rewarding. However, there are tangible benefits as well. Business is built on relationships with the suppliers, customers, employees, and other groups. The strength of these relationships is largely a function of the amount of trust the parties have in each other ..... Studies have shown that the firms which maintain ethical standards perform much better than others due to the good relationships they have with their suppliers, customers, employees and general public. Thus, ethics are cornerstone of business success."[18]

Ethics in health administration is vital for the health and medical personnel otherwise it would become difficult to take care of patients. We get a moral government by creating those conditions within which a moral government can operate. This is done by making it possible for health persons to acquire the necessary traits and by the practice of the same. An exemplary health and medical personnel, to be specific, is not simply one who obeys the laws and behaves within the confines of law but is also one who strives for a moral atmosphere. Such is the duty of those who wish to be involved in the difficult and complex world of health development. This is the essence and basis of a moral state.[19]

Public life is in a desperate state today, with vice-regal regalia dominating it with its fierce ferocity and crushing criminality, sounding the death-knell of ethicality, morality, and value-system. We have seen the killing of hundreds of children being killed in Nithari, in Gaziabad. There is dire need to save it. Public men—at whatever station of life they function—must be men for the public; leaders must lead; and, most importantly, politicians must stop 'politiking'. Public opinion—which is often branded as meaning neither public nor opinion—must be built up against acceptance and tolerance of unethical behaviour and action by anybody, howsoever high and mighty he may be. Crisis of confidence—which admittedly is a unction of culture—must be restored in public life; otherwise, the ancient civilization that we boast of will be no more; there will remain no public, no life, worth-living, without ethics.[20] A large number of cases are coming where doctors and paramedical staff are indulging in non ethical practices.

We must remember that it is the top men in each department who set the tone of the administration. It is they who set the example for those at the top become tainted, when their reputation becomes shady, they will not be able to enforce high standards of integrity in those below them. It is, therefore, imperative that men at the top should present the highest standards of personal integrity, probity and rectitude. As Sir Ivor Jennings observed, the most elementary qualification demanded of a minister is honesty and incorruptibility. It is, in addition, necessary not only that he should possess this qualification but also that he should appear to possess it.[21]

An action is noble because of the ideal which one strives, in itself an action is neither good nor bad. It is the motive in the heart of man that makes an act either good or bad. Once we are careful to choose for ourselves the right type of motive to inspire our activities, the achievement is not only spectacular, but the entire effort becomes rewarding in terms of the feeling of peace and sense of fulfilment that floods the bosom. When we work joyously to gain a great ideal or goal. Our efficiency increases—Chinmaya.

If Administrators work with ethics in their heart and soul, we are sure to make India a heaven on this earth where people from other parts of the world would seek spiritual, ethical and moral pleasure.

SKM Maeilanandhan rightly comments that the essence of vedic scriptures emphasize God realization and attainment of everlasting peace, as the main aim of human life. All religions aim at the following:

- People must live in harmony without harming others.
- Help people who are suffering.
- Love other living beings as they love themselves.
- Share whatever they get, with others.
- Show love and compassion towards fellow beings.

Humanitarianism will blossom only when all people realize the fact though place, appearance and name separate us. We are basically one and united with the soul and source. Let us mediate, analyze, realize and be in Peace and Happiness.[22]

Swami Swabhananda beautifully talks about peace. To quote him:

The force that can hold society together is moral force, Dharma, the consideration for the other person. This deep value in mankind, which enhanced becomes altruism, is possible only in an atmosphere of toned down materialism an assertion of the spirit. If the individuals value sense gratification and money, the society will be materialistic; if the individuals value intellectual pursuits, the society will be advanced in science and technology; if the individuals value the arts, the society will be cultured. Only if the individuals place the highest value on spiritual awakening, will the society be a peaceful one.

The fundamental nature of man, says Vedanta, has two important characteristics: freedom and equality. These two aspects have found expression in man's urge for freedom and equality in the social realm as well. Each of the two main ideals of social and political systems of the world, democracy and socialism, emphasizes one of these fundamental urges of mankind.

Modern science now accepts the theory that the essence of all matter is energy, a theory which unifies the physical world. Long before the birth of Einstein, this unity was declared by the sages of the Upanishads who realized this through inspiration, or intuition. Their philosophy, Vedenta, teaches that the essence of all existence is the eternal, changeless Brahman—Existence, Knowledge, Bliss absolute. In the Chandogya Upanishad we read, "All this is verily Brahman", that is, not merely mankind, but all creation is the manifestation of the same Reality.[23]

Rabindranath Tagore wrote, "When we become merely man, but not man in the universe, we create bewildering problems. But this cannot go on foreover. Man must realize the wholeness of his existence, his place in the infinite."

HRD must realize that efficiency is a virtue, but our success in invention, industry, commerce, and the professions, the vigor of our public life, depends on other virtues—including trust, integrity and civility—that transcend a simple calculus of profit and loss. Acting otherwise, we have lost much of the popular confidence our professions and institutions once enjoyed. If the next twenty years renew our recognition of the importance of such non-economic virtues by HRD programmes, we will be much better off. This will be a permanent enjoyment for persons engaged in these activities.

All the ills from which health Administration is suffering can be solved to a great extent, if we follow the principles of administrative ethics in our HRD programs and in our personal and official life. All these priceless values are contained in all the religions of the world and especially in our ancient Sanskrit literature—Gita, Vedas, Mahabharata, Dharamshastras, Ramayana, etc. The need is to following them sincerely to enable the people of this country to lead a healthy life of bliss. This depends to a great upon health professionals.

Notes and References

1. Oto Kirchheimer, "The Historical and Comparative Background of the Hatch Act," in *Public Policy*, Cambridge Mass, 1941, p. 365.
2. James M.C. Canny, The Administration of American Foreign Affairs, 1950, p. 335.
3. John W. Gardner, "Excellence", New York, 1961, Harper and Brothers, p 154.
4. Medical Ethics, "A viewpoint from the Developing World:" By J.S. Neki, *World Health*, July, 1979.
5. UN Sales No ST./TAO/M 152/Add I, p. 53.
6. UN Inter-Regional Seminar on Administration of Management Improvement Services, (Vol. I), Copenhangen, Denmark, 28 Sept. 1970 (pp. 6-7, STITAOM/56).
7. M.L. Mishra Contemporary Management Thinkers, Associated Publishing House, New Delhi, 1980, pp. 120-29.
8. Paul H Douglas, Ethics in Government, Harward, 1953, p. 27.
9. A.D. Moddi, The Brahmanical Culture and Modernity, Asia Publishing House, New York, pp. 106-14.
10. *The Tribune*, November 29, 1980.
11. *The Tribune*, November 24, 1980.
12. Khalil Gibran, Between Night and Morning, The Philosophical Library, New York, 1972, pp. 8-9.
13. *The Tribune*, Nov. 30, 1980.
14. Jawaharlal Nehru, and Public Administration, Ed. By Prof. V. Jagnnadham, I.I.P.A., New Delhi, 1975.
15. *Ibid*.
16. H. Finer, The Civil Service and Modern State.
17. Graham Wallas, The Great Society, pp 273-74.
18. Swami Jagadatmananda, *Learn to Live*, Vol. 2, Sri Ramakrishna Math, Chennai, p. 3.
19. S.K.M. Maxilanandhan, Activities and Practical Strategies of SC for Peace and Harmony in ALIYAR, 2002, *op. cit.*, pp. 68-69.
20. Swami Swabhanand, "Peace" in Pravrajika Vrajaprana (ed.) Living Wisdom, Vedanta in World Community, Sri Ramakrishna Math, Madras, 1994, pp. 88-89.
21. *Ibid*.
22. S.K. M. Maxilanandhan, Activities and Practical Strategies of SC for Peace and Harmony in ALIYAR, 2002, *op. cit.*, pp. 88-89.
23. Swami Swabhanand, *op. cit.*, pp. 88-89.

Part B

FINANCE

Health Financing in India through Government Allocations

There are no two opinions on the issue that without adequate resources, health development would remain only on the paper. Finance is the fuel of health administration, as all activities for the development of health need finances directly or indirectly. We know that health is wealth. Health is basic component of socio-economic development and hence the investment in health is sure to bring rich dividends.

Although health is recognized as a human right to be made available to all the members of the society, however, the fulfilment of this right depends upon the availability of adequate finances. Dr. Brain Abel Smith in his article, "Global perspective on Health Service Financing" has rightly mentioned the reasons of low priority of health financing. To quote him:

The financing of health services is now a subject of major concern to governments all over the world. The causes are not hard to identify. The world economic crisis has lowered rates of economic growth. And in a number of countries particularly in Africa and Latin America, gross national product per head has been falling or national product had declined in absolute terms. The international debt problems of many developing countries are now formidable and when help has to be sought from the International Monetary Fund, cuts in public expenditure are often required as part of the price for further loans. Public expenditure on health services is one possible target for finding the savings which are required.[1]

Investment in health is thus of vital significance, especially in the developing countries like India, for enriching the quality of human life which in turn can promote economic development. It has been rightly said that not gold but only men can make a nation great and strong. The deleterious consequences of non-investment or inadequate investment in health are indeed very serious. Charaka, the renowned Ayurvedic physician has said that health is vital for ethic, artistic, material and spiritual development of man.

Debate on the allocation of public health resources should focus on making choices between interventions that: (a) deal with important health problems, (b) are cost-effective, (c) are targeted to the poor, and (d) are mostly public goods. In a situation of limited financial resources, it is important to base the allocation of public health funds criteria that promote equity, effectiveness, and efficiency, three tenets that shape most recent health care reforms.

There should be no presupposed preferences as to where and by whom these interventions are delivered. Many cost-effective interventions, which contribute significantly to reducing the burden of disease, require integrated provision of care at both primary and secondary levels, and policy-makers should not assume that prevention is always more cost-effective than cure. In addition, they must move from a model of isolated and competitive health care sub-systems to one of health care provider networks. For example, sick child programs and safe motherhood programs are both cost-effective interventions for reducing infant and maternal mortality and morbidity that demand good integration between the primary health clinic and the district hospital at the secondary level.

When selecting which problems should take priority and which interventions should be publicly financed, the World Bank recommends three broad criteria: (a) the dimension of the health problem, (b) the problem's amenability to available health interventions than can be provided at reasonable cost, and (c) the social value of the problem. The World Bank (1993) has operationalized the first two criteria in terms of the burden of disease, measured in disability adjusted life years (DALYs), and the cost-effectiveness of health interventions. As for the third dimension, social value, the discussion about how to best target resources and services to the poor and how to best focus public investments on public goods is still ongoing.[2]

We have to ensure adequate finances for development of efficient public health services. Any society should consider that a high quality of life, and happiness of the people, which can only be obtained through a sufficient level of health, is not only a basic need to development but should be the lone objective of development.

Financing health care is a critical concern for rich and poor countries alike, as health care systems account for 9 percent of global production. Developing countries face particularly serious challenges as they attempt to improve the well-being of their populations, achieve economic development objectives, and integrate themselves with the global economy. Health care financing is a particular concern for these countries, which account for 84 percent of the world's population and 93 percent of its disease burden but only 18 percent of its income and 11 percent of its health expenditures. Imbalances between spending and the disease burden will be exacerbated as a result of the changing composition of illness toward non-communicable diseases and injuries, which by 2020 will account for almost 80 percent of these countries' disease burdens, compared with just over 50 percent now. These diseases are more expensive to treat and harder to prevent than the infectious diseases that were previously the leading causes of illness and death.

Understanding how countries finance their health care systems is of critical importance for industrial and developing countries alike. The methods used to mobilize the resources that support basic public health programs, provide access to basic health services, and configure health service delivery systems affect people's health status-as well as every aspect of a country's social, economic, and political well-being. Moreover, health care systems account for 9 percent of global production and a significant portion of global production and a significant portion of global employment. Health care systems also affect imports and, in some countries, exports.[3]

Goals of a Health Care System

- Improving a population's health status and promoting social well-being.
- Ensuring equity and access to care.
- Ensuring microeconomic and macroeconomic efficiency in the use of resources.
- Enhancing clinical effectiveness.
- Improving quality of care and consumer satisfaction.
- Assuring the system's long-run financial sustainability.

Policy-maker must have some way to evaluate the performance of their country's health systems against those of other countries or regions at comparable income levels. One approach is to divide the performance of health financing mechanisms into three broad categories (Chart 8.1). The first category is concerned with how efficiently and equitably revenues are raised, and what effect they have on the size and distribution of the resources available to the health sector. The second category involves evaluating how efficiently and equitably resources are used to provide health services. The third category relates to the effects health expenditures have on health outcomes. This last measure is tied to intersectoral factors such as education, water and sanitation, and women's status, since health services are just one factor among many that determine a population's health status. This paper focuses on issues related to the first group of measures.

Insufficient health expenditure on delivery of health services remains the predominant cause of the poor health delivery system. In addition to this proper utilization of available sources adds to the problem. Even Bhore Committee before Independent India provided that:

CHART 8.1

Difference Ways of Measuring Performance in Health Financing

Revenue generation	**Health services output**	**Health status and outcomes**
Key issues: Efficiency, stability, and sustainability in revenue generation; effectiveness in risk pooling and redistribution.	*Key issues:* Efficiency in service output per dollar invested; access; quality; patient satisfaction and patient choice.	*Key issues:* Intersectoral determinants of health including medical care, household behaviour, women's status and education, water and sanitation, environment, nutrition, and lifestyle changes.
Examples of instruments: Burden of taxation, distribution of public subsidies, extent of insurance coverage. (Formal and Informal)	*Examples of Instruments:* Unit cost of effective services by different facilities, payment system, organizational and management structures.	*Examples of Instruments:* Mortality and morbidy rate reduction (increase in life expectancy, reduction in infant mortality, life years saved per dollar).

It is the duty of the state to provide access to universal health care and to ensure that no one is denied health care, because of inability to pay.

Health Sector Spending: Levels and Trends

India's public health expenditure is estimated at 0.9 per cent of GDP, well below the average of 2.8 per cent for low- and middle-income countries, and the global average of 5.5 per cent.[4]

Financing of health is very difficult task as the resources in India are limited and the needs are abundant. Programmes of health lie at the base of efforts to harness the energies of the people. The Union and State Governments provide health finances under plan and non-plan schemes.

Restructuring of the health care infrastructure, redeployment and skill development of the manpower, development of referral network, improvement in the health management information system, development of disease surveillance and response at district level are some of the critical steps that have to be taken up by the State Government in order to improve the functional status and efficiency of the existing health care infrastructure and manpower in the states.

Let us now examine the financing of health in India.

The Ministry of Health and Family Welfare consisted of three departments viz. the Department of Health, Department of Family Welfare and Department of AYUSH. The Departments of Health and Family Welfare have since been merged under the single line department in the modified version of Allocation of Business Rules.

Achieving an acceptable standard of health for general population has been the objective over the plan era in the Health sector. In line with this objective, there has been a steady increase in the allocations made for this Sector from the 1st Plan onwards. The allocation for Health and Family Welfare during the 9th Plan was of the order of Rs. 20,238 crores. This saw a substantial step up during the 10th Plan with the original outlay being Rs. 36,378 crores showing a step up of 81%. Against the actual allocations made for the 10th Plan, the increase is even more significant with the step up being 105%. In the table below is captured the financial outlays and expenditure for Health and Family Welfare for the 9th and 10th Plans and the individual years (2002-07).

There is a need to convince the planners, political leaders to allocate more for health finances as it comes in priority area. To maintain quantity and quality of health services, adequate allocations is a must.

Empirical Findings

- Overall health spending in India is estimated at 4.5 per cent of GDP, less than the average of 5.6 percent for low and middle-income countries.
- Public spending on health in India is 0.9 percent of GDP, among the lowest in the world.
- Out-of-pocket private spending dominates health expenditures, with 82 percent of all health spending from private sources.
- Hospitalization frequently results in financial catastrophe, especially in the absence of risk pooling. About 10 percent of Indians, most of them employees in government or elsewhere in the formal sector, have some form of health insurance.
- The gap in public financing for health between rich and poor states in widening and threatening to expand the gaps in outcomes.[5]

Healthcare is one of the seven thrust areas under the National Common Minimum Programme. The special emphasis given to the Health sector in the CMP has been very clearly reflected in terms of financial allocations received during the last two years of the 10th Plan. The CMP has *inter-alia* focused on increased public spending on health to at least 2-3% of GDP over the next 5 years with focus on primary healthcare. Accordingly, a National Rural Health Mission has been launched in April 2005 to effect an architectural correction in the healthcare delivery system with the convergence of six programmes including four disease control programmes namely National Vector Borne Disease Control Programme, Revised National TB Control Programme, National Leprosy Eradication Programme, National Programme for Control of Blindness; and Iodine Deficiency Disorders Control Programme and Integrated Disease Surveillance Programme. However, the outlay for these programmes was shown under Health till 2005-06. From 2006-07, the outlay of these programmes has been shown under NRHM. Accordingly Demands for Grants has separated into Health (other than NRHM) and NRHM.

TABLE 8.1

(Rupee in Crores)

Plan Period	*Approved Outlay*			*Expenditure*		
	Health	*F.W.*	*Total*	*Health*	*F.W.*	*Total*
9th Plan (1997-2002)	5118.19	15120.00	20238.19	4906.80	12968.72	18875.52
10th Plan						
Original Outlay	9253.00	27125.00	36378.00			
Revised Outlay	10252.00	26126.00	36378.00			
Existing Status	10521.00	31064.00	41585.00			
2002-03	1550.00	4930.00	6480.00	1359.82	3916.63	5276.45
2003-04	1550.00	4930.00	6480.00	1325.81	4409.27	5735.08
2004-05	2208.00	5780.00	7988.00	1772.36	4862.09	6634.45
2005-06	2908.00	6424.00	9332.00	2253.72	5672.53	7926.25
2006-07$	2305.00	9000.00	11305.00	2048.92*	7951.08*	1000.00*
11th Plan (2007-12) (P)	36947.81	131169.00	168116.81			
2007-08 (P)	5415.66	12866.62	18282.28			

* Revised Estimate.

$ Figures shown as Health and NRHM from 2006-07.

P Proposed.

Source: Annual Report, Ministry of Health and Family Welfare, 2006-07, p. 3.

The Scheme-wise break-up of Actual Expenditure during 2005-06 and Outlay for 2006-07 for the Health and NRHM-6 is given at Statement I and II.

Allocation of Finances for Health Development

The plan outlay during the last Eight Five Year Plans has been increasing from 65.20 crores in First Five Year Plan to 7582.20 crores in 8th Plan which comes to 3.33% and 1.75% respectively. In case of Family Welfare it has ranged from 0.10 crores in 1st Plan (.01%) to 6500 crores in 8th Plan (1.50). These figures clearly reveal the low priority accorded to health.

The Centrally sponsored disease control programmes and the family welfare programme provide funds for additional critical manpower and equipment; these have to be appropriately utilized to fill critical gaps, the ongoing and the proposed EAPs are additional resources. Health is one of the priority sector for which funds are provided in the central budget under the head Additional Central Assistance (ACA) for basic minimum services. The States can utilize these funds for meeting essential requirements for operationalising urban and rural health care.

Health is one of the sectors identified under the Special Action Plan. In addition to the funds available from Domestic Budgetary Support, several centrally sponsored disease control programmes are receiving funds from EAPs. Taking all these factors into consideration, the Department of Health has been provided with an outlay of Rs. 5118.19 crores for the Ninth Plan period. The outlay for the annual plans will be adjusted depending upon the requirements of the department and the availability of funds including reimbursement from EAPs.[7]

The non-plan funds are very meager. Even the funds allocated are not made available and thus the actual expenditure is less as compared to allocation. For example, out of a outlay of Rs. 125.6 crore provided in 8th Five Year Plan in Haryana, the actual expenditure was Rs. 82.69 crore (65.8%). In Karnataka, the expenditure on health has increased from 249.59 crores in 1990-91 to 600.41 crore in 1995-96.

Let us discuss the allocations made by Punjab Government under Plan Scheme to health sector. In Eighth Five Year Plan, a provision of Rs. 25475 lakh was made, out of which only Rs. 11866.91 lakhs was spent, which is a very sad reflection on Government and Health Department. The money allocated during Ninth Plan is 63615.50 lakhs out of which 21562.00 lakhs are for capital content. This reflects the poor thinking of planners towards health as a component of socio-economic development.

Existing Mechanisms

Around the world, health services are financed through four main channels, of which two are private: out-of-pocket payments and voluntary insurance; and two are public: compulsory insurance (or social insurance) and funding from general government revenues. Social insurance, either publicly managed or heavily regulated by governments, also receives funding from general government revenues, and is hence classified as public[8].

Health Financing in Poor Countries: Cost Recovery and Cost Reduction

The problem of financing health services in the developing countries is currently being looked at as one of cost recovery. This is the approach taken by, in particular, the World Bank, whose activities as a pressure group are currently aimed at getting the countries to which it furnishes health assistance to undertake four policy reforms:

TABLE 8.2

Department of Health and Family Welfare Health Sector Scheme-wise Break-up of Actual Expenditure during 2005-06 and Outlay for 2006-07

(Rs. in crores)

Sl. No.	*Name of the Schemes/Institutions*	*Annual Plan 2005-06 Expenditure*			*Outlay for 2006-07*		
		Plan	*Non-Plan*	*Total*	*Plan*	*Non-Plan*	*Total*
I.	CENTRALLY SPONSORED PROGRAMMES	731.42	6.12	737.54	998.0	25.00	1003.02
	Control of Communicable Diseases:	520.12	0.01	520.83	705.67		705.67
1.	National AIDS Control Programme and National STD Control Programme	520.82	0.01	520.83	705.67		705.67
	Control of Non-Communicable Diseases	118.16	6.11	124.27	137.00	5.00	142.00
2.	Cancer	71.99	6.11	71.10	17.00	5.00	92.00
	(i) National Cancer Control Programme	71.99	6.11	71.10	17.00	5.00	92.00
3.	National Mental Health Programme	46.17		46.17	50.00		50.00
	Other Programmes	92.44		92.44	155.35		155.35
4.	Assistance to State for Capacity Building	35.17		35.17	45.00		45.00
	(i) Taruma Care	35.17		35.87	45.00		45.00
5.	Assistance to States for Drug and PFA Control	56.57		56.57	75.35		75.35
	(i) Drugs Control						
	(ii) PFA Control						
6.	New Initiatives under C55				35.00		35.00
	(i) Initiatives taken during 2006-07						
	Telemedicine				15.00		15.00
	National Programme for Prevention and Control of Diabetes, Cardiovascular Disease and Stroke				5.00		5.00
II.	PURELY CENTRAL SCHEMES	913.84	1200.84	114.68	1306.98	1217.83	2524.81
	Contral of Communicable Diseases	42.49	27.01	69.50	39.4	30.85	10.30
7.	National Institute Couunincable Diseases	20.33	9.53	29.06	12.17	10.15	23.02
	(i) On-going activities (including Guineaworm Yaws Eradication)						
	(ii) Strengthening of the Institute						
8.	National Tuberculosis Institute, Bangalore	0.41	2.69	3.10	2.12	2.80	4.93
9.	B.C.G. Vaccine Laboratory, Guindy, Chennai	2.99	3.45	6.44	1.27	4.00	5.27
10.	Pasteur Institute of India, Coonoor	3.98		3.98	10.00		10.00
11.	Lala Ram Sarup Institute of T.B. and allied diseases, Mehrauli, Delhi	12.00	5.98	17.98	9.55	6.00	15.55
12.	Central Leprosy, Training and Research Institute, Chengalpattu (Tamil Nadu)	1.31	3.18	4.49	2.00	4.35	6.35
13.	Regional Institute of Training, Research and Treatment under Leprosy Control Programme	1.47	2.18	3.65	2.33	2.85	5.18
	(a) R.L.T.R.I., Aska (Orissa)	0.02	0.95	0.97	0.55	1.30	1.85
	(b) R.L.T.R.I., Raipur (M.P.)	0.13	1.23	1.36	0.18	1.55	1.73
	(c) R.L.T.R.I., Gauripur (W.B.)	1.32	1.23	1.36	0.18	1.55	1.73
	Hospitals and Dispensaries	150.03	440.60	590.63	186.64	418.96	605.60
14.	Central Government Health Scheme	23.40	293.26	316.66	35.00	274.00	309.00
15.	Central Institute of Psychiatry, Ranchi	7.69	10.70	18.39	18.70	11.65	30.35

16. Institute for Human Behaviour and Allied Sciences, Shahdara, Delhi				1.00		1.00
17. All India Institute of Speech and Hearing, Mysore	6.58	3.57	10.15	8.00	2.90	10.90
18. All India Institute of Physical Medicine and Rehabilitation, Mumbai	3.52	3.67	7.19	5.60	3.45	90.5
19. Safdarjung Hospital and College, New Delhi	79.61	73.62	153.23	78.00	74.58	152.58
20. Dr. R.K.L. Hospital, New Delhi	29.23	55.78	85.01	40.34	52.38	92.72
Medical Education	363.36	527.78	891.14	572.12	544.47	1116.59
21. All India Institute of Medical Sciences and its Allied Departments, New Delhi	637.19	606.99	1244.18	811.31	626.50	1437.81
22. P.G.I.M.E.R., Chandigarh	40.00	121.00	161.00	40.00	122.00	162.00
23. J.I.P.M.E.R., Pondicherry	33.36	44.29	77.65	70.00	46.00	116.00
24. Lady Harding Medical College and Smt. S.K. Hospital, New Delhi	16.49	45.39	61.88	28.00	49.00	77.00
25. Kalawati Saran Childrens' Hospital, New Delhi	6.99	11.44	18.43	10.94	11.00	21.94
26. Indira Gandhi Institute of Health and Medical Sciences for North-East Region at Shilong*	30.00		30.00	126.27		126.77
27. N.I.M.H.A.N.S., Bangalore	43.73	19.70	63.43	50.00	21.00	71.00
28. Kasturba Health Society, Wardha	13.00		13.00	13.80		13.80
29. V.P. Chest Institute, Delhi	8.00	9.00	17.00	7.00	9.00	16.00
30. National Medical Library, New Delhi	0.31	1.09	1.40	13.00	2.60	15.60
31. National Academy of Medical Sciences, New Delhi	0.35	0.17	0.52	0.65	0.17	0.82
32. National Board of Examinations, New Delhi	6.77		6.77	4.60		4.60
33. Medical Council of India, New Delhi	1.00	0.60	1.60	1.00	0.60	1.60
34. Medical Grants Commission				1.00		1.00
35. Pharmacy Council of India		0.10	0.10		0.10	0.10
(b) Training	18.83	3.21	22.04	22.19	4.03	26.22
36. Development of Nursing Sciences	17.57		17.57	20.00		20.00
37. Nursing Colleges						
(i) R.A.K. College of Nursing, New Delhi	0.50	2.45	2.95	0.76	3.05	3.81
(ii) Lady Reading Health School	0.26	0.66	0.92	0.43	0.88	1.31
38. Indian Nursing Council	0.50	0.10	0.60	1.00	0.10	1.10
39. (a) Indian Council of Medical Research, New Delhi	255.00	76.00	331.00	217.00	78.00	295.00
Other Programmes	84.13	69.28	153.41	269.58	85.74	355.32
40. All India Institute of Hygiene and Public Health, Calcutta (All H&PH) and Serologist and Chemcial						
(i) All H&PH, Calcutta	1.17	5.86	7.03	1.50	7.14	8.64
(ii) Serologist and Chemical Examiner, Calcutta	0.15	1.58	1.73	0.30	1.89	2.19
41. Central Research Institute, Kasauli	3.98	12.01	15.99	8.12	12.25	20.37
42. National Institute of Biological, NOIDA (U.P.)	44.25		44.25	34.40		34.40
43. Health Education	0.02	1.29	1.31	1.50	1.65	3.15
44. Health Intelligence and Health Accounts						
(i) Intelligence	0.54	0.51	1.05	1.14	0.75	1.89
(ii) Accounts				1.10		1.00
45. Prevention of Food Adulteration	2.65	2.19	4.84	3.10	2.50	5.60

46. Central Drug Standard and Control Organisation	9.51	6.70	16.21	12.65	7.50	20.26
47. Port Health Authority						
(i) Jawaharlal Nehru Port Sheva	0.32		0.32	0.46		0.46
(ii) Setting up of offices at 8 new by created international Airports		7.47	7.47	1.00	8.80	9.80
48. Strengthening of D.G.H.S./Ministry:						
(i) Strengthening of Depts under the Ministry	2.10	14.25	16.35	3.00	24.10	27.10
(ii) Strengthening of DGHS	0.92	17.42	18.34	1.30	19.16	20.46
49. Health Sector Disaster Preparedness and Management	14.00		14.00	10.00		10.00
50. New Initaitives under Central Schemes (Institute of Public Health)				65.00		65.00
51. Pradhan Mantri Swasthya Suraksha Yojana	2.52		2.52	75.00		75.00
52. Bhuj Hospital	2.00		2.00	10.00		10.00
53. Emergency medical relief (Avian Flu)				40.00		40.00
Other Schemes		56.96	56.96		55.78	55.78
Indian Red Cross Society		0.10	0.10		0.20	0.20
St. John Ambulance		0.02	0.02		0.08	0.08
International Conference on Medical and PH		0.06	0.06		0.09	0.09
Discretionary Grant		0.43	0.43		1.00	1.00
Dental Council of India		0.18	0.18		0.18	0.18
Original Book in Hindi		0.02	0.02		0.02	0.02
Child Care Trg. Centre, Singur		5.26	5.26		4.82	4.82
New Delhi TB Center		1.00	1.00		1.05	1.05
Deratisation of Ships		0.03	0.03		0.15	0.15
Delegation to International Health Conference		0.77	0.77		0.80	0.80
National Illness Assistance Fund		2.84	2.84		2.30	2.30
Assistance for Hospitalization of the Poor		3.00	3.00		3.50	3.50
International Cooperation		7.57	7.57		7.00	7.00
Feasibility Testing Scheme of Vitamins		0.12	0.12		0.14	0.14
Procurement of Meningitis Vaccine		16.35	16.35		8.45	8.45
Medical Store Depot		16.22	16.22		23.62	23.62
Departmental Drug Expenditure		1.21	1.21			
Clearance and Handling of Intl. Store		1.78	1.78		2.38	2.38
Transferred/Weed Out						
Hospital Waste Management						
GRAND TOTAL	1645.26	1206.96	2852.22	2305.00	1222.83	3527.83

Source: Ibid.

Charge users of government health facilities, especially for drugs curative care

"This will increase the resource available to programs, encourage better quality and more efficiency, and increase access for the poor" (who will be protected by reduced fees and will be "the principal beneficiaries of expanding resources for and improved efficiency in the government sector)." (cf. [1] p. 3).

TABLE 8.3

Department of Health and Family Welfare Health Sector

National Rural Health Mission (NHRM)

Scheme-wise Break-up of Actual Expenditure during 2005-06 and Outlay for 2006-07

(Rs. in crores)

Sl. No.	*Name of the Schemes/Institutions*	*Annual Plan 2005-06 Expenditure*			*Outlay for 2006-07*		
		Plan	*Non-Plan*	*Total*	*Plan*	*Non-Plan*	*Total*
	CENTRALLY SPONSORED SCHEMES	5975.62	12.33	5987.95	8681.55	14.21	8695.76
A.	DISEASE CONTROL PROGRAMMES	569.20	5.20	574.40	1721.00	6.47	727.47
1.	National Vector Borne Disease Control Programme	256.61	5.08	261.69	371.58	6.47	378.05
2.	National T.B. Control Programme	188.12		188.12	202.17		202.17
3.	National Leprosy Eradication Programme	23.09	0.12	23.21	42.25		42.25
4.	Iodine Deficiency Disorder Control Programme	8.44		8.44	15.00		15.00
5.	National Programme for Control of Blindness	92.94		92.94	90.00		90.00
B.	FREE DISTRIBUTION and SOCIAL MARKETING OF CONDOMS FOR NACO				200.00		200.00
C.	FAMILY WELFARE	5406.42	7.13	5413.55	7760.55	7.74	7768.29
1.	Direction and Administration	229.89	5.10	234.99	249.45	5.11	254.56
2.	Rural FW Services (Sub-Centres)	1231.06		1231.06	1556.68		1556.68
3.	Urban Health Centres	122.74		122.74	125.00		125.00
4.	Grants to State Training Institutions	83.70		83.70	91.15		91.15
5.	Free distribution of contraceptives	163.61		163.61	100.00		100.00
6.	Procurement of Supplies and Materials		0.02	0.02	250.00		250.00
7.	Routine Immunisation	162.58		162.58	345.00		345.00
8.	Pulse Polio Immunisation	918.07		918.07	1049.00		1049.00
9.	IEC (Inf., Edu. and Communication)	122.89	2.01	123.90	130.10	2.63	132.73
10.	Area Projects	360.12		360.12	215.27		215.27
11.	Flexible Pool for State PIPs	2011.76		2011.76	3648.90		3648.90
	(i) RCH Flexible Pool	2011.76		2011.76	1705.72		1705.72
	(ii) Mission Flexible Pool				1943.18		1943.18
12.	National Drug De-Addiction Control Programme						
	CENTRAL SECTOR SCHEMES	303.49	22.02	325.51	316.43	19.22	335.65
A.	DISEASE CONTROL PROGRAMMES	39.26		39.26	102.00		102.00
1.	Integrated Disease Surveillance Programme	39.26		39.26	102.00		102.00
B.	FAMILY WELFARE	264.23	22.02	286.25	214.25	19.22	233.65
1.	Social Marketing Area Projects				1.00		1.00
2.	Social Marketing of Contraceptives	107.65		107.65	49.50		49.50
3.	F.W. Training and Res. Centre, Bombay	0.68	0.86	1.54	5.00	0.98	5.98
4.	NIHFW, New Delhi	5.06	9.01	14.07	6.05	9.79	15.84
5.	IIPS, Mumbai	1.65	4.60	6.25	2.90	4.60	7.50
6.	Rural Health Training Centre, Najafgarh		3.39	3.39	1.31	3.85	5.16
7.	Population Research Centres	5.62		5.62	8.00		8.00

8. CDRI, Lucknow	2.75		2.75	3.00		3.00
9. ICMR and IRR	34.00		34.00	40.00		40.00
10. Travel of Experts/Conf./Meetings, etc. (Melas)	0.55		0.55	1.00		1.00
11. International Co-operation	1.49		1.49	1.64		1.64
12. NPSF/National Commission on Population	2.80		2.80	6.00		6.00
13. NGOs (Public-Private Partnership—PPP)	49.45		49.45	32.91		32.91
14. FW Linked Health Insurance Plan	8.26		8.26	10.00		10.00
15. RCH Training	29.73		29.73	7.38		7.38
16. Other Schemes	14.54	4.16	18.70	38.74		38.74
Schemes Weeded/Transferred	1.88		1.88	2.02		2.02
1. Sterilization Beds	1.88		1.88	2.02		2.02
2. District Projects						
3. Community Incentive Scheme						
4. Transport						
5. New Initiatives						
GRAND TOTAL	5280.99	34.35	6315.34	9000.00	33.43	9033.43

Source: *Ibid.*, p. 43.

Provide insurance or other risk coverage

"In order to help mobilize resources for the health sector while simultaneously protecting households from large financial losses. A modest level of cost recovery is possible without insurance. But in the long run, insurance is necessary to relieve the government budget of the high costs of expensive curative care; governments cannot raise government hospital charges close to costs until insurance is widely available." (cf. [1] p. 4).

Use non-government resources effectively

"Encourage the non-government sector (including non-profit groups, private physicians, pharmacists, and other health practitioners) to provide health services for which consumers are willing to pay. This will allow the government to focus its resources on programs that benefit whole communities rather than particular individuals...Any prohibitions or restrictions on non-government providers should be reviewed. Unnecessary paper work and the regulations relating to non-profit providers should be reduced." (cf. [1] p. 5).

Decentralize government health services

Decentralize planning, budgeting and purchasing for government health services, particularly the services offering private benefits for which users are charged. When setting national policies and programs, use market incentives where possible to better motivate staff and allocate resources. Allow revenues to be collected and retained as close as possible to the point of service delivery. This will improve both the collection of fees and the efficiency of the service." (cf. [1] p. 6).

These reforms are expected to have a favourable impact on the solution of three essential problems, all of which are said to be due to the efforts of governments to cover the full costs of health care for everyone from general public revenues:

- Insufficient spending on cost-effective health activities;
- Inefficient use of resources in public programs; and
- Inequity in health-care distribution.

The World Bank is not, however, the only organization to preach cost recovery. Since 1984 the World Health Organization has concerned itself with disseminating these ideas (cf. [2]). The technical discussions that took place during the Fortieth World Health Assembly (Geneva, May 1987) concerned "economic support for national health-for-all strategies," and the ways of increasing health services financing were on that occasion were grouped into four categories: public revenues, insurance schemes, community financing schemes, and user charging (cf. [3] pp. 62-79). The schemes and mechanisms put forward under the heading of "community financing", while highly diverse, have one feature in common: the effort is borne by the people, most often the sick. In other words, the term "community financing," which no doubt pleases certain experts and certain audiences, accords perfectly with cost recovery systems (and even sometimes the special case of user charging).

Similarly, the activity announced by UNICEF in September 1987 under the title "Bamako Initiative" is based on recovering a multiple of the cost of essential drugs and thereby generating a margin sufficient to finance certain primary health-care activities (cf. [4], [5], [6]). The fact that this proposal is based mainly on the use of essential drugs is not without significance: this explicitly introduces the prospect both the rationalizing prescribing to some degree, very necessary in all countries and especially the poorest, and of a perhaps decisive reduction in average prescription cost.

On reflection it is clear that solution of the problem posed by the inability of governments to finance health services can be sought in two directions: the view can be taken either that the costs are a given and new financing sources must be found to cover them (direct: cost recovery, or indirect: insurance), or that costs can be reduced and the solution lies at least in part in eliminating waste that has been tolerated up to now. Should efforts therefore be directed to recovering costs as they are or else to first lowering them before trying to recover them[9]?

BASED UPON THE CHILE EXPERIENCE WORLD BANK CAME TO THE CONCLUSION

This last measure intended to increase coverage will necessarily require improvements in the government's ability to track the incomes of the self-employed and enforce compliance. The government may find that many of those that it will be able to easily capture—among the more "formal" self-employed professionals—already are affiliated to an ISAPRE, and that and thus that there will be little additional coverage. Argentina's experience of trying to enforce the participation of the self-employed has not been positive. Financing minimum health package through taxes with a wider base, such as the value added tax, would be more efficient, and might even allow a reduction in Chile's payroll taxes.

The government expects an increase in participation and compliance from the creation of an explicitly guaranteed minimum package of services and quality of care. Thus, while developing greater enforcement capacity will still be important, the government expects that a large portion of Chileans who currently evade or choose not to participate in the health insurance system, will seek cover. This expectation may be well founded. Public health insurance is regularly cited in surveys and opinion polls as a high priority, even among the poor who find it difficult to pay premia. Evidence presented in the next section of increases in participation in the pension system linked to changes in the health system, indicate that the government might expect a small increase in affiliation to FONASA and perhaps even the ISAPRES. However, a significant portion of the currently uninsured might still remain uninsured for structural reasons. Thus the move toward guaranteeing minimum care and financing these guarantees through broad based taxes are extremely positive.[10]

I. Existing Mechanism

Budgetary Support out of the revenue collected through taxation at the union and state levels, a small percentage of it is allocated to health, which is highly inappropriate. The State Governments account for 75 percent of this expenditure. In this context we may keep the following in view:

The basic criteria for evaluating alternative financing modalities are:

- *Economic efficiency*: the tax system should not interfere with the efficient allocation of resources.
- *Equity (fairness)*: the tax system ought to be fair in its treatment of different individuals.
- *Administrative simplicity*: the tax system ought to be easy and inexpensive to administer.[11]

In summary, developing countries need to replace narrow, distorting tax bases that have high and widely differentiated rates and numerous loopholes with broader tax bases that generate higher revenues at lower rates and do not discriminate against the various sources and uses of income. Doing so would result in the simultaneous achievement of efficiency, administrative simplicity, and horizontal equity (Thirsk forthcoming). Moreover, effective tax reforms can only take place if they are accompanied by reforms in tax administration.[12]

Overview of Health Care Financing

Revenue Allocation

Resources for health care financing come mainly from the government's general revenue, accumulated through various forms of taxation, social health insurance contribution, user charges and other collections. Even though health policy-makers realized that the increase in the level of funding to the health sector depends largely on the rate of economic growth and the efficiency of taxation, which are outside their immediate control, they often ask what would be the optimal level of investment in health, both by public and private sources, with a view to soliciting a public debate. Health policy-makers tend to raise issues such as: "What is the right amount for a country to spend?" or "How much of a nation's gross national product (GNP) or gross domestic product (GDP) should be devoted to health care?"

In 1981, an indicator, "the number of countries with at least 5 per cent of GNP spent on health," was proposed for the purpose of monitoring and evaluation of the global strategy for health-for-all by the year 2000 (HFA-2000).[13] While WHO and its Member-Countries have not been able to formally adopt this indicator, the numerical level, i.e. "5 per cent of GNP spent on health", was used as frequently as possible in many policy debates and even mentioned in some cases as "WHO recommended target."

According to World Health Report 2001 (WHR-2001), the countries of the Region, on an average, had a total health expenditure (THE) of around 2-8 per cent of GDP. In reality, except four countries—Bhutan, India, Maldives and Thailand—others could not spend more than 5 per cent of GDP on health. Similarly, many countries around the world never achieved this "fictitious target." A recent IMF study suggested that effective health coverage would require around 12 per cent of GNP in low-income countries in order to meet the international development goals.[14]

An appropriate percentage benchmark or target for health spending, like the fictitious target above, is extremely difficult to set. Research is under way to better define the *minimum amounts* of finance that countries should invest in order to optimally develop their health systems. In its report in 2001, the WHO Commission on Macroeconomics and health (WHO-CMH) recommended that the low-income countries should increase their domestic spending on health by an additional 1 per cent of GNP by 2007, rising to 2 per cent by 2015, keeping in view existing and future trends of economic growth.[15] Good governance, strong political leadership and political will of all stakeholders are required for increasing investment in health.

While many countries rely on general revenue for financing health care, many others bank on the creation or expansion of *compulsory health insurance contributions*, generally referred to as "social health insurance", usually based on pay-roll deductions, with additional support from the government via general tax revenue.

2. User Charges

In a traditional public finance context, individuals pay user charges (based on the principle of cost recovery) for a publicly provided good or service. Such charges should be used whenever a publicly produced good or service has benefits that can be assigned to an individual. Taxes are more appropriate to finance public goods with collective (rather than individual) benefits, to compensate for market failures, and to achieve distributional objectives (World Bank, 1988).

User charges should be evaluated using the same criteria used to evaluate taxes (economic efficiency, equity, and administrative simplicity). Although user charges for publicly provided services are a source of government revenue, from a national health accounts perspective they are technically private expenditures for publicly provided services. In this context they are no different from direct private out-of-pocket payments for non-government services, discussed below. But since they have implications for public financing and government policy, user charges for publicly provided services are analyzed in this section.

Evidence on user charges in developing countries is extensive and varied. The findings indicate:

- A strong utilization response to user charges, with disproportionately larger reductions in utilization on the part of the poor.
- Exemptions from user charges often benefit high-income groups.
- User charges need to be considered in the context of time costs and managerial and administrative capacity.
- Although user charges can be used to supplement public revenues for curative care at the facility level, total revenue generation has not met expectations (being on the order of 5 per cent of total revenues).
- Effects on health status and efficiency are less clear, although there is some evidence of adverse effects on health outcomes.
- People appear more willing to pay for tangible benefits (such as drugs).
- User charges for public services have elicited higher prices for private services, resulting in declines in total utilization (see Gertler and Hammer in this volume; Wang' Ombe in this volume; Gertler and van der Gaag, 1990; Creese and Kutzin, 1995).

In other words, user charges can increase efficiency and ensure equity if the systems are designed carefully and generate tangible benefits for individuals. But time costs, administrative capacity, and impacts on private pricing policies must be analyzed carefully. Moreover, while revenue generation can have important effects at the facility level, overall revenue generation may be lower than original expectations.[16]

However, in India the yield from user charges is small but increasing since its introduction.

The World Bank 2001 report identifies four main hurdles to major expansion: the lack of appropriate mechanism for user charge review; the minimum level cost recovery due to low fee structure and inadequate collection mechanisms; the difficulty of implementing targeting mechanisms to exempt the poor from user charges; and the lack of adequate mechanisms to ensure fund utilization at point of collection.[17]

Since the introduction of user charges, the efficiency of health institutions has improved due to the following reasons:

(1) The in charge of health institution can take care of emergencies out of user funds and thus can provide proper facilities to patients.
(2) The In charge can maintain the building properly out of these user charges.
(3) Proper arrangement for sitting and lavatory, drinking water can be installed.

However, proper accounting procedures may be developed to take care of pilferage or wrong use.

Most of the developing countries were providing free health services as it was very difficult for the poor to afford payment. It was feared that poor people with infectious diseases can create health problems for the community. However, it is being realized now that people must pay a part of the expenditure incurred in providing services to them. It should not be totally free. The users can pay for diagnostic tests, hospital admissions, OPD consultations, etc. There is now virtually no country in Western Europe which allows free medical care. Besides supplementing health resources, it promotes people's participation. However, user charges should be kept low keeping in view the per capita income of the people. Referred patients may not be charged to encourage referral system.

Karnataka Health Systems Development Project in its report rightly mentions the rationale for cost sharing. The appropriateness of adopting cost sharing principles depends on the type of services provided. Hospital services are mostly patient-related curative services. There is a scope to charge on curative services, provided a mechanism exists to adjust fees depending on the patients ability to pay. However, the additional revenues generated by cost sharing may not be adequate to cover fully the expenditure in improving quality through better facilities in terms of equipment and drugs. The argument for cost sharing is based on efficiency. If no fee is charged there will be an "excess demand" for services, especially hospital beds. Government hospitals are crowded and often the resourceful but the undeserving people get free access, whereas the poor have to incur "transaction costs" to get treatment or a hospital bed. Graded cost recovery from the non-poor is expected to restrict demand for beds thereby releasing beds for the poor. Thus, cost sharing may be a step in restoring equity; the poor may benefit proportionately more than the non-poor.

Charging fees for services may only slightly affect the demand negatively for health services, because demand for in-patient and out-patient care is highly inelastic. However, consumers will be more responsive to the quality of care, time costs and the relative prices of alternative types of care givers. Cost sharing will augment resources for the health sector and should, therefore, lead to improvements in supply, both in qualitative and quantitative terms. Sustainability would also be promoted to a large extent because the revenue realized would finance a portion of the .operational costs, thereby relieving the budgetary constraint. Cost sharing would result in improvements in the quality of care if the resources generated internally by a hospital are ploughed back for improving the availability of drugs and equipment in that hospital.

However, the experiment at Rajindra Hospital, Patiala is very disheartening. The user charges are not being used properly. To quote the report by Japinderjit Singh (*Chandigarh Tribune*, dated March 15, 2000)—Vacant wards, empty corridors, reduced number of patients at the OPDs in a government hospital after a hike in the hospitalization and treatment charges is a common knowledge now. Often the official version is that the situation is due to the hike. However, enquiries revealed that patients do not mind paying a few bucks more, provided they get commensurating treatment and care like that offered by private clinics.

The treatment and care at the hospital stands still due to the omnipresent problem of non-functioning of several machines due to one fault or another. The faulty machines cause harassment to the patients, as the treatment continues in the hospital, .while check-ups have to be done outside.

The list of such non-working machines is long. It is headed by the CT-Scan equipment. Ever since its purchase, it has remained in news due to some irregularity in its purchase or non-working. Then, there is the dialysis machine which is out of order for years now. Due to its non-working, patients with the kidney disorders have avoided the hospital.

The Ultrasound machine in Orthopedics Department, ventilators in the emergency unit, X-ray machines, EEG machine in the Neurology Wing, Cabalt plant used for cancer therapy, the fluorescence Angiography Unit, Lasic Laser, exima laser, ultrasound and retinascope in the Eye Department are all out of the order. Little wonder that the wards present an empty look.

Sources in the hospital said when the government had hiked the fee charges, it had said the generated revenue would be reinvested in the hospital. However, now almost a year after the hike, only some part of the revenue has been reinvested. This share, source say, has been spent on paying the electricity and other bills and not on the repair of the machines.

Most of the states have delegated the powers to the hospital authorities to make use of the user charges for the promotion of quality health care. Under this system, there is a danger of misuse of funds. The better method would be to collect users charges from all institutions at the state level and then provide amounts out of these funds as contingency grants to hospital authorities. This would encourage transparency, accountability and good governance.

3. Grant Assistance

Grant Assistance is subject to the budgetary situations and political agendas of donors. As a result, while grant assistance is an important financing source in the short-run for may countries to purchase essential health services and develop critical infrastructure capacity, it is not a reliable long-run source of financing. Thus it cannot be relied on to ensure long-term financial sustainability.

However, Grants received from World Bank, UNDP and bilateral assistances are not utilized properly causing waste of rare resources. The author conducted USAID Study in Hamachal Pradesh in three districts in which 11 crores were spent for improving primary health care. An evaluation study revealed that there has been no improvement after 5 years of financial input in health sector.

4. Borrowing

Borrowing, like grant assistance, can be either a public or private financing mechanism. When the government is the borrower, it is a public revenue source. When a private entity is the borrower, it is a private revenue source. Funds can be borrowed from either domestic or foreign sources. Foreign sources of health financing include international development organizations, bilateral donor assistance agencies, private commercial institutions, and foreign medical suppliers. Such lending may include a significant grant (donor) element or may be at full market rates. The essential feature of borrowing is that the funds eventually must be repaid. Borrowing, in effect, imposes a burden on future generations.

Borrowing money by Government for health promotion must be used economically and efficiently. At present, many state governments in India are receiving 3000 crores of rupees from World Bank but the impact on State Health is not as desired.

Borrowing, like other potential forms of revenue raising, requires careful consideration of inter-temporal tradeoffs. Borrowing imposes a burden on future generations and so must be carefully considered in the context of economic growth and development objectives. Given the poor balance of payments situations in many low-income countries as well as higher-priority development needs, borrowing for social programs, except where such borrowing is on a confessional basis, is likely to be quite limited. Moreover, concessional borrowing from international organizations (such as the World Bank) generally has policy conditions attached.[18]

5. Donations by Foundations

International Civil Society Including Foundations and Associations, play an important role in financing health, especially in the area of prevention and promotion. The Rockefeller Foundation, the Nippon Foundation, Rotary International, MSF, Help International, and many others are assisting the countries in prevention and control of diseases such as poliomyelitis, leprosy, TB, HIV/AIDS, malaria and other tropical diseases. In addition, multinational pharmaceutical corporations such as Novartis, SmithKline, Merck, etc., are donating their products and finances to help the global elimination of major communicable diseases such as leprosy, river blindness, filariasis, soil transmitted helminthic infections and other diseases.

The recent entry of Rotary Club members and other national and international entrepreneurs as private philanthropists, in health and other social sectors such as the Sasakawa Health Trust, the HP Foundation, the Ted Turner UN Foundation, the Bill and Melinda Gates Foundation, Rotary Club, with multi-billion dollar contributions to specified funds and programmes for global health development, are making health an important investment for development. Presently, their inputs are usually aimed at special health development funds or programmes and/or assigned for certain geographical areas.

Similarly, national and sub-national non-governmental organizations and other civil societies have played a major role in mobilizing human and financial resources for health. In most countries, community trust funds and foundations have been established at both national and local levels in order to protect the financial risk for health care, especially for poor patients (Help Aid for Blind, National TB Union, etc.).

A few funding pools by public voluntary donations are earmarked to provide support for prevention and control of specific diseases, especially noncommunicable ones, such as cancer, diabetes and renal diseases, like National Cancer Foundation, National Diabetes Association, National Kidney Foundation or National HIV/AIDS Association/Foundation. The extent of such contributions by these national funding sources, whether they would be able to cover essential health care for these specific needy groups, has not yet been properly accounted for, although efforts to do this with in the NHA framework are under way. There is also a possibility of double counting since governments are also financing many international and national NGOs including foundations. A few countries have created drug revolving funds or community trust funds for the purchase of drugs and other essential supplies for the poor, mainly at the local level.[19]

6. Ineffective Utilization of Resources

The most serious problem in India is not as much of Resource mobilization as that of resource utilization. The resources are not producing the desired impact.

K.N. Rao, in a paper on "Health in Developing Countries" pointed out: "It may be stated, however, that even funds allocated by WHO and UNICEF are not fully utilized in some developing countries including India due to administrative and procedural difficulties."[20]

Thus, a quantitatively inadequate or qualitatively deficient system of public administration will not merely retard the development process, but may defeat the entire development effort in an even more decisive manner than any temporary shortage of capital, or inadequate technical skills, or an unfavourable monsoon.

Nigro has also remarked in this connection that "management experts from the highly developed countries find that these are serious obstacles to improvements." He adds that some developing countries in Latin America which have succeeded substantially in improving their respective administrative system, have been able to make better use of international assistance."[21]

Let us understand the nature of these problems. There have been a large number of administrative challenges and problems, which impede and bedevil the effective functioning of the governments in the developing countries. Let us mention some of them:

(a) Lack of effective policy-making, planning and decision-making to exploit the human and financial resources for the welfare of the people.
(b) Lack of effective manpower planning resulting in the poor utilization of human resources.
(c) Lack of coordination among the allied agencies and within the various units of a department resulting in duplication and wastage of financial resources.
(d) Lack of reliable, timely and suitable information systems for the formulation, implementation and evaluation of financial policy.
(e) Widely scattered funding mechanism with little control over costs.
(f) Lack of effective mechanism to involve the employees and beneficiaries in the policy-making and implementation of the programme of an organization.
(g) Use of outdated methods and procedures in the operation of the financial administration.
(h) Lack of interest to improve financial administrative structures and procedures.
(i) Absence of innovative leadership, administrative capability and competence in general and financial administration in particular. and
(j) Lack of equity of distribution and adequacy of coverage in relationship to need.

Resources mobilization and utilization can be improved to a great extent through improved administrative system, especially in the sphere of financial administration. Besides, all the resources must be utilized economically and efficiently and the expenditure on unproductive resources must be curbed.

We may conclude by saying that the policy-makers, planners and decision-makers may attend to the following carefully to husband all resources and to accomplish as much as possible with what is available:

(i) to identify who (action agents) needs how much money (cost) and for what (activities);
(ii) to define criteria for and priority in allocation of budgetary resources among different activities and different organizations responsible for performance of activities;
(iii) to provide flexibility in budgeting and financing, if necessary, beyond bureaucratic control;
(iv) to ensure the timely availability of funds to the programme activities of field level;
(v) to design Management Information System to get timely information on the utilization of resources;
(vi) to arrange statistical analysis to bring out what the performance data truly signify;
(vii) to explore and recommended possibilities of reducing costs with due regards to the maintenance of efficiency and quality;
(viii) to ensure the development of effective linkages among financial, personnel, materials and other resources; and
(ix) to ensure the full impact on the main objective, socio-economic development and modernization.

SUGGESTIONS

Though the public health services in India play a vital role, their contribution to total health services in the country is low. The proportions of public and private expenditure to total expenditure on health and related parameters, are presented in the following Table 8.4.

Public expenditure as a percentage of total expenditure on health is very low in India, compared with some of the neighbouring countries and generally in Asia. Bangladesh and Sri Lanka have a higher proportion on health out of total public expenditure. The comparatively higher outlay in the public sector, combine with the efficiency of the health services, is reflected in the per capita expenditure in international dollars in the countries. The figures do not reflect the sections of society that are deprived of better health services. In India, clearly, the low scales of outlays result in the rural areas and the economically weaker sections being so deprived. There is a case for higher public expenditure on health services in the country.

It is also necessary to provide sufficient funds for the maintenance of assets and continuation of the activities created under externally aided projects. The latter constitute an injection of large funds over a short period which are not allocations made from the normal revenues of the State. However, at the end of the project period, it would be essential to provide

TABLE 8.4

Public and Private Expenditure on Health in some elected countries

Country	Public Expenditure as % of total expenditure on health	Private Expenditure on health as % of total expenditure on health	Public Expenditure on health as % of total Public expenditure	Per Capita Public Expenditure on health in International dollars
India	13	87	3.9	11
Bangladesh	46	54	9	32
Pakistan	22.9	77.1	2.9	16
Sri Lanka	45.4	54.7	5.2	35
Malaysia	57.6	42.4	5.1	116
Indonesia	36.8	63.2	3	21
Singapore	35.8	64.2	5.5	26.8
Philippines	48.5	51.5	7.2	48
China	24.9	75.1	5.5	18
Cuba	87.5	12.5	10	96
Japan	80.2	19.9	16.2	1410
France	76.9	23.1	13.8	1634
Canada	72	28	15.3	1322
United Kingdom	96.9	3.1	14.3	1156
USA	44.1	55.9	18.5	1643

Source: From Table 8, World Health Report 2000—Health Systems—Improving Performance, WHO.

by way of enhancement of the budget funds for sustaining the gains of these projects. The additional funds for this purpose would have to be found and the budget allocations enhance to the extent necessary. In this context, a review of the condition of the vehicles must be made to condemn, repair and replace them as may be necessary to enhance supervision capability.

Equally important is the need for both adequate and timely releases of allocations. Such releases, in combination with sufficient financial delegations, would go a long way towards maintaining and improving the health services.

The question of sustainability of the desired enhanced level of funding needs attention. In times of financial constraints, it has been the practice to impose budgetary cuts on the social sectors, with education and health being the worst hit. This is most unfortunate because the establishment of the health services and their being built up to reasonable levels of efficiency takes effort and time. Unlike sectors in which the creation of fixed assets is predominant, in the health sector the placement of doctors, their training and local acceptance are processes over time. Abrupt cuts in allocations destroy continuity and waste expertise and experience, with long-term effects on the services. It is, therefore, recommended that budgetary cuts should not be made in the health sector.[22]

7. International (Multi-lateral and Bilateral)

World Health Organization through it South-East Asia Regional Office provides assistance to a number of projects in priority areas through expertise equipment and fellowships.

State Health Systems Development Projects are being implemented in the following States with World Bank Assistance: (i) Andhra Pradesh (from 1995 for 6 years) 608 crore; (ii) Karnataka (1996 for 5 years) 456 crores; (iii) East Bengal (1996 for 5 years) 689 crores; (iv) Punjab (1996 for 5 years) 425 crores; (v) Orissa (1998 for 5 years) 415.58 crore.

State Health Systems Development Projects with World Bank Assistance

State Health Systems Development Projects started with the World Bank assistance are aimed at improving/upgradating secondary level health care facilities. The details of these projects which have been completed/under implementation is as under:

The objectives of the above projects are to provide quality health care services to the people in the rural areas: to provide viable first referral mechanism, i.e. at the level of the community health centers, sub-division hospitals and district hospitals to improve the health status of especially the poor and the under served (women, SC/ST, elderly) by reducing mortality, morbidity and disability, and to improve efficiency in allocation and use of health resources through policy reform and institutional development.

In addition to these, there are many specific programmes assisted by other countries on bilateral basis.

WTO Cell

The WTO Cell in the Ministry of Health and Family Welfare began working since July 2004. The aim of the WTO Cell is to help in ascertaining impacts on public health due to globalization and suggest ways to formulate effective legislation and policy initiatives to deal with it. In particular, the functions of the WTO Cell includes:

- To provide technical assistance to the MoH&FW in the area of international trade-related agreements, such as TRIPS, GATS, SPS and TBT.
- To review the existing system, available data and information, identify the data gaps and provide evidence-based information, intervention options, and potential solutions/strategies with respect to trade-related agreements and its impact on health issues.
- To conduct quantitative and qualitative studies related to international trade agreements and health issues, and further

identify relevant stakeholders and institutions and interact with them.

- To participate, organize, conduct workshops, seminars, meetings and document the process.
- To understand what other ministers/departments/agencies, at Centre and State levels have done in this field, which can be useful for the Ministry of Health.
- To enhance the culture of inter-sectoral involvement in international economic policymaking and subsequent national law/policy making.[23]

Based on discussion, it was found that most of the funds are not utilized properly. Because of administrative obstacles, the foreign assistance fails to produce the desired impact.

8. Employer's Liability

Many autonomous institutions provide free medical services to their employees. The central and state Government employees get either fixed medical allowances or free treatment or reimbursement. In industry, there is an ESI scheme, wherein the expenditure on health is shared among employees, employers and government.

9. Central Government Health Scheme (CGHS)

The Centre organizes facilities for health care of its employees and pensioners living in the capital and other major cities through Central Government Health Scheme and Public Hospitals.

Objective of the Scheme

The Central Government Health Scheme (CGHS) was started in 1954 with the objective of providing; (a) Comprehensive medical care facilities to the Central Government Employees and their family members; (b) To avoid cumbersome system of medical reimbursement.

Extent of Application

Besides Central Government Employees, the scheme also provides services to: (1) Members or Ex-members of Parliament; (ii) Judges of Supreme Court and High Courts (sitting and retired); (iii) Freedom Fighters; (iv) Central Government Pensioners, employees of Semi-Autonomous bodies/Semi-Government Organizations; (v) Accredited Journalists; (vi) Ex-Governors and Ex-Vice-Presidents of India.

The Scheme which was initially started in Delhi was subsequently extended to Ahmedabad, Allahabad, Bangalore, Bhopal, Bhubaneswar, Chandigarh, Chennai, Guwahati, Hyderabad, Jabalpur, Jaipur, Kanpur, Kolkata, Lucknow, Meerut, Mumbai, Nagpur, Patna, Pune, Ranchi, Shillong, Thiruvanthapuram and Dehradun.

Number of Dispensaries, etc.

As on 31st March 2006, there are 244 Allopathic dispensaries for 9.11 lakh card holders and 33.01 lakh beneficiaries of CGHS. In addition to the allopathic dispensaries, the CGHS facilities to the beneficiaries has also been provided in Indian System of Medicine and Homeopathy through dispensaries/units in Ayurveda, Homeopathy, Unani, Siddha and Yoga for which 85 dispensaries/units are there. Apart from this, 19 Polyclinics, 65 Laboratories, 17 Dental Units and 5 Allopathic First Aid Posts are functioning under CGHS. One Maternity Hospital and Two Maternity Centers are also functioning under CGHS.

Facilities provided under CGHS

Facilities of outpatient care in all systems and emergency services in allopathic system, free supply of necessary drugs, laboratory and radiological investigations, domiciliary visits to the seriously ill patients, specialists consultatation both at the dispensary and hospital level, family welfare services, treatement in spcialized hospitals, both government and CGHS recognized private hospitals, etc. are being provided to the beneficiaries through dispensaries, polyclinics and government/CGHS recognized private hospitals/diagnostic centers. There are special facilities for the convenience of pensioners and senior citizens entitled to CGHS. Pensioners can obtain a 'whole life' CGHS card by paying 10 years' subscription. Those living in the nearest CGHS covered city. Credit facilities are also available to the pensioners for treatment taken in private hospitals/ diagnostic center approved under CGHS with permission from CGHS. Also facilities are given to Pensioners to obtain medicines for chronic ailments up to three months at a stretch. In emergency cases recognized private hospitals are also provided credit facilities to all beneficiaries on production of valid CGHS card and claim reimbursement from parent Department/ CGHS as the case may be as per approved rates. In non-emergency cases on production of valid permission, CGHS recognized hospitals shall provide credit facilities to Pensioners including freedom fighters, etc. and submit the bills subject to the ceiling approved rates to the offices of the Head of CGHS covered cities for payment. The CGHS has recognized the private hospitals and diagnostic centers throughout the country for the benefits of the beneficiaries whereby these hospitals/diagnostic centers cannot charge more than the agreed rates for which an agreement has been executed with the units by the CGHS.

Budgetary Provision

A provision of Rs. 35.00 crores has been made in the budget during 2006-07 under Plan and Rs. 276.50 crores in the budget of Min. of Health and Rs. 300 crores for Pensioners from the Department of Pensioners under Non Plan, Min. of Home Affairs.[24] The city-wise breakup is as given in Table 8.5.

TABLE 8.5

Central Government Employees Health Scheme Finance

(Rs. in thousands)

Sl. No.	City	Plan	Non-Plan	MH-2071-PROB(NP)
1.	Ahmedabad	400	32512	16600
2.	Allahabad	800	57185	38000
3.	Bangalore	0	120575	89000
4.	Bhopal	7870	0	15000
5.	Bhubaneswar	7750	15610	5500
6.	Chennai	1500	110660	110000
7.	Chandigarh	19100	0	35000
8.	Delhi	106815	1375190	160000
9.	Dehradun	7715	0	10000
10.	Hyderabad	0	199719	250000
11.	Guwahati	22100	0	6700
12.	Jaipur	775	59050	60000
13.	Jabalpur	29440	0	60000
14.	Kanpur	0	99493	75000
15.	Kolkata	1875	150831	132200
16.	Lucknow	13970	59706	28000
17.	Meerut	660	55660	50000
18.	Mumbai	3090	209002	153500
19.	Nagpur	800	92705	63000
20.	Patna	0	54660	50000
21.	Pune	0	65000	119000
22.	Ranchi	7640	7332	6000
23.	Shillong	7900	0	2500
24.	Trivandrum	29800	0	25000
	Computerization of CGHS, Delhi	80000	11000*	
	Total	350000	2765000	3000000

* Rs. 1,10,000 retained with the Dte. G.H.S.

Source: Ministry of Health and Family Welfare.

10. Private Sector

Private sector possess immense potentially to provide decent health care to the people. We are witnessing the mushroom growth of Nursing homes, complex hospitals like Appolo, Cadila, Wochard Fortis, etc. They are making a good contribution. However, we should take care that they may not exploit the people. The charges in private hospitals are so high that only selected people can avail of their benefits. Even these have become cheating devices of specialists. It is high time that the Union Government should come out with a legislation to provide control over these institutions so that they serve the people and jot resort to profit making and fleecing the people.

11. NGO's Role

There are many institutions run by voluntary organizations. It has been seen that most of the NGOs get the money from Government. Such NGOs should be discouraged and asked to raise their own resources. Only those NGOs should be encouraged, which can raise more than 50% to finances themselves. We should encourage such organizations like Ramakrishna Mission, which has been providing excellent health services and was awarded by Government of India for its dedicated services. Ramakrishna Mission Branch at Chandigarh runs a mobile van to provide free health care in villages. Dr. H.V. Jindal, Former Deputy Director, Health, Punjab, provides honorary services on holidays. The state should award such individuals to set example of service. There are many other religious organizations like Khalsa Panth, Sanatan Dharam, Christianty, etc. which also provide such services.

12. Philanthropy

Charity is one of the oldest and most common in India. Individual donors give donations to hospitals and institutions and business men and industrialists to develop health institutions from their personal assets.

Many private individuals are providing health facilities purely from their personal resources like Mohan Dai Cancer Hospital, Ludhiana, a premier institution set-up by Lala Vidya Sagar Oswal in memory of his wife, who died of cancer. Similarly, many industrialists like Birla, Tata have set-up such institutions. Many individuals give funds for additions in existing health institutions like Dr. P.N. Chuttani, who donated huge funds to PGI.

13. Curtailment of Wasteful Expenditure

Wasteful expenditure, especially in institutions run by government is very high. A serious problem in this area is of inefficient use of allocated resources and non-utilization of actual and potential resources judiciously and properly. Huge resources are being wasted because of selection of inappropriate technology, inefficient management and unsatisfactory control mechanisms.

It is necessary that public revenue should be raised in an equitable manner and spent economically so that the tax payers may get full value for their money.

Dr. N.S. Deodhar in his article, "Potential for Resources Mobilization for Health Care Financing in India" rightly mentions the following suggestions which merit the attention of government.[25]

Better fiscal management and monitoring cost-effectiveness are the measures of high potential for internal resource mobilization. This can be achieved in several ways. These are:

(a) Improving efficiency by laying emphasis on achieving results in real terms of effective services, and discarding the present approach of incurring targeted or budgeted expenditure without considering the outcome.
(b) Ensuring total coverage of the unorganized communities, the under-privileged and deprived, i.e. attending the have-nots.
(c) Replacing the top down health care delivery system by the bottom up health care delivery, i.e. primary health care approach with due financing. Appropriate system would have to be economical, cheaper to the beneficiaries, mainly preventive rather than mainly curative, and above all community-oriented. The urban-rural differences should be reduced. Blind adoption of the Western systems which are too costly, far too individualistic, not relevant, and much wasteful would be unwise.
(d) Rationalizing expenditure on items such as highly sophisticated medical care to only a few (in urban areas), non-essential and unethical drugs, etc.
(e) Emphasizing immediate provision of services and purchase of equipments and material rather than the construction of buildings and other physical facilities such as hospital beds. In fact, if the population is given training about home nursing and post-operative care for minor surgeries, may be at the secondary school level, the necessity and requirement of hospital beds can be minimized.
(f) Ensuring full utilization of the trained manpower and available equipments.
(g) Discarding ineffective and out-dated strategies and practices in favour of efficient and/or more rational approaches and alternatives, e.g. shifting emphasis from the chemical control to environmental control of the mosquitoes as a strategy for the National Malaria Eradication Programme.

The *Indian Express* dated March 15, 2000, has quoted the case of BYL Nair Hospitals at Mumbai, where money is being spent on bricks and mortar and not on patient care. To quote, "The BYL Nair Hospital at Mumbai Central has pulled-off the impossible. It has opted for a multicore makeover even as it admits patients to its 32 wards sans drugs and surgical equipment.

The secret to the crippling shortage of drugs and supplies is to ask patients and their relatives to make the purchases themselves and to depend on the generosity of doctors who volunteer to pitch in. Despite pasting lists of ever-expanding 'out-of-stock' drugs on the walls of each of the 32 wards, doctors say the Diabetic Patients Department has no insulin injections, the Trauma Ward has no Depin (an antihypertension drug) and anaestheticians complain patient) ran out long ago."

There are a number of reasons which result into wasteful expenditure. Firstly, the health system is not well organized. Because of inadequate referral system, there is lot of duplication, overlapping and improper use of services resulting into huge costs. Tertiary health care, which is highly costly, is being used for primary health care. This also results in poor manpower utilization.

Secondly, there is maldistribution of health resources. Most of the health budgets (about 80 per cent) are being spent only on a few people (20 per cent). This deprives the people living in rural areas and urban slums. A WHO study group on the Financing of Health Services, which met in Geneva from 21 to 25 November, 1977, mentioned the following characteristics, which reflect the situation in the developing countries:

(a) Disproportionate concentration of expenditure on health services in urban areas compared with expenditure in rural areas.

(b) Heavy concentration of expenditure on secondary and tertiary care services compared with expenditure on primary care services.

(c) Heavy concentration of expenditure on curatives services compared with expenditure on preventive services.

We can correct this imbalance through the innovative health policies developed in tune with the needs of the country rather than based on any foreign model.

The objectives of financial control are to ensure: (i) that no wastage of resources occurs; (ii) that public money is not misused; and (iii) that intended results are obtained with the money spent. We can exploit the potential resources through careful planning and management. The traditional system of medicine can be of immense value to provide health care at a very low cost, provided this is properly tapped by the designers of health services. It was reported in a UN Survey (1976), that these adverse trends are despite the higher percentage of government expenditure being devoted to health, compared with 1960s and the fact that ratio of population to the number of beds and of medical personnel have moved favourably. Essentially, the continuance of poor health standards is indicative of a less-than optimal use of resources available. Some aspects of this are the emphasis on curative, as opposed to the preventive techniques embodied in the existing hospital systems, the inadequate development of indigenous medicine system on which there is a continued reliance and the limited coverage of available medical facilities, particularly in rural areas.

In a paper presented by M. Siegel, Assistant Director General, Department of Administrative and Finance, WHO, Geneva to the Advisory Group on Nursing Administration (16 Dec. 1975), he has rightly remarked.

If the resources for health work, in trained person and in finances, were unlimited the need for constant attention to these factors would not be so great. But the limitation in the number of trained personnel and the lack of adequate financial resources are major obstacles to greatly improved health in the world today. We must therefore, husband our resources carefully to accomplish as much as possible with what we have available.

The third serious challenge in this field is the rising cost of health services, beyond the reach of most of the people inhabiting the developing societies. It is very difficult to afford the costly urban-based hospitals using highly sophisticated technology. A huge amount is being spent on costly buildings and equipment, which the developing countries cannot afford. The only services, which can meet the health needs of the people, are low cost services, which should be efficient and effective. This is possible if we use methods and equipment appropriate to the socio-economic environment existing in a country, e.g. the people can contribute voluntary labour to maintain health services. This would reduce the cost. We must take decisions and think of alternative solutions to provide health care to the people as financing and decision-making are complementary functions. The health administrator should encourage the low cost service programmes beneficial to the larger section of the community.

The fourth problem in this connection is the lack of coordination among different agencies financing health care services. This may result in wasteful duplication of efforts. Besides, many health services may not get the desired financial allocation because of this wastage. The situation can be improved through proper coordination among such agencies. Fifthly, a serious problem in health care administration is the absence of cost consciousness among the staff of public health administrations. All over the world, health service staff—even of the highest professional cadre—are taught little about the economics of health services and know little about the costs of the equipment and supplies they use. Doctors tend to employ what is new without regard to cost. It is a fashion to prescribed costly drugs. They are also subjected to considerable sales pressure from manufacturing firms. A cheaper drug or cheaper equipment may give just as good a result for the vast majority of patients. Cost consciousness is not just a matter for central administrators or planners but should be inculcated in all those working in health care. More people can be provided with services if no services cost more than what is a must to provide the necessary level of care. The price paid for high cost technology for a few is not technology at all for the many.

Sixthly, the problem is the use of hospital services non-judiciously. In the more developed countries, the majority of secondary care is generally given in hospitals, and increasingly the hospitals in which it is provided tend to be large, i.e. 500 beds or more. The larger hospital offers the opportunity for a high degree of specialization and for achieving the fullest use of expensive specialized equipment. The larger the hospital and the more specialized its work, the larger catchments area it needs to serve. The higher average transport costs for staff and patients may be justified by the quality of service that a large hospital should be able to provide.

In the developing countries like India, where the bulk of the population lives in rural areas, with limited public or private facilities for long distance travel, such transport is costly, except for the few patients who can be transported to hospital in vehicles travelling for other purposes. Moreover, in-patient care must be provided much more selectively if it is not absorb an excessive share of the health budget. It must be confined to those with a high probability of deriving clear and lasting benefit from it. The emphasis should be on ambulatory service.

For these reasons, hospitals should on average be smaller in developing countries than in more developed countries and they should not be used to provide the most sophisticated technology. Costs can be saved if limited number of relatives accompany the patient and take responsibility for preparing food and providing basic patient care. But many developing countries have followed the example of more developed countries and concentrated on a high proportion of their health service expenditure on large urban hospitals, many of them teaching hospitals, equipped to provide tertiary care with high technology. These hospitals have been set-up before smaller district hospitals have been developed and as transport is not normally developed, they tend to be sued to provide secondary care to the urban population. Moreover, they are mainly used for patients who do not need their special facilities, e.g. the chronically disabled, children suffering from malnutrition, and patients with minor illness who could be treated in a much simpler hospital or at home. In some countries, the out-patient department of a regional hospital is used to provide primary care as there is no referral system and time of super specialists is wasted on minor problems, which could be dealt elsewhere. It is suggested that the referral system must be made statutory to screen the patients.

B.B.L. Sharma in his article, "Financing Health Care Reforms" in *IJPA*, Oct.-Dec. 1999, suggested the following reforms in financing health services, based upon his analysis of various Five Year Plans. He stresses the following reforms:

- In view of resource constraints, there is need for raising financial resources to maintain quality of health-care services and to meet the rising expectations of the people.
- The concept of free medical care requires reviewing and people are required to pay, even of partially, for the health services.
- The payment system requires to be so designed that truly indigent population are able to get free or highly subsidized medical care. Innovative approaches/practices and a system of medical audit should be developed.

- Maximum cost-effective utilization of existing services should be an important agenda item.
- In accordance with the new policy of the government to encourage private initiatives, private hospitals and clinics should be supported, subject to minimum standards and suitable returns for tax incentives.
- Norms for minimal facilities and accreditation of private hospitals should be developed to maintain quality of care.
- At the cost of other different categories of personnel, over-emphasis on super-specialization training and its financing has been given, which has created imbalances and it needs to be checked.
- The pertinent remark about family planning is that it is being run as a 100 per cent centrally sponsored scheme. The entire outlay is included in the Plan with the result that a major proportion, 60-70 per cent of the outlay, goes towards meeting the expenditure of maintenance nature, leaving very little scope for expansion and strengthening of the programme for new initiatives.

The developing countries give low priority in the allocation of resources to the health care of their people. We can see from the figures given earlier that the allocation has been very low. The health expenditure to the total expenditure has been very low in South-East Asian countries, i.e. 1.6 per cent in Indonesia, 2.1 per cent in India, 3.8 per cent in Bangladesh. Mongolia has been spending 10 per cent for the health care of its people. There is a need to raise the health allocations to improve the quality of life. Dr. White has rightly said that, "Nothing can be done without the expenditure of money...Available financial resources set a maximum limit on administrative activity as a whole and on each of its separate parts."

A sound state of finance is of paramount importance to the political health of a nation...The soundness of public finance depends both upon the right policy and good organization, but a great deal upon the latter. The scarcity of resources affect all aspects of the health delivery system. There is a need to step up the health allocations to the minimum of 10 per cent of the total budget.

CRITICAL APPRAISAL

Finances for health care not being allocated and spent prudently and rationally. We mention some of the facts and suggestions, which can improve the financial health of health care systems in the new millennium:

1. Undue Expansion Leading to Dilution of Services

There has been undue expansion of health infrastructure, without proper facilities, because of financial constraints. For example, the number of sub-centres has increased from 84376 to 144988 (from 1.4.85 to 30.6.2006). Similarly, primary health centers have increased from 9115 to 22669 during the same period. There are 3910 CHC as on 31.3.2006. It is time to consolidate and equip the already existing facilities fully. This would save the money for future expansion.

2. Low Time Utilization by Health Workers

The output of workers is very less in terms of health care delivery system. Strict disciplinary action may be initiated against those workers who are habitually late or are in the habit of wasting time. Besides, unessential activities may be withdrawn so that they can concentrate on essential services. It is no use paying salaries without any output. This may be strictly ascertained through supervision, performance appraisal, surprise checks, etc.

3. Less Emphasis on Preventive Services

The main activity of primary health care is preventive care and not curative. The health workers should focus attention on ensuring provision of cheaper preventive services having lasting impact.

4. Improper Maintenance of Equipment

Equipment at health centers generally remains out of order; inspite of the fact that the equipment supplied is not old. Healths workers do not take due care and also do not handle properly the equipment, resulting in the equipment going out of order. They should maintain equipment in good condition.

5. Intersectoral Coordination Missing

Many of the activities in the domain of primary health care can be better handled by some other agencies or Panchayat Raj System. There is a need to involve more and more other agencies like ICDS.

6. Performance Budgeting to make the best use of Resources

Performance budgeting is very useful in developing countries. It facilitates better programming, decision-making, review and control for a more intelligible presentation of governmental activities to the public and the legislature. Broadly speaking, the main purposes sought to be served by performance budgeting are:[26]

(a) to correlate the physical and financial aspects of every programme/activity;
(b) to improve budget formulation, review and decision-making at all levels of management in the government machinery;
(c) to facilitate better appreciation and review by the legislature;
(d) to make possible more effective performance audit; and

(e) to measure progress towards long-term objectives as envisaged in the plan; and to bring annual budgets and development plans closely together through a common language.

CONCLUSION

In developing countries several issues merit particular attention:

- Taxes and other public revenue sources must be evaluated in terms of economic efficiency, equity, and administrative simplicity.
- The inherently agrarian/rural nature of much economic activity, the small and transient nature of urban formal sector firms, and the openness of their economies generally preclude heavy reliance on the more efficient and progressive income taxes used in most industrial countries.
- Limited taxable capacity and inefficient administration limit revenue generation potential.
- Broadly based taxes with limited rate differentiation and few exemptions, deductions, and exclusions applied to commodities, as well as entities that display little responsiveness to the tax, are preferable for economic efficiency and equity.
- A broadly based value added tax with limited rate differentiation, exemptions for the poor, and non-discrimination between domestically produced and imported goods ranks high in terms of equity, economic efficiency, and administrative feasibility.
- Public financing of personal health services pools risks, eliminates adverse selection, and ensures equity but reduces choice and imposes excess burdens.
- Since developing countries can only generate about two-thirds the revenue generated in industrial countries (relative to GDP), in the absence of regulated private insurance markets developing countries could improve welfare by organizing these markets so that people who are able to pay can purchase health insurance at an actuarially fair price.
- User charges can be used to enhance public revenues where the services in question have individual (rather than collective) benefits. But such charges need to be carefully structured to balance equity, efficiency, and revenue generation objectives.

Developing countries will continue to rely on public and private revenues to finance their health care systems. The instruments used will affect economic efficiency, the distribution of income, and the revenues generated. Limited administrative capacity and infrastructure hinder implementation of effective policies. Dealing with these impediments to fiscal and health financing reform should be a priority; otherwise the effects of economically and politically "correct" policy prescriptions will be marginal. Moreover, implicitly underlying these technical and administrative concerns is the need for a stable and sustainable political environment.[27]

Although this paper has focused on health care financing in terms of public and private revenue sources, national policies must also be concerned with the management and uses of such funds. Still, strictly from the financing side, a number of health policy prescriptions have emerged that apply to all countries and regions:

- Revenue-raising efforts involve tradeoffs between equity and efficiency.
- Administrative capacity is an essential component of revenue-raising efforts.
- Since raising revenue imposes significant economic costs, governments must maximize the returns on the uses of such funds.
- A government's ability to raise revenue increases significantly as income increases.
- The structural characteristics of labor and industry in low-income countries limit the instruments available to these governments to raise significant revenues.
- For reasons of equity and economic efficiency, broadly based taxes with few loopholes should be the preferred tax approach in developing countries.
- User charges that are properly designed and focused on services with tangible benefits to consumers and service facilities can lead to increased financing and better services, although user charges are not equitable unless they are applied to income-elastic goods and services.
- Public health services should be publicly financed or subsidized.
- The advantages of health insurance as a means of polling risks and the random nature and potentially high costs of treating many illnesses make public and private insurance the preferred vehicles for financing personal health services.
- Given these advantages, their limited revenue-raising capabilities, and the importance of private financing, governments in developing countries should increase their institutional capacity to ensure the availability of efficiently run and privately financed health insurance to supplement government efforts.
- Informal risk-pooling schemes, often voluntary and sponsored by local governments, appear to be viable mechanisms for pooling risks in poor rural areas.

- Recent innovations in managing health revenues—including managed competition and medical savings accounts—may help promote the efficient use of resources and can offset some of the problems inherent in insurance markets in countries with sufficient administrative capacity and developed financial markets.
- Priority needs to be given to collecting information on public and private sources of health care revenues and expenditures in all regions. National health accounts are essential for effective policy-making.[28]

Health is the most important component of socio-economic development beet still the Governments spend negligible for health promotion. Whatever is allocated to health is not spent properly causing further strains. Central and Eastern Europe are facing crisis in their health system. These countries are trying other methods.

All countries studied have reduced capital expenditure for health dramatically during the transition. This is an appropriate short-term response to fiscal crises which have undermined operating expenditures for basic health services. In the medium-term, however, the health systems of the transition countries need massive investment to replace and upgrade equipment and facilities which are often outmoded and/or near the end of their economic life. At the same time, most countries are seeking to alter the public/private mix of health services, and redefine central government and peripheral responsibilities. However, they have not yet adopted the policy framework to do so, nor significantly restructured the physical capacity of the public sector network to increase its efficiency and sustainability. Development of a long-term strategy for public investment is dependent on decisions in these areas. The current downturn in capital spending for health is an opportunity for governments to develop appropriate objectives and criteria for future public investment.

Adjustment of health system in Central and Eastern Europe in response to economic and fiscal contraction has been characterized by: (i) diversification of revenues to include insurance contributions, co-payments and user fees; (ii) compression of recurrent public spending (where economic decline has been severe); and (iii) dramatic declines in capital spending. However, implementation of the reform agenda for improvements in efficiency and effectiveness of health systems has scarcely begun, despite abundant rhetoric and support from international agencies such as the Bank. Most countries are moving very slowly—with Hungary and Croatia as the front runners—to introduce new reimbursement mechanisms which provide incentives for efficiency and cost containment, transfer ownership of some assets to the private sector, build management capacity and provide necessary managerial autonomy. Little action has been taken to limit the scope of basic health insurance coverage and restructure the public sector network of health facilities, both necessary—

but politically difficult-steps to improve the financial sustainability, efficiency and effectiveness of health services. Until financial incentives are in place, restructuring the operational reforms are unlikely to take place.[29]

Towards Better-run Hospitals

From 50% to 80% of all health expenditure in countries go to the hospitals. Public hospitals usually absorb more than 50% of government spending on health. The bigger the hospital, the harder it seems to keep the costs under control. So their role in the health system needs to be re-examined to make sure that they are more effective and better adapted to changing health situations.

The role of the big teaching hospitals in particular needs to be reassessed, since the poorer sectors of the population have always had only limited access to basic and intermediate care, and very rarely benefit from the technology and high-level competence of these institutions. Better management is called for it every domain.

The present trend towards privatization does not resolve all the problems. Hospitals should, in fact, be an integral part of the national health systems and their role and functions clearly stated and monitored, allowing firm control to be exercised on investments in high-tech medicine and on imports of costly drugs by countries. Hospitals should provide a well-defined number of interventions and an agreed level of performance and quality, and adhere to a list of essential pharmaceutical substances.

Courses in management should be included in the training of all health personnel, and the hospitals themselves could call in financial experts—two measures that would serve to avoid the risks of unnecessary waste. As for hospital staff, their role in health care needs to be much more fully recognized and they should be rewarded accordingly.[30]

This shift from hospital to community services as units of organization, particularly for primarily for primary health care, could be an example to both developing and developed countries. The dominance of hospitals in all countries, particularly in the developing world, requires a major shift to empower community-led and community-managed primary health care to take its rightful and central place in all health systems. The approach in New Zealand could serve as a model.[31]

Government of India and State Government in India must provide health care to the people directly through its revenue and other methods like social insurance to the poor and under privileged and private insurance for those who can pay. Her Government must regulate the insurance system.

NOTES AND REFERENCES

1. Brain Abel-Smith, "Global Perspective on Health Services Financing" in India Society on Health Administrators, Bangalore, Proceedings of the Fifth Annual Conference, 1984 (Dec. 13-15, 1984), p 48.

2. Joana Godinho, World Bank, Integrated Cost-Effective Care: The Missing Link between Community, Primary and Secondary Care, Economic Development Institute of The World Bank, Implementing Health Sector Reform in Central Asia, pp. 43-44.
3. George Schieber and Akiko Maeda, A Curmudgeon's Guide to Financing Health Care in Developing countries in George Schieber (ed.) Innovations in Health Care Financing Proceedings of a World Bank Conference, March 10-11, 1997. World Bank discussion paper No. 365, Washington DCFSA, preface.
4. World Bank 2001.
5. Better Health Systems for India's Poor, The World Bank, Washington, D.C., Financing Health, p. 234.
6. Ministry of Health and Family Welfare, GOI, Annual Report, 2006-07, National Rural Health Mission, "Funding for the Programme", pp. 37-43.
7. Ninth Five Year Plan, *op. cit.*, pp. 186-87.
8. WDR, 1993.
9. J. Brunet-Jailly, Population and Human Resources Department, The World Bank, May 1991, WPS 692, Health Financing in the Poor Countries, Cost Recovery or Cost Reduction? Working Paper 1991.
10. The Risk of Poverty from Health Shocks, A World Bank Country Study, Household Risk Management and Social Protection in Chile, p. 55.
11. To other criteria for evaluating taxes are flexibility: the tax system should be able to respond easily (in some cases automatically) to changed economic circumstance; and political responsibility: the tax system should be designed so that individuals can ascertain what they are paying so that the political system can more accurately reflect the preferences of individuals (see Stiglitz, 1988, p. 390).
12. A Curmudgeon's Guide to Financing Health Care in Developing Countries, "George Schieber and Akiko Maeda", World Bank Discussion Paper No. 365, p. 22.
13. WHO, Health for all 2000 (HFA-2000) Series No. 4, Development of indicators for monitoring and evaluation of HFA-2000, and health for all 2000 Series No. 3, Global strategy for Health for All by the Year 2000.
14. IMF study "Public spending on Health Care and the Poor", 2001.
15. WHO, Report of the Commission on Macroeconomics and Health, Macroeconomics and Health: Investing in Health for Economic Development (WHO-CMH), 2001, pp. 18-19 and 108-111.
16. A Curmudgeon's Guide to Financing Health Care in Developing Countries, "George Schieber and Akiko Maeda", 'World Bank Discussion Paper No. 365, pp. 22-24.
17. Health Finance, India Health Report, Rajiv Misra, Rachel Chatterjee, Sujatha Rao, p. 151.
18. A Curmudgeon's Guide to Financing Health Care in Developing Countries, "George Schieber and Akiko Maeda", World Bank Discussion Paper No. 365, pp. 25-26.
19. Originally issued as document SEA/PDM/Meet.40/TD/1.3 dated 25th July 2003, Social Health Insurance, Working Paper, pp. 22-23.
20. Dr. K.N. Rao, "Health in Developing Countries," *Indian Journal of Public Administration,* Chapter III.
21. Felix A. Nigro: Chap. III: Administration and Culture, Modern Public Administration, (New York, 1966), p. 70.
22. Karnataka Towards Equity, Quality and Integrity in Health, Final Report, Health Financing, Report of the Task Force, April 2001, pp. 323 and 328-29.
23. International Co-operation for Health and Family Welfare, Annual Report 2006-07, pp. 288-90.

24. Annual Report 2006-07, Ministry of Health and Family Welfare, NRHM, pp. 159-160.
25. Indian Society of Health Administrators, *op. cit.*, pp. 224-25.
26. ARC: Report of the study team, Financial Administration, May 1967, Chapter III.
27. A Curmudgeon's Guide to Financing Health Care in Developing Countries, "George Schieber and Akiko Maeda", World Bank Discussion Paper No. 365, pp. 26-27.
28. A Curmudgeon's Guide to Financing Health Care in Developing Countries, "George Schieber and Akiko Maeda", World Bank Discussion Paper No. 365, p. 36.
29. Ellen Goldstein, *et. al.*, Trends in Health Status, Services, and Finance, The Transition in Central and Eastern Europe, Vol. I, World Bank Technical Paper No. 341, Social Challenges of Transition Series, pp. 35-36.
30. Humberto M. Novaes, Hospital trends in Latin America, *World Health*, 47th Year, No. 5, September-October 1994, p. 16.
31. Laurence Malcolm, Replacing the hospital, *World Health*, 47th Year, No. 5, September-October 1994, p. 14.

*Financing of Health Services: Social Insurance**

Bhore Committee (1946) mentioned that it is the duty of the state to provide access to Universal Health Care and to ensure that no one is denied health care because of inability to pay. Many families in rural areas and medium and small towns become indebted due to high cost of medical care as well as cheating by doctors. It is big problem for poor families. What is the way out? Here we examine the concept of social insurance.

In many countries, the out-of-pocket payments (OOP) form a major part of the total health expenditure (THE). Analysis from the NHA Tables in WHR-2002[1] indicated that in 60 per cent of countries with incomes below $1000 per capita, OOP consist of 40 per cent or more of THE, whereas only 30 per cent of middle and high income countries depend as heavily on this kind of financing. Most countries in the Region have more than 50 per cent of THE coming from out-of-pocket payments.

While people have the freedom of choice to pay out of their pockets for health care—and it might provide, especially the rich, with high satisfaction—there is no guarantee that the majority of the population can afford to pay for health care needs by out-of-pocket payment. The real situation in many developing and even in developed countries is the issue of a high proportion of catastrophic expenses of households in all income deciles, especially among the lowest and the highest deciles.

People become impoverished due to higher and rising cost of medical bills, because of the uncertainty of the amount of expenditure to meet health care needs on individual basis. In some cases, people have to spend 'under-the-table' expenditure for getting access to public health facilities. And, in

* Mostly Based upon South-East Asia Regional Office of WHO, "Social Insurance", New Delhi, 4-5 September 2003.

CHART 9.1

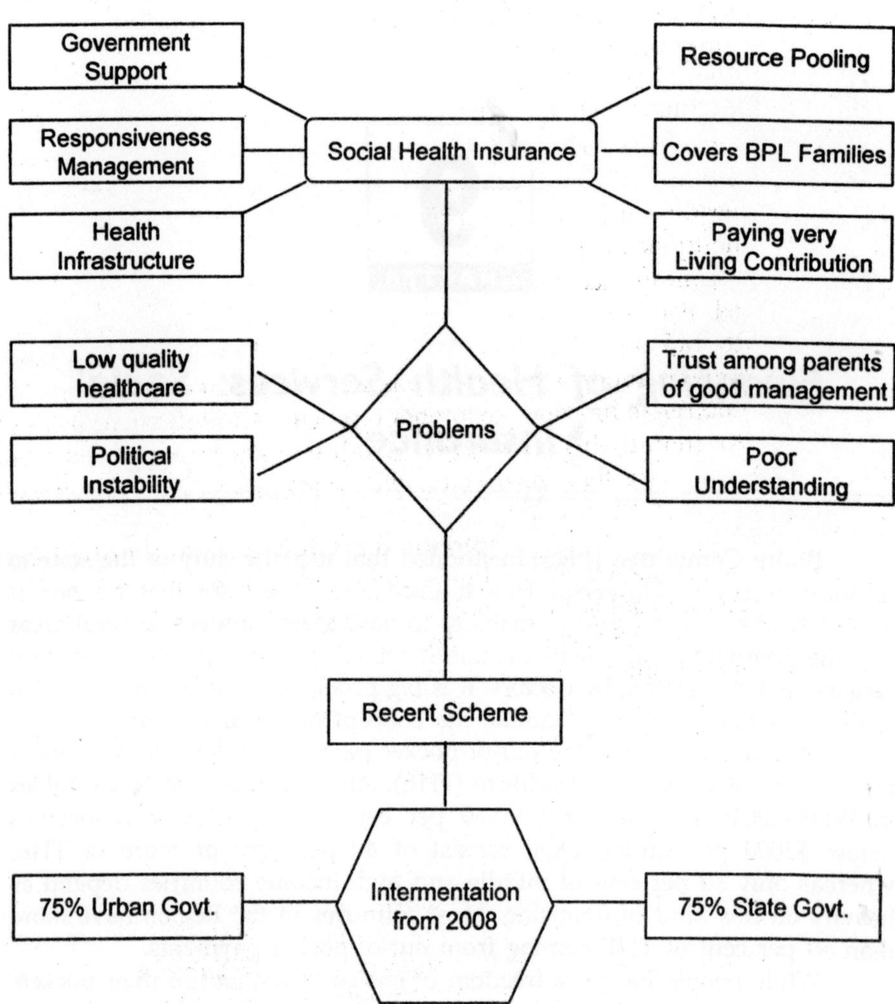

other cases, the unskilled and unqualified private providers might charge higher rates for their service in the exploitation of quick and easy access and convenient service hours. Strong stewardship of the government is required to rationalize the provider consumer relationship. In fact, strong purchasing power could play a better role in controlling health care costs to a certain extent.[2]

It is a method to provide health care to the community wherein individuals, enterprises and the Government contribute to pool the resources. In India, Employees workings in the factories are provided social insurance under Employees State Insurance Act, 1948. (To be discussed in detail in Chapter 4)

BASIC CONCEPT

Social health insurance is a mechanism for financing and managing health care through pooling of health risks of its members on the one hand, and the financial contributions of enterprises, households, and the government, on the other.[3] SHI is generally perceived as a financial protection mechanism for health care, through health risk sharing and fund pooling for a larger section of the population.[4] It usually forms part of a broader *social security* framework, covering all contingencies, which need financial protection and risk sharing. SHI is not merely a new method to collect money to co-finance services. It is a method that is able to achieve a stable financing for a package of health services (health insurance benefits), while at the same time achieving greater access to health care among the population.

FEATURES OF SOCIAL INSURANCE

SHI must have certain characteristics to be used with the terms "social" and "insurance." Countries, which implement various SHI schemes on a national scale usually adopt broad social security policies and legislative framework, within the policy framework stipulated under the National Constitution. In some cases, the policy framework is determined by society consensus. The major characteristics of SHI schemes are:

(a) Compulsory or mandatory membership of individuals and/or groups or households, initially targeted to cover civil servants, and other formally employed people, from public and private, commercial, semi-commercial, industrial and agricultural establishments and their dependents; and, usually expanding coverage to informally employed people, non-working people, retirees and even students (*inclusion of target population does not necessarily depend on the structure of the economy*);

(b) Responsibility for contributions by the members (employees) with proper organizational arrangement to collect regular income-related contributions or flat-rate contributions from individuals/groups, with added contribution from employers and the government (*earmarked deduction as insurance contribution*[5] *from regular pay-roll or pre-set collection amount from individuals or groups*);

(c) Contribution according to the ability to pay (based on economic means) and not related to health risks of individuals, households or employment groups;

(d) Choice of health care according to the health needs (*Basic benefit packages usually set by many countries, which also allow the members to make co-payment or purchasing supplementary health care services in addition to basic packages*);

(e) Solidarity across the population; risk equalization and cross subsidization;
(f) Arrangement for social assistance to cover vulnerable populations (young and old aged, disabled, pregnant women). *Contributions by these groups may be partially or totally subsidized by the government through general revenue;*
(g) Covering a large segment of the population, and
(h) Funds collected from contributions are pooled into single or multiple fund arrangements administered by a quasi-independent public body that would act as a purchaser of health care.

According to the International Labour Organization (ILO) Convention No. 130, its Member Countries are free to choose different "Social Security Schemes-SSS" inclusive or with a separate SHI scheme. A country will fall into the category of "those with SHI" only if the major proportion of the population of that country is legally covered under a SHI scheme with a designated (statutory) purchaser through non-risk-related insurance contributions separated from general taxes or other legally mandated payments.

SHI schemes ensure to all people who make contributions a predefined entitlement to health care, irrespective of their income or social status.[6] The schemes usually cover the minimum health and financial risks (basic package for health care and its expenditure) that, in the absence of insurance, would entail a financial burden on the households as a result of the cost of health care.

The SHI schemes and the general revenue-based health care financing system[7] share similar characteristics of pooling risks. In SHI, people as members of insurance schemes are directly aware of their insurance contributions (*explicit*). Usually people contribute from their daily, weekly, or monthly pay-roll. Such contributions are the pre-set proportionate pre-paid collection from employees, employers and the governments.

In the general revenue-based or tax-funded systems, the resources for health care come directly from general revenue and, in some cases, from special or earmarked taxes or revenue. In this method of financing, people or enterprises contribute from their income, but in an indirect way via general taxation. Thus, people are not aware of the amount they contribute solely for health care (implicit).[8]

I. Resource Pooling

"Pooling of resources" refers to "the accumulation of health assets on behalf of a population." By pooling of resources, the financial and health risks are spread and transferred among the population. Good pooling can improve health conditions by sharing health resources effectively between individuals so that people can get access to services when needed. By pooling, the financial resources are no longer tied to a particular contributor.

The term "universal coverage" means "effective protection of health and financial risk for all citizens." It is the provision of essential and affordable health care packages to everybody according to needs and preferences, regardless of income, social status or residency (coverage by essential health care for all and not all possible care for whole population) (see WHR-2000, *op. cit.*, p. 15). Joe Kutzin further defined it as "effective health risk protection at the least cost possible and the coverage may be in depth—the range of affordable health care packages, and in breadth—the proportion of people that would effectively protect from health risks. (Sanguan, N. and A. Mills, *Achieving Universal Coverage of Health Care, 1998*).

2. Membership

Most SHI schemes run with compulsory or mandatory membership. This ensures inclusion of certain underserved groups such as the poorest and vulnerable people, who are usually left out in voluntary private health insurance schemes. The compulsory scheme would guarantee an appropriate mix of good and bad health risks. Private health insurance schemes usually base contributions on the level of good or bad health risks of the individuals or groups of consumers. People who are at a higher risk pay more and each scheme may adopt a different benefit package (like insurance for car and house).

SHI schemes aim at reaching *universal coverage.* Once the target is achieved or near achievement, there is a strong potential to foster efficiency and effectiveness of health systems performance, by pushing forward the *monopsony* of purchasing power, in ensuring the quality of care and efficient resource consumption. Many countries with SHI schemes that relied on fee-for-services payment mechanisms are modifying them into more closely regulated payment mechanisms, such as capitation, global budget and Diagnosis Related Groups (DRG). It is more of a self-sustaining health care financing mechanism, provided it is properly managed.

3. Purchasing

In order to have an effective and efficient health insurance, the essential health care packages should be available to the consumers literally free-of-cost, rather than fee-for-services and arrangement for reimbursement, in addition to having a large amount of co-payment. The insurance agency or agency managing insurance fund must make various arrangements for purchasing services from health care providers, on behalf of consumers (insured). Health care providers from national public or private health care systems should ensure that the health care packages, which they provide have to be responsive and financially fair. This can be achieved through strategic purchasing.[9]

1. Insurance must maintain highest standards of behaviour so that their actions and decisions result in the benefits for industry, employees, customers, shareholders and society.

2. Health and service must conform to the commitment promised to customers. Insurance must be realistic and truthful in stating claims.
3. Customers must be given best possible service and treated with respect and fairness.
4. Best way of promoting high standards of business practices is through self-regulation. The Code has been designed as an instrument of self-regulation to serve as voluntary guideline towards better quality of life and higher standards of business practices.
5. Holding of a public office requires that its incumbent is willing not only to acknowledge the moral responsibility for his/her actions but also to accept the accountability for such actions. Deflecting responsibility does not make action and its consequences disappear. Nothing is more damaging to public trust than justifying fraud and deception in the name of national security, government needs, or nation-building. Problems are more pervasive at the top simply because it is there where more is to be gained. That is why moral leadership had to come from people at the top. The absence of such leadership breeds cynicism and generates tolerance of hypocrisy, greed, and self-indulgence. The State (and finally society at large) becomes the victim of those individuals holding public offices who are unable to put the public business above their selfish leanings.
6. Enlightened Citizens believing in Ethical values. Without the co-operation of citizens, nothing can be achieved. They have to be vigilant and enlightened.[10]

Attitude Changes among Personnel Responsible for Delivery of Services

A democratic reorientation of the attitudes of the official towards the citizens has become very much necessary for both the prevention of the citizen's complaints and their prompt redress. Administrators should pay great attention to the opinions of the people. Reorientation of the attitudes of the officials towards the citizens is a very difficult task. It will require thinking on several fronts such as in service training, recruitment from a wider social base, special assignments in rural areas and the like. The Public Servant of today should not only possess traditional service virtues like efficiency, integrity and loyalty but should also shake off all the feelings of exclusiveness and superiority. There should be a desire to establish contacts with the citizens to understand their problems. Unless the change in the attitudes of civil servants as a whole is brought about, all other measures to deal with the citizen's grievances will be of limited use.

(1) *Standards*: Setting, monitoring and publication of explicit standards for the services that individual users can reasonably

expect. Publication of actual performance against these standards.

(2) *Information and Openness*: Full, accurate information, readily available in plain language, about how well they perform and who is in-charge.

(3) *Choice and Consultation*: The public sector should provide choice wherever practicable. There should be regular and systematic consultation with those, who use services. User's views about services and their priorities are to be taken into account for final decisions on standards.

(4) *Courtesy and Helpfulness*: Courtesy and helpful service from public servants who will normally wear name badge. Service available equally to all who are entitled to them and run to suit their convenience.

(5) *Putting Thing Right*: If things go wrong, an apology, a full explanation, and a swift and effective remedy to be offered. Well published and easy to use complaint procedures with independent reviews, wherever possible to be introduced and maintained.

(6) *Value for Money*: Efficient and economical delivery of public services with in the resources, the nation can afford an independent validation of performance against standards.

4. Regular contribution from the pay-roll

The SHI contributions come from regular deductions from the pay-roll and accumulated as a "Health Fund." Although the total contribution is calculated as a percentage of the monthly income, the amount is normally split between the employee and employer, and sometimes even through an additional subsidy by the central or state government, depending upon the national policy and social consensus. One actuarial issue is what proportion of salary should be compulsorily deducted (along with other deductions like pension and provident fund, income tax, etc.).

5. The Health Infrastructure

The SHI schemes act as main purchasers and can help to ensure that those covered receive appropriate health care. The schemes have to work in an environment where health care facilities are functioning in an adequate manner so that access to health care by the insured people is not denied for any reason. It does not mean that the schemes themselves should establish their own health care facilities. Traditionally, social security schemes in India and Myanmar established their own health care facilities in order to fill the gaps left by public health care providers. Similarly, big state or private enterprises like mines, railways, electricity, petro-chemical industries and other heavy industry complexes have established their own health care facilities. Some even have secondary and tertiary health care facilities that inadvertently led to inequity. Those population groups who are not insured (due to differences in their employment status, especially people in the informal sectors and mainly from agricultural, fishery and animal husbandry sectors) are often not able to get appropriate health care due to their inability to pay contributions regularly or, in most cases, because of lack of social health insurance coverage. Thus, the main aim of SHI schemes is to add on the health financing resources for universal coverage, but not for just an alternative.

6. The Management Infrastructure

The SHI schemes need a large *social capital* in all aspects: appropriate human resources with skill and knowledge in social science, commerce and economics, disease burden, clinical management, public health management, banking and financial management (i.e. health economists, insurance mathematicians, actuarial scientists, social economists, accountants, demographers, epidemiologists, medical record-keepers and statisticians, information specialists, public health legislators). Many countries do not have much national capacity to fulfil the requirement of national social capital. Regional solidarity may be required to improve and strengthen the capacity of social capital. In addition to the need for setting up appropriate collection of funds, there must be a nationally approved mechanism for managing this fund. It is critical to ensure the independence of the "Health Fund" from the general management of public finance. There is also a need to ensure transparency in how the fund is being managed, particularly to strengthen the people's trust in public management of fund. Some countries are still keeping the social security agency or agency managing social health insurance as an integral part of government public departments. They collect the contribution and put them into the general revenue. The Fund Agency has to compete with other public agencies for their annual budget, thus limiting the scope and work of the agency. In many middle income countries, the SHI fund is usually managed by an independent single agency or multiple agencies, as parastatal bodies or private enterprises (with their own budget, legal status and management). However, they all should be under strict legislative control.[11]

Advantages:

(a) It can supplement the Government resources which are very less to meet the health needs of the people;
(b) It can award rights to people to get health services and thus can be challenged in consumers courts if service are not proper or there is doctor's negligence.
(c) It can ensure equity as well as access.
(d) It can work with greater independence and is not tied to the rules and regulations of the government, which cause delays and inefficiency.
(e) It can ensure efficient delivery of health services.

(f) The premium to be paid is less, as it is a subsidized scheme.
(g) Regard for Public Comfort and Convenience.
(h) Transparency, Citizen Centric.
(i) Responsiveness.

However it has not become popular in India, as people want the Government to provide complete health care.

The main reasons for adopting the SHI scheme, in general, are:

(a) It can provide a stable source of revenue for health care.
(b) It would ensure self-reliance financing of health care compared to loans, grants and other external sources.
(c) The flow of funds into the health sector is visible.
(d) It can assist in establishing patients' rights as customers.
(e) It combines risk pooling with mutual support, by allocating services according to need, and distributing financial burden according to the ability to pay.
(f) It can operate within government health policy goals; yet maintain a degree of independence.
(g) It can be associated with efficient provision of health services.
(h) It solves equity and affordability of health care financing contribution which private health insurance fails to facilitate.

Problems

- *Poor understanding of basic conceptual framework of social health insurance and lack of nation-wide consensus* between stakeholders is a major issue in the adoption of SHI as a means of achieving universal coverage. An appropriate policy framework has to be adopted to ensure the basic concept and ground rule of SHI, i.e. to guarantee equitable health benefits to those with similar health needs, regardless of the level of contributions.
- *The need for building trust by potential members of the fund (its creation and management)* is also another major hurdle. Consumers (beneficiaries) have to fully understand the basic concept, the contributory obligation, agreement of benefit packages and how easy it is for them to be in the system, etc.
- *Inadequate or ineffective health care* provided to the insured members may be another constraint in expansion. If the existing health care system is not able to provide an essential basic health care package, it makes little sense to start an SHI scheme.
- *Insufficient or lack of human capital* or social capital leading towards inefficient and ineffective managerial or administrative capability or capacity to organize nation-wide SHI schemes, could lead to inadequate collection, reimbursement, capitation payment, inefficient management of revenues and assets

collected, or lack of monitoring the necessary health and financial information.

- *Political instability,* usually linked with national internal politics, social and economic insecurity is the main hurdle. In some cases, there is also a lack of policy debates between high-level policy-makers and beneficiaries.

  While a few countries in the Region might face similar impediments in the expansion of SHI schemes, there are many examples where opportunities could be exploited to facilitate the acceleration of SHI implementation, or transition from other financing options to social health insurance.

  The main ingredients of successful expansion of SHI schemes are:

- *Political stability:* Stability in governance, with a strong political and social commitment towards adopting SHI policies by the stakeholders as a solidarity measure, within the national framework of social security and welfare policy, will be the *raison d'être* for the success of the SHI programme.
- *Economic growth*: There is no doubt that economic growth has an impact on the speed of expansion of insurance coverage. If the growth spreads more equitably within the country, the willingness and ability to pay SHI contributions could be enhanced.
- *Level of income*: Once the general population has access to better income, they tend to participate in health insurance schemes and to make higher contributions. If people are willing to pay and can afford to pay even a small amount, it would be prime time to start with.
- *Expanding risk pools (universal coverage)*: The challenge for countries, which do not have a higher coverage of risk pooling is the enormous task of expansion that would require significant political will and an enhanced managerial and technical capacity. There is a need to increase the risk pool by expanding the beneficiaries or adding essential packages. Partnerships of employers, employees, families and enterprises will ensure that the direct burden of financing is spread more widely among them.
- *Solidarity*: There is no general rule about the proportion of the population to be covered with SHI schemes. No single country starts with a clean slate. There are historical, political and technical reasons for not covering the whole population. It is a measure of social solidarity to protect every citizen against financial and health risks. If people accept this, it facilitates in arriving at a general consensus faster, on the type of SHI, premium and the benefit package to be made available.

- *Relative size of the informal and formal sectors*: The larger the size of the informal employment sector, the more difficult it is to determine and collect contributions and to provide appropriate benefit health care packages to reach them effectively and efficiently. For the SHI schemes covering only employees from the formal sectors, it could easily be expanded to dependents, pensioners and workers who are temporarily unemployed.
- *Managerial capacity*: Adequate capacity of financial sectors such as banking and financial transactions, including actuarial and managerial arrangement, is essential for the success of SHI schemes.
- *Transparent policy debates*: For the success of SHI, a thorough political process of debates is required before any policy is adopted, especially the type of social health insurance, the level of the premium, what proportion of contribution to be made by the government, employers and employees, what are the benefit packages, how to contain costs, who are the providers and how they are paid, and what are the total financial returns, etc.
- *Globalization and liberalization of multilateral trade and commerce*: There are increasing concerns that liberalization of multilateral trade and commerce in services, especially promoting foreign competition in the financial and health sectors through Multilateral Trade Agreements like TRIPS Agreement and General Agreement on Trade in Services (GATS) could pose risks to equity, access to health services, and the quality of health care. However, countries could easily handle these concerns through appropriate rules and regulations. Governments can regulate 'the private insurance market including those financial institutions handling private/ commercial health insurance, by ensuring that they offer supplementary to basic minimum health care packages. It should also be ensured that they are not "dump" high-cost patients on the public health care systems and that they ease the exclusion criteria and encouraging them to ease exclusion criteria.
- *Democratization and decentralization*: Even though SHI schemes do not have the widest coverage in least developed countries, experience shows that they could consolidate, expand, and catalyze various local-level community-based health insurance schemes and transform other community-based health financing schemes to expand risk sharing. Within the context of democratization and decentralization, there could be fewer hurdles in administrative and managerial capacity and financial capability.
- *Institutional arrangements*: Establishment of appropriate institutions to be responsible for governance, technical skill

development and administrative and management capacity as well as monitoring and evaluation SHI schemes is vital.

- *Time implications*: Experience indicates that more than two to three decades are needed to reach the target of universal coverage. Appropriate strategic development plans are required, as most countries of the Region would take several decades to achieve universal coverage.[12]

India introduced the Employees' State Insurance Scheme (ESIS) in 1948, as part of the mandatory social security benefit to workers in the formal employed sectors (earlier to all power-using non-seasonal industrial establishments employing 10 or more people, and later extended to cover employees in all non-power using factories with 20 or more people, including people working in service sectors like hotels and restaurants, cinema houses, road transport and newspaper printing, but not covering people working in mines and plantations or any other establishments offering health care as good as or better than ESIS package). The scheme now covers more than 33 million employees and retirees. The pre-payment contribution is based on the proportion of pay-roll tax by employees (1.75 per cent), employers (4.75 per cent) and state governments (12.5 per cent). ESIS provides health care from its own network of health establishments, and if not accessible, the members are entitled for reimbursement for fee-for-services.

India also established a Central Government Health Scheme (CGHS) in 1954, providing comprehensive health care to employees of the Central Government (Civil Servants) and their families. The premium is progressive with salary scales ranging from Rupees 15 to 150 per month. The beneficiaries include nearly 4.5 million central government civil servants and their families.

Since 1986, the General Insurance Corporation (GIC) of India, a public sector undertaking, along with its subsidiaries, has offered various voluntary health insurance schemes (*Mediclaim Plan and others*), usually as health riders to other insurance packages. Some national and private commercial establishments have created their own health facilities in order to provide basic and specialist health care packages and they have created their own "reimbursement of health expenses" to employees. Since 1995, a series of private insurance companies, as major parts of larger insurance corporations or financial institutions, have introduced specialized private health insurance schemes, with a lot of adverse selection criteria.

In addition, the central and state governments have initiated a series of initiatives for expanding social health insurance coverage for target vulnerable groups, such as family planning acceptors, people below the poverty line, etc. with the aim of providing financial protection to the poor. Some state governments have established a multitude of community-based health insurance schemes with an estimated coverage of 30-50 million people.[13]

The main reasons for adopting the SHI scheme, in general, are:

(a) It can provide a stable source of revenue for health care.

(b) It would ensure self-reliance financing of health care compared to loans, grants and other external sources.

(c) The flow of funds into the health sector is visible.

(d) It can assist in establishing patients' rights as customers.

(e) It combines risk pooling with mutual support, by allocating services according to need, and distributing financial burden according to the ability to pay.

(f) It can operate within government health policy goals, yet maintain a degree of independence.

(g) It can be associated with efficient provision of health services.

(h) It solves equity and affordability of health care financing contribution which private health insurance fails to facilitate.[14]

RECENT DEVELOPMENT: HEALTH INSURANCE FOR UNORGANIZED SECTOR IN INDIA

For workers in the unorganized sector, social security is an alien concept. But the government took a small step towards improving their lot by announcing the guidelines of a health insurance scheme for those who live below the poverty level or on Rs. 12 per day.

Once implemented, the Rashtriya Swastha Bima Yojana (RSBY) would cover 1.2 crore families, comprising husband, wife and three children, in the first year, beginning 2008.

The families would be covered for Rs. 30,000 per year and they would access the insurance through smart cards. The card would hold good for migrating workers as well.

Under the scheme, all existing diseases would be covered. Hospitalization, surgery and daycare services would also be covered. The Centre (75 per cent) and the State (25 per cent) would share the cost. "In the first year, the cost is expected to be Rs. 751.50 crore. But provisioning for social welfare schemes will not derail fiscal deficit targets for this year and the next fiscal. We will adhere to the 3.3% target of fiscal deficit," said Finance Minister P. Chidambaram while unveiling the programme, along with Labour Minister, Oscar Fernandes.

Chidambaram said that states would implement the scheme. Over the next six months, state governments are expected to finalize details of the scheme. They will identify hospitals, public and private and insurance providers. It would also be the responsibility of the state administration to verify the eligibility of BPL families.

Keeping in mind that there are nearly 40 crore workers in the unorganized sector, it is surely a small beginning.[15]

Bill for Unorganized Sector

Eleven Schemes for unorganized labour form the core of the Unorganized Sector Social Security Bill, 2007.

The Bill envisages advisory boards at national and state levels with representation from all stakeholders. These Boards will advise on future projects to be taken up for unorganized labour. The Aam Admi Bima Yojana, the National Old Age Pension Scheme and a Health Insurance Scheme for Below Poverty Line (BPL) families are among the schemes included in the Bill.

Under the Aam Admi Bima Yojana, all the rural landless households would be provided life and disability insurance cover. The cover will be Rs. 75,000 on death/permanent disability due to accident. In case of partial disability, it would be Rs. 37,500. Upon the death of a member, prior to the terminal date, Rs. 30,000 will be the insurance amount. The premium charged would be Rs. 200 per year of which 50 per cent will be contributed by the Centre and the remaining by states.

The National Old Age Pension Scheme would be extended to all BPL persons, above 65 years. A pension of Rs. 200 would be provided and states will be requested to add another Rs. 200. An amount of more than Rs. 4,000 crore per year will spent under the scheme which will be administered by the Ministry of Rural Development.

A Health Insurance Scheme has been formulated for BPL workers and will cover six crore families, progressively in the next five years. In all, more than 30 crore workers will be benefited. Each family would be entitled to health care worth Rs. 30,000 per year. During the first year the scheme would incur an expenditure of about Rs. 700 crore and this will go up to more than Rs. 3,500 crore by the end of five years when all the six crore BPL families would be covered.

A provision has been made for issuing smart cards to each of these families, which would carry a unique identification number. Both public and private health facilities will be utilized for providing medical services and there would be cashless transactions to ensure that there is no harassment of the beneficiaries.

The Bill also envisages setting up of advisory boards at the national and state levels having representation from all the stakeholders.

CONCLUSION

It is important to emphasize the need to attend to the process of health financing reform and its related transitions because such a reform requires changes in institutions, management, accountability mechanisms and population behaviours that take time and resources. SHI is not merely a new method to collect money to co-finance services. It is a method that can achieve stable financing for a package of health services (health insurance benefits), while at the same time achieving greater access to health care for the population. While SHI is a promising alternative source of financing in order to promote equity and efficiency, it cannot be the main solution to bridge the gaps of financial resources required for additional health funding. SHI schemes are not a panacea or remedy to replace other mechanisms or forms of health care financing, particularly financing based on general tax revenue. The government should not shirk its responsibility to ensure and regulate the provision of health care including essential public health functions, whether directly or by public or private health care providers.

We should take care of the following facts:

1. Poverty—People in General cannot afford to pay the contribution to social insurance. They even cannot maintain their basic needs.
2. Government in developing countries is also starved of funds as they are spending already on health institutions. In addition, the Government lacks clarity and will.
3. There is a lot of corruption in health institutions.
4. The quantity and quality of service available is very poor and disgusting.
5. People are not treated with courtesy and respect.
6. Services are not prompt.

From the above discussions, it is clear that Social Insurance may not be suitable to our country. What is needed is to make the existing health infrastructure at Primary, Secondary and tertiary levels responsive, efficient, citizen centric and provide decent health care services. More attention in Government-run institutions may be gives to poor, women, children and the aged.

Universal Health Insurance Scheme (UHIS)

The four public sector general insurance companies have been implementing Universal Health Insurance Scheme for improving the access of health care to poor families. The scheme provides the reimbursement of medical expenses upto Rs. 30,000 towards hospitalization floated amongst the entire family, death cover due to an accident for Rs. 25,000 to the earning head of the family and compensation due to loss of earning of the earning member @ Rs. 50 per day upto maximum of 15 days. The Universal Health Insurance Scheme (UHIS) has been redesigned targeting only the BPL families. The premium subsidy has been enhanced from Rs. 100 to Rs. 200 for an individual, Rs. 300 for a family of five and Rs. 400 for a family of seven, without any reduction in benefits.[16]

My recent visit the China in 2007 found that people in villages are running co-operative health service, which is efficient in operations. We may follow the Chinese Pattern. It may also be observed that an excellent infrastructure for health exists in India. Whatever we are spending on this infrastructure is going waste largely. Why can we not make it efficient? Without injecting efficiency in Health Care system, even Social Health Insurance would be farce. Swami Ranganathananda rightly feels:

It is in this context that the problems of administrative efficiency in our newly established democracy become urgent. That efficiency is to be measured by only one test, namely, its dynamic responsiveness to the national urges. This is achieved only by the administrative personnel, representing a cross-section of the national intelligentsia, getting trained in imaginative sympathy and national dedication. It is self-centeredness and lack of concern for others that lead to corruption; and that evil is already afflicting man and society alike in India. We are not required to forego all concern for ourselves and become ascetics. We are only called upon to put this concern for ourselves in the context of a larger concern for others. This changes the whole aspect of our life and work. This is called enlightened self-interest in political philosophy. It is self-interest, but with a touch of spiritual enlightenment, resulting in the recognition of mutuality, inter-dependence and the spirit of service, as the truth of all healthy social processes.[17]

We are now experimenting on human welfare, human development, in our country. We had never done it before on the colossal scale that we are doing today. We had the necessary philosophy and ideas; but the implementation was arrested in later centuries. Therefore, the stress today should be on practical implementation, faster and still faster, and watching a new India, healthy and strong, rising on the horizon. This should be the great watchword of all administration in the Centre and the States, down to the zilla parishad and gram panchayat institutions, in our country.[18]

The existing health machinery run by Government with more finances can meet the needs of people. Since the introduction of user charges, more funds are available. Which must be spent efficiently.

World Health Organization also recommended Social Insurance for the poor. The key challenge are low and inefficient investment in health, high levels of out-of-pocket expenditure and substantial inequities in financial access to health care. To meet these challenges, a consultative strategy on health care financing was developed in collaboration with the Western Pacific Region for 2006-10. The consultative process identified the following core and functional strategies for countries of the SEA Region for universal financial coverage.

Core and Functional Strategies of Universal Financial Coverage

Core Strategies:

- Increasing investment in health, particularly public spending in areas that address the public health needs of the poor;
- Establishing social protection in health, especially for the poor, through effective financing mechanisms based on pre-payment, risk pooling and cross-subsidies; and
- Securing sustainability in financing efforts, including reliance on domestic sources.

Functional Strategies:

- Supporting the review of health expenditure in countries;
- Exploring/piloting innovative financing within broader social protection in the longer term; and
- Assisting in support mechanisms for sustaining core strategies, e.g. capacity building, legislation and regulation.[19]

Planning Commission, Government of India, New Delhi, in its Document, 'Towards Faster and More Inclusive Growth', An approach to the 11th Five Year Plan Suggests:

Financing Health Services

Energizing health systems involves additional government expenditure. The existing level of government expenditure on health in India is just under 1 percent, which is unacceptably low, and effort should be made to increase the total expenditure at the Centre and the states to 2-3% of GDP. This must be accompanied by innovative financing mechanisms, which incentivize performance. The quality of publicly supplied healthcare depends on how healthcare providers are paid. Providers should be paid only if they actually perform a service or satisfy the customer (the patient or the village health committee). Such systems linking payment to performance will increase accountability and should be encouraged.

The 11th Plan should experiment with different systems of private-public partnership, of which many examples already exists in some states. We could explore the possibility of an entitlement system for pregnant women to have professionally supervised deliveries. This will empower them to exercise choice, as well as create competition in the health service sector. Contracting out well-specified and delimited projects such as immunization can help enhance accountability. This does not mean that the state will withdraw from the health sector. Studies across the country have shown that expenditure on healthcare is a primary cause of indebtedness. Due to inadequate and non-performing public health infrastructure, the poor are forced to approach private practitioners who charge exorbitant fees. It is thus vital to ensure access to functioning public sector healthcare facilities.

Experience has shown that severe ill health can lead to disastrous outcomes for individuals and their families especially for the poor. These problems are best handled by health insurance. Community Based Health Insurance (CBHI) is emerging as a promosing concept and existing experience in different states has shown that well managed pre-payment systems with risk pooling are effective in protecting the poor from impoverishment due to high medical costs during catastrophic health events. CBHI initiatives based on some individual contributions to the premium, plus a government subsidy, deserve to be supported, as they would improve the quality of healthcare and expand the healthcare interventions as per requirements. We also need to look at alternative approaches such as comprehensive risk pooling packages through the public system and through accredited private providers. This is possibly an area where multiple experiments need to be encouraged so that we can come to firmer conclusions about what model will work best.[20]

Notes and References

1. The World Health 2002, Reducing Risks, Promoting Healthy Life, Annex Table 5, 2002.
2. Social Health Insurance, *op. cit*, pp. 23-24.
3. Carrin G. *et al*, Social Health Insurance Development in low-income developing countries Building Social Security: the challenge of privatization, X. Scheil-Adlung (ed.). Transactions Publication, London 2001.
4. This model of health care financing is popularly known as "Bismarck Model" that is applied in most EU countries like Germany, Belgium, Austria and Netherlands (based on a system of entitlement to health insurance on employment status and payment of contributions).
5. There is some fundamental difference of "prepaid" or "prepayment" for insurance with other "prepaid" services like "prepaid telephone card" or "prepaid goods." The money spent for the goods or services by the consumers in such cases is limited to the amount prepaid, whereas, in health insurance, the goods/services received by the consumer might get will be costing many times the actual value prepaid. The term "insurance contribution" may be better used than "prepaid." (Personal communication with Professor T. Hasbullah).
6. WHO, The World Health Report, 2000, *Health systems: Improving performance*, WHO, Geneva, 2000.
7. The general revenue-based or tax-funded health care financing model is popularly known as "Beveridge Model", applied by western European countries like Denmark, UK, Ireland, Italy, Portugal, Spain, and Sweden.
8. Social Health Insurance, *op. cit.*, pp. 27-29.
9. "Purchasing" refers to the transfer of pooled resources to service providers on behalf of the population for which funds are pooled. It means not only to include explicit purchases from public and private entities, but also to include management processes that allocate funds to providers within public agencies.
10. See UK Foreign and Commonwealth Office, "Raising the Standards: Britain's Citizen's Charter and Public Service Reform, London, Citizens' Charter Unit, November, 1992, p. 6.
11. Social Health Insurance, *op. cit.*, pp. 24-25.
12. Social Health Insurance, *op. cit.*, pp. 55-59.
13. Social Health Insurance, WHO, 40th Meeting of CCPDM, New Delhi, 4-5 September 2003, p. 31.
14. Modified from Normand, C. and Weber A, Social Health Insurance: A Guide for Planning, WHO/ILO 1994 (WHO/SHS/NHP/94.3), p. 15.
15. Health Insurance for unorganized sector in India, *Hindustan Times*, Oct. 2007.
16. Annual Report, 2006-07, Ministry of Finance, Government of India, p. 56.
17. Swami Ranganathananda, "Democratic Administration in the light of Practical Vedanta, p. 21.
18. *Ibid., op. cit.*, p. 75.
19. WHO: Regional Office for South-East Asia, The Work of WHO in South-East Asia Region, Report of the Regional Director, 1st July 2006-30 June 2007, New Delhi, 2007, p. 60.
20. Planning Commission, GOI, New Delhi, in its document, "Towards Faster and More Inclusive Growth, pp. 68-69.

Health Financing in India through Private Insurance

MAJOR CONCERNS AND FUTURE CHALLENGES

Although Singapore has come a long way in improving its health indicators and standards of medical service, many concerns and challenges remain. These include:

- Increasing costs of providing health care as a result of advances in medical knowledge and technology, leading to increased specialization and sub-specialization and greater use of medical technology.
- Rising expectations and demand for better and more sophisticated health services by an increasingly well-informed and more affluent public.
- Rapid aging of the population, with the portion of people 60 years and above estimated to increase from 9 percent at present to 25 per cent by 2030.
- Shortage of staff such as nurses and health therapists, as young people become more attracted to less demanding jobs than those in the health care services.[1]

From these figures one can easily realize that Private Health Insurance is the only way to provide quality health care for those who can pay premium. Health Insurance is found to grow at a fast rate with many companies entering the field.

Financing of Health Services—Private Insurance

Like all forms of insurance, health insurance is a system of protection against financial loss. In a health insurance system a group of individuals

CHART 10.1

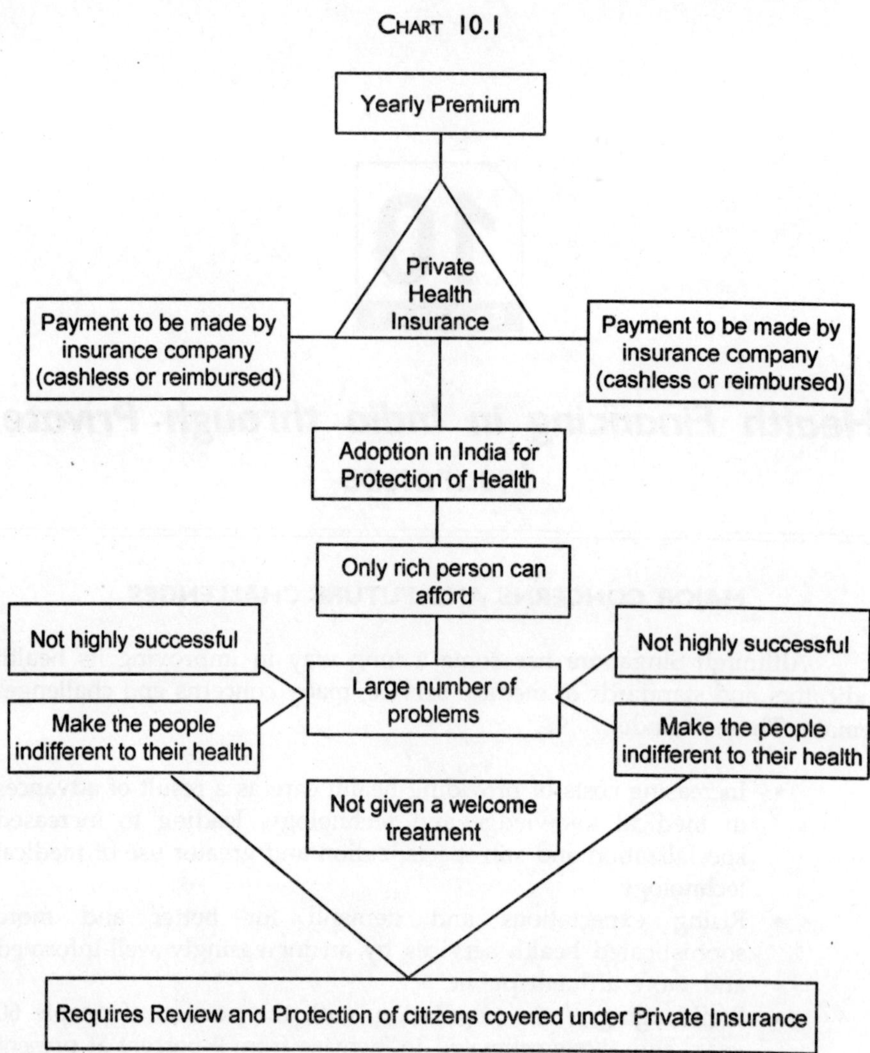

agree to pay certain sums for a guarantee that they will be compensated for costs related to the use of specific kinds of health care. Formal health insurance contracts typically stipulate the covered health care services must be medically necessary and provided by appropriately trained health care professionals. Because health providers generally prefer to see patients who are insured rather than risk non-payment for care, in many countries having health insurance (private or public) is equated with having access to health care.

The premise of health insurance is simple: individual health care needs can be unpredictable and costly, but relatively few people need health care at any particular time. Thus, by pooling the risk of large health care expenditures over many people, health insurance can make necessary health care affordable to all.[2]

The rich population of developing and developed countries as well as employees engaged in well off and multinational companies are resorting to private health insurance to avoid the delays and poor health services available in Public Sector. Private Health Insurance provides quick and quality health service through A Grade hospitals in the private sector. Many multinational companies employ doctors in various specializations to provide quality services within the premises of the company. For example, in India, there has been mushroom growth of good hospitals in the private sector. Hence, people who can afford better health services or their employers can provide them better private health insurance. The private insurance is becoming popular in India as well among rich class.

In a nation like India, where there is no worthwhile social security system in place (notwithstanding high tax rates) healthcare and health insurance assume magnified importance. Without this, even the loudest screams and chest thumping on the 'India growth story' will sound hollow. The private sector has an estimated premium potential of over Rs. 4,500 crore. This is found to increase.

One of the fastest growing and most potent sectors in India is the health-care sector: India is fast becoming a preferred medical destination for patients in the Middle East, Africa and even the West.

There is now growing global realization that Indian hospitals can provide world-class care at competitive rates. Today, India has big names of healthcare like the All India Institute of Medical Sciences (AIIMS), Apollo Hospitals and Shankara Netralaya.

Permissible depreciation rates for medical equipment under income tax laws have been increased to enhance cash flows of corporate hospitals in the private sector. Interest on lending for private sector hospitals exceeding 100 beds will improve access to low-cost funding for hospitals.

Notwithstanding healthy competition, several big corporate houses have ventured in and the Indian healthcare sector is slowly but surely, coming of age. The entry of big pharmaceutical companies is a clear sign of strong corporate focus on this sector.[3]

Fueled by rising incomes and growing dissatisfaction with publicly financed (and often publicly delivered) health care services, private insurance coverage typically begins among large company managers in white-collar industries, and in multinational companies with large numbers of employees. However, informal insurance arrangements exist even in the poorest countries, reflecting a universal desire for financial protection and, in some countries, access to better-quality health care than is offered in the public system.[4]

Even in India, persons from business community or private employment are getting themselves insured through private insurance like mediclaim, ICICI Bank, HDFC Bank, etc. It is steadily becoming popular among the people.

To provide health insurance, private insurance companies would compete with one another to attract customers; people would pay the insurance premiums either out of their own income or as a fringe benefit from their employer; and the insurance company would determine the amount of the premium for each individual based on its assessment of the probability or risk of a claim by the individual concerned.[5]

A private insurance market can offer a number of advantages over a purely public system of health care financing. It can allow governments to develop and maintain smaller and targeted system of health care financing to serve people who do not have access to private insurance. Private insurance can help health care providers (private and public) rebuild infrastructure and amortize needed investment when government payments for health care are inadequate. In the best cases private insurance encourages health care system-both the financing and the delivery of care—to innovate and to become more efficient, and offers a point of reference for improving the quality and efficiency of care in the public system. Typically encumbered by politics and bureaucracy, governments may find it difficult to innovate without a private market to lead the way.[6]

The principal arguments in favour of this system relate to the criteria of quality and efficiency. As people would be free to choose their providers, doctors and hospitals that provided low-quality treatment for high prices would lose customers to those who provided better and/or cheaper services. For instance, a doctor who acquired a reputation for making wrong diagnoses, holding half-hearted consultations, or keeping patients waiting a long time would lose patients to other doctors who were known for their medical successes and ease of access. Similarly, a hospital that did not use cost-saving technology would have to charge higher prices than its more efficient competitors, and would eventually be driven out of business. Thus medical practitioners of all kinds would have a strong incentive to improve their standards of service and reduce their costs.

Furthermore, patients would have freedom of choice. People could choose the doctor, the hospital, and the treatment that suited them best. Doctors and hospital staff would be attentive to their patients' desires and preferences, knowing that their incomes depended on it. The result would be a system of health care financing and delivery that delivered high-quality care at the least possible cost: a system that was both macro-efficient and micro-efficient. Moreover, this private model would have advantages relating to some of the other criteria; namely, it would accord with the benefit principle of equity, because those who benefited would be those who paid, and it would not involve any administrative costs for the government, because the government would not be involved.[7]

In 2001 with entry of various private insurance companies now the customers have choice of buying this insurance from 14 insurance companies. The Companies, which offer Health or Mediclaim Insurance, are:

1. Apollo DKV Insurance Company Limited;
2. Bajaj Allianz General Insurance Company Limited;

3. Cholamandalam MS General Insurance Company Limited;
4. HDFC Chubb General Insurance Company Ltd.;
5. ICICI Lombard General Insurance Limited;
6. IFFCO Tokio General Insurance Company Limited;
7. National Insurance Company Limited;
8. New India Assurance Company Limited;
9. Oriental Insurance Company Limited;
10. Reliance General Insurance Company Limited;
11. Royal Sundram Alliance Insurance Company Limited;
12. Star Health and Allied Insurance Company Limited;
13. TATA AIG General Insurance Company Limited (Overseas Health Insurance only); and
14. United India Insurance Company Limited.

Health insurance companies are offering innovative products to their customers these days. The latest product in this line is cashless hospitalization. Here individuals do not have to pay for their hospital bills in case of hospitalization; the insurance company settles the bill directly. But certain conditions like the hospital needs to have a tie-up with the insurance company, the documents need to be in order, etc. have to be met.

Leading a happy life, involves good planning for your health. Accidents happen and you need to be prepared for such situations. In times of high health cost, you need to get covered for health risks.

Viju, B. in his article, "Medical bills swell under cashless insurance cover," discuss the state of affairs of Private Health Insurance.

Vijay Kothari was admitted to a Mahim hospital for two days for a piles operation. The hospital said the total expenses amounted to Rs. 2.5 lakh. A shocked Kothair protested and after several rounds of bargaining the bill was brought down to Rs. 1.7 lakh. Not that it mattered to Kothari; he was covered under a cashless insurance policy and the insurance firm would pick up the tab.

Sheetal Patil was admitted with viral fever to a South Mumbai hospital. Three days later when she was discharged she got a rude shock when presented with a bill of Rs. 1.5 lakh.

These are merely two random examples of private hospital and nursing homes charging exorbitant amounts the moment they discover patients are insured under a cashless scheme. Insurance firms say that ever since they started facilitating cashless insurance cover under the Mediclaim policy there has been an upswing in the number of cases where patients have been charged unreasonably high fees for minor ailments and operations.

Patients under such cover can avail of treatment without depositing an advance since their claims are settled by an intermediate agency called the Third-Party Administrator (TPA).

Insurance companies on their part have passed the cost burden on to their customers, ensuring that the money is eventually recovered from the larger pool of clients. Several insurance companies have hiked the premium for cashless medical polices, making the consumer pay for private health-care's avarice and their own losses. Association of Hospitals spokesman Colonel Manish Masand, however, denied hospitals were issuing inflated bills in cashless transactions. "Bills may be higher than expected because of treatment needed for associated complications," he said.

"The hospital refused when I asked it for a copy of the detailed bill. Officials told me that the TPA would take of the claims," Kothari said. He then approached the director of the hospital and lodged a complaint. "The bill was brought down to Rs. 1.7 lakh after a protracted argument," Kothari said. There are instances galore of a different set of billing rules for insured patients in hospitals.

When Sunil Mehta's wife was admitted to a nursing home in Andheri, the doctor asked him whether she had a Mediclaim policy. The nursing home had two different rate-cards for insured and non-insured patients; it was okay to have a higher rate-card for insured patients, as they were not paying the money out of their pockets, the doctor explained.

There are eight insurance players in the market, four of them public sector, and insurance experts say the scam will easily run into hundreds of crores. "We recently got a bill for a surgery from a doctor. He charges Rs. 50,000 in one hospital and Rs. 1 lakh in another though both hospitals have the same facilities," an insurance official said.[8]

Insurance firms say that ever since they started facilitating cashless insurance cover under the Mediclaim policy there has been an upswing in the number of cases where patients have been charged high fees for minor operations.[9]

Despite these advantages, private insurance presents a number of problems. First, health insurance can be unaffordable for low-income people. In principle, governments can develop subsidies to help low-income people buy insurance, but such systems can be difficult to design and to administer. Second, insurers may want to deny coverage to people who are sick, and to limit coverage for high-cost conditions or services. By refusing people who are sick or by deterring them from seeking coverage, private insurance can contribute to higher average costs in public financing programs that enroll larger populations and serve as the insurer of last resort. The selection of low-cost patients into private insurance can cause serious problems for the public financing system (or the health care delivery system that it finances) if it cannot readily adjust to higher average costs-even when total costs decline. Governments can require private insurers to accept sick people, restrict how insurers price coverage, and require insurance plans to cover various types of high-cost health care. However, insurers may be unwilling to enter or remain in markets with such requirements.

Other problems with private insurance derive from the complexity of insurance contracts. Consumers typically do not understand many aspects of insurance contracts. Because consumers usually are unable to detect which insurers are unscrupulous or financially unsound, the market can attract these insurers. Consequently, insurance regulators play an essential role in stabilizing a competitive private insurance system. However insurance regulation is more art than science. It should encourage innovations that improve efficiency and service, but it must require financial integrity and discourage practices that threaten the stability and effectiveness of the health insurance system—and, in turn, the health care system that it supports.[10]

Group coverage

To limit the amount of adverse selection that can occur in a health insurance pool, many insurers prefer to insure people who have grouped themselves for reasons other than the purchase of insurance. Such groups typically include employees of a particular firm, members of a professional or trade association, or even members of a social organization. Many insurers require that the sponsoring organization pay a significant share (at least half) of the cost of coverage for group members to ensure that even the lowest-risk group member would find enrolling advantageous. Also, insurers may require that a minimum percentage of the group (for example, 80 per cent) enroll in the plan regardless of the sponsoring organization's contribution, further reducing the chance that adverse selection will occur within the group.[11]

Private Health Insurance is not popular in India:

1. People are poor and cannot afford high premium, which is beyond their means.
2. The premium is very high as compared to the benefits.
3. The hospitals where insurer can get the benefit do not provide adequate services. They try to inflate the bills and are highly expensive.
4. The contract agreed upon between the individuals and the private Insurance Company is made to the advantage of the Private Insurance Company.
5. Treatment is not adequate and the quality is poor.
6. There is very little regulations of Government to ensure quality health care.

Most health sector regulations in developing countries are weak, and regulatory structures (where they exist) are often un-enforced or inappropriate. Weak regulations discourage private insurance because there is a dearth of competent providers from whom to purchase health care services. Moreover, when payers and providers merge (as they do under managed care), regulations on the organization and delivery of health services have an increasing impact on health insurance regulation, its structure, and enforcement. Hence, although a separate issue, regulation of providers (hospitals, clinics, physicians, and other health professionals) has a direct bearing on health insurance regulations and the regulatory environment in general.

The lapses—either in terms of impeding growth of the private sector or allowing it free rein with no controls or policy signals from government-lead to an uncertain business environment and an inhospitable climate for private investment in health insurance.[12]

Disadvantages of Private Health Insurance

1. Private Health Insurance is not based on equity, i.e. according to the ability to pay. It also does not provide same treatment to all. The quality of treatment differs according to the premium paid for private health insurance. In this way, there is a lot of cheating by Private Health Insurance Companies.
2. It is difficult to measure the quality and efficiency as patients are not experts and hence get exploited. The model's quality and efficiency claims are also suspect. For a health care market to work in the way posited, consumers would have to have sufficient medical knowledge to assess quality, otherwise they would not be able to decide who was offering good treatment and who was offering poor treatment. In practice, for consumers to have the necessary information would be almost impossible. In consequence, they would be in no position to reward good providers and to penalize bad ones by shifting their customer from one to the other. Thus the engine of competition driving quality improvements would have broken down. Insofar as providers will compete with one another, competition will not be based on the quality of medical care as such, but on factors that are easily observable to consumers, such as the quality of "hotel" facilities in hospitals and well-publicized pieces of high-technology equipment.[13]
3. The hospitals would provide extra services, which is not required to inflate the bills as the bills are to be paid by the Private Insurance Company and not the patient. Moreover, the presence of poorly informed consumers gives doctors an incentive to increase their incomes by over treatment. This incentive is increased if patients are insured, because the doctor knows the insurance company will be paying, not the patient. This is the so-called moral hazard problem of insurance markets. Moral hazard is the phenomenon that once people are insured against an eventuality, their actions make it more likely to occur. It arises in the case of private health care, because neither doctors nor patients have any incentive to economize on treatment. The insured may visit the doctor for frivolous ailments; the doctor, secure in the knowledge that the patient does not have to pay, may recommend highly expensive

treatment. Both these factors may raise utilization and costs well beyond the efficient level.[14]

4. Administrate costs of Private Health Insurance companies are very high. There is a need of high publicity and employ agents and administrative staff to handle all the processes, which add to the cost.
5. Hospitals give priority to their regular patients as compared to insured people as they cannot go to any other place.
6. Behaviour of doctors towards insured is not sympathetic.

Private systems of health care are therefore likely: (a) to provide quality care in terms of easily observable factors, such as hotel facilities in hospitals, but not necessarily in terms of the quality of medical care; (b) to engage in over treatment, thus causing both macro-inefficiency and micro-inefficiency; and (c) to have large groups of uninsured people, thereby creating inequity. They are also likely to have high administrative costs and, especially for countries with a history of free care, to be politically difficult to implement. By contrast, private systems are likely to be technologically innovative and highly sensitive to consumers' desires and wants.[15]

Insurers can lower the price of a health insurance contract in four ways:

- By trying to insure only low-risk people, denying coverage to people who are sick, or excluding coverage for some conditions.
- By offering less coverage, limiting the scope or extent of covered services.
- By discouraging excessive use of covered health care services.
- By reducing the administrative costs of the plan.[16]

Private insurance provides greater freedom of choice to consumers and greater quality assurance. In order to attract larger population, especially the self-employed, there is a need to establish products with standard benefits and standard prices upon which insurance companies should compete. Some of the aspects which could make private insurance attractive is if it includes: (i) Outpatient treatment, maternal care, preventive care, chronic diseases and catastrophic illnesses; (ii) Assured renew ability and limited exclusions for pre-existing conditions; (iii) Fee structure for both the outpatient and inpatient treatment should be formalized and monitored; (iv) Individual rating of premiums should be avoided as much as possible; and (v) Indemnity insurance, for treatments with large payments, must be avoided.

Quality standards and treatment protocols should be made public and quality ratings of providers should be available. Proper monitoring and accreditation of private providers is required. Quality control system should also be followed-up with public providers when tie-ups with public providers are made.

Consumer redress mechanisms should be made simple and cheap. Sophisticated administrative infrastructure, uniform accounting procedures for hospitals, accurate clinical record system, computerized claim auditing, adequate health information, technical capacity to calculate premiums actuarially, know-how on underwriting methods to prevent adverse selection and risk selection, and procedures to detect fraud and abuse need to be developed. Regulations, reforms and a set-up of basic administrative structure are prior conditions to liberalize India's private health insurance market.[17]

Insurance mechanisms, however, are not without risks of market failure. Several characteristics of the health care market may lead to cost escalation:

- Information gaps between providers and patients may create incentives to provide more care than may be medically appropriate, especially in a regime of pure indemnity insurance. The information gaps make the patient, and insurers for that matter, less willing to question the doctor's recommendations (Arrow, 1963). The problem will be greater in situations in which the patient can choose his or her doctor and treatment freely and then present the bill to the insurer for reimbursement.
- Health insurance reduces the incentive of individuals to guard against poor health and thus tends to drive up demand for more expensive care. The covered individual may know that he or she is taking more risks, but the insurance company may not (the insurance term used for this information gap is "moral hazard)."
- Another information gap is that patients are likely to know much more about their health status and future needs than insurers. Thus, people expecting to incur significant health expenditures in the near future will figure disproportionately among those who choose to get insured (the insurance term used for this information gap factor is "adverse selection)."
- Without minimum capital reserves and incomplete epidemiological information about the population, which is the case in most developing countries, insurance companies risk long-term failure by guessing wrong and charging premiums that are too low in comparison to the benefits offered in a competitive environment.
- Empirical evidence exists that health spending per capita is positively associated with the proportion of the population covered by private insurance.

The contribution of an insurance scheme, whether public or private, to improving the quality of health care depends on whether the scheme is able to influence the licensing of medical personnel and facilities and the entry of highly skilled individuals into the health sector. For equity, the main concern is that private insurers will try to sell only to low-risk customers. But an expansion of private health insurance could eventually improve access to public facilities by those unable to get private insurance.[18]

Private (Voluntary) Health Insurance

Voluntary health insurance schemes for individual and corporations are available primarily through the General Insurance Corporation (GIC) of India and its four subsidiaries—and this essentially is a government owned monopoly. These schemes are financed from household and corporate funds. GIC offers Mediclaim policy for groups and individuals; Jan Arogya policy mainly covering poorer individual and families; and Bavishya Arogya policy covering individual and spouses for old age security...These policies are annual policies mainly covering hospitalized treatment and there are exclusions and pre-existing disease clauses. Furthermore, the scheme are of indemnity type, which makes it unattractive for many, and providers have to be paid by the insured who are in turn, reimbursed by the insurer. Premiums are risk rated according to age and individuals up the age of 75 can buy policies under Mediclaim and only up to age of 70 under Jan Arogya. Only policy available to provide insurance after 75 years of age is Bavishya Arogya of GIC and Senior Citizens Unit Plan of Unit Trust of India (UTI). The have to be bought between the ages of 18 to 55 for psot retirement benefits up to Rs. 50,000 for hospitalization coverage. These policies have had only limited success in India covering only 1.7 million people in 1998. Some of the innovations in these policies are no-claim bonus, group discounts (under Mediclaim), tax exemptions and no in-limits within the sum insurred for. Other schemes like overseas medical insurance and personal accident insurance also exist and some private insurance companies have recently started schemes to cover catastrophic illness. Asha Deep Policy of Life Insurance Corporation (LIC) covers individuals between ages 18 and 50 for four major ailments—cancer, paralytic stoke, renal failure and coronary artery disease.

Some of insurance schemes also work through community financing. Community financing can complement formal social security schemes that cover regularly employed or self employed, particularly in rural communities. Based on the review of some of the NGOs by Ford Foundation (1994) and Garg (2001).[19]

Medical Policy-holders may get claim on preexisting diseases too, "Our Bureau", Kolkata:

> Medical insurance policy-holders can now rejoice. Insurance companies are reviewing claims settlement norms in case of preexisting diseases. This means, insurers may soon no longer deprive mediclaim holders for claims under the clause of "non-disclosure of diseases."

Accordingly, policyholders who never underwent treatment nor showed symptoms of a disease before signing a policy document are likely to get the medical policy benefits in future.

At present, insurance companies often decline to settle insurance claims in case policyholders are diagnosed to have contracted the disease prior to the signing the mediclaim policy.

This is likely to change. The General Insurance Council of India, in consultation with all insurers, is working on the appropriate definition of preexisting disease. "Policy-holders who did not undergo any diagnosis or treatment or show indications of a disease prior to the signing of a contract should not be considered in the know of having any preexisting diseses," said Mr. B. D. Banerjee, a member of the committee, appointed by Insurance Regulatory and Development Authority (IRDA) for examining issues related to health insurance for senior citizens.

He was talking to reporters on the sidelines of an interactive session on health insurance, organized by Bengal Chamber of Commerce and Industry here on Saturday. The Seven-member committee is likely to submit its report by the first week of November, it is started to meet in Mumbai from October 9 to 11.

The insurance regulator was formed by the committee in May this year in the wake of a over 200% hike in premium for medical insurance policies after September 2006. The insurers increased the premium for senior citizens defying the regulator's advice not to hike it more than 70%.

Mr. Banerjee felt, "most private insurers turn down health policies to people aged above 60. Among the public sector insurers, only Oriental Insurance as of now does not offer health insurance policies to senior citizens. It has, however, applied for a policy for senior citizens to IRDA.

CONCLUSION

Private health insurance has both benefits and pitfalls relative to purely public financing systems. Private insurance can improve the availability and quality of health. It can help health care systems rebuild infrastructure and amortize needed investment when government financing for health care is inadequate. It can offer consumers a choice of providers, and thereby generate incentives that reward high-quality providers and penalize poor quality (at least as perceived by consumers). Similarly, private insurers are becoming increasingly adept at distinguishing efficient from inefficient providers, and can develop methods that systematically reward efficiency. (By contrast, public financing systems often reward efficiency and inefficiency alike). Finally, although private insurance can siphon off lower-cost people and leave the public sector with higher average costs, it can reduce the total financial burden on government.

Private health insurance offers benefits and costs to society. Its importance and applicability vary by country and culture, but in most countries it is well established. The challenge to governments is to regulate private insurance effectively: to assure the financial stability of insurers and the integrity of insurance contracts, and to strike a balance between the social acceptability of private insurance and insures' competitive drive toward economic efficiency.[20]

Notes and References

1. Kai Hong Phua, "Medical Savings Accounts and Health Care Financing in Singapore", World Bank Discussion Paper No. 365, March 10-11, 1997, p. 249.
2. Deborah J. Chollet and Maureen Lewis, "Private Insurance: Principles and Practice," World Bank Discussion Paper No. 365, March 10-11, 1997, p. 78.
3. "AK-NOMICS," Health is Wealth, in *Hindustan Times*, September 17, 2007.
4. Deborah J. Chollet and Maureen Lewis "Private Insurance: Principles and Practice, World Bank Discussion Paper No. 365, March 10-11, 1997, p. 77.
5. Julian Le Grand, London School of Economics and Political Science, "Financing Health Care", Economic Development Institute of the World Bank, Implementation Health Sector Reform in Central Asia, p. 78
6. Deborah J. Chollet and Maureen Lewis, "Private Insurance: Principles and Practice, World Bank Discussion Paper No. 365, March 10-11, 1997, p. 77.
7. Julian Le Grand, Financing Health Care, in Implementing Health Sector Reform in Central Asia, Economic Development Institute of the World Bank, Washington D.C., 1999, p. 78.
8. Viju B. in his article, in Newspaper, *The Times of India*, New Delhi, Wednesday, Sept. 19, 2007, p. 13.
9. *Ibid.*, in newspaper, *The Times of India*, p. 13.
10. Deborah J. Chollet and Maureen Lewis, "Private Insurance: Principles and Practice, World Bank Discussion Paper No. 365, March 10-11, 1997, p. 77.
11. *Ibid.*, p. 83.
12. *Ibid.*, pp. 100-01.
13. Julian Le Grand, Financing Health Care, p. 78.
14. *Ibid.*, *op. cit.*, pp. 78-79.
15. *Ibid.*, *op. cit.*, p. 79.
16. Deborah J. Chollet and Maureen Lewis, "Private Insurance: Principles and Practice," World Bank Discussion Paper No. 365, March 10-11, 1997, p. 81
17. Charu C. Garg, "Is Health Insurance Feasible in India?: Issues in Private and Social Health Insurance, Securing Health for All Dimensions and Challenges, pp. 447-48.
18. Better Health Systems for India's Poor, World Bank, 2002, Human Development Network, Financing Health, pp. 245-46.
19. Charu, C. Garg, Is Health Insurance Feasible in India? Issues in Private and Social Health Insurance, Securing Health for All, Dimensions and Challenges, eds., Sujata Prasad and C. Satyananda, pp. 433-34.
20. Better Health Systems for India's Poor, Human Development Network, Financing Health, *op. al.*, pp. 101 and 103.

Appendix 10.1
Health Insurance Experiment

Karnataka Health System Development and Reform Project received a credit from World Bank to implement Health Insurance in Karnataka. During the Project preparation the GOK expressed strong interest in expanding Health Insurance for the poor in the state possibly through additional subsidies through the development of new schemes. However, development of the large Health Insurance schemes for the state is rendered difficult due to the lack of sufficient knowledge of appropriate benefit design and implementation, to provide comprehensive coverage to the poor and rural population. As such it was agreed that the KHSDRP would finance a significant Health Insurance Experiment, which could help fill the major knowledge gaps and provide valuable experience in how to develop and implement health insurance for the poor. The Health Insurance Experiment will develop and test several different models of HI designs and implementation including variations in the benefit package, household contribution and subsidies.

Objectives

General Objective

To improve the health status, access to health care and financial security of poor rural families in Karnataka.

Specific Objectives

- To design and implement a health insurance experiment intended to provide a significant package of financial protection against health expenditures related to hospitalization and primary care to approximately two million vulnerable individuals in selected rural areas of Karnataka over a period of two-three years.
- To develop and test several different models of insurance design and implementation, including variations in benefit package, household contributions and subsidies, and scheme administration.
- To thoroughly document the technical analysis and implementation process steps and lessons learned in developing a rural health insurance project in India.
- To rigorously evaluate the schemes in terms of impact on health services' utilization, health indicators, poverty, and labor force effects through a combination of appropriate implementation design, periodic surveys, and routine monitoring.
- To use the resulting documentation and analysis to strengthen health financing policy in Karnataka, India, and the wider international health community.

The Current Situation in Karnataka in Terms of Health Insurance

There are a number of schemes currently being implemented in Karnataka to provide health insurance or similar types of financial risk protection for health-related events. Some of the main ones include:

Yeshashvini

This is self-standing group benefit scheme run by a non-profit trust (the Yeshashvini Trust) which is closely linked to the state Department of Cooperatives. The scheme is in its fourth year of operation but has experienced stagnant enrollment in the last two years. When launched in 2003, Yeshashvini enrolled something over 1.6 million members, which then expanded to 2.02 million in year 2. Enrollment fell to 1.47 million in the third year and increased again to 1.85 million in year four.[1] The scheme initially collected a premium of Rs. 60 per person, which was supplemented by a premium contribution from the Dept. of Cooperatives of Rs. 30, totaling Rs. 90 per person. The benefits are primarily surgical, in approved network hospitals. The scheme has set-up a network of 100+ hospitals around the state, mostly private institutions. Members are also entitled to free ambulatory care visits (no consultation charge) in those same hospitals. Membership is open only to cooperative society members. In general, premia are paid by the cooperative society on behalf of all its members, rather than by individuals or families enrolling. During its first year, the scheme had a significant surplus, but in its second year claims rates increased significantly.[2] In 2004, the premium was raised to a total of Rs. 120 per person and the state government de-linked its contribution from enrolments, switching to a lump-sum subsidy. In later years, the scheme has been looking for additional revenue sources, such as a tax on profitable cooperative societies and charitable donation.

NGO-run micro-insurance schemes

There are a number of schemes run by NGOs at community-level or higher, which provide risk coverage for health. These schemes use a range of different models include freestanding group benefit approach, and also working through established insurance companies and third party administrators (TPAs).

Mediclaim

A number of insurance companies offer *mediclaim* type policies, primarily in urban areas. Benefits under these policies are predominantly administered by TPAs, in keeping with the prevailing regulations.

UHIS

In July, 2005, the Department of Health, GoK launched its own program to expand coverage of UHIS and to supplement the premium

1. International Labour Organization, "Yeshashvini Cooperative Farmers' Health Scheme: A typical example of adverse selection", New Delhi, Feb. 2007.
2. The reason for increased claims, both frequency and severity, has been attributed to increasing awareness about the scheme on part of the members.

subsidy provided by the national government. The 2005-06 budget envisaged premium subsidy to approximately 250,000 households statewide. The subsidy was to be provided to SC/ST households' below-poverty line with women members who belong to Self-help Groups (SHGs). The program was administered through United Insurance Company, a public sector insurance company and a TPA, Family Health Plan, which also administers the Yeshashvini scheme. The scheme was marketed through the existing government health and nutrition infrastructure that is using Anganwadi workers, ANMs, PHC staff, etc. Results were very disappointing; with environment only a fraction of what was expected. In 2007 the GoK abandoned the scheme.

The SKDRDP [Shree Kshetra Dharmasthala Rural Development Project]

The SKDRDP [Shree Kshetra Dharmasthala Rural Development Project] is a rural development project in the coastal belt of Karnataka spanning Uttar Kannada, Udipi and Dakshina Kannada. It is a rural livelihood support project run by the Dharmasthala Temple Trust, where all low income farmers, landless agricultural workers in the target area covered (mostly BPL population) with total membership 4.2 lakh individuals (about 40% of members of the trust). This hospitalization benefit provides upto Rs. 5000 coverage per member; floating coverage for family with no limit on number of episodes of utilization including maternity and pre-existing diseases. There is no TPA, but the trust enjoys a lot of goodwill that allowed it to network with providers, which include about 40-50 private hospitals that are regularly monitored by trust representatives.

Design of the Health Insurance Experiment under KHSDRP

General design considerations

The primary focus of the insurance experiment is to provide financial protection for poor rural families in the face of unexpected health care costs to provide coverage to prevent "catastrophic" health expenditure at the household level.

Out-of-pocket spending in India is high. About two thirds of this spending is for outpatient care and drugs, and one-third for hospitalization-related expenses. Hospitalization-related expenses are much less frequent and much larger when they do occur. Also, some share of spending reported as drug purchases and diagnostics is probably also related to hospitalization, since it is not unusual for hospitals to require patients to purchase additional supplies and tests. Hospitalization is the most important cause of large financial impacts on households and so will be the main focus of the health insurance experiment. One option under the experiment will allow households to combine hospitalization benefits with outpatient/primary care benefits. Household data from India indicate that the poor are much more likely to be seriously affected by high household, spending than the non-poor. However, they also show that the poor use less hospital services than the non-poor, which likely reflects their response to the risks of high spending. This non-use of services is also a cost to the poor, with effects on household's health and therefore their economic status.

Reaching the poor with health insurance is a difficult challenge. First, their ability to pay for health insurance is very limited. This requires that premiums be subsidized. Second, the poor pose additional risks to the viability of a health insurance scheme. They tend to be sicker, may have more pre-existing conditions, which are often excluded from traditional insurance products, and because of their chronic under use of services may experience a larger increase in demand under insurance than the non-poor population. They may also perceive significant benefit from types of coverage often excluded, such as maternity-related benefits. This requires that any insurance scheme targeting the poor must be prepared to compensate for higher than average benefit payout. Third, the poor may know and understand less about insurance, and may be more difficult to reach with information and administrative services. This requires that a scheme plan for increased marketing and distribution costs, and consider innovative strategies such as enrolment of groups, like village self-help groups, rather than individuals.

The health insurance experiment will incorporate strategies to address all these concerns.

- The core benefit package will cover hospitalization-related expenses. The experiment will augment this with alternatives for benefits of high perceived value (like maternity benefits), higher levels of financial coverage, and coverage for ambulatory care expenses.
- The insurance products will be subsidized significantly to enable the poor to purchase them. Financing will be provided to cover pre-existing conditions and to support additional marketing and administration costs.
- After initial discussions it was tentatively agreed that subsidies will be targeted to the official "below-poverty-line" (BPL) population. However, more precise criteria to identify the poor who will receive a subsidy to their premium are still being discussed. Products will be available to the non-poor population without subsidy.
- Enrollment will be voluntary, but the experiment will explore strategies to encourage group enrolment, like that of federation of self-help groups at village level.
- Geographic coverage will be limited to no more than three to five districts, to enable the experiment to benefit from economies of scale in administration and management.

Source: Dr. G.Y. Nagaraj, Joint Director (Health Insurance), Karnataka Health System Development Reform Programme: Orientation Workshop, pp. 45-49.

Employees' State Insurance Corporation

ESTABLISHMENT OF EMPLOYEES' STATE INSURANCE CORPORATION

(1) With effect from 1st October 1948 as the Central Government, by notification in the Official Gazette has established for the administration of the scheme of employees' state insurance in accordance with the provisions of this Act a Corporation to be known as the Employees' State Insurance Corporation. The Corporation is a body corporate by the name of Employees' State Insurance Corporation having perpetual succession and a common seal and shall by the said name sue and be used.

Constitution of Corporation

The Corporation shall consist of the following members, namely:-

[(a) a Chairman to be [appointed] by the Central Government;
(b) a Vice-Chairman to be [appointed] by the Central Government;
(c) not more than five persons to be [appointed] by the Central Government;
(d) one person each representing each of the [States] in which this Act is [in force] to be [appointed] by the State Government concerned;
(e) one person to be [appointed] by the Central Government to represent the [Union Territories];
(f) [ten] persons representing employers to be [appointed] by the Central Government in consultation with such organizations of employers as may be recognized for the purpose by the Central Government;
(g) [ten] persons representing employees to be [appointed] by the Central Government in consultation with such organizations of

CHART 11.1

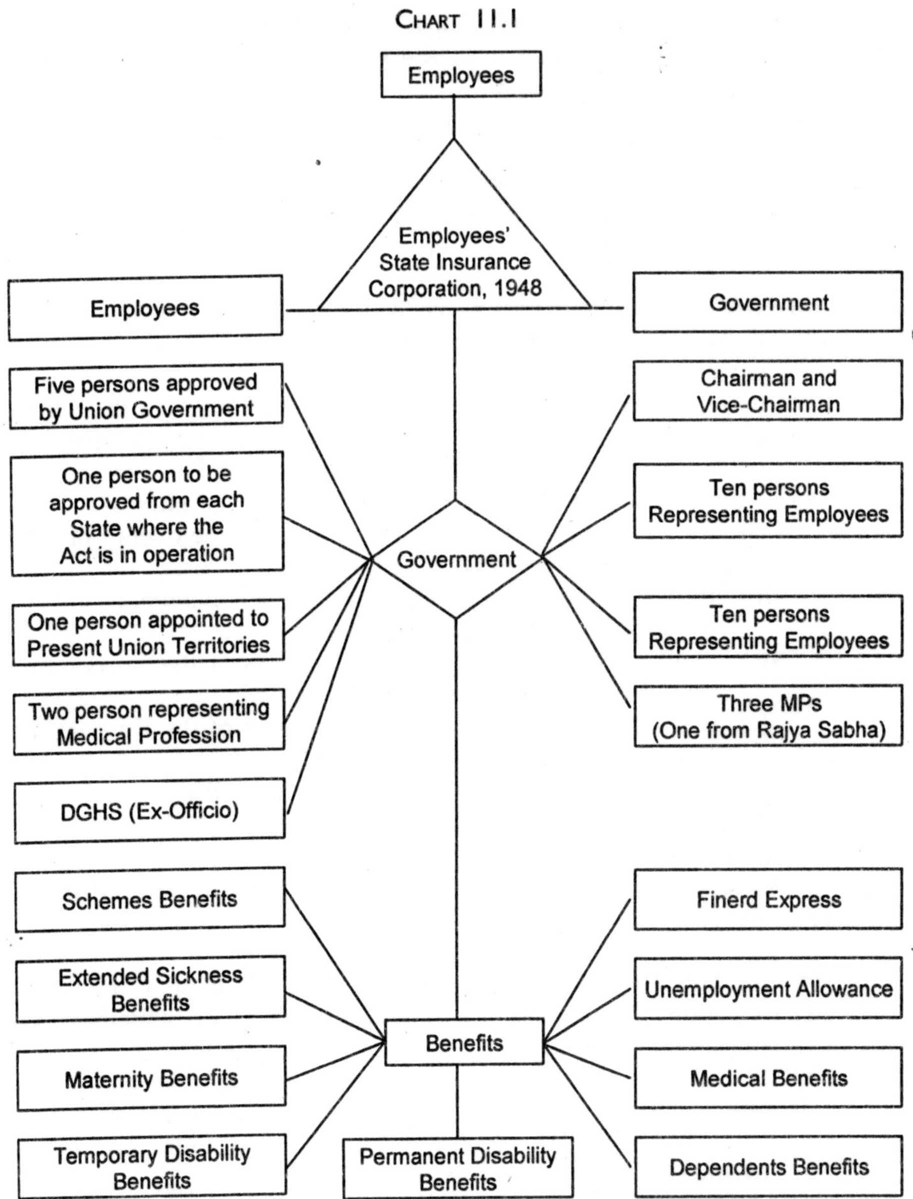

employees as may be reorganized for the purpose by the Central Government;

(h) two persons representing the medical profession to be [appointed] by the Central Government in consultation with such organization of medical practitioners as may be recognized for the purpose by the Central Government;

(i) three members of Parliament of whom two shall be members of the House of the People (Lok Sabha) and one shall be a member of the Council of States (Rajya Sabha) elected respectively by the members of the House of the People and the members of the Council of States; and

(j) the Director-General of the Corporation *ex-officio*.

Constitution of Standing Committee

A Standing Committee of the Corporation is constituted from among its members, consisting of—

(a) A Chairman, [appointed] by the Central Government;

(b) three members of the Corporation [appointed] by the Central Government;

[(bb) three members of the Corporation representing such three State Governments thereon as the Central Government may, by notification Gazette, specify from time to time;]

(c) [eight] members elected by the Corporation as follows—

(ii) [three] members from among the members of the Corporation representing employers;

(iii) [three] members from among the members of the Corporation representing employees;

(iv) one member from among the members of the Corporation representing the medical profession; and

(v) one member from among the members of the Corporation elected by [Parliament];

[(d) the Director General of the Corporation, *ex-officio*.]

Medical Benefit Council

(1) The Central Government shall constitute a Medical Benefit Council consisting of—

(a) the Director General, Health Services, *ex-officio*, as Chairman;

(b) a Deputy Director General, Health Services, to be [appointed] by the Central Government;

(c) the medical commissioner of the Corporation, *ex-officio*;

(d) one member each representing each of the [States (other than Union Territories) in which this Act is in force] to be [appointed] by the State Government concerned;

(e) three members representing employers to be [appointed] by the Central Government in consultation with such organizations of employers as may be recognized for the purpose by the Central Government;

(f) three members representing employees to be [appointed] by the Central Government in consultation with such organizations of employees as may be recognized for the purpose by the Central Government; and

(g) three members, of whom not less than one shall be a woman, representing the medical profession, to be [appointed] by the Central Government in consultation with such organizations of medical practitioners as may be recognized for the purpose by the Central Government.

Employees' State Insurance Scheme of India

Employees' State Insurance Scheme of India, is an integrated social security scheme tailored to provide protection to workers in the organized sector and their dependants in contingencies, such as, sickness, maternity or death and disablement due to an employment injury or occupational disease. Towards this objective the scheme of health insurance provides full medical facilities to insured persons and their dependants, as well as, cash benefits to compensate for any loss of wages or earning capacity in times of physical distress.

Applicability of the ESI Act

The ESI Act (1948) applies to the following categories of factories and establishments in the implemented areas:

Non-seasonal factories using power and employing ten (10) or more persons.

Non-seasonal and non-power using factories and establishments employing twenty (20) or more persons.

The "appropriate Government" State or Central is empowered to extend the provisions of the ESI Act to various classes of establishments, industrial, commercial, agricultural or otherwise in nature. Under these enabling provisions most of the State Governments have extended the ESI Act to certain specific classes of establishments, such as, shops, hotels, restaurants, cinemas, preview theatres, motor transport undertakings, newspaper and advertising establishments, etc., employing 20 or more persons.

Infrastructure

The Central headquarters of the Corporation is located at New Delhi. For purpose of coverage, revenue collection, extension of the scheme to new classes of establishments, implementation of the scheme in new areas, coordination with the State Governments and general administration the Corporation has established Regional, Sub-Regional and Divisional Offices across the country mostly located in the State capitals.

Regional Offices of the Corporation

Jammu
Pawanoo
Dehradun
Chandigarh
New Delhi

Patna
Ranchi
Kolkata
Guwahati
Bubhaneswar

Faridabad
Kanpur
Jaipur
Indore
Raipur
Ahmedabad
Mumbai
Hyderabad
Chennai
Pondicherry
Bangalore
Panaji
Thrissur

Sub-Regional/Divisional Offices

Rohini (New Delhi)
Okhla (New Delhi)
Nandnagari (New Delhi)
Ambala
Gurgaon
Pune
Nagpur
Thane (Mumbai)
Marol (Mumbai)
Aurangabad
Vadodra
Surat
Hubli
Vijawada
Coimbatore
Madurai
Salem
Tirunelveli
Kollam
Barrackpore
Noida
Varanasi

Given the huge number of beneficiaries—about 354 lakhs now the Corporation has set-up a wide spread network of service outlets for prompt delivery of benefits in cash and kind that includes full medical care.

Medical facilities are provided through a network of 1422 ESI Dispensaries, over 2000 Panel Clinics, 307 diagnostic centers besides 144 ESI hospitals and 42 hospital annexes with over 28,000 beds. For providing super-specialty medical care the Corporation has tie up arrangements with advanced medical institutions in the country, both in the public and private sector. The medical benefits is administered with the active cooperation of the State Governments.

The payment of cash benefits is made at the grass roots level through as many as 825 Branch Offices and Pay Offices that function under the direct control of the Corporation.[1]

Contribution

The ESI Scheme is mainly financed by contributions raised from employees covered under the scheme and their employers, as a fixed percentage of wages. As of now, the rates of contribution are:

(i) Employer's Contribution : 1.75 percent of wages
(ii) Employer's Contribution : 4.75 percent of wages

Employees' earning upto Rs. 50 a day as wages are exempted from payment of their part of contribution.

The State Governments Bear one-eighth share of expenditure on Medical Benefit within the per capita ceiling of Rs. 900 per annum and any additional expenditure beyond the ceiling.

Wage Ceiling

Employees of covered units and establishments drawing wages upto Rs. 10,000 per month come under the purview of the ESI Act, 1948 for multi-dimensional social security benefits.

Human Resource Development, besides seminars and conferences, following training arrangements made.

Setting up of National Training Academy (NTA)

During the period 2005-06 NTA was set-up at New Delhi. The main objective of ESIC National Training Academy (NTA) is to do TNA (Training Need Analysis) from time to time and to design and execute training interventions needed for various levels of Personnel.

In-House Training Programmes

The Central Training Institute organized 12 Trainings/Workshops for I.Is./Branch Managers and the total number of 304 participants attended the said trainings/workshops during the year 2005-06.

The Zonal Training Centres, in all arranged 41 training programmes for 1152 Participating officials during the year 2005-06. Three induction training programmes were organized for 83 Group 'D' Staff by the Regional Directors.

Out-House Training Programme

During the year 2005-06, 192 Officers of the ESI Corporation were deputed to attend special training programmes sponsored by the various national level management institutions/organizations of repute such as Administrative Staff College, Hyderabad, Landmark Education India, ISTM, New Delhi, NIC, New Delhi, I.I.M, Ahmedabad, National Academy for Training and Research in Social Security (NATRASS), New Delhi and Delhi Productivity Council, etc. The capsule training programmes ranged from Stress Management to e-governance and social security, etc.[2]

Working of ESI Scheme

The total number of beneficiaries till the year 2005-06 was 354.97 lakhs through 728 centres. The total number of employers were 3,05,294 by 2005-06.

Employees' State Insurance Scheme of India is a multidimensional social security system tailored to provide socio-economic protection to worker population and their dependents covered under the scheme. Besides full medical care for self and dependents, that is admissible from day one of insurable employment, the insured persons are also entitled to a variety of cash benefits in times of physical distress due to sickness, temporary or permanent disablement, etc. resulting in loss of earning capacity, the confinement in respect of insured women. Dependents of insured persons who die in industrial accidents or because of employment injury or occupational hazard are entitled to a monthly pension called the dependents benefits.

At an average the ESI Corporation makes 40 lac individual payments each year amounting to about Rs. 300 crores through its wide spread network of Local Offices in the implemented areas. For availing cash benefit in different contingencies insured persons or their dependants have to compete some minimal formalities and follow certain set procedures. Therefore, to ensure smooth and straight flow of benefits, an attempt has been made in the following paragraphs about the procedure to be followed by the ESI beneficiaries for claiming the benefits as and when the need arises:

Benfits

I. Sickness Benefit

A claim for Sickness Benefit can be made only on the basis of Medical Certificate issued by the authorized doctors under the Scheme. In exceptional cases alternative evidence of sickness or temporary disablement is accepted by the Corporation—

(a) An Insured Person is required to deposit his medical certificate in the box provided at the Dispensary or the Local office. Or he should ensure that the certificate is presented to the Local Office within 3 days of its issue.

(b) He/she should fill-up claim form for Sickness Benefit printed on the certificate itself or on claim form available at Local Offices, when he/she goes to Local Office for collecting payment or while submitting the certificate at the pay office, as the case may be.

(c) Local Office staff will assist in filling the claims if so required. In case of pay-offices, Dispensary staff will assist in filing the claims.

(d) If the claim is accepted, the same shall be paid immediately by the Local Office and if not found eligible a regret slip will be issued in ESIC-15. In case of Pay-Offices the cashier visits the pay office on an appointed day and disburses the payment. Insured Person can also get payments through money order if they so desire and send a written request to the Local Office.

The total number of employees entitled to claim sickness benefit during the year 2005-06 is estimated about 74.59 lakhs. During the year 2006-07 an amount of Rs. 83.25 crores was paid as sickness benefit.[3]

2. *Extended Sickness Benefit*

Same procedure is to be followed as is applicable for claiming Sickness Benefit. However, in this case the Insured Person is supposed to appear before the Medical Referee when referred by the Local Office Manager for the purpose of confirmation of the diagnosis/examination for allowing Extended Sickness Benefit from 124 to 309 days. Further an insured person is required to appear before the Medical Board for deciding the case beyond 400 days but upto a maximum period of two years.

The All India incidence of extended sickness benefit claims during the year 2005-06 was 0.66 per 1000 employees per annum as against 0.72 reported last year.[4]

3. *Maternity Benefit*

An Insured women claiming Maternity Benefit during the employment is to submit following documents either personally or by post:

(e) A certificate of expected confinement (Form-21), issued by an authorized doctor.
(f) A benefit claim in Form-22 duly completed.
(g) In addition to above, she has also to submit a certificate of confinement in Form-23 within 30 days of the date of confinement.

In case of claiming payment after confinement insured women has to submit a certificate Form-23 alongwith the claim form in *Form*-22.

In case of miscarriage she has to submit a certificate of miscarriage alongwith claim in Form-22. Certificate of miscarriage has to be submitted within 30 days. Insured Women can draw Maternity Benefit on weekly basis. At the time of final payment she should submit Form – 28 duly completed by her employer which will be issued by the Local Office Manager.

The estimated number of women employees deemed eligible for Maternity Benefit, increased from 12.86 lakh in 2004-05 to 13.13 lakh in the year 2005-06. The total amount paid as maternity benefit during the year under report was Rs. 2146.82 lakh as against Rs. 2102.13 lakhs paid in the previous year. The average amount of cash benefit payment per maternity claim increased from Rs. 10,247 in *2004-05* to Rs. 10,635 in 2005-06.the number of claims per thousand insured women employees, decreased from 15.95 in the year 2004-05 to 15.38 in 2005-06. The incidence of the claims per thousand women employees was the highest in Pondicherry at 25.42 and lowest in Punjab at 2.58.[5]

4. *Temporary Disability Benefit*

(i) Procedure regarding submission of Regulation Certificate and claiming the benefit remains the same as shown above against Sickness Benefit.

(ii) In addition, an Insured Person who sustains employment injury has to give a notice of such injury to the employer immediately either in writing or orally and also ensure that the employer has given the accident report to the concerned Local Office well in time in the prescribed form—Form-16.

The number of employees exposed to employment injury was 79.85 lakh as against 73.26 lakh in 2004-05. The amount paid as temporary disablement benefit, during the year 2005-06 was Rs. 2880.24 lakh as against Rs. 3073.37 lakh in 2004-05. the average number of fresh spells per employee per annum is 0.01 during 2005-06 and 0.02 during 2004-05 and the average number of benefit days per employee per annum decreased from 0.44 during 2004-05 to 0.38 during 2005-06.

The average daily benefit rate of TDB during the year 2005-06 increased to Rs. 95.21 in the year 2005-06 from Rs. 94.68 in the previous year. The average duration per spell of temporary disablement benefit was 29.17 days as against 28.27 days in the previous year.[6]

5. Permanent Disablement Benefit

(i) An Insured Person should submit an application for reference to the Medical Board on plain paper to the Local Office Manager after the termination of temporary disablement benefit. This may be done at the time of submitting the final certificate or within twelve months from the termination of temporary disablement.

(ii) He should ensure that he also gives his age proof to the Local Office Manager alongwith the application.

(iii) Form B.11(a) indicting residual incapacity will be issued by the I.M.O./I.M.P. at the time of final certificate. It is required to be submitted alongwith an application for appearing before a Medical Board. If it has not been obtained at the time of issue of final certificate is should be obtained at the time of applying for Medical Board.

(iv) The Medical Board sends its decision to the ESIC Regional Office directly or through Local Offices as the case may be and the Regional Office issues the sanction for periodical payments of P.D.B. One copy of the sanction order is endorsed to the Insured Person should submit the claim form in the Local Office for payment of P.D.B. This payment will be made to him every month as long as he is alive.

(v) In case his rate of P.D.B. is Rs. 5 per day or less an insured person can apply for lump sum communication of the payment provided that the total commuted value does not exceed Rs. 30,000.

(vi) An Insured Person should apply for commutation within a period of six months from the date of possible option. Then only the Local Office Manager shall be able to send the request to Regional Office immediately. Otherwise the Insured Person will be referred to the Medical Referee for certifying normal expectancy of life, and only after such certificate is obtained, the Insured Person's case will be processed for sanction of commutation.

(vii) The original sanction order of commutation is sent to the Insured Person with a copy to the Local Office. The Insured Person should produce the original copy at the Local Office at the time of payment.

The incidence of permanent disablement benefit cases registered is 13,675. The number of fresh cases admitted during the year under report registered an increase from 12,470 PDB cases during 2004-05 to 13,675 in 2005-06. The incidence of permanent disablement benefit per thousand Insured Persons increased to 1.71 in the year 2005-06 as compared to 1.70 cases per thousand employees in the previous year. Likewise the number of claimants of permanent disablement benefit have increased from 1,54,132 to 1,64,408 during the period under report the period under report *vis-à-vis* the previous year. The actual amount disbursed as cash benefit for permanent disablement benefit was decreased to Rs. 9216.19 lakhs (including the commuted amount of Rs. 1014.24 lakhs) from Rs. 10509.35 lakhs (including the commuted amount of Rs. 3429.09 lakhs) in the previous year.

The capitalized value of permanent disablement benefit claims in respect of fresh cases admitted during the year were Rs. 9469.94 lakh as against Rs. 8002.41 lakhs in the previous year.

The number of claimants of permanent disablement benefit, who opted for receipt of commuted value in lieu of periodical payment, have decreased to 6877 in 2005-06 from 10854 in 2004-05.

On the basis of analysis of 13675 cases of permanent disablement benefit cases admitted during the year 2005-06 it has been revealed that the highest number of accidents were reported in Textile industry followed by Engineering and Metallic Mineral Industry respectively.[7]

6. *Dependants Benefit*

(i) Dependents of a deceased insured person should contact the Local Office for claiming the dependant's benefit. The claim clerk will receive them and supply them necessary Forms and furnish all information needed by them. He will also assist them in filing the Claim Form (Form-18).

Dependents are required to submit:

(h) The evidence of death of the Insured Person having occurred due to an employment injury.

(i) Evidence that claimants is/are dependent(s).
(j) Evidence of age of claimant(s).
(k) Evidence that female dependants (widows/daughters) has/have not remarried or married after the death of an Insured Person.
(ii) These claims after scrutiny are forwarded to the Regional Office and the Regional Office communicates its decision to all the persons who claim the Dependents Benefit. To those who are not found entitled, a letter in Form ESIC-146 will explain why their claim has been rejected. The letter in Form ESIC-147 will indicate the daily rate of benefit of each dependant. For minor dependent the information is sent through the guardian.
(iii) The dependents should approach the Local Office with the letter (ESIC-147) for claiming the first payment.
(iv) Subsequently they can collect Dependents Benefit on first of each month either in person or by Money Order by submitting claims in Form-18A.
(v) If dependants are staying in far-off places, they can opt for payment from the nearest Local Office. The Local Office Manager will transfer all the records to the concerned Local Office from where payment has been desired to be made by the beneficiary.
(vi) At the time of claiming Dependent Benefit for the month of June and December every year, the claimant should submit a declaration in Form-27 duly attested by the authorities mentioned therein.

The number of fresh claims admitted for Dependants' Benefit during the year 2005-06 increased to 912 from 843 in year 2004-05. The total number of persons admitted as dependants during the year is 1,715. The category-wise distribution of all the dependants entitled to dependants' benefit at the beginning and at the end of the year 2005-06 is give below:

An amount of Rs. 4328.07 lakh has been paid as Dependants' Benefit during 2005-06 as against Rs. 4205.68 in the previous year. The capitalized values in respect of Dependants' claims admitted during the year was Rs. 3217.80 lakh asa against capitalized values of Rs. 3052.05 lakhs in the previous year.[8]

Let us discuss the various benefits under ESI Scheme.

7. Medical Benefit

An insured person and his dependant family members become eligible to claim medical facilities under the ESI Scheme from day one of entering insurable employment.

For availing the medical facility for self or any of the declared dependants an insured person has to produce the temporary identification certificate issued by the ESIC Local Office on taking insurable employment.

Description	As on 31st March	
	2005	2006
Widows	24419	25116
Sons/Daughters	30923	31484
Fathers	4300	4474
Mothers	5534	5728
Widow Mothers	382	481
Other Dependants	1903	1893

This temporary identity certificate is thereafter replaced with a family photo identify card that carries the photographs and other particulars of the family members and the insured person. Failure to obtain the permanent card or its non-production at dispensary/hospital can result in deprivation of medical care.

It is also to be borne in mind that dispensary is the base point for availing medical facilities. The reference for specialist treatment or diagnostic investigations is made by the ESI dispensary, itself to the concerned hospital. It is only in extreme emergency or at odd hours when the dispensary is closed that the insured person/dependant can report at the Emergency Department of an ESI hospital directly but should not fail to produce his/her photo identity card.

All medicines are issued free of cost by the dispensary to which an IP is attached. However, in case of non-availability of prescribed drugs at the hospitals/dispensary an insured person can purchase the medicines from local market if so advised and submit such claim to the dispensary for reimbursement.

By the end of March 2006, the Corporation had commissioned 18,860 beds in 144 ESI hospitals and 42 hospital annexes. An additional, 4396 beds had been reserved in various State Government hospitals for exclusive use of ESI beneficiaries.

For out-patient services, 1422 ESI service dispensaries have been commissioned. 2041 private medical practitioners have also been empanelled for providing primary medical care to ESI beneficiaries.

Out Patient Services

Out patient medical care under the scheme is provided either through the service system, i.e. ESI dispensaries administered by full-time staff of the State Governments, or through panel system, i.e. private medical practitioners called Insurance Medical Practitioners (IMPs) working part time for the Scheme. As on 31.3.2006, there were 6992 Insurance Medical Officers (full time IMOs) and 2041 Insurance Medical Practitioners (IMPs).[9]

8. *Unemployment Allowance*

The ESI Corporation had decided to provide Unemployment

Allowance to the Insured Persons who have been rendered unemployed involuntarily due to closure of the factory/establishment retrenchment or permanent invalidity arising out of non-employment injury. The Scheme has been named as "Rajiv Gandhi Shramik Kalyan Yojana." It shall apply to an Insured Person who becomes unemployed on or after 1st April, 2005.

Kinds of Unemployment covered under the Scheme

Unemployment which arises due to following reasons shall be covered the Scheme:

(a) Retrenchment as defined in the Industrial Disputes Act, 1947.
(b) Closure of the factory/establishment as defined in the Industrial Disputes Act, 1947.
(c) Permanent invalidity not less than 50% arising out of non-employment injury. The invalidity should be duly certified by a Medical Board constituted by the Central or State Government.

Eligibility Conditions

(a) The applicant should have been Insured Person under the ESI Act on the date of loss of insurable employment on account of retrenchment, closure of the factory/establishment or permanent invalidity arising out of non-employment injury, ad defined above.
(b) Contribution in respect of him/here should have been paid/ payable for a minimum period of five years prior to the loss of employment. The duration of a year in this context would mean a period of 156 days or more. An Insured Person who has lost employment and in respect of whom the contribution was paid/ payable for 156 days or more in any two consecutive contribution periods in this reckoning will be deemed as having worked for one full year. Similarly, those who have paid contribution for 78 days or more in a contribution period will be deemed as having served for a half year.
(c) The period of service of an Insured Person need not be continuous with one employer. The Insured Person shall be entitled to this allowance irrespective of the fact whether part of his/her service as employee was rendered in the insurable employment with any other employer in the same or in any other region.
(d) The Insured Person need not satisfy and qualifying conditions afresh for claiming unemployment allowance for any subsequent spells provided to him/her but he/she should be an Insured Person on the subsequent dates of unemployment. The unemployment allowance in the subsequent spells shall be at the same rate as has already been decided/paid.

(e) As specified in Section 65 of the Act, an Insured Person shall not be entitled to any other cash benefit and the Unemployment Allowance simultaneously for the same period. However, he/she may opt for either of the two, i.e. cash benefit or unemployment allowance. The term 'cash benefit' excludes periodical payments of Permanent Disablement Benefit under ESI Act and Regulations.

(f) As specified under Section 61 of the ESI Act, an Insured Person who is in receipt of unemployment allowance shall not be entitled to receive any similar benefit admissible under the previsions of any other enactment.

(g) There will be one-month waiting period after the retrenchment.

The number of claims admitted in 2005-06 was 179 and the expenditure on this scheme in the year 2005-06 is Rs. 23,31,049.

9. Funeral Expenses

Claim in Form 25(A), duly attested by the competent authority as mentioned in the claim form itself, be submitted to the Local Office alongwith the death certificate for claiming the funeral expenses on the death of an insured person. Reimbursement of expenses upto a maximum of Rs. 2500 is admissible.

Under the ESI Scheme, payment is made in lump-sum upto a maximum of Rs. 2500 in case of death of an Insured Person as assistance for defraying expenditure on funeral of the deceased I.Ps. During the year under report, a sum of Rs. 212.88 lakhs was paid on this account as against Rs. 210.85 lakhs in the previous year. The incidence of funeral expenses claims, expressed as number of claims per thousand employees decreased from 1.16 during 2004-05 to 1.06 during 2005-06.[10]

10. Other Benefits

Some other benefits under the Scheme are:

- Old age medical care for self and spouse at a nominal contribution of Rs. 120 per annum.
- Physical rehabilitation with free supply of artificial appliances.
- Vocational rehabilitation on permanent disablement.
- Immunization, Family welfare services besides pre-natal and post-natal care in respect of female beneficiaries.

Grievance Redressal

If any ESI beneficiary feels harassed in the process of availing lawful benefits or if the delivery of benefits is wilfully delayed at any level he/she is advised to contact or write to:

1. Pubic Grievance Officer of the region concerned.
2. Regional Director of the region concerned.
3. Director Public Grievances ESIC head quarter's New Delhi.

CRITICAL APPRAISAL

We have examined the structure and functions of Employees State Insurance Corporation set under ESI Act, 1948. It is doing a useful service to workers in industry. This combines the features of Private and Social Insurance. This is the biggest organization in terms of persons served and medical benefit available. However, on personal discussion with the Employers and Employees, we mention here some facts and suggestions to make this corporation effective and efficient:

(1) Corrupt Practices

The Doctors indulge in corrupt practices to recommend award of cash benefits. The employees pay to get certificate of illness, etc. This must be examined to save the resources.

(2) Doctors are not responsive to patients

The behaviour of the doctors with the patients in unsatisfactory. Workers are from lower strata of society and hence the doctors do not care for them.

(3) Restricted coverage

It serves those who become the members of the ESI Scheme. It should be mandatory for all employees.

(4) Workers coverage based on salary is not justified

The ESI scheme fixes the scale for benefits entitlement. When the facilities are in existences, why not to cover all the employees irrespective of pay scales. They can be offered services at high rates. This would make the scheme beneficial to all the persons employed in industry.

(5) Top leadership not serious

It has been seen that there are many persons *ex-officio* who have plenty of work in their own office—such people cannot contribute much. Only such person must be put at the top level who understand the role and can devote time.

(6) Depending upon Private facilities inefficient

Corporation is big institution and can set-up all facilities from its own funds as private facilities charge too much and provide second rate services.

However, ESI Corporation is doing a useful work for workers in industry. It can be improved and made more efficient.

Conrol of lax Certificate and Misuse of Cash Benefits

The Corporation has been regularly monitoring the Centre-wise and State-wise incidence of Sickness and Temporary Disablement Benefit to control lax certification and misuse of cash benefits. The All India average incidence of Sickness Benefit and Temporary Disablement Benefit for the year 2005-06 was 1.34 and 0.36 days per employee per annum respectively. Wherever incidence was found to be higher compared with the all India average, concerned State Governments were alerted and requested to take measures to curb any laxity in medical certification.

During the year 2005-06, the average incidence of Sickness and Temporary Disablement Benefit was found to be higher in the States/areas of Andhra Pradesh, Assam, Ahmedabad, Bihar, Chandigarh, Chhattisgarh, Jharkhand, Jammu and Kashmir, Hubli, Kerala, West Bengal, Madhya Pradesh, Maharashtra, Punjab and Pondicherry-Yanam-Mahe, when compared with the all India average incidence. Since the average incidence of sickness benefit in West Bengal continued to be abnormally high for the last several years, the issue was taken up by the Secretary Government of India, Ministry of Labour and Employment with the Chief Secretary to the Government of West Bengal. The Regional Directors and Sr. State Medical Commissioners/State Medical Commissioners were also advised to liaise with the respective State Governments regularly for keeping a check on the high incidence of certification.

Special measures have been suggested to the State Government to control lax certification which include, withdrawal of certification powers from Medical Officers indulging in lax certificate and requiring them to refer cases to the specialists wherever necessary; seeking second medical opinion of Medical Referee or Medical Superintendent of the nearest Hospital more frequently and careful monitoring of Insured Persons availing more than 25 days of Sickness Benefit in one benefit period and 40 days in two consecutive benefit periods.

In order to control the incidence of Temporary Disablement Benefit wherever it was found to be high, the Regional Director were asked to advise the employers to submit the accident reports under the signature of the person authorized as principal employer under Section 2 (17) of the ESI Act and request the Chief Inspector/Inspector of factories to investigate whether proper safety measures were in place in the factories reporting high number of accidents.[11]

Financing Health Services

Energizing health systems involves additional government expenditure. The existing level of government expenditure on health in India is just under 1 percent which is unacceptably low and effort should be made to increase the total expenditure in the Centre and the State to 2-3% of GDP. This must be accompanied by innovative financing mechanisms with incentivise performance. The quality of publicly supplied healthcare depends on how healthcare providers are paid. Providers should be paid only if they actually perform a service or satisfy the customer (the patient or the village health committee). Such systems linking payment to performance will increase accountability and should be encouraged.

The 11th Plan should experiment with different systems of private-public partnership, of which many examples already exist in some states. We could explore the possibility of an entitlement system for pregnant women to have professionally supervised deliveries. This will empower them to exercise choice, as well as create competition in the health service sector. Contracting out well-specified and delimited projects such as immunization can help enhance accountability. This does not mean that the state will withdraw from the health sector. Studies across the country have shown that expenditure on healthcare is a primary cause of indebtedness. Due to inadequate and non-performing public health infrastructure, the poor are forced to approach private practitioners who charge exorbitant fees. It is thus vital to ensure access to functioning public sector healthcare facilities.

Experience has shown that severe ill health can lead to disastrous outcomes for individuals and their families especially for the poor. These problems are best handled by health insurance. Community Based Health Insurance (CBHI) is emerging as a promising concept and existing experience in different States has shown that well managed pre-payment systems with risk pooling are effective in protecting the poor from impoverishment due to high medical costs during catastrophic health events. CBHI initiatives based on some individual contributions to the premium, plus a government subsidy, deserve to be supported, as they would improve the quality of healthcare and expand the healthcare interventions as per requirements. We also need to look at alternative approaches such as comprehensive risk pooling packages through the public system and through accredited private providers. This is possibly an area where multiple experiments need to be encouraged so that we can come to firmer conclusions about what model will work best.[12]

Notes and References

1. Employees' State Insurance Scheme, Citizen's Charter, ISO 9001-2000, New Delhi, January 2007, pp. 2-3.
2. Annual Report, 2005-06, Employees' State Insurance Corporation, New Delhi, p. 85.
3. Annual Report, 2005-06, Employees' State Insurance Corporation, New Delhi, p. 45.
4. Annual Report, 2005-06, Employees' State Insurance Corporation, New Delhi, p. 45.
5. Annual Report, 2005-06, Employees' State Insurance Corporation, New Delhi, pp. 45-47.
6. Annual Report, 2005-06, Employees' State Insurance Corporation, New Delhi, p. 47.
7. Annual Report, 2005-06, Employees' State Insurance Corporation, New Delhi, p. 47.

8. Annual Report, 2005-06, Employees' State Insurance Corporation, New Delhi, p. 49.
9. Annual Report, 2005-06, Employees' State Insurance Corporation, New Delhi, p. 33.
10. Annual Report, 2005-06, Employees' State Insurance Corporation, New Delhi, p. 51.
11. Annual Report, 2005-06, Employees' State Insurance Corporation, New Delhi, p. 51.
12. Planning Commission, GOI, 17th November 2006, Towards Faster and More Inclusive Growth, An Approach to the 11th Five Year Plan, p. 73.

Appendix 11.1

ESIC at a Glance

Particulars	*As on* *31.3.2005*	*31.3.2006*	*Variation during 2005-06*
1	*2*	*3*	*4*
States/Union Territories Covered	25	27	2
No. of Centres	718	728	10
No. of Employees	75,70,200	84,00,526	8,30,326
No. of Insured persons/family units	84,98,250	91,48,605	6,50,355
No. of Insured women	15,43,250	16,22,600	79,050
Total Beneficiaries	3,29,73,200	3,54,96,600	25,23,400
No. of Employers covered	2,80,871	3,05,294	24,423
Coverable Employees in Non-Implemented area	8,93,780	9,01,095	7,315
Branch Offices/Pay Offices	628/183	646/179	18/(-)4
Inspection Offices	258	248	-10
ESI Hospitals	144	144	—
ESI Annexes	42	42	—
No. of ESI Beds			
(i) Constructed			
(a) ESI Hospital	23,063	23,063	—
(b) ESI Annexes	849	849	—
(ii) Reserved in other Hospitals	3,187	4,396	1,209
Total	27,099	28,308	
ESI Dispensaries	1,427	1,422	(-)5
Insurance Medical Officers	6960	6992	32
Insurance Medical Practioners	2135	2041	(-)94

Capital Constructions

(Rupees in Lakhs)

Sanctioned	66365.86	67400.39	034.5312
Advanced	57882.33	58385.88	503.55

Income and Out-go

(Rupees in Lakhs)

Revenue Income	2,24,606.05	2,41,061.77	16,455.72
Revenue Expenditure	1,25,819.53	1,27,896.16	2,076.63

Source: Annual Report, Employees' State Insurance Corporation, 2005-06, p. 13.

APPENDIX 11.2

Citizen Charter

1. Introduction

Employees' State Insurance Scheme of India, is an integrated social security scheme tailored to provide social protection to workers in the organized sector and their dependants in contingencies, such as, sickness, maternity or death and disablement due to an employment injury or occupational disease. The scheme tailored to suit health insurance requirements of workers provides full medical facilities to insured persons and their dependants, as well as, cash benefits to compensate for loss of wages or earning capacity in different contingencies.

2. Applicability of the ESI Act

The ESI Act, (1948) applies to the following categories of factories and establishments in the implemented areas:

- Non-seasonal factories using power and employing ten (10) or more persons; and
- Non-seasonal and non-power using factories and establishments employing twenty (20) or more persons.

The "appropriate Government" State or Central is empowered to extend the provisions of the ESI Act to various classes of establishments, industrial, commercial, agricultural or otherwise in nature. Under these enabling provisions most of the State Governments have extended the ESI Act to certain specific classes of establishments, such as, shops, hotels, restaurants, cinemas, preview theatres, motors transport undertakings and newspaper and advertising establishments, etc., employing 20 or more persons.

3. Organisation

As provided under the ESI Act, the scheme is administered by a duly constituted corporate body called the Employees' State Insurance Corporation (ESIC). It comprises members representing Central and State Governments, Employers, Employees, Parliament and the medical profession. Union Minister of Labour functions as Chairman of the Corporation whereas the Director General, as chief executive, discharges the duty of running the day-to-day administration.

A Standing Committee representing all stakeholders is elected from the body corporate for managing the affairs of the scheme and monitoring the progress of implementation of various decisions and policies, etc. from time to time.

The Medical Benefit Council, a statutory body advises the Corporation on matters related to administration of medical benefit under the ESI scheme.

4. Infrastructure

The central headquarters of the Corporation is located at New Delhi. For purpose of coverage, revenue collection, extension of the scheme to new classes of establishments, implementation of the scheme in new areas, co-ordination with the State Governments and general administration the Corporation has established Regional and sub-Regional Offices across the country mostly located in State capitals.

Given the huge number of beneficiaries—about 329 lakhs now—the Corporation has set-up a wide spread network of service outlets for prompt delivery of benefits in cash and kind that includes full medical care.

Medical facilities are provided through a network of 1427 ESI Dispensaries, over 2100 Panel Clinics, 307 diagnostic centres besides 143 ESI hospitals and 43 hospital annexes with over 27,000 beds. For providing super-speciality medical care the Corporation has tie up arrangements with advanced medical institutions in the country, both in public and private sector. The medical benefit is administered with the active co-operation of State Governments.

The payment of cash benefits is made at the grassroots level through as many as 800 Branch Offices and Cash Offices that function under the direct control of the Corporation.

5. Contribution

The ESI Scheme is mainly financed by contributions raised from employees covered under the scheme and their employers, as a fixed percentage of wages. As of now, the rates of contribution are:

(i) Employees' Contribution	:	1.75 percent of wages
(ii) Employers' Contribution	:	4.75 percent of wages

1. Employees' earning upto Rs. 50 a day as wages are exempted from payment of their part of contribution.
2. The State Governments bear one-eighth share of expenditure on Medical Benefit within the per capita ceiling of Rs. 900 per annum and any additional expenditure beyond the ceiling.

6. Wage Ceiling

Employees of covered units and establishments drawing wages upto Rs. 10,000 per month come under the purview of the ESI Act, 1948 for multi-dimensional social security benefits.

7. Social Security Benefits

Quantum, Scale and Contributory Conditions

Employees covered under the scheme are entitled to medical facilities for self and dependants. They are also entitled to cash benefits in the event of specified contingencies resulting in loss of wages or earning capacity.

The insured women are entitled to maternity benefit for confinement. Where death of an insured employee occurs due to employment injury or occupational disease the dependants are entitled to family pension—the dependants benefit.

Various benefits that the insured employees and their dependants are entitled to, the duration of benefits and contributory conditions therefore, are as under:

I. Medical Benefit

Full medical facilities for self and dependants are admissible from day-one of entering insurable employment. Whereas, the primary, out-patient, in-patient and specialist services are provided through a network of Panel clinics, ESI dispensaries and hospitals, super-speciality services are provided through a large number of advanced empanelled medical institutions on referral basis.

Eligibility to Medical Benefit

- From day-one of entering insurable employment for self and dependants such as spouse, parents and children, own or adopted.
- For self and spouse on superannuation subject to having completed five years in insurable employment on superannuation or in case of having suffered permanent physical disablement during the course of insurable employment.
- The rate of contribution for superannuated/disabled IPs is Rs. 120 per annum payable in lump sum at Branch office for availing full medical care for self and spouse.

II. Sickness Benefit (Cash)

Sickness Benefit is payable to an insured person in cash, in the event of sickness resulting in absence from work and duly certified by an authorised insurance medical officer/practitioner—

- The benefit becomes admissible only after an insured employee has paid contribution for at least 78 days in a contribution period of six months.
- Sickness Benefit is payable for a maximum of 91 days in two consecutive contribution periods (one year).
- Payment is to be made by the Branch Office within 7 days of certification of sickness at a standard rate, which is not less than 50 per cent of the wages.

(a) Extended Sickness Benefit (Cash)

Extended Sickness Benefit is payable to insured persons for the period of certified sickness in case of specified 34 long-term diseases that need prolonged treatment and absence from work on medical advice.

- For entitlement to this benefit an insured person should have been in insurable employment for atleast two years. He/she should also have paid contribution for a minimum of 156 days in the preceding four contribution periods or say two years.
- ESB is payable for a maximum period of two years on the basis of proper medical certification and authentication by the designated authority.
- Amount payable in cash as extended sickness benefit is equal to about 70 per cent of the daily wages.
- The benefit is payable within 7 days following the submission of complete claim papers at the Branch Office concerned.

(b) Enhanced Sickness Benefit (Cash)

This cash benefit is payable to insured persons in the productive age group for undergoing sterilisation operation, viz. vasectomy/tubectomy—

- The contributory conditions are same as for the normal Sickness Benefit.
- Enhanced Sickness Benefit is payable to an Insured women for 14 days for tubectomy and for 7 days in case of vasectomy in respect of male IPs.
- The amount payable is double the standard sickness benefit rate, that is, equal to full wages.

III. Maternity Benefit (Cash)

Maternity Benefit is payable to insured women in case of confinement or miscarriage or sickness-related thereto—

- For claiming the benefit an insured woman should have paid contribution for at least 70 days in two consecutive contribution periods, i.e. one year.
- The benefit is normally payable for 12 weeks which can be further extended upto 16 weeks on medical grounds.
- The rate of payment of the benefit is equal to full wages or double the Standard Sickness Benefit rate.
- The benefit is payable within 14 days of submission of duly authenticated the claim papers.

IV. Disablement Benefit (Cash)

Disablement Benefit is payable to insured employees suffering from physical disablement due to employment injury or occupational disease.

- An insured person should be an employee on the date of the accident.
- **Temporary disablement** benefit @ 70 per cent of the wages is payable till temporary disablement lasts and is duly certified by authorised insurance medical officer.
- In case of **permanent disablement**, the cash benefit is payable for life. Amount payable is worked out on the basis of loss of earning capacity determined by a medical board.
- Disablement benefit is payable within one month of submission of the complete claim papers.

V. Dependants' Benefit (Cash)

Dependants benefit (family pension) is payable to dependants of a deceased insured person where death occurs due to employment injury or an occupational disease—

- A widow can receive this benefit on a monthly basis for life or till her re-marriage.
- A son or daughter can receive this benefit till eighteen years of age.
- Other dependants like parents including a widowed mother, etc. can also receive this benefit under certain conditions.
- The rate of payment is about 70 per cent of the wages shareable among dependants in a fixed ratio.
- The first instalment is payable within a maximum of three months following the death of an insured person and thereafter, on a regular monthly basis.

VI. Other Benefits

Some other benefits offered by the Scheme are:

(a) **Funeral expenses** on death of an I.P. subject to a maximum of Rs. 2500 payable at the Branch Office.

(b) **Vocational Rehabilitation** in case of disabled insured persons under 45 years of age with 40 percent or more disablement.

(c) **Free supply** of physical aids and appliances such as crutches, wheelchairs, dentures, spectacles and other such physical aids.

(d) **Preventive health care** services such as immunisation, family welfare services, HIV/AIDS detection, treatment, etc.

(e) **Confinement Allowance** @ Rs. 1000 is paid to an insured woman or in respect of the wife of an insured person in case she does not avail medical facilities of the scheme for child delivery.

8. Rights and Duties of Employers

(a) Duties of Employers

- An employer will apply in Form-01 for coverage under the ESI Act, within 15 days after the Act becomes applicable to a factory or establishment.
- The employer will submit Declaration Form in respect of all coverable employees in the unit.
- The employer will collect temporary identity cards from the Branch Office concerned followed by permanent photo identity cards and pass them on to the employees' concerned.
- The employer will deposit both employees and employers contribution as per specified rates within 21 days of the following month.
- The Employer will maintain an Accident Book and submit accident reports to the Branch Office, involving insured worker(s) on the job, within 24 hours of an accident.
- The Employer will maintain all such records and registers as are required under the Act and produce them for verification/ inspection before the authorised officers of the Corporation.
- The employer will facilitate proper inspection of records/ registers and the premises by visiting officers of ESIC as and when so required.
- The employer shall submit half-yearly Return of Contributions (RC) by 12th May/11th November every year with all columns properly filled.
- The employee shall indicate insurance number of IPs in chronological order in the return of contribution and his own code number in all correspondence.
- The employer will not make any false declaration or misrepresentation of facts, concerning the applicability of the Act, or, admissibility of benefits to employees—regular, hired or contractual.
- The Employer will ensure that contribution is paid in respect of all contract labour, badli and casual workers drawing wages upto Rs. 7500 a month.
- The employer will promptly report the date of closure of a factory/establishment to the ESIC Branch Office/Regional Office, preferably within seven days of such closure and clear ESI liabilities.
- The employer will report any change in business activity, address, ownership or the management to ESIC authorities forthwith.
- An employer will also ascertain the liability towards ESI dues, while taking over the ownership of a factory/establishment

through purchase, gift, lease, licence or otherwise as the new owner is liable to discharge past liabilities.

(b) Rights of Employers

- Exemption from applicability of Workmen's Compensation Act, 1923 in respect of employees covered under the scheme.
- Exemption from applicability of Maternity Benefit Act, 1961 in respect of insured women.
- Right to be represented on ESI Corporation, Medical Benefit Council and other important committees of the Corporation that may be formed from time to time.
- Right to be supplied requisite Forms as may be required for fulfiling any obligation under the ESI Act.
- Right to recover employees' share of contribution on the spot from the wages of insured persons.
- Right to appeal to Employees' Insurance Court in case of any disputes.
- Right to seek exemption from the applicability of the Scheme in case benefits provided by the management are similar or superior to those available under the ESI Scheme.
- Right of access to all essential information concerning the applicability of the Act, benefits, contribution, inspections and other procedures.

9. Safeguards for Insured Employees

(i) Right to receive payment of any benefit under the Act shall not be transferable or assignable.

(ii) Cash Benefits payable under the Act are not liable to attachment or sale in execution of any decree or order of any court.

(iii) Employer shall not dismiss, discharge or reduce the wages or otherwise punish a covered employee during the period he/she is in receipt of Sickness Benefit or Maternity Benefit, etc.

(iv) By reason of his liability to pay his share of contribution under the ESI Act, no employer shall directly or indirectly reduce the wages of a covered employee.

(v) Right to register their grievances/complaints at any level for immediate redressal.

(vi) Right to approach ESI Court against any action/decision of the Medical Board, etc.

10. Role of ESIC in Delivery of Benefits

The ESIC is to ensure that:

- The quality and quantity of benefits is as per norms and standards laid down by the Corporation for the purpose.

- The benefits are made available within the given time frame to insured persons and beneficiaries.
- No harassment is caused to the beneficiaries across the counter at the grass root level by way of word or deed.
- All requisite information, procedural guidance, etc. is made available to the beneficiaries for claiming benefits.
- All types of forms, etc. are made available to the beneficiaries free of cost as may be required by them for filing claims, etc.
- No beneficiary is exploited at any level in any way in the process of delivery of benefits.
- Office hours as notified for ESIC/ESIS establishments are strictly adhered to by the staff and displayed prominently so as to avoid any inconvenience being caused to the beneficiaries in smooth flow of benefits.
- Drugs, dressings, injections, etc. as prescribed by the authorised doctors are made available timely.
- A complaint box is fixed within the office premises for posting written complaints.

11. Role of ESIC in Servicing Employees

- To develop a responsive, purposive and productive relationship with employers.
- Seek their active involvement in the improvement of the scheme as a confidence building measure.
- Provide them necessary guidance in fulfiling their lawful obligations under the ESI Act.
- Make available to them requisite Forms and proformae as may be required by them from time to time.
- To ensure that any lax medical certification on part of ESIC does not bring down the productivity of a factory or establishment.
- To ensure that in case of any difficulty, doubt or misunderstanding employer is given a chance to be heard at an appropriate level.
- To ensure that all correspondence emanating from the employer is responded to, timely and objectively.
- To ensure that an employer is not being harassed by any official of the Corporation authorised to inspect the premises or the records.
- To ensure that any grievances received from employers are looked into promptly and pointedly for speedy redressal.

12. Redressal of Public Grievances

ESI Scheme, being a multi-discipline service intensive social security programme for workers, an estimated 3.5 lakh beneficiaries visit the service outlets at the grassroots level daily, either for treatment or for availing cash benefits. In such a highly interactive and dynamic system there is sufficient scope for any inadvertent or wilful harassment being caused to the beneficiaries. The Corporation has, therefore, set-up an elaborate system for speedy redressal of public grievances and complaints at various levels. Grievances can be reported in writing, on telephone, by post or in person to any of the following officers:-

Source: Citizen's Charter, Revised Edition, January 2007, Employees' State Insurance Corporation Headquarter (ISO 9001-2000 Certified), New Delhi.

Appendix 11.3
Some Useful Tips for Employees

Employers are among the most important stakeholders in the ESI Scheme. Their productive cooperation is the major source of strength for the success of the Scheme.

Employers may find the following tips, useful towards fulfiling their obligations under the ESI Act:

- Get your factory/establishment registered within 15 days after the Act becomes applicable. Submit 'From 01' to the Regional Office for this purpose. Obtain 'Employer's Code No. for use in all ESIC Forms/documents and correspondence with the offices of the ESI Corporation.
- Fill up Declaration Forms in respect of all coverable employees and submit the same the Regional Office/Local Office of the Corporation well before the 'Appointed Day' and obtain Insurance Numbers from the concerned Local Office Regional Office.
- All fresh entrants into the insurable employment should be advised to furnish two postcard size family photographs (of IP and dependants only) with the Declaration, Form to the appropriate local Office for issuance of Identity Cards.
- Pending receipt of identity cards/identity certificate you may issue 'Certificate of employment' in Form 86 to the covered employee(s) enabling them to avail medical benefits.
- Deposit ESI contributions (Employers' share @ 4.75% of the wages and the employees' spare @ 1.75% of the wage) with the designated Bank within 21 days of the month following, in which the wages fall due.
- Maintain an 'Accident Book' as prescribed under the Factory Act/ESI Act. Submit an "Accident Report" to the Local Office/ESI Dispensary concerned immediately in respect of accidents that could result in death or disablement within 24 hours of its occurrence.
- Grant leave to insured employees on the basis of sickness certificates issued by an authorized ESI medical officer/practitioner.
- Whenever events, such as, marriage, birth or death entails any additions or deletions in the family particulars of an insured person, the requisite information should be conveyed by the employer in 'Form 1-B' to the Local Office within 15 days.
- On re-entry of a person into insurable employment or, where an insured person had been disentitled to medical benefit due to non-submission of Return of Contribution, the employer may issue a 'Certificate of re-employment' or 'continuing employment' to such person in Form ESIC 37. This certificate

will enable the Insured Person to avail medical benefit from the date of issuance.

- If an insured employee needs a change of dispensary due to any valid reasons, an application may be made in Form 'ESIC-53'.
- Whenever an Insured Person goes, out of station on duty or leave he may be issued a certificate in Form ESIC-105. This will enable him and his family to avail medical treatment in ESI Dispensaries/hospitals elsewhere, or from State Government Hospitals, etc.
- If any insured person is in need of a duplicate identity card, an application may be made to the Local Office Manager in Form ESIC 72.

  The following records/registers should be maintained properly for purpose of inspection:

  (i) Attendance Register in respect of all the employees including employees engaged through immediate employer/ contractor;

  (ii) Register of wages;

  (iii) Register under Regulation-32;

  (iv) Accident Book;

  (v) Cash Book/Books of Account, Ledgers, petty cash book including bills and vouchers;

  (vi) Other relevant records to show the labour charges paid to the labour engaged in construction, repair and maintenance, etc.;

  (vii) Inspection Book;

- Furnish any requisite information promptly when asked for by the Regional Office/Local Office/any other office of the Corporation/Scheme.
- Facilitate proper inspection factory/establishment by any authorized officer of the Corporation and produce before him all relevant records on demand.
- Intimate the date of closure or shifting (temporary or permanent) of the factory/establishment, to the Regional Office/Local Office within seven days of its closure or shifting.
- Promptly report any change in the business activity, ownership of the concern or its management.
- Ascertain the liability towards ESI dues, while taking over the ownership of any factory/establishment by purchase, gift, lease or licence or in any other manner whatsoever as new owner is liable to discharge the past liabilities if any.
- Maintain, proper sanitation for a hygienic and healthy environment within the workplace and residential quarters if allotted to the insured persons.

Source: Public Relations Department, Employees' State Insurance Corporation, Panch Deep Bhavan, New Delhi-110 002.

Appendix 11.4

IT Enabled Services of ESI Corporation

The Employee's State Insurance Corporation is a pioneer social security organization always looking for new initiatives and innovations to serve the working class in the organized sector.

The ESI Corporation provides full medical care ranging from primary health consultancy to super-speciality treatment, and also a bouquet of cash benefits to provide security to the individual workers and his/her family in times of need.

In its endeavour to serve its Insured Person and the employers covered under the scheme, the ESIC has launched a project to provide IT enabled Services. Information Technology ennoblement of ESIC is being done through the National Informatics Centre (NIC), Ministry of Information Technology, Government of India. Initially the pilot project of IT enabled services is being launched for covering States of Delhi and Haryana.

Once the pilot project is completed the IT enabled services will be rolled out to all other ESI Establishments throughout country in a phased manner.

Objectives

- Better delivery of services to beneficiaries and other stakeholders of the scheme.
- Improved flow of information, faster communication, online delivery of services and online monitoring of physical and financial progress.
- Networking of all the office of ESIC for optimum utilization of the infrastructure.
- Interface with the beneficiaries and the employers through ESIC's bilingual portal-based website (www.esic.nic.in) for dissemination of information and providing online services.
- Having an integrated data center of ESIC.

Facilities

The IT Enabled Services will provide—

- Online registration of employers under the ESI Act, 1948.
- Online registration of Insured Contribution by the Employers through gateway of State Bank of India.
- Option of access to ESIC's website (www.esic.nic.in) in Hindi as well as in English.
- Payment of Cash Benefits of all types.
- Facilitation of Medical Care.

Steps to be followed to avail online facilities

A. *Online registration of employers*

- The employer's is required to open the internet and visit the site of ESIC at www.esic.nic.in.
- The employer has to click the line 'employer's registration.'
- The employer registration module will open asking the employer to fill in various details.
- The employer fills in required details and submits the filled in form.
- Employer's application for registration is completed and a message is shown on the screen that he would receive necessary registration intimation from the concerned office.

B. *Online payment of ESI contribution*

- The employer similarly visits the ESIC website at www.esic.nic.in
- He chooses the link of 'online payment of contribution'.
- The window asking for user ID and password, opens.
- Employer fills in the user ID and password, which employer has to get from ESIC.
- He presses the inter-button and he is taken to secure site.
- On secure site he is asked to fill in the type of payments and other details.
- The employer fills in the details and submits for making payment.
- The employer is asked to confirm whether he want to proceed.
- The employer confirms and then he is taken to gateway of State Bank of India.
- The employer is asked to provide user ID and password, which he has to obtain from State Bank of India for operating his accounts.
- The employer fills I the user ID and password and submits for effecting payments.
- Payment is effected which is confirmed.
- The employer has option to print the confirmation of payment. After payment is effected, an acknowledgement is taken by the employer and he is put back on ESIC's website.

C. *Employees' registration*

- The employer furnishes the Declaration Form in the Branch Office.
- Branch Office Officials receive the Declaration Form and enter them into employer's details of the employer.

- Branch Office has facility to print Temporary Identity Card (TIC).
- TIC is printed and given immediately to the employer's representative for enabling receipt of benefits by employees and his/her family.

D. *Payment of Cash Benefits of all types*

- IP, Dependant or his representative visits the Branch Office.
- He fills in claim form and submits to Branch Office.
- The claim clerk will diaries the claim online on the computer and identify the claimant.
- He will also check the eligibility of the IP for Cash Benefits online—
  (a) On finding ineligible, he will prepare the regret letter.
  (b) On finding eligible he will prepare payments as well as payment docket on computer itself and submit.
  (c) He will also prepare RM-I/ESIC-10 on computers.
- The same will be submitted for approval.
- Branch Manager/Head Clerk will approve the regret letter or the payment online on the computer as well as on docket. The claim clerk will had over the regret letter to IP/Dependant/Representative.
- Cashier will call the IP/Dependant/Representative and disburse the payment after obtaining the acquaintance on docket.
- The Cashier will also handover RM-1 if found necessary.

Medical Services: Dispensary

- The IP or his family visits Dispensary, whose eligibility is checked at Registration Counter.
- He is registered electronically and given a token number with location of Doctor to see.
- Patient is called in by the Doctor, examined and the Doctor may prescribe medicines or tests or both.
- In case of prescription of medicine the patient is issued with a computer printed prescription slip indicating medicines, dosages, duration, etc. with advice.
- In case of tests Patient is directed to concerned Laboratory.
- Patient visits the laboratory and gives the sample for examination.
- Laboratory conducts the test and files the report online.
- The patient then calls on the Doctor again.
- The Doctor while examining the Patient refers to the tests results available online and prescribes the medicines/treatment. The

Patient is issued with prescription with name of medicine, dosages and other instructions.

- Patient visits the pharmacy and produces the slip.
- The Pharmacist checks the stock online enters the quantity of the medicines prescribed by the Doctor and issues the medicines to the Patient by online entry and acknowledgement from the Patient. The Medicine stock is updated automatically.
- In case of referral need, Doctor advises the Patient over the instructions printed on the prescription slips in such situation to visit the referred ESI Hospital.
- Patient visits the referred Hospital for referral cases.

Hospital

- The IP/family visits hospital with ESI Card either on reference from the Dispensary or directly.
- OPD/Emergency registration checks the IP status to deal with the case accordingly.
- If IP/family is entitled for Medical benefits as per online checking of eligibility conditions, he/she is registered for treatment.
- The IP/family is given a token number and directed to the concerned Medical Officer/Examination Room.
- The Doctor examines the patient and may prescribe medicines and advices.
- The IP/family is issued with computerized prescription and advice to take medicines from Pharmacy.
- In case of tests the Doctor advises the patient to go the laboratory. Investigation required is logged online by the Doctor, and can be given on printed slip.
- Patient reaches lab and submits samples, etc. for test.
- The lab files the report online for viewing by the Doctor when the patient would call on him next.
- In case of outside tests the authority is issued by the Doctor in the form of a computer printed advise slip.
- In case of need for admission the Patient is referred to admission section.
- The admission section checks the bed availability, etc. online and allocates the bed to the Patient.
- In case of need of operations and procedures the same is prescribed online and concerned referral Doctor examines the case and schedules the operation by blocking the slot online.
- The patient on discharge is issued with a discharge summary and advice.

Source: Public Relations Branch, ESIC, Head Quarter Office, Employees' State Insurance Corporation, New Delhi – 110002.

No. of Insured Persons & Beneficiaries (2002-2006)

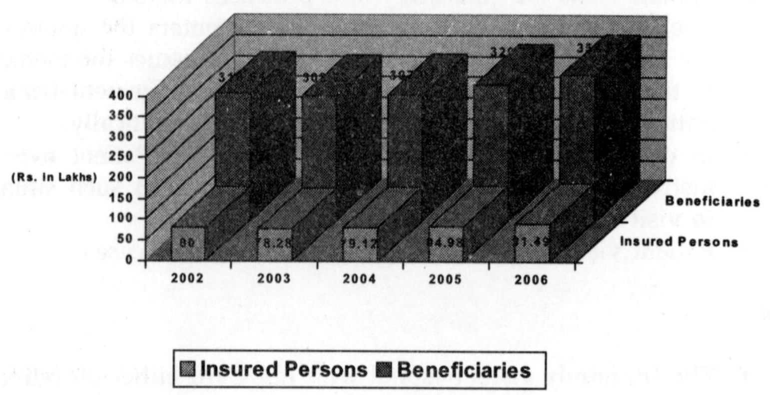

Number of Employees Covered under the ESI Scheme (2002-06)

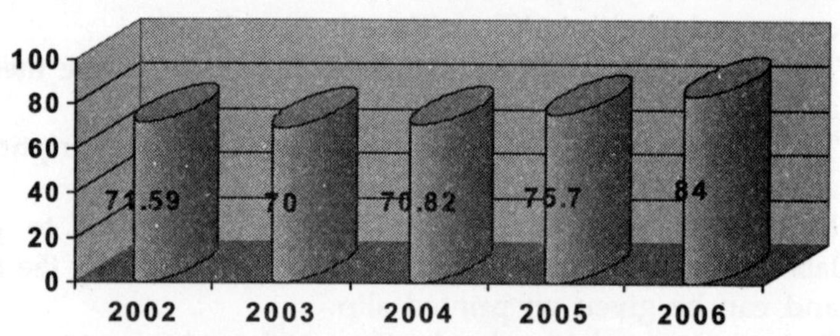

Expenditure on Cash Benefits—At a Glance (2002-2006)

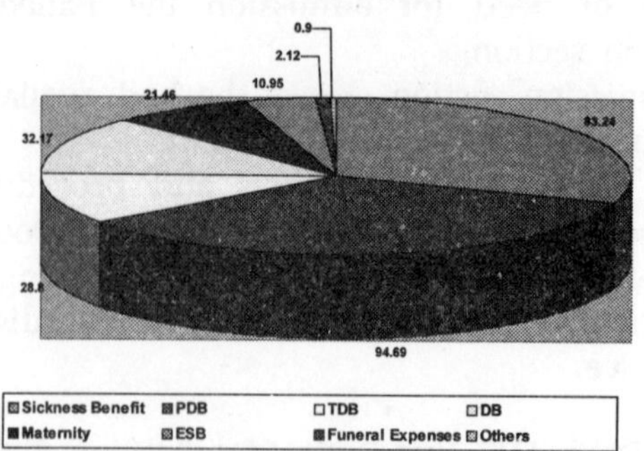

12 CHAPTER

Performance and Zero-Base Budgeting including Human Resource Accounting and Audit

As already discussed, the allocation to health sector by Union and State Governments is very low. The more important is that whatever money is allocated is not utilized properly. The most important component of health allocation is salary of medical and health staff. They remain absent frequently and spend less time as compared to their duty hours. In addition, there is great corruption in purchases of equipment, medicine and other articles. Thus the expenditure on health is wasted and need analysis. The Government itself has reported about it time and again. Most of the equipment is underutilized or unserviceable. People are unsatisfied and that is why private practice is flourishing.

How to ensure that the:

> "In the management or administration of any enterprise, the quality, quantity, timing, and cost of the work necessary to reach the objectives of the enterprise are inter-related factors which must be given constant attention. If the resources for health work, in trained persons and in finances, were unlimited the need for constant attention to these factors would not be so great. But the limitation in the number of trained personnel and the lack of adequate financial resources are major obstacles to greatly improved health in the world today. We must, therefore, husband our resources carefully to accomplish as much as possible with what we have available."[1]

A serious problem in health care administration is the absence of cost-consciousness among the staff of public health administrations. All over the world, health service staff-even of the highest professional cadre-are taught little about the economics of health services and know little about the costs of the equipment and supplies they use. Doctors tend to employ what is new without regard to cost. It is a fashion to prescribe costly drugs. They are also subjected to considerable sale pressure from manufacturing firms. A cheaper drug or cheaper equipment may give just as good a result for the vat majority of patients. Cost-consciousness is not just a matter for central administrators or planners but should be inculcated in all those working in health care. More people can be provided with services if no services cost more than what is a must to provide the necessary level of care. The price paid for high-cost technology for a few is no technology at all for the many.

How to tackle these problems? There is a need of introducing performance Budgeting and Zero-Base Budgeting as well as Human Resources Accounting and Audit.

The thriving significance of budget reforms has been a hallmark of many newly independent developing countries since the early 1950s. As alluded to earlier, most of these states were in search of budget mechanisms that could respond to their changing political and economic conditions. Consequently, budget reforms shifted their emphasis from control and accountability to performance measurement, a key deficiency manifested by the traditional budgeting. As Donald Axelrod explains, "Without performance measurement, it is impossible to determine the cost, efficiency, and effectiveness of programmes and projects and agency compliance with legislative appropriations. A performance budget, in essence, is a budget system which epitomizes the purposes and objectives and quantitative data measuring the accomplishments and work performed under each programme. For developing countries, the measurement of performance was viewed as a key factor in determination of effectiveness and efficiency of programmes."[2]

Performance Budgeting

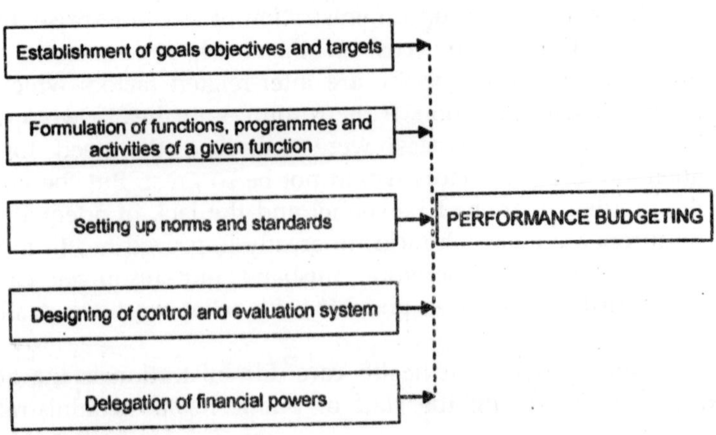

PERFORMANCE BUDGET

The budget is a blue print of the projected plan of action expressed in financial terms for specified period of time. It serves as a valuable aid to the management (through policy-making, planning, co-ordination and control. The Institute of Cost and Management Accounts of England and Wales defines budget as "A financial and/or quantitative statement prepared prior to a defined period of time of the policy to be pursued during that period for the purpose of obtaining a good objective." George R. Terry has described the budget as "an estimate of true needs arranged according to an orderly basis, covering all the activities of an enterprises for a definite period of time." The purpose of budget is generally:

(a) To aid in financing the enterprises,
(b) To clarify the operations of a programme,
(c) To promote co-ordination among different branches of the enterprise,
(d) To help in future planning, and
(e) To measure efficiency.

According to Wildavsky, "a budget can be a political Act, a plan of work, a prediction, a source of enlightenment, a means of function, a mechanism of control, an escape from restrictions, a means to action, a brake on progress."

The existing health budgets have been mainly designed to ensure financial and legal accountability to the legislature and within the executive, observance of similar accountability on the part of each subordinate agency. Budgets are generally prepared with an emphasis on the subjects of expenditure constituting the primary units of appropriation such as pay of officers, pay of establishment, allowances and honoraria, etc. It lays more emphasis on the cost aspects without any indication of the results. The traditional budget reveals what Government purchases but not why; it indicates what Government buys, but not what the Government does. In short, the traditional budgeting fails to provide adequate link between the financial outlays and physical targets. According to Mr. S.S. Visvanathan, an expert in the field of performance budgeting, there are the following four shortcomings in the conventional budget which arise mainly out of systems of classification:[3]

(a) The classification does not serve as an adequate base for informed decision-making at each level of management. It does not help management to control and appraise performance of the various programmes, projects, activities and schemes (programme activity and classification is suggested to remedy this);

(b) It is difficult to see from the existing budget and account heads for what broad purposes and objectives resources are being allocated (functional classification is suggested to remedy this);

(c) The classifcation does not permit a proper analysis of the impact of government transactions on the total national economy (this is sought to be remedied by an economic classification); and

(d) It is not helpful as a basis for judging the progress towards the achievement of goals and objectives as envisaged in the development plans.

For example, we do not find the impact of health budget on the health status of the people.

Meaning

To overcome the negative points of traditional budget, the concept of performance budgeting has been mooted. Let us understand its meaning.

It has been mentioned by the report of the ARC Study Team that "Performance budgeting as is generally known is essentially a technique of presenting government operations in terms of functions, programmes, activities and projects. Through such a meaningful classification of transactions governmental activities are sought to be identified in the budget in the financial and physical terms so that a proper relationship between inputs and outputs could be established and performance assessed in relation to costs.[4] According to Shri S.S. Visvanathan, "Performance budgeting is a comprehensive operational document conceived, presented and implemented in terms of programmes, projects and activities with their financial and physical aspects closely inter-woven."[5] The most important objective of this technique is the precise definition of the work to be accomplished or service to be rendered and a correct estimate of what that work or service will cost in financial terms.

Principles

There are three interrelated considerations or basic steps in the development of performance budgeting in an organization. They are:[6]

(a) evolving a meaningful classification structure in terms of programmes, projects and activities under each function entrusted to an organization in order to show precisely its objectives, the work done and the organizational responsibilities;

(b) bringing the system of accounts, reporting and the prevailing financial management practices in general into accord with the new classification and requirements of performance budgeting; and

(c) establishing suitable work units for physical measurement of work done, or services under each programme and activity and developing suitable norms, standards and other performance indicators for appraisal of performance.

In fact performance budgeting seeks to integrate the planning, budgeting, costing, reporting, and control system of the organization.

Significance/Purpose

Performance budgeting is very useful for developing countries. This facilitates better programming, decision-making, review and control for a more intelligible presentation of governmental activities to the public and the legislature. Broadly speaking, the main purposes sought to be served by performance budgeting are:[7]

(a) to correlate the physical and financial aspects of every programme/activity;
(b) to improve budget formulation, review and decision-making at all levels of management in the government machinery;
(c) to facilitate better appreciation and review by the legislature;
(d) to make possible more effective performance audit;
(e) to measure progress towards long-term objectives as envisaged in the plan; and
(f) to bring annual budgets and development plans closely together through a common language.

PROCESS OF PERFORMANCE BUDGETING

The process of performance budgeting includes the following:

(a) Establishment of goals, objectives and targets.
(b) Formulation of functions, programmes and activities of a given function.
(c) Setting up of norms and standards.
(d) Designing of control and evaluation system.
(e) Delegation of financial powers.

(a) Establishment of Goals, Objectives and Targets

The formulation of goals, objectives and targets are policy decisions to ensure socio-economic development. This requires a lot of data to ensure the availability of inputs. At this stage, the top management must answer these questions. What is to be achieved? Why it is to be achieved? When it is to be achieved?

(b) Formulation of Programmes and Activities

After stating the objectives and goals, we must analyze the work of the government into functions, programmes and activities. Let us explain the meaning of these terms.

Function

The function is generally a broad division of the total assessed efforts of the Government. Thus, each of the following: Education, Public Health, Defence and Agriculture may be defined as a function.

Programmes

Programme is a significant segment of a function, usually having an end object. The purpose of programmes is to contribute to the achievement of the objectives of the function to which it belongs, e.g., control of communicable diseases is a programme of the function of Health.

Activity

Activity is a division of programme into homogeneous types of schemes. An activity contributes to the attainment of the end results of the programme to which it belongs; activity is usually identifiable with a lower operating level organization, e.g. Malaria Eradication Programme.

(c) Setting up of Norms and Standards

The third step towards performance budgeting is to determine performance standards. It may be clearly understood that there is no single yardstick for determining performance standards. The fixation of standards should be tentative and flexible. It should be based on a thorough understanding of the nature of the work allowing for deviation within tolerable limits. These must be refined and made exact and scientific on the basis of experience and research.

(d) Designing of Control and Evaluation System

An adequate system for performance reporting is necessary adjunct to performance budgeting. Performance budget requires periodic assessment of physical and financial progress of Governmental activities to ensure timely implementation of programmes.

Thus, the objectives of a reporting system under performance budgeting as regards progress activities are:

(a) to find out the physical achievements and ascertaining how these can be improved;
(b) to enable formulation of future plans of action in a realistic manner;
(c) to facilitate a quantitative and qualitative assessment of the work; and
(d) delegation of more financial powers to lower levels.

A necessary adjunct to performance budget is the delegation of adequate financial powers commensurate with the functions and duties entrusted to various levels of operating officials. This is necessary for the accomplishment of targets at various operational levels of performance. The delegation of powers to the operating officials should be the maximum possible and not the minimum necessary in order to enable them to fulfil their assignment without frequent reference to the higher authorities.

The reporting system with regard to capital projects is based on 'Control Schedules' prepared in connection with the projects. The techniques may be the Critical Path Method (CPM) or Project Evaluation and Review Technique (PERT). There are two types of reports prepared in connection with the capital projects-Project Status Report and Cost Reports.

Format of Performance Budget

Any format to be used for performance budget should consist of three parts.

The first part or introductory part should include the statement of the objectives and goals of an organization in quantitative terms. This part is to give briefly the idea of the origin, set-up, scope of organization concerned so as to get an insight into the functioning of the department.

The second part deals with preparing the budget according to functions, programmes and activities as well as terms of the objects of expenditure. This part should also indicate the sources of financing the activities and programmes. It has, therefore, three sections:

(a) Programme activity classification showing the range of work classified in meaningful categories by programmes and activities;
(b) Object-wise classification giving a different angle in terms of broad items of expenditure groupings;
(c) Sources of financing indicating the several Demand Numbers and Major Heads under which the outlays for the programmes and activities are included in the appropriation structure.

The total of the three sections, i.e. A, B, and C will be the same.

The third part of the budget format should provide the explanation of financial requirement. A performance budget becomes meaningful and useful to management only if this part is taken care of properly. In this part, each programme activity will be explained with necessary data to justify funds asked for.

Limitations

According to the A.R.C., performance budgeting has some limitations. The more important of them are briefly mentioned below:

(a) Performance budgeting enables only a quantitative and financial evaluation of programmes and activities. This limitation is not, however, peculiar to this technique, since no budgetary technique can make qualitative evaluation possible. This is to be achieved through other appropriate devices.

(b) Its usefulness is somewhat limited in respect of activities that are not measurable in any precise manner. It is true that performance budgeting may not be as effective in non-measurable fields such as research, police, law and order, etc. as in development or construction areas where units of measurement are available. Nevertheless, even in such non-measurable areas, suitable bases can be developed to explain performance in a meaningful manner so that effectiveness of money spent may be known, though no value judgment is possible. At any rate, as a technique of presentation, it has its own advantage over the present system.

(c) The success of performance budgeting depends upon well-organized departments and agencies identifiable with specific programmes and activities. However, in practice, precise categories of functions and programme corresponding to organizational units are rather difficult to achieve. A synchronization of function and programmes with organization though desirable in the long-run, is neither a precondition nor an essential ingredient of a performance budgeting system.

(d) Performance budgeting provides no remedy for the administrative deficiencies in the budget process. It is no panacea for the administrative and organizational short-comings.

CRITICAL APPRAISAL

Peter N. Dean rightly mentions that: "Performance budgeting was not tried, tested and proven as an operational system at the time developing countries adopted it. On the contrary, dissatisfaction was beginning to emerge in USA about its usefulness. When it was exported to developing countries, those countries reservation were suppressed. Instead exaggerated claims were made about what it accomplished. Developing countries tried to fulfil these claims but they encountered a range of difficulties similar to those already experienced in the United States."[8]

The efforts of the Central Government and State Governments have so far been concentrated mainly on the preparation of performance budget documents by conversion of the figures in the existing Demands for Grants into a new formation as a post-budget exercise. In this connection, the Estimates Committee asked the Government to give their comments on the following observations made by an expert on performance budgeting, "Apart from the inadequacies of data regarding targets, norms and other relevant performance indicators which are inherent in first attempts of this kind and of which Governments themselves are aware, the questions covered so far, performance budgeting has been really introduced. The answer is a definite No. We have only partially succeeded in converting the existing Demand for Grants into the format of a performance budget with whatever data that could be had. This does not amount to installing the technique in any sense of the term."[9]

The Estimates Committee rightly pointed out that, "The technique of performance budgeting has yet to be perfected and that we have reached so far only first stage of defining the activities of department in a certain meaningful manner. In fact, the second stage of classifying the Accounting Heads in order to relate them to the performances budget has yet to be completed. The third stage, which is really one of intimate and significant interest to members of Parliament of working out and prescribing norms and standards, which could enable them to evaluate and critically review the work has yet to be evolved. The Committee cannot too strongly stress the need for ensuring that all these stages for making Performance Budget a useful document are completed without further delay and that concrete action should be taken to see that performance budget is prepared by all ministries/departments who are charged with departmental and other plan activities."[10]

It clearly indicates that we are still far from the performance budgeting in the real sense of the term. We have so far adopted the performance budget in letter only and not in spirit. As Presidential Assistant Joseph Califano has put it, "The name is not important, the approach is." There is need, therefore, to ensure the following to make the performance budgeting useful and fruitful.

(a) Streamlining Accounting Structure

In order to make the scheme of performance budgeting successful, it is essential that the concept of performance budgeting must also be reflected in the structure of Accounts. A functional classification of accounts under heads as correlated with the budget heads would prove to be of direct help to management.

(b) Effective Management Information System

The success of Performance Budgeting presupposes the communication of the approved budgetary system to various drawing and disbursing Officers, prevention of over and under-spending, and adhering to time-schedule for expenditure and work. Besides, the management information system must provide the feedback to ensure physical progress.

(c) Effective Management at all Levels

There must be effective and efficient management to get the advantage of the data made available through performance reporting. It should be the endeavour of the top management to devise new methods, procedures, techniques of operation, system of internal audit, etc., so as to bring about effectiveness and economy in operation or output of goods and services. We must discard the old methods and procedures, which have become obsolete and out-dated.

(d) Separating Capital Outlays and Current Operating Costs

Capital cost is an expenditure for the acquisition, construction or improvement of property or equipment (fixed assets), such as land, buildings, plants or machinery. Operating costs is an expenditure, other than capital cost, incurred in carrying out of specific programme or activity. These two types of costs are different in character and should appear separately under each major activity. In the words of Hoover Commission, "While a capital project may be carefully analyzed for usefulness, timeliness and total probable costs at the time of original authorization, total remaining costs, of all capital projects should be set forth in the budget each year, together with costs incurred to date. These costs should be revised in succeeding years to keep them current with latest developments."

(e) Effective Relationship between the Finance Ministry and Administrative Departments

The emphasis of Performance Budgeting is not only on the financial implications but also on the physical performance. Therefore, there is need for greater collaboration, consultation and co-ordination between the Finance Ministry and other Administrative Departments to ensure the success of Performance Budgeting.

(f) Training in Performance Budgeting

There is a need to create a specialized cadre of the persons in government, who can deal with the art and science of Performance Budgeting. Besides, the officers of Government dealing with the budget should be given a brief training to understand the mechanics and applications of Performance Budgeting. The Government must adopt an organization, where the performance budgeting has been adopted in all seriousness as a pilot programme and use this organization as a field area to propagate the merits and utility of such budgeting.

M.J.K. Thavaraj, in his article on "Performance Budgeting in India" has rightly said that: "It should, however, be remembered that performance budgeting is a tool and not a panacea. Whether it is manageable or unwieldy depends largely on the skill of the tool-maker. How effectively it is applied depends on the skill, imagination, energy and strength of purpose of the user. All it can provide is a meaningful basis for administrative planning, executive co-ordination, legislative decision and administrative accountability at all levels of government. It is by means a substitute for responsible public administration."[11]

(g) Effective Control by the Parliament Committees

The three Financial Committees—Public Accounts Committee, Estimate Committee, Standing Committee and Committee on Public

Undertaking keep a watch on Government spending and performance as best as they can. But apart from calling attention to the cases of wasteful expenditure, these committees do little to prevent a recurrence of the lapses. The attitude of the Centre and the States have caused havoc, with financial indiscipline permeating at all levels. However, there is ample scope to prune and economize, by curbing wasteful expenditure. Many instances care quoted each year by these Parliamentary Committees, but the waste of public funds, caused by bureaucratic indifference and lack of adequate control, continues.

A. Sekawat has rightly said that Performance Budgeting was seen as an alternative to the traditional budget approach as budgeters and administrators sought alternative 'suitable' techniques of budgeting. However, after several years of implementation, it became apparent that performance budgeting "did not live up to its expectations" as its usefulness as a planning and performance measurement mechanism became questionable by legislatures and public administrators.

M.J.K. Thavaraj has rightly said that "If performance budget is to be of operational significance, it must be built from operating levels of responsibility and summarized suitably for higher levels of management. Moreover, the absence of proper measures of workload might prove to be the Achilles' heel of performance budgeting. Unless suitable norms and yardsticks are developed, performance budget will be like a castle built on quicksand."

In any case, performance budgeting still manifests ample room for improvement and success in those countries that have exerted considerable effort to implement it. It promises to provide valuable detailed financial information that legislators and auditors needs, and has the potential for the ultimate realization of full scale measurement of performance of individual units of government.

ZERO-BASE BUDGETING (Z.B.B)

Meaning

Zero-Based Budget requires that health organizations while preparing their budgets should not take earlier years expenditure for granted and therefore should start afresh. In this process, the examination of existing programmes and activities has to be done in the same manner as would apply to newly proposed ones. To quote E.V. Srinivasan:

"ZBB can be defined as an operating planning and budgeting process which requires each manager to justify his entire budget request in detail from a scratch (hence—Base), and shifts the burden of proof to each manager to justify why he should spend any money at all."

Zero-base budgeting is thus a rationalization of the regular budgeting process to ensure accountability and maximum utility. It demands a total re-justification of every financial activity from zero.

Essentials

(a) Need of eliminating redundant expenditure, which is not serving the existing purpose.
(b) To identify and remove duplication or multiplication of expenditure.
(c) To search for alternative device to save expenditure.
(d) Optimize expenditure by making it productive and efficient.
(e) An appropriate administrative structures to ensure fruitful application of new budgetary aspects.
(f) To design an effective communication system in the organization.
(g) To design an adequate information system.

Methodology (Refer Chart 12.1)

It involves the following major steps:

(a) Identification of Decision Units.
(b) Formulation and Development of Decision Packages.
(c) Evaluating and Ranking Decision Packages in order of priority.
(d) Preparation of budget by allocating resources to activities or decision packages.
(e) Follow up and Revision.

CHART 12.1

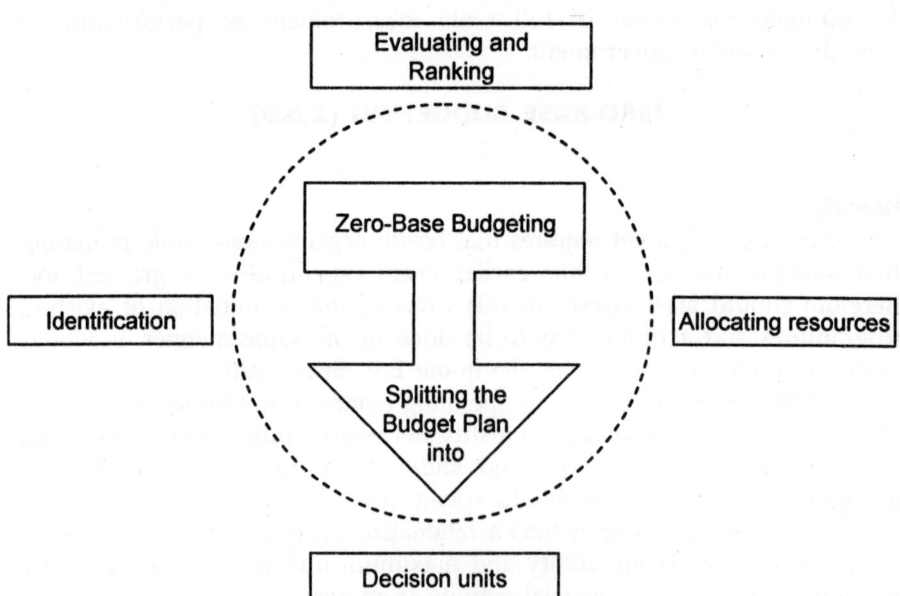

(a) Decision Unit

A decision unit is a distinct segment of an organization for which budget is prepared. This segment may be human or a programme activity, project but it should neither be too big nor too small so that it can be evaluated meaningfully in terms of expenditure.

(b) Formulation and Development of Decision Packages

A decision package includes comprehensive justification for budget estimates of an activity. To quote from the Government of India's letter, a decision package is a budget proposal, which should contain the following:

I. A description of the function or activity of the decision unit.

II. The goals and objectives of the various functions/activities of the Unit.

III. Benefits to be derived from financing the activity/programme.

IV. Relevance's of the activity/programme to the objectives of the organization/Department in the present context.

V. The consequences of its non-funding.

VI. The projected/estimated cost of the package.

VII. The yearly phasing of the proposed expenditure/project cost.

VIII. Alternative ways of performing the same activity or achieving the same objectives.

For each activity different levels of funding need to be analyzed to examine use of inputs with the resulting output for each level of funding. The Government of India in their letter mentions three levels of funding, i.e. the minimum level, current level and enhanced level. It is at this level that an acceptable level of funding has to be selected. A decision package helps decision unit manager in defining his objectives and to ensure their implementation.

(c) Ranking of Decision Packages

We need to ensure that the ranking process enables the available resources to be allocated according to consciously decided priority among decision packages, financing high priority decision packages.

(d) Preparation of Budget

Based upon ranking decision, budget may be prepared. The decision packages evaluated in terms of their costs and benefits are ranked in order of priority and are consolidated with those of other decision units through the management hierarchy and thus the budget for the organization is finalized.

(e) Follow-up and Review

A continuous follow-up helps in assessing performance and to local deviations and their causes. These causes may be removed through necessary review. A review has to be adequently quick so that its effect can bear fruit.

(f) Problems

Zero-Base Budgeting may face the following problems in the Indian context:

(a) It would increase a lot of paper work and would be a costly and time-consuming exercise.

(b) There is dearth of well-trained personnel in this area.

(c) It would require a well organized Management Information System.

(d) Re-deploying of resources from low priority to high priority is a very sensitive issue, as it involves the manpower.

(e) Plan and Non-Plan expenditure distinction carries no significance in this exercise.

(f) Center-state relations in finance create problems of utilization.

These and other suggestions mentioned earlier would help us to:

I. Identify our normal objectives and goals with precision and on a continuing basis.

II. Select among those goals the ones that are most urgent in the socio-economic development of the country.

III. Adopt those programmes, which can be achieved at comparative low cost or least cost.

IV. Measure the cost of programmes in financial terms for the present and the future.

V. Measure the performance of our programme *vis-à-vis* money spent.

VI. Make available to top management more concrete and specific data relevant to broad decisions.

VII. Spell out clearly and more concretely the objectives of government programmes.

VIII. Produce total rather than partial cost estimates of programmes.

IX. Present on a multi-year basis the prospective costs and accomplishment of programmes.

X. Review objectives and implementation analysis on a continuing, year round basis.

In health departments at Union and State Levels, Medical Personnel do not devote time to their duties due to the Charm of Private Practice. The Government must make use of Human Resource Accounting and Audit to get work out of health and medical personnel.

Human Resource Accounting and Audit are the latest terms to evaluate personnel in an organization. Human Resource Accounting is the term used to describe the accounting methods, systems and techniques, which coupled with special knowledge and ability, assist personnel management in the valuation of personnel in financial terms. This term has been defined by different scholars. Human Resource Accounting is the measurement of the cost and value of people for the organization.

It is based on the presumption that there exists a great difference among personnel in their knowledge, ability and motivation in the same organization and from organization to organization. There are some individuals who are able to produce more as compared to others in terms of goods and services. It means that there are some who may be a liability. Human Resource Accounting would provide all this information to facilitate decision-making about the personnel either to keep the personnel or dispense with their services or give promotion or to provide training.

The Manpower Audit is conducted to ensure that the manpower implementation plans are being executed and the objectives meet. If these are not being achieved, it became necessary to 'flag' that important assumption and analyse it to take corrective measures.

Human Resource Auditing is the continuous and systematic process of ascertaining whether personnel policies are being put into action as designed. The objects of such auditing are:

(a) To confirm that the policies of personnel management are being properly executed and to draw attention to those areas where policies appear to be inadequate.
(b) To verify that the information used by personnel management to control human resources is both adequate and accurate.
(c) To conduct a systematic survey and analysis of all operative functions of personnel, with a summarized statement of findings for correction of deficiencies.

S.A. Sapre says that an organization should be built on the strength of the people; not on their weakness... trees die from the top, so do the organization, for want of integrity in the manager (*Financial Express*, July 7, 1992).

There is a real need to reform the current personnel policies in government, semi-government, private, co-operative organizations through intellectual and idealistic approach. The day-to-day personnel administration is the responsibility of the personnel department, but, the major policy decisions in the form of rules or regulations would require the approval of the chief executive. Most of the personnel in an organization agreed that the personnel administration is passing through a crisis caused by the antiquated procedures backed by unwillingness and incapacity to introduce the desired reforms.

The performance of the personnel functions by the personnel department is limited in practice because of the following drawbacks:

(a) Inadequate understanding and appreciation of the basic and the essential problems of personnel management;
(b) No future personnel planning resulting in the absence of timely corrective measures;
(c) Lack of control and supervision over the personnel especially of the field personnel;
(d) Lack of effective decentralization to substantive departments resulting in delays and confusion;
(e) Absence of effective participation of the employees resulting in a gulf between the management and the staff;
(f) Lack of a manual setting out all the rules and regulations clearly and fully in a single document; and
(g) Lack of effective communication between the staff and management.

CONCLUSION

For a developing country like India, ZBB is very essential to ensure the optimization of financial resources. The existing budgetary system is responsible for a huge wastage as many activities for which finances are being allocated are not productive. ZBB would also indirectly inject many reforms in out-dated administrative health set-up to generate social change and modernization. However, its success would depend upon the co-operation, dedication and hard work of politico administrative leadership. It can help in genuine allocation of financial resources and controlling of expenditure.

Poor people in India are suffering, as they do not get satisfactory health service. There is a need of strictness on the part of the Government to ensure decent health care services. The Government can make use of performance budgeting, Zero-Base Budgeting, Human Resource Accounting and Audit, and other techniques to ensure utilization of health services.

Notes and References

1. H.A. Goddard, Principles of Administration applied to Nursing Service, World Health Organization, Geneva, 1958, p. 84.
2. Quoted in Alex Sekhawat, Budgetory Approaches in Developing Countries, in *IJPA*, Oct.-Dec., 1992, pp. 572-73.
3. S.S. Visvananthan: Performance Budgeting in Government: An Illustrative Guide, I.I.P.A., New Delhi, September 1972, pp. 1-2.
4. ARC: Report of Study Team, May 1967, pp. 160-61.

5. S.S. Visvanathan, *op. cit.*, p. 2.
6. *Ibid.*, pp. 2-3
7. ARC: Report of the Study Team: Financial Administration, May 1967, Chapter III.
8. Dean N. Peter, Government Budgeting in Developing Countries, London, Routledge Publishing, 1990, pp. 3-4.
9. Government of India, Lok Sabha Secretariat, Estimates Committees, 1972-73, Fifth Lok Sabha, 24th Report, November 1972, New Delhi. P. 19.
10. *Ibid.*, pp. 20-21.
11. M.J.K. Thavaraj, Performance Budgeting in India, in Management in Government, Edited by B.C. Mathur, K. Desh, C. Chandrasekharan, New Delhi, GOI, Ministry of Information and Broadcasting, Publication Division, 1976, p. 328.

Part C

MATERIAL

Materials Management: Techniques of Purchasing and Classification

A. MATERIALS MANAGEMENT

Introduction

Men, Money and Materials are the keys to development. We generally find that senior functionaries of health do not pay the desired attention to the materials management resulting in inefficiency. They even forget that 40 per cent of resources are spent on expendable and non-expendable equipment. "Materials management is one of the key factors for improving performance of any health unit. Higher inventories like medicines saddle an organisation with avoidable costs besides blocking scarce funds which might be required by the health institution for its own operations for some other essential development programmes. Proper Management of materials, therefore, assumes considerable importance in functioning of health services as well as in national economy." There are eight primary and seven secondary objectives which can ensure the best performance and use of materials (Equipment and Drugs). Many of these objectives conflict with each other. Balancing of these various conflicting objectives is one of the main tasks before the materials manager. The better this balance is done, the better the efficiency of the materials management:

B. ESSENTIAL PRINCIPLES

Broadly, we can say that there are seven principles of material management which must be kept in mind to ensure good results. Health managers must follow these principles or rights. We can decide about these rights by using the Management Techniques mentioned later:

(a) Right items,
(b) Right-quantity,
(c) Right price,
(d) Right source,
(e) Right delivery,
(f) Right method, and
(g) Right people.

Materials can essentially be categorised under three heads, viz.. vital, essential and desirable. These three categories must determine how much quantity of each item should be in stock for a store-keeper. Various techniques are available to decide on the right items, quantity, price, sound delivery, methods and people. The techniques are as follows:

CHART 13.1

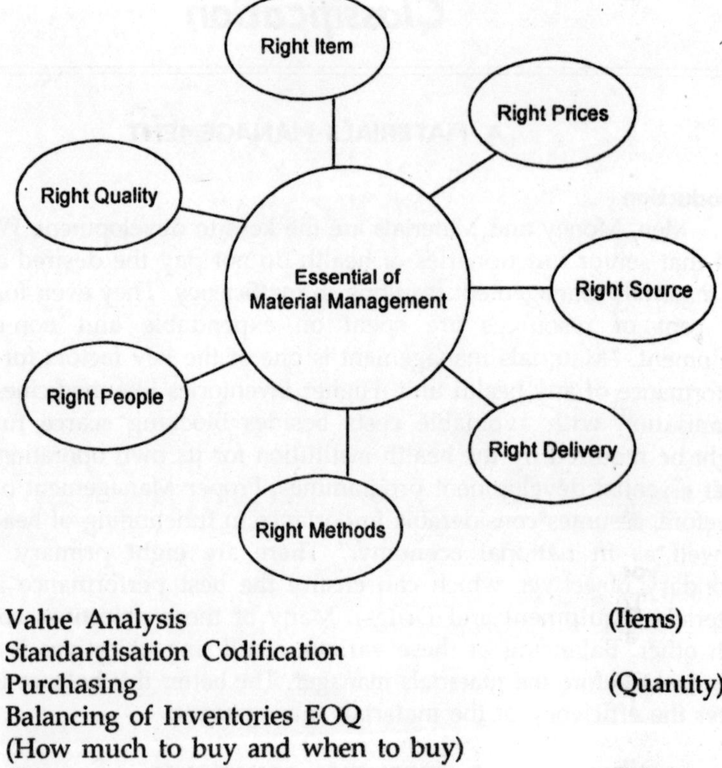

(1)	Value Analysis Standardisation Codification	(Items)
(2)	Purchasing Balancing of Inventories EOQ (How much to buy and when to buy)	(Quantity)
(3)	Cost Price Value Analysis	(Price)
(4)	Market Research Purchasing Techniques Selection	(Source)

(5) Procurement Techniques (Delivery)
Follow-up
PERT/OR

(6) Work Study (Methods)
Systems Analysis
ABC Analysis
Management Information Systems

(7) HRD (People)
Organizational Analysis
Behavioural Sciences

(1) Essentials

Materials management ensure the fulfilment of the following objectives:

(a) To develop a system of supplies whereby there will be right quantity of stock of items properly stored, easily retrievable and distributed close to the points of usage, whenever required, at a given time. In case, there is not enough stock the work in the organisation may have to be stopped and the men and equipment will remain idle. On the other hand, if there is overstocking of materials, it will unnecessary block capital in inventories.

(b) The reduction in inventory costs—both carrying cost and ordering cost.

(c) To ensure that the resources available are used most effectively and the stores are purchased at the most economical price consistent with the quality.

(d) To bring about co-ordination among the various sections in the organisation, i.e. in a hospital to bring co-ordination among the Doctor, Nurse, Storekeeper and the Medical Superintendent.

(e) To ensure that the formulations do not suffer.

(2) Procedure

To achieve these objectives the procedures can be enumerated as a Cycle, and in sequence of events, as follows:

(a) To determine the categories of stock required in terms of the quantity and quality of each item.

(b) To procure the items necessary from the best, reliable and authentic sources either within or outside the country at most economical prices.

(c) To ensure timely supply from these sources.

(d) To ensure good storage for effective delivery.

(e) To develop an effective control mechanism through good record keeping.

(f) Effective distribution at the points of usage.
(g) To ensure plugging of loopholes and the leakage.
(h) Employment of trained personnel to handle materials management.
(i) Enforcement of performance rather than legal audit.

(3) Principles of Inventory Management

Management has to decide about the following two issues:

(a) *Determination of Order Quantity*: At the time of placing an order. what quantity should be purchased? That is, what is the most economical quantity to order'?

(b) *Determination of re-order Point of Record Level*: At what time order should be placed in relation to existing inventory levels. Let us new turn to two important areas of Inventory Management in details, i.e. Economic Order quantity and classification of materials.

(4) Economic Order Quantity

The dictionary meaning of the word "inventory" is stock of goods. The classical definition of inventory is that it is an idle resource of any kind having an economic value. It case money to hold stock, it costs money in terms of storage, space, equipment, personnel, insurance, deterioration and obsolescence, and above all the cost of capital involved in financing stocks. Inventory management is the procedure and the body of knowledge which can help us in planning to maintain an optimum level of the idle resources. Before this, we may explain briefly some terms which influence Economic Order Quantity.

(a) Order Costs

These are the costs incurred to get the materials into the inventory of an organisation. The cost includes the costs on stationery, advertisement, salaries of personnel. If we examine the ordering cost in case of the organizations, we find the major components of ordering cost are salaries. To control the ordering cost, the number of men dealing with purchasing should be kept to the minimum.

(b) Carrying Costs

All the costs incurred to maintain inventories are termed as Carrying Costs. There are also known holding costs The cost is usually expressed as a percentage of the average investment in inventory. The chief component of costs are cost of capital invested in Inventory, cost of storage due to the rents and depreciation charges, salaries to stores personnel, obsolescence, losses due to pilferage and breakage, insurance costs, etc.

(c) Lead Time

It is the period that elapses between placing an order and receiving the same. These can be classified as administrative lead-time, manufacturing lead time, transporting lead time and inspection lead time. Any strategy to control lead time must try to control the administrative and inspection lead time. Others, too, can be controlled to a lesser extent.

(d) Buffer Stock

Buffer stock is the quantity of stores set apart as an insurance against the variations in demand and procurement period. This quantity of the item is to be kept as an emergency for unforeseen demands. It is calculated by multiplying the difference between maximum and average consumption rate per day with the lead time for the items.

(e) Reorder Level

This term is used to denote the stock level at which fresh order has to be placed. This is equal to the average consumption per day multiplied by lead time plus buffer stock. By ordering at the time when stock reaches the reorder level, we are fairly assured that the chances of 'stock out' are practically nil.

(f) Stock Turnover

Another aspect of inventory control is to see that there is proper turnover of items stocked and to see that the items are used up before the time expiry of the warranty period. Special efforts should be made to issue items on first come first out basis. Expiry date on control sheets to keep a control against keeping out-dated material on the shelf should be maintained. In case, there is no possibility of using the stocks of short life items within the expiry period, efforts should be made to deploy the stock to other institutions so that they could be issued before the expiry time.

Codification and Standardisation

In any undertaking having a large number of items, codification is essential. It hardly needs any emphasis that codification of items is a pre-requisite for introduction of mechanization in stock control and purchases and stores accounting. There are two systems which are commonly used for the purpose—'Birch' system and the 'Kodak' system. The major objectives of the codification are:

1. The classification of items on functional basis to ensure that one items is kept under one code.
2. To bring together the items according to their degree of similarly to reveal excessive variety and the substitutes available.
3. To list items as per National/International standards instead of vendor's number wherever possible.

4. To prepare a catalogue indicating the necessary details for procurement action and also which can be used as a reference by the users.

The purpose of inventory management is to find the appropriate levels for holding inventories and the ordering sequence and the quantities so that the total cost is minimised. Economic Order Quantity is that quantity at which the cost of ordering the annual requirements of an item and the inventory cost are nearly equal, i.e. when the total of the two costs is lowest Example: Let us assume that a hospital will need Rs. 30,000 of certain medicines in a year. The cost of ordering is Rs. 25 per order and the carrying cost is 20 per cent of the average.

This table clearly indicates that the hospital should order 10 times during a year. The ordering quantity is Rs. 3000. Here, carrying cost is Rs. 250 and ordering cost is Rs. 300. The total cost is Rs. 550. We can also determine it mathematically by the formula:

TABLE 13.1

No. of Orders per year	Order size (Rs.)	Average inventory 50 percent of order quantity	Annual carrying cost	Amount ordering cost at Rs. 25 per order	Total cost
1	30,000	15,000	3,000	25	3,025
3	10,000	5,000	1,000	75	1,075
5	6,000	3,000	600	125	725
10	3.000	1,500	300	250	550
15	2,000	1,000	200	375	575
20	1,500	750	150	500	650
25	1,200	600	120	625	745
30	1,000	500	100	750	850

$Q = 2RC_2/UC_1$ or $2RC_2/RC_1$.

(If R and Q are in rupees)

where R Annual requirement in units.
C_2 Ordering cost per order.
C_1 Carrying cost in per cent of average inventory.
U Unit price or Unit cost.
Q Order Quantity in units.

Using the Data of previous example. we have:

R = Rs. 30,000
C_2 = Rs. 25
Q = (.2 × 30,000 × 25)/.2
= 2 × 30,000 × 25 × 10
About Rs. 2750
Or nearly Rs. 3000

C. COST COMPARISON APPROACH

This methods has not taken into consideration the discount for bulk purchases. Here, we can use the cost comparison approach. In this method, the total cost of inventory carrying costs and ordering costs using an optimum purchase basis or economic ordering quantity is compared to the total cost of ordering and carrying under conditions which qualify the buyer for the quantity discount.

D. RE-ORDERING SYSTEM

The main principle of inventory control is that items for which annual consumption is high, orders are placed frequently so that the inventory level is as low as possible Items whose annual consumption value is not high, sufficient stocks are maintained and orders placed less frequently.

There are two universally organized systems of inventory control. They are:

(a) Cyclic system
(b) Bin System

Let us explain them

(a) Cyclic System/Fixed Order

This system has a fixed and ordering interval and the size of the order may vary with the fluctuation in demand. Under this system. It would be necessary to ensure that the stock could not fall between reviews to a level less than the usage during the lead time-taking the example just given less than 20 x 300 = 6000 units. If we assume the stock to be reviewed every 20 days, this means it must be above, 6000 + 20 × 30 = 12,000 units. So adding on buffer stock of 700, we have a 12,700 ROL

(b) Bin System/Fixed Order Quantity

In this system, the order quantity is fixed and the frequency of ordering varies and is determined by the fluctuation in demand. Under this system, simply multiply lead time by usage per unit of time and add the buffer stock. If, for example, the lead time is 20 days. The daily usage 300 units a day and 700 units buffers stock is held. Then the ROL is = 20 × 300 + 700 = 6700 units.

The fixed-order size system is more suitable for C and low value B items. The Fixed-Order-Interval system with its frequently and careful: reviews is suitable for A and high value B items. For a given risk of stock out the Fixed-Order-Interval system requires more of safety stock as compared with the Fixed-Order-Size system.

E. METHODS OF CLASSIFICATION

Methods can be chosen from the Exhibit depending upon the objective of control e.g., if we want to control the value or the consumption, we can use the ABC analysis. Besides, we can use some of the methods simultaneously to fulfil the different objectives of inventory control. This approach is simple and helps in selective control. The principle of selective inventory management recognizes that it is impossible to manage and control every item in inventory holding in the same way and still meet the two broad objectives referred to earlier.

Take care of the forest, the tree will take care of itself should be the motto of an inventory controller. Classification of inventory can help in effective control, i.e. concentrating on items which are most important, as it is difficult to give equal attention to all the items in the inventory. This is also known as "Management By Exception", which is a system of identification and communication that signals a manager when and where his attention is primarily needed. The primary objective of such a system is to simplify the management process itself, i.e. to enable a manager to identify and isolate problems that call for decisions and action on his span and avoid dealing with less critical problems, which can better be handled by those at a lower level in the organisation hierarchy.

F. ABC ANALYSIS

It is found that in most inventories some items have a much higher annual usage value than others. ABC analysis separates inventories into A. B and C items. In order to make such an ABC analysis. the list of all the stored items and their annual consumption in value is tabulated on the basis of the latest available records. Each individual item and its annual consumption value is listed separately and then this list is rearranged in a descending order, beginning with the items of highest value and ending with the items of lowest value. When such an analysis is made, it is usually seen that the 1st 10 per cent of the items (A) approximately account for 70-80 per cent of the value. Next 20 per cent of items (B) 15-20 per cent and the last 70 per cent of items (C) only 5-10 per cent of the value. The analysis can be used as a guide for economizing purchases and controlling stores by having concentrated attention on the inventory control of A and B items. The ABC concept tries to isolate the vital few and concentrate on them.

TABLE 13.2

Selective Inventory Control Exhibit

S. No.	Title	Basic	Main uses
1.	ABC (Always Better control)	Value of Consumption	To control raw material components and works in progress inventories In the normal course of business
2.	HML (High, Medium Low)	Unit price of the Material	Mainly to control purchases
3.	XYZ	Value of items in storage	To review the inventories and their uses at scheduled intervals
4.	VED (Vital, Essential desirable)	Criticality of the components	To determine the stocking levels of spare parts
5.	FSN (Fast Moving, Show moving, Non-moving)	Consumption pattern of the components	To control obsolescence
6.	SDE (Scarce Difficult, easy to obtain)	Problems faced in procurement	Lead time analysis and purchasing strategies
7.	GOLF (Govt., Ordinary, local, Foreign)	Source of the material	Procurement strategies
8.	SOS (Seasonal) Off seasonal)	Nature of supplies	Procurement/holding strategies for the seasonal items like agriculture Products.

Procedure

The steps computing A-B-C analysis are:

(a) First we are trying to prepare a list of items and calculate their annual usage in rupees. This can be obtained by multiplying the quantity (number of units) of the item consumed in one year by its unit price.

(b) Arranging all these items in the descending order of their individual usage in rupees. That means the first item in the list will now show the maximum annual usage in rupees. the second item the second maximum, the third item the third maximum and so on. After having done this, the total of annual usage in rupees is put at the bottom of the list.

(b) Those items which together form about 70 percent of the total annual usage may be categorised as A items. Similarly, Items which contribute the next 20 to 25 per cent of the aggregate are listed as B items. The rest which contribute 5 to 10 per cent of the total percentage of annual usage are called C items.

(c) Arranging on the basis of this classification.

Example: Let us explain with the help of an example from a hospital 'X', which has 10 items mentioned in the Table 13.2.

Table 13.2 shows a representative A-B-C analysis where 10 items have been studied and annual usage extended by unit cost to get annual usage in rupees. Table 13.3 shows the ranking and assignment of A, B and C categories for items.

TABLE 13.3

A-B-C Analysis Usage in Rupees

Items	*Annual usage units*	*Unit cost in Rs.*	*Annual Usage Rs. (2 x 3)*	*Ranking*
1	2	3	4	5
101	20000	0.25	5000	4
102	30000	0.20	6000	3
103	1000	0.10	1000	6
104	500	0.20	150	9
105	50000	0.20	10000	2
106	8000	0.05	400	2
107	60000	0.40	24000	1
108	700	1.00	700	7
109	9000	0.50	4500	5
110	50	2.00	100	10
TOTAL				Rs. 51,580

Table 13.4 is a summary of A-B-C analysis showing that 20 per cent of the items represent 65.57 per cent of annual usage. 20 per cent of the items represent 21.21 per cent of the annual usage; and 60 per cent of the items represent 13.22 per cent of the annual usage.

A items are ordered more frequently and in small quantities (i.e., few weeks requirement) while C items are ordered just once or twice a year to obtain the entire year's requirement. Without A-B-C analysis, the ordering

TABLE 13.4

A-B-C Ranking

Ranking	Items	Annual Usage (Rs.)	Cumulative Annual Usage (Rs.)	Cumulative Percentage	Category
1	107	24000	24000	46.28	A
2	105	10000	34000	65.57	A
3	102	6000	40000	77.14	B
4	101	5000	45000	86068	B
5	109	4500	49500	95.47	C
6	103	1000	50500	97.39	C
7	108	700	51200	98.14	C
8	106	400	51600	99.51	C
9	104	150	51750	99.81	C
10	110	100	51800	10000	C

TABLE 13.5

Summary A-B-C Analysis

Class	Item	% of items	Rs. Per group	Cumulative percentage
A	107,105	20	34000	65.57
B	102,101	20	11000	21.21
C	109,103,104	60	6850	13.22

policy of an undertaking may be to order all items once a quarter and position would be somewhat as represented by Table 13.6.

TABLE 13.6

Category	No. of orders per year	Annual requirements in Rs.	Quantity ordered each time in Rs.	Average Inventory in Rs.
A	4	40000	10000	5000
B	4	4000	1000	500
C	4	400	100	50

The average total inventory in the above case is 5550 and adding 20 per cent carrying cost the total inventory cost works out to be 5550 plus 1110 = Rs. 6660. Now, if A-B-C analysis is applied. the ordering policy would be different as shown in Table 13.6. Though the total number of order placed during the year is the same as before.

TABLE 13.7

Category	*No. of orders per year*	*Annual requirements in Rs.*	*Quantity ordered each time in Rs.*	*Average Inventory in Rs.*
A	4	40000	4000	2000
B	4	4000	800	400
C	4	400	400	200

Average total inventory is now Rs. 2600 and adding 20 per cent inventory carrying cost the total inventory cost works out to be 2600 + 520 = 3120, which is 3540 lower than the corresponding cost in the first instance.

G. VED ANALYSIS

VED Analysis is used for medical stores, spare parts inventory, etc. Those items, the absence of which even for very short duration will stop production/work are known as vital products, e.g., life saving drugs. Essential items are those, the absence of which cannot be tolerated for more than a day or so. The desirable items are those which are definitely needed, but with their absence, the work can continue. This type of analysis helps in deciding on the confidence level.

This technique was first developed in General Electric Company of USA by Lawrence D. Miles. Its purpose is to red lice the total cost of a product through the provision of the alternative means of achieving the functions that are desired and required. It may be defined as the systematic study of the function of a material, part, component to identify areas of costs that can be eliminated without impairing the capacity of the items. The definition used by the British Productivity Council brings out the main features of the techniques:

> "Value analysis is the study of the relationship of the design, function and cost of any product, material or service with the object of reducing cost by modified design or material specification, more efficient process, change in source of supply (external or internal) or possibly elimination of a component or its incorporation into a related item. The overriding consideration is that quality and reliability must be maintained."

Let us mention some examples. An Institute was mailing lessons to students. Two pages were useless in every lesson, i.e. the first page contained only lesson number while the last page contained a list of questions only. Based on the suggestions, given, these two pages redesigned as the lesson number was mentioned on the lesson material itself and in the questions were given. This exercise saved Rs. 50,000 per year. The complete process comprised of the following eight main stages:

SELECT	: the item to be studied
GATHER INFORMATION	: about the item
ANALYSE	: what it does and its value for money
SPECULATE	: to generate alternative ideas
ASSESS	: the worth of these ideas
REACH CONCLUSIONS	: as to what should be done
IMPLEMENT	: get it done
EVLUATE	: check the expected benefits that have materialized

The value analysis would require the interest, co-operation and motivation from the of all functional departments in an organisation. The work of a value analysis team facilitated if there is a good suggestion scheme in operation in an organisation. Such a scheme involves all employees in cost reduction effort and suggestions which come from men on the job and are generally useful and practical. The essence of this process depends upon the scientific attitude of the members, i.e. to keep an open mind to any suggestion that may be made by any of the team members.

We have not covered the area of storing, proper handling and disposal as these are self-explanatory. Disposal must be done fast and carefully otherwise, there may be many outdated materials (like medicines) which can be very harmful and besides, these may occupy space which is needed for fresh arrivals.

CRITICAL APPRAISAL

Materials management is one of the most neglected area of management in the Government organizations and public sector. In most of the organizations surveyed by the writer, it was found that the organization are either suffering because of heavy inventory or because of non-availability of certain materials in the inventory. There is a need to encourage the use of inventory management systematically to ensure the best use of inventory. We mention here some of the problems which need the attention of the experts to ensure implementation of the principles of materials management:

1. There is a tendency to use jargons and terms by specialists not comprehensible to the administrators and experts in other lines. These jargons instead of helping improvements confuse the administrators. There is a need to devise simple terminology.
2. Studies in materials management are more theoretically-oriented and have less of practical application. We must devise ways and means to solve the existing difficulties.
3. Materials managers are not trained properly. No person should be recruited to handle materials management without a proper training. Besides, the existing personnel must be trained in the art and science of materials management.
4. Suitable literature based on real case studies may be got prepared by the government and circulated among the administrators and experts for review and action.
5. An effective information system needs to be designed to suit the materials management in an organisation.
6. We must introduce standardization to optimize the number of items and reduce inventories.
7. The top management does not take keen interest in inventories as the effects of poor inventory are not visible on the operating statement. The top management must attend to it seriously as the basic responsibility for inventory control lies with them.
8. There are generally delays in supply which affect inventory levels. Expediting delivery of supplies on orders has a major effect upon inventory levels since the influence is directly connected with lead time or the procurement cycle time. There is a need to ensure expediting of orders. There is a need to integrate inventory control with buying functions and field expediting.
9. In the production inventory, we may use the technique of line of balance to avaoid imbalance among different components of one product. Line of balance a managerial tool applying the concept of management by exception to ascertain and maintain a balance in the components of the production in process.
10. The materials managers are prone to the influences of business houses resulting in the manifestations of commercial bribery. Managers must exhibit and believe in honesty to ensure quality of goods. The purpose should be to obtain the maximum value for the expenditure.
11. Most of the organizations revealed that the inventories are not stored properly and large items become unserviceable or scrap causing loss to the organisation. The top management and the materials managers must ensure that the materials are properly stored and biological and non-biological damages may be avoided through carefull handling, storage and retrieval. While storing we may keep the following in mind:

(i) Efficient space utilization and flexibility of arrangement.
(ii) Ease of physical counting.
(iii) Ready and easy accessibility.
(iv) Avoiding deterioration and pilferage.

12. In a multi-echelon Inventory systems like Electricity Boards, Health Department, etc., there is a need to look at the inventory management for the system as a whole rather than treating each storage location independently. Loss of expensive items may be avoided through careful handling, storage and retrieval.

Let us mention some examples. Suppose medicine A is very costly but medicine B serving the same function is very cheap. Then recommend medicine B. Doctors in order to earn money from Pharmaceutics recommend costly medicines write cheap medicines serve the same purpose.

H. CONCLUSION

A thorough understanding and use of the techniques of materials management would help in ordering supplies when needed. Controlling their use. Keeping them safely are in working order, and also motivating the personnel in the best use of equipped and drugs. This also prevents the chance of non-availability of equipment and drugs as being out of stock of these reduces the usefulness of the hospital system. Since the modern health institutions are becoming complex it is advisable for the health experts who are managing these institutions to make use of these techniques for better equipment and drugs management.

Drugs Management

The provision of appropriate drugs of good quality at affordable cost is essential for the success of disease control programmes. Equally important is to restrict, and if possible, elimination of the use of irrational drug formulation, detect and eliminate spurious drugs. The Central Government is responsible for the control over the quality of imported Drugs, control over the manufacture and import of new drugs into the country amendments to the Drugs and Cosmetics (D and A) Act and Rules, coordinate the activities with the State Drug Control Authorities for uniform implementation of D and A Act and Rules, laying down standards for drugs and updating Indian Pharmacopoeia. training of drugs analysts and drugs inspectors and licensing of whole human blood and blood products, large volume parenterals, sera and vaccines. Provisions for strengthening Drug Control Organsiation in the States and the Centre were made in the Eighth Plan. However, the implementation of the Scheme has been patchy and tardy.

At the rational use of medicinal drugs is critical to the most important primary and preventive health care measures. At the same time, unless there is a regular supply of safe and effective drugs, public trust—and interest—in primary health care will rapidly deteriorate. Yet half the world's population lacks regular access to the most needed medicines. Over the past decade, progress has been particularly difficult in the developing world because of adverse economic conditions and at the same time ineffective legislation and regulations, poorly coordinated drug policies and strategies, inefficient procurement, uneven distribution, unaffordable prices and inappropriate drug use. Although some 75% of the world's population live in those countries, they consume less than 20% of the total pharmaceutical market, valued at US $ 170,000 million. The more developed a country is, the more drugs it consumes.

Of course the need for drugs in poor countries is just as great as, if

CHART 14.1

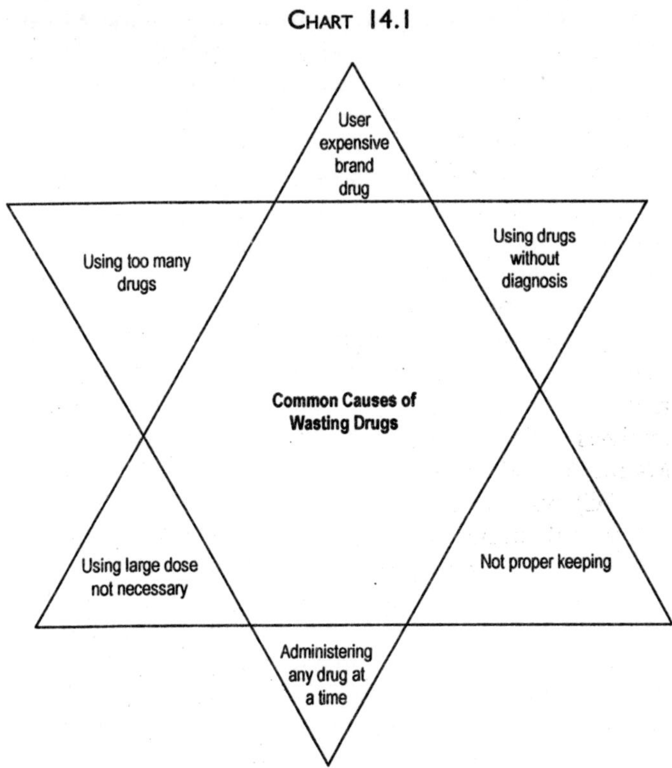

not greater than, the need in the richer countries. The only difference is that the developing world lacks the finance to pay for the medicines it needs. Just over a decade ago, WHO—through its action Programme on Essential Drugs—began to provide technical and financial support to developing countries seeking to improve the availability and rational use of drugs. In addition to its operational work, the Action Programme has played a major advocacy role in promoting the essential drugs concept as a tool to make the most of scarce resources, to improve health care, and to contribute to greater social equity. At present 64 developing countries have operational essential drugs programmes, and another 28 are in the process of drawing up national programmes.

Many other development and relief agencies now also apply the essential drugs concept to their health activities. An increasing number of countries are setting up comprehensive national drug policies. with clearly defined Objectives, which draw together the different components in the chain of drug supply and use. Such policies will typically include: legislation to ensure drug safety and quality and to regulate marketing and dispensing; centraized procurement on the basis of a national essential drugs list; the provision of non-commercial drug information; and strategies to improve the education of both prescribes and the public in rational drug use.

But despite significant progress in many parts of the world, the need remains for stricter and enforceable legislative control, greater coverage of the population, lower prices, improved quality and better use of drugs. Unfortunately, widespread social and economic deterioration in the developing countries stands in the way of effective, efficient and sustainable programmes. The public domain has been especially hard hit, rigorously jeopardizing the goal of universal access to essential drugs.

If these difficulties worsen, the drug situation also can only deteriorate. In such circumstances, the essential drugs concept. with its focus on equity and meeting real health needs, becomes even more convincing. National drug policies and essential drugs programmes are now. and in the foreseeable future. the best means we have available of pursuing and eventually attaining the dual objectives of rational management of drug resources and better health for all.[1]

Supply of essential drugs, vaccines/device holds the key to success in any disease control programme. Funds for drugs used for primary, secondary and tertiary care centres come partly from the State funds and partly from Central Plan funds (CSS). Procedures for procurement and distribution vary and bottlenecks in these at the national and State level have been recurrent problems. Inefficient indenting procedures adversely affect drug procurement. Poor inventory management results in unsatisfactory drug procurement and distribution. Some states such as Tamil Nadu have attempted strengthening drug procurement and distribution through formation of a Medical Services Corporation. This Corporation has drawn up an essential drug list, improved purchase and storage of drugs and organised efficient drug distribution within the states and has brought about effective inventory control. During the Ninth Plan efforts in improving procurement and inventory control and distribution for drugs at Central and State level are to receive priority.

The problem of irrational use of anti-bacterial drugs is both complex and many-faceted. But whatever its complexity, it should not be underestimated because it has a harmful influence on the possibilities of successfully treating certain highly prevalent infectious diseases. It is therefore no exaggeration to call on the international community to give high priority to drawing up a global policy on the rational use of antibiotics.

A coherent policy should promote simple and inexpensive measures that could have a considerable effect on the optimal use of antibiotics. Such measures include:

- orienting the initial training and regular retraining of prescribers and dispensers so that they learn the best ways of effectively combating infectious diseases;
- providing simple and inexpensive equipment to laboratories so that they can give valid bacteriological information;
- improving the supply and distribution of antibiotics in

accordance with the principles of an essential drugs policy, thus making drugs available at locally affordable prices;

- controlling information and marketing in such a way to promote the most efficacious antibiotics and those best adapted to the local epidemiological situation; and
- carefully studying cultural attitudes so that the right kind of education and information can be deployed to encourage people to accept the most appropriate treatments for each illness.

Such a line-up of measures could form the basis of an international campaign for the rational use of antibiotics, spearheaded by the health authorities and WHO; this would help to limit as much possible the appearance and spread of resistant strains, which in the long-run threaten our chances of effectively controlling the infectious diseases.[2]

Drugs are very important in a hospital and, therefore, these must be used with due care, skill, knowledge, and need. The drugs can be dangerous if not administered properly. Wasting of drugs also results in wastage of scarce resources of the hospital. Every state must prepare a list to suggest the quantity and quality of drugs required at different levels of health institutions in the country. A World Health Publication has rightly summed up the purpose of Drug Management from different angles which are mentioned below.

> "The purpose of management of drugs is to use drugs wisely and avoid wasting drugs, and therefore to have enough for patients needs."[3]

Y.C. Simhadri, Vice-Chancellor, Andhra University, Visakhapatnam delivered the Inaugural address of the Refresher Course in Pharmaceutical Sciences and Medical Lab Technology at the Academic Staff College, Andhra University, Visakhapatnam on 13.10.2003. He said, "A well informed society expects accountability, transparency and sound professional services from the health care providers. This requirement is fulfiled by professionalism and ethical practices of profession. The core element of a profession is a specialized body of knowledge and commitment to service. Integrity of knowledge base and its expansion through research and ensuring the highest ethical standards in its use in the best advantage of the patients is a professional commitment of a pharmacist. Any failure in his duty is an indicator of falling standards of the profession. Licensing bodies and professional associations have the responsibility and social obligation to discipline unprofessional and incompetent pharmacists. Society believes that the profession places the welfare of society above that of the profession. The educational institutions have an important obligation to inculcate these values in their graduates."

For a national drug policy to bear fruit it must be firmly rooted in the community with at its core the goal of equitable access to essential drugs.

It will need the full involvement of all health professionals and the support of the pharmaceutical industry. The media have an important role to play in keeping the public informed about the rational use of drugs, while schools and universities are the key to creating critical mass of knowledgeable patients and prescribes. Above all, the Government must offer strong support to the national drug policy as a keystone of its national health policy.

From these basic roots spring the different Interlocking segments that will guarantee the functioning of the drug policy. There must be unstinting political will on the part of the government. as it draws up and puts into effect the necessary legislation and regulations. Drugs should be selected and made available to meet the real health care needs of the community, and a system developed to ensure that they are of good quality.

Procurement should be centralized and carefully coordinated to obtain economies of scale and optimal prices supply and storage facilities must guarantee available and safeguard drugs in all weathers. As well as during transport from central medical stores to the remotest health post. Information about all drugs and vaccines used is essential for the health professionals prescribing them; and the public must be educated in their proper use. Finally, transfer of technology is needed to share out the benefits of new pharmaceutical developments. Now the drug policy will be ready to bear Furit! The public on confident that the drugs prescribed to them are death safe and effective. And are guaranteed quality, thus ensuring that they get appropriate treatment. They will also know how to make better use of the drugs available, and can feel that they are getting value for money. Because there will be efficient distribution of the essential drugs. They should be accessible to all, and there will no longer be unfair gaps in availability. In the long-run, the rest fruit of all to grow on this sturdy tree will be: Better health for all.[4]

COMMON CAUSES OF WASTING DRUGS AND MONEY

1. Using too many different drugs on one patient.
2. Using expensive, brand-named drugs when cheap or standard drugs are equally effective.
3. Using drugs without a proper diagnosis, "Just to try it."
4. Using a larger dose than necessary.
5. Giving drugs to patients who do not believe in them and who throw them away, or who forget to take them.
6. Ordering more drugs than are needed, so that some drugs become "expired" on the shelf.
7. Not caring for the refrigerator, so that vaccines are no longer effective.
8. Exposing drugs to damp, heat or light.
9. Giving out (Issuing from store) many drugs at one time so that they are stolen or used extravagantly.

EDUCATING STAFF IN THE USE OF DRUGS

Drugs are important, powerful and expensive. For these reasons, all health workers using drugs should be well-informed about them and should develop a mature and responsible attitude towards their use.

A health-worker manager can educate staff about drugs in the followings ways:

1. Put one or more copies of a simple book on pharmacology in the library.
2. Make notes on the common drugs used, explaining their uses and side-effects. Give copies of these notes to all staff.
3. Set out the correct doses of common drugs on wall boards.
4. Hold staff meetings to discuss causes of drug wastage.
5. Inform all staff about the cost of various drugs.
6. Make a lecture/discussion programme and discuss one drug each week in the staff meeting.

EDUCATING PATIENTS ABOUT DRUGS

Very often patients take drugs in a wrong way. They either reduce the dose to make the treatment last longer or increase it hoping for a quicker cure. They use the drugs at wrong times or forget a dose. Patients on long courses of treatment then stop them too soon. They do this because they do not understand the action of drugs in the body. The result is that they are sometimes not cured and the drug is wasted. Health workers should explain very carefully to patients how to take their drugs.

How to use medicines safely

- Only use a medicine when it is needed. Rest, good food and lots to drink are often enough to help a person get better.
- Don't insist on injection. Although in some countries injections are commonly regarded as more effective, in fact most drugs work just as well or other better when taken by mouth. Injections cost more and can be dangerous. If administered by an untrained person or if needles and syringe are not properly sterilized.
- Don't buy medicines from unauthorized sources, such as street pedlars. Only use medicines from proper packages with instructions labels.
- Take the medicine at the right times and in the right amounts.
- Always finish the full course of medication even if you feel better.
- Don't use someone else's medicine and don't share your own.
- Keep all medicines in a cool place out of the reach of young children.

Suggested action by teachers

Have you thought of including basic information about medicines in your health education activities? You could invite the local pharmacist or health worker to talk to the children about the safe use of medicinal drugs (and about how to avoid the illicit drugs that can only do them harm). A visit to the nearest clinic or health centre could also be very instructive. You could also do some of the following with the children:

- Make up a play or a puppet show; for example, acting the story of a false "doctor" who comes to the village with bottles full of different coloured water. He makes a long speech which the people believe: they buy his medicines and he goes away with a lot of money, but no one gets better. He comes back next year but this time the people chase him away.
- Draw posters to show the rules about safe use of medicines. described above.
- Make up songs or stories with the medicine safety rules and teach them to friends.
- Find an advertisement for some kind of medicine and discuss it. What does it say? What does the picture tell us? Should we believe it? Why, or why not?
- Find out the cost of a bottle of "tonic" (medicine which is claimed to make us strong). What does it contain? Compare the price of one bottle of tonic with an orange, a kilo of green leaves, or other local nutritious foods which could be eaten instead of taking the tonic. Which is the best use of the money?[5]

EXPLAINING TO PATIENTS THE USE OF DRUGS

They should also explain in a simple way why a drug must be taken in a particular way. Thus, patients could learn that:

1. Each drug has a particular action, a drug used for one condition will not help another.
2. The size of the dose is very important. If it is too little it acts too weakly to cure the condition: if it is too much it may poison the patient. The dose for children are smaller than those for adults.
3. Treatment must be regular. This means that the desired level of the drug in the body is maintained.
4. The whole course of treatment must be completed. If it is not, the patient may relapse into an even more serious condition than before.
5. Drugs must be kept out of reach of small children. They may eat them as sweets and poison themselves.

Special Education

Patients with tuberculosis and leprosy who have to take drugs too many months need a great deal of explanation and encouragement. They must continue to take tablets even when they feel better, in case the disease becomes active again.

CONTROLLING LIFE-SAVING DRUGS

Sometimes a patient's condition is so acute, severe or critical that only the immediate use of certain drugs can save his life.

It is of vital importance that such drugs are always in stock. The absence of such drugs in an emergency may result in patient's death.

This is an unnecessary tragedy and a failure of health-service management. Such a tragedy can be avoided by:

1. Making a list of vital or life-saving drugs;
2. Placing them together on one shelf;
3. Checking the shelf frequently or whenever drugs are issued; and
4. Ordering a new supply when stocks reach the half-way point (use the ABC or double-shelf system described above).

PRE-PACKAGING DRUGS FOR THE OUT-PATIENT'S DEPARTMENT

This means that a full course of treatment with a certain instruction is put in small envelope or folded papers, before the clinic or out-patient session. It is ready when the patient needs it. This has a number of advantages:

1. The patient receives the correct and full course of treatment.
2. Its saves time and avoids waiting and queuing while tablets are counted.
3. Printed (or duplicated) instructions can be given with the packet or written on the envelope. This tells the patient how and when to take the tablets, and assists his memory. Special signs must be designed for patients who cannot read: e.g., the sun rising to the horizon represents morning.

It is very useful in special clinics where standard treatments are given to every person, e.g., iron and folic acid tablets to pregnant women. It makes it easy to observe and control the issue of drugs.

Besides the Government must streamline the manufacturing of drugs and limit the number of drugs. The World Health Organisation has recommended the manufacture of 295 drugs which can meet the requirements of India while India produces about 60,000 different types of drugs. Mr. S.P. Sharma in his article on "Land of Drugs" in *The Tribune* dated 24-6-98 has rightly quoted Herben M. Shelton who says: "It is not illness that is expensive. It is the naive idea that the healing powers of the body require absurd purchasing of "treatment", "reliefs" and other high priced drugs that make suffering a lavish luxury. When man grounds his behaviour in illness on commonsense instead of seeking illusive "cures" recovery will be far more rapid and without disastrous "costs due to ever changing status of disease, there is a need of constant research in the area of drug management to combat the changed disease pathology."

Based upon personal visits, observation and discussion, we mention here the problems and suggestions to ensure quality drugs management.

1. Lack of Clarity about the Quantity and Quality of Drugs

It has been seen that drugs are purchased at different levels or supplied from above to different institutions without examining their requirements, leading to either over stocking or understocking. Some of the medicines become time barred leading to wastage of resources. Therefore, there is a need of advance planning.

2. Pilferage of Drugs

It has been found that the hospital staff sell the medicines in market. which were meant for free distribution. Patients always complain of non-availability and all are not supplied the medicine.

3. Poor Quality of Drugs

Drugs in Primary Health Centres and hospitals are of very poor quality and sometimes even beyond consumption. There is a need to order good quality medicines so that quality health care can be assured.

4. Lack of Clear-cut Communication regarding the Procedure to take Medicine

Doctors do not clearly intimate the patients about the procedure and importance of medicine taking resulting in their not taking it medicine or taking it wrongly or irregularly.

5. Heavy Doses Prescribed

It has become a fashion to prescribe large number of medicines resulting in over-dosing and high expenditure. They must be used with skill, knowledge and accuracy, otherwise they can become dangerous.

6. Action Programme

The WHO Action Programme on Essential Drugs and Vaccines helps less developed countries to utilise the Model List: in association with UNICEF, WHO responds to requests from Member-States for procurement of drugs contained in the list at a very reasonable cost, much lower than the market price. Moreover, the two agencies encourage group purchasing, which further reduces prices. An experiment in group purchasing with obvious advantages in terms of cost has been under way for several years in the Gulf States.

The Action Programme provides, in addition, other useful services in the drug field, including helping Member-States to formulate their National drug Policies, assure the quality of imported drugs and train personnel. WHO has also, through its Certification scheme. been active in helping developing countries which lack quality control facilities to ensure the quality if imported products.

Other UN agencies cooperate in expanding the services provided through the Action Programme. UNCTAD and UNIDO, for example, are offering their expertise in technology transfer and in other areas of local pharmaceutical production.

A further development arising from use of the Model List is the encouragement to use generic names of drugs instead of trade-names. A generic name is approved official name for a certain chemical entity; it relieves the user of the need to memorise a multitude of trade-names for the same Drug. It also facilitates, to a great extent, the work of procurement officers, enabling them to choose the best available medicine at the most reasonable price; and it largely relieves the pressures exerted by manufacturers at the moment of tender.[6]

7. Drug Safety

Benefits for countries

The extent to which a country is able to use the Model List and benefit from the Action Programme depends largely on its stage of development. At least some, if not all, of the following advantage should be obtainable:

1. Assistance in formulating a National Drug Policy which satisfies the needs of the national health policy and reflects the country's socio-economic conditions.
2. Establishment of local quality control facilities to guarantee safety and efficacy of drugs. In some cases, regional cooperation may be established.
3. Improvement of systems of procurement, storage and distribution of drugs, to ensure ready availability at the lowest cost.
4. Encouragement of local production of pharmaceuticals, within the framework of the National Drug Policy, starting with simple formulations which may gradually be developed as feasible. Some Third World countries already produce over 80 per cent of their drug consumption; some have also introduced production of certain pharmaceutical chemicals and packaging materials.
5. Promotion of research capabilities in various pharmaceutical, pharmacological and clinical fields. Simple pharmaceutical research includes investigation of the stability of dosage forms

under local weather conditions, and the most suitable and economic packaging. Pharmacological research includes aspects of drug behaviour in the body, effects and adverse reactions. Clinical research requires the cooperation of clinical pharmacologists clinicians to evaluate the theratic effects and cost/benefit ratio of drugs when used by the local population under specific genetic and environmental conditions.

Experience so far with the Model List has been more than gratifying; the advantages are scientific, educational and economic. On the scientific and educational side, an EDL leads to a more rational use of drugs and facilitates, the production of a national drug formulary. On the economic side, an EDL reduces expenditure on medicines, avoids drug misuse, encourages local production of pharmaceuticals, and increases the proportion of the health care budget that can be devoted to other items. Already, a large number of Third World countries have their own EDLs; many of them have national formularies, and some are enjoying certain of the above-mentioned advantages. To say the least, the concept of the EDL has been widely accepted the Action Programme has been well utilised and the rational use of drugs has been gaining ground.[7]

Drugs are biologically active substances. Used imprudently they may do harm rather than good, but considerable efforts are made to ensure that marketed products meet the claims which are made for them, and that they are acceptably safe. It would be misleading to suggest that absolute safety is attainable, or that every potential danger can be spotted before a new drug is released for general use. Indeed, from time to time, drugs are withdrawn from use because they are found to hold previously unsuspected dangers. But it would also be wrong to cast into question the undeniable benefits that pharmaceutical innovation has yielded since organic synthetic chemistry became established some 50 years ago.

Life is beset by hazards, but drug induced injury holds a particular pathos. Clinicians mindful of their Hippocratic oath are concerned not with statistics but with individuals. Their first consideration is never to do harm. However, in reality, they are concerned in virtually every intervention with an assessment of benefit and risk. It is ultimately for society, rather than the professions, to judge what risks are acceptable in the conquest of naturally occurring disease.[8]

8. Quality Control

Small-scale laboratories can be linked up to a reference laboratory located in the same region, so that suspect drugs requiring more detailed analysis can be referred to the reference lab from the whole region. This concept of regional laboratories has been under serious consideration by some countries: one has been established in the Caribbean area; East and West African countries are also discussing a similar facility. The author of a feasibility study made on behalf of the West African Pharmaceutical

Federation has proposed that countries like Gambia, Sierra Leone and Liberia could establish their own small-scale national quality control laboratories for example, at the Royal Victoria Hospital, Banjul, Gambia, where certain analytical facilities could be shared with the existing clinical biochemical laboratory. A similar one may be established in Sierra Leone, using the central government hospital in Freetown. These small-scale quality control laboratories are expected ultimately to become independent and grow into larger and more sophisticated labs, if the resources are available and the demands on them justify the expansion.

It is important for a country to announce in the national drug policy its intention of supplying good-quality essential drugs to its citizens. It must then be prepared to allocate money for the establishment of a quality control system. To calculate the financial commitment involved, a feasibility study should be conducted to spell out both the capital and recurrent expenditures, and the manpower involved. For countries with limited budgetary provision, it may be necessary to phase the project over a certain length of time.

Making a start

Once there is a national drug policy to protect people from poor-quality drugs, the drug testing programme can begin by making special arrangements to use the facilities of existing national laboratories in another country—an example of technical cooperation among developing countries (TCDC). An interesting arrangement has been made among Member-States within the West African Pharmaceutical Federation. Drug samples from Gambia, Sierra Leone and Liberia, where at present there are no national quality control laboratories, are sent to Ghana or Nigeria for testing. It is better for countries to start somewhere, using available resources—the WHO Certification Scheme, and existing laboratory facilities—than to have no scheme at all and risk wasting any of the drugs they have purchased at such high cost to the nation and its people.

Drug regulation is concerned with quality, safety and efficiency under the umberalla of International Conference of Drug Regulatory Authority (ICDRA)

India's need for essential drugs is still not fully met. Patent laws do not cover over 95% of the essential drugs. Bulk manufacture of the generic drug and dispensing them in inexpensive packages to bulk consumers like hospitals will substantially reduce the budget needed to meet the drug cost in public health system. The possibility of providing a dual pricing system for generic and brand drugs will be explored so that essential drugs under generic name are available at affordable cost. This approach can subsequently form the base and basis of "drug cooperatives" as community-managed institutions.[9]

NOTES AND REFERENCES

1. Hiroshi Nakijama, How Essential is an Essential Drugs Policy, *World Health*, March-April, 1992, p. 3.
2. John Daniel Rainhorn and Maimuna Bah Sangare, Antibiotics: an Overwebed Remedy, *World Health*, March-April, 1995, p. 15.
3. WHO On Being Incharge, Geneva, 1980, W 100-61 and 174-75.
4. WHO: *World Health*, A Drug Policy that bears fruit, March-April, 1995, pp. 16-17.
5. WHO: Ideas for Action, *World Health*, March-April, 1995, p. 26.
6. A.W.E—Borolossyn Advantages of an EDL, *World Health*, Dec. 1985, pp. 3-6.
7. *Ibid.*, p. 6.
8. John Dunne, Fore-Warned is Fore-Armed, *World Health*, December 1985, p. 26.
9. Ninth Five Year Plan, p. 183.

APPENDIX 14.1

Model List of Drugs Brought up-to-date

The use of essential drugs, no. 722 in WHO's Technical Report Series contains the latest version of the WHO Model List of Essential Drugs. The Model List is revised periodically by the members of the WHO Expert Committee on the Use of Essential Drugs.

Besides giving the Model List in full with explanatory notes. The use of essential drugs also includes guidelines for establishing a national essential drugs programme. Criteria for selection of drugs and dosage forms, and a list of information services offered by WHO. The following are some interesting extracts from this new WHO publication.

Criteria for the selection of essential drugs

Essential drugs are those that satisfy the health care needs of the majority of the population; they should therefore be available at all times in adequate amounts and in the appropriate dosage forms.

The choice of such drugs depends on many factors such as the pattern of prevalent diseases; the treatment facilities; the training and experience of the available personnel; the financial resources and genetic, demographic, and environmental factors. Only those drugs should be selected for which sound and adequate data on efficacy and safety are available from adequate clinical studies and for which evidence of performance in general use in a variety of medical settings has been obtained.

Each selected drug must be available in a form in which adequate quality, including bioavailability, can be assured; its stability under the anticipated conditions of storage and use must be established. Where two or more drugs appear to be approximately similar in the above respects, the choice between them should be made on the basis of a careful evaluation of their relative efficacy, safety, quality, price, and availability. In cost comparisons between drugs the cost of the total treatment and not only the unit cost of the drug, must be considered. In some cases the choice may also be influenced by other factors, such as comparative pharmacokinetic properties, or by local considerations such as the availability of facilities for manufacture or storage.

In the great majority of cases essential drugs should be formulated as single compounds. Fixed-ratio combination products are acceptable only when the dosage of each ingredient meets the requirements of a defined population group and when the combination provides a proven advantage over single compounds administered separately in therapeutic effect safety or compliance.

Essential drugs and primary health care criteria for the selection of drugs for primary health care

The Expert Committee on the Selection of Essential Drugs in its first report recommended the compilation of a separate list of drugs appropriate for use in primary health care. After broad consultation, and having regard to situations in which a traditional healer or community health worker rather than a qualified doctor is the patients' first point of reference, the present Expert Committee has selected 23 substances from main list that might be considered this purpose. They are listed below. It cannot be emphasized too strongly that, in practice, the selection must be determined nationally since the training and responsibilities of these workers vary within wide limits. The following factors. However, will inevitably influence the content of the list:

(1) *Existing systems of medicine*: The establishment of primary health care services should not result abrupt disruption of prevailing cultural patterns in rural communities. But the work of traditional healers should be adapted and supplemented in such a way as to ensure that innovation is successfully integrated into existing systems of care.

(2) *The national health infrastructure*: The type of primary health care service that a country requires is dependent upon the proximity and nature of the first referral facilities. It is still not unusual in some countries for the nearest permanently manned health post to be one or more days travelling time from isolated villages in its catchment area.

(3) *Training and supplies*: The numbers of trained personnel, the facilities placed at their disposal, and the supplies entrusted to them determine both the scope and the limitations of the primary health care system. Workers with one or more years' vocational training can obviously accomplish more than personnel reliant upon an intensive course of practical instruction lasting only a few weeks. But, whatever the circumstances, little can be accomplished unless continuity of essential supplies and information is assured.

The pattern of endemic disease: The prevalence of major endemic infections and parasitic diseases may vary from region to region within a country in conformity with climatic, geographical, topographical, social, economic, and occupational factors. Careful planning and in some cases, epidemiological surveys are required to ensure that the most effective drugs are provided and to obtain benefit from limited resources.

A model list of drugs for primary health care

- Acetylsalicycle acid
- activated charcoal
- an antacid
- an antihaemorrhoidal drug

- atropine (antispasmodic)
- benozoic acid + salicylic acid
- benzyl benzoate
- calamine lotion
- chlorhexidine solution
- chloroquine
- chlorphenamine
- ephedrine (asthma)
- ergometrine (postpartum haemorrhage)
- gentian violet also known as crystal violet
- (International Nonproprietary Name: methylrosanilinium chloride)
- Iodine
- ipecacuanha
- iron/folic acid (nutritional supplement during pregnancy)
- lindane
- mebendazole
- oral rehydration salts
- paracetamol
- piperazine
- tetracycline eye ointment

The selected drugs which should be available in the dosage forms specified in the main list, can be used effectively and safely by responsible individuals with little formal medical knowledge. The list is adapted to the needs of a malarious area (free from chloroquine resistance) where helminthic infections are also endemic, and the instructions for using the drugs can be based upon the recognition of a few basic clinical signs and symptoms.

Highly trained workers might use a wider range of drugs appropriate to their diagnostic skills with acceptable safety. However, where there is no scarcity of medical manpower, the provision of comprehensive emergency and domiciliary services involves the use of many potent drugs. Decisions regarding the availability of specific drugs to community health workers can be taken only when all relevant locally operative factors have been taken into account. In ideal circumstances antibiotics for instance, should be used only by individuals with advanced diagnostic skills and with access to appropriate microbiological facilities. However, the need for these drugs is as great in isolated rural communities as elsewhere, and health administrators have a prime responsibility to ensure that, as far as possible, basic medical services are brought within the reach of the whole population.

Source: WHO: *World Health*, Dec. 1995, pp. 28-29.

APPENDIX 14.2

National Drug Regulatory Authorities

No drug should be offered for sale unless persuasive assurances can be offered regarding its quality, efficacy and safety. It is the responsibility of national drug regulatory authorities to ensure that quality, efficacy and safety are rigorously maintained. Close contacts between these authorities and WHO serve as an important channel for the exchange of information.

Essential Drugs

Countries with limited resources need to rationalise drug procurement in order to make their health care systems effective. WHO has produced a Model List of some 250 Essential Drugs to meet basic health care needs. Countries are invited to adapt the model list to their own specific national needs.

Drug Monitoring

Everyone who prescribes or uses drugs should be aware that they are biologically active agents which are never totally devoid of risk. Adverse effects of drugs need to be closely monitored to make sure that unexpected hazards are identified. For many years, countries with highly evolved monitoring facilities have been coordinating their activities under the aegis of WHO.

Drug Names

A single drug is often sold under many brand names, possibly differing from country to country. The drug may also be combined with other drugs in yet more branded products. Some widely used drugs are available globally in well over 100 products with totally different names. There should never be any doubt, however, about the composition of a medicine. Every proprietary product should carry, in addition to the brand name, an officially approved non-proprietary or generic name for each ingredient. WHO's list of 5,000 international non-proprietary names (INNs), compiled over the last 30 years, has brought about the world-wide standardization of drug nomenclature.

Good Manufacturing Practice (GMP)

Drug manufacture is a complex and exacting task: every stage must be carefully controlled. WHO has therefore issued a ode for Good Practices in the Manufacture and Quality Control of Drugs (GMP). The guidance given sets a standard for government inspectors. No aspect of the process escapes attention: the GMP code covers not only the manufacturing operations themselves, but the layout of premises, hygiene and sanitation. Staffing measures taken to assure quality, labelling and packaging routines, and maintenance of records and procedures for handling complaints.

The WHO Certification Scheme

Countries importing drugs need to know that they have been produced according to the WHO guidelines on good manufacturing practice. The WHO Certification Scheme on the Quality of Pharmaceutical Products Moving in International Commerce was devised to provide this assurance. The governments of most drug exporting countries have acceded to this scheme by agreeing to provide, on request, an attestation on whether a factory has been inspected, and whether a product is available for sale in the country of origin.

Quality Control Laboratories

There is usually no simple way of detecting a sub-standard, degraded or spurious drug. The countries most vulnerable to unacceptable products are those without a national drug quality control laboratory that would be a cost-effective investment in virtually every country.

The International Pharmacopoeia

In producing the International Pharmacopoeia, WHO has aimed to support the concept of the modest quality control laboratory. The IPh provides for a full analysis of all the drugs on WHO's Model List; 70 per cent of these tests can be performed in the simplest of the recommended laboratories.

Source: WHO: *World Health*, Dec. 1995, pp. 16-17.

Managing Equipment

Upto eighty percent of the medical equipment in developing countries is permanently out of order. Fortunately a new breed of maintenance technicians is undergoing training in France.

Equipments in hospitals are essential for diagnosis and treatment. Without these, it would be impossible for the health experts to conduct their activities and ensure good health care. However, these equipments are becoming very complex and costly. Thus, there is a need of good equipment management in the hospitals. M. Mohan Murali, Professor, Bio-medical Engineering, Department of Electronics. University College of Engineering, Osmania University, Hdyderabad rightly says that quality and delivery of health care depends to a large extent upon proper management of biomedical equipment. Health authorities have given a very low priority to this important need. Hence, one of the pressing problems is proper regular maintenance of Bio-medical equipment, 60 per cent of which are in an unserviceable state, especially, in the government health institutions, due to lack of in-house maintenance set-up.

Medical institution requires utilization of wide variety of equipment ranging from the simplest to the most complicated for diagnostic, therapeutic and it is becoming complex day-by-day because of the scientific and technological revolution.

There are five major procedures used in managing equipment, i.e. ordering, storing, issuing, controlling/maintaining and standardization:

(i) Ordering Equipment

The first important requirement for ordering equipment is to analyze requirements based on past experience and future requirements. This has to be done carefully, otherwise this can result in unnecessary purchases and thus less money would be available for buying for important equipments. After this analysis, we may balance the requirements with the resources available so that one can remain within budgetary limits. This process can be facilitated with the help of catalogues, which are easily available and this would avoid the chances of forgetting important items. After this, an order or a requisition form is prepared in all details and specifications to avoid later complications.

(ii) Storing Equipment

Equipment must be stored carefully, otherwise there is a danger of pilferage or breakage. Equipment can be stored either in a proper store or at the place of use. Inventory of the store must be well maintained and proper accounts must be maintained through stock ledger. Care must be taken to enter each item in a ledger on a separate page so that the entry for similar new items added or issued can be done on that very page and the stock position can be analysed at a glance.

(iii) Issuing Equipment

Each hospital has many wards, laboratories, etc., where equipment is required. Each ward or unit must be responsible for the equipment issued to them. They should keep liaison with the store to replenish the consumed articles or repairs of some other articles. The person who signs the issue voucher takes responsibility for the care of the apparatus or equipment. issue vouchers must be filled and a copy kept in the store. It has been mentioned by many stores officers in the hospitals that the various units articles issued without requirements and sell them in the market. There is a need to keep a proper control through surprise check of the use of these articles.

(iv) Controlling and Maintaining Equipment

This is the most important aspects of equipment management as it has been observed that most of the non-expendable equipment remains out of order for a long time. There have been cases where the machinery remains out of order for years together. Therefore, there is a need to educate the staff in the proper up keep of the equipment. Besides, there is a need to take action to get the equipment in order if some mechanical defect enter into its working. This is a very serious problem in most of the hospitals. If a list is got prepared of the non-working equipment in health units, it may come to near about 60% which is very serious as it affects the working of these units. It has also been mentioned by some (During Discussion) that the equipment is intentionally made unworkable in connivance with the private practitioners so that the patients can be directed to them for examination.

The maintenance and controlling of equipment should be done from the headquarters. Karnataka Health Systems Development Project assessed the existing set-up of equipment maintenance in Karnataka health system and suggested some steps which need implementation. The same is true about other states. Let us quote from this report. The existing Health

Equipment Repair and Maintenance Unit in the Directorate is inadequate when compared to the vast range of equipment spread all over the state. There are only nine persons under the Health Equipment Officer. There is only one X-Ray technician, two semi-skilled artisans and one dark room assistant. The remaining five are administrative and Group D Staff.

It is proposed to revamp this unit by inducting qualified Mechanical Biomedical/Electrical/Electronics engineers who have adequate familiarity with hospital equipment systems. The same is needed in other states.

The objectives of the revamped unit will be to:

1. Provide expert technical services and advice on the purchase of equipment, spares, service contracts, etc.;
2. Procure, install, commission, maintain and service biomedical and other hospital equipment for diagnosis, monitoring, analysis and therapy, etc.;
3. Maintain and service heating, ventilation, air-conditioning (HVAC) systems, power systems, etc.;
4. Carry out minor maintenance works related to buildings, electrical and sanitary fixtures;
5. Organise training programs for biomedical technicians and users;
6. Modify existing equipment, if required, by the doctors; and
7. Maintain records for administration and management purposes.

The technical services of the unit would be effectively used in:

(a) Studying the equipment needs;
(b) Selection of equipment based on technical evaluation;
(c) Preparation of sites and basic utilities;.
(d) Installation, commissioning and acceptance;
(e) Preventive maintenance, wherever required; and
(f) Training of users.

Professional management of the system will ensure that there is no procurement of obsolete systems, which may prove to be ineffective and uneconomical, involving huge operational costs. Other shortcomings such as inadequate radiation protection, uneven load distribution, noise and vibration level of equipment, lack of temperature and humidity controlled environment, electrical leakage. Explosion hazards due to gases, etc. should also be avoided. Besides, the staff dealing with equipment should be convinced of the need for maintenance. For this purpose following actions need to be taken:

(a) To convince staff of the importance of cleaning, inspecting and keeping equipment in good order; of reporting defects immediately; and of returning equipment to its correct place after use.

(b) To use an inspection check-list and inspection schedule.
(c) To detect discrepancies and explain them.
(d) There is no easy way to convince staff of the need to clean equipment and keep it in good condition. The best way is for the supervisor (health-worker manager) to set a personal example and to emphasize that equipment must be cared for.
(e) To prevent transmission of infection, e.g., by a dirty instrument.
(f) To keep it in good condition (dirty or damp equipment deteriorates more rapidly than equipment that is kept clean and dry); and to economize.

(v) Codification and Standardisation

In any undertaking having a large number of items, codification is essential. It hardly needs any emphasis that codification of items is a pre-requisite for introduction of mechanisation in stock control and purchases and stores accounting. There are two systems which are commonly used for the purpose—Brich System, the Kodak System. The major objectives of the codification are:

1. The classification of items on functional basis to ensure that one item is kept under one code.
2. To bring together the items according to their degree of similarity to reveal excessive variety and the substitutes available.
3. To list items as per National/International standards instead of vendor's numbers, wherever possible.
4. To prepare a catalogue indicating the necessary details of procurement action, which can be used as reference by the users.

Medicine today depends increasingly on instrument technology, but the equipment used must be carefully selected to be appropriate to its site, and needs competent maintenance and repair. The lack of technicians and spare parts, misinformation, poor instructions, inappropriate, poor instructions, purchases and donations—these and other problems all contribute to the current lamentable situation, where upto 80 percent of medical equipment in developing countries does not work.

ANALYSIS AND SUGGESTIONS

It is a matter of great concern that most of the equipment in hospitals either remains out of order or is not available. What are its consequences? This leads to insufficient utilisation of manpower and inefficient health services. It is very distressing to note that a number of Bio-medical Equipments used in our hospitals are lying unserviceable and there seems to be no proper organisation and arrangements for care and maintenance of these sophisticated apparatus. This is the foremost problem faced today by many of these hospitals. Medical development creating a demand, for, further complex medical equipments for diagnoses, therapy, monitoring visualization, prosthesis, life support system, etc., which depend on a technology in which few hospitals have knowledge or training. Without proper maintenance, no equipment can perform satisfactory functions. As more and more sophisticated Bio-medical equipments come into use, the requirement of specialised services for maintenance and repair will become more critical and bring with it the need to recognise Bio-medical Engineering (BME) support. This would ensure that bio-medical equipment is always in a condition fit for its purpose.

WHO in its technical report suggests the following:

1. There is a real need for the relevant technology in the community.
2. There is a suitable place in which to install the equipment.
3. All necessary support in the form of electricity, water and air conditioning, if required, is available and of reliable quality.
4. The equipment has a genuine warranty period, even if it is a gift.
5. A user's manual is supplied in a language that can be understood by the users.
6. Spare parts and maintenance supplies are readily available.
7. Consumable supplies used with it are readily available and affordable.
8. Technicians or engineers, who can maintain the equipment are available.
9. There are staff who know how to use the equipment or can be trained to use it.

Preventive maintenance is a continuous maintenance procedure wherein the condition of the equipment is watched through a systematic inspection mechanism and preventive action taken to reduce the incidence of breakdown. The necessity for either major or minor repairs is determined to prevent unscheduled interruptions or deterioration of equipment. The fundamental activities of preventive maintenance are:

(a) Periodical inspection of the equipment to discover conditions of deterioration.
(b) Upkeep of equipment to remove or repair such conditions while they are still in a minor stage.

The salient advantages of such a system have been identified as:

(a) Continuous availability of equipment.
(b) Increased life of the equipment.

(c) Prolonged service.
(d) Timely replacement of spares.
(e) Timely availability.
(f) Satisfactory quality of services.
(g) Safety of operation.
(h) Savings in Costs of repairs.

Training for medical technicians

Mays L. Swicord and Diana Gibson in their article "On the Mend" in *World Health,* July 1986 observes that the training courses in France and Cyprus for medical technicians are a necessary first step towards dealing with the maintenance problems of the developing countries. However, the size of the problem calls for much more strenuous efforts, beginning with the establishment of stronger ties between the Lyon and Nicosia centres, national health authorities and the WHO regional offices.

National health authorities can identify the need for particular skills and select individuals to be sent for training. The WHO regional offices can help in this process, and should be willing to sponsor the trainees with WHO fellowships. Then, possibly with WHO support, the countries can set-up local workshops where returned trainees undertake both maintenance and repairs.

The few centres in existence today cannot possibly meet the demand for trained medical equipment technicians. WHO hopes, therefore, that in future the workshops set-up in developing countries will themselves become training centres addressing specific local needs. These centres will depend on Lyon (for French speaking countries) and Nicosia (for English speaking countries) for technical direction and for the training of instructors.

The hospital equipment technicians course in Lyon does not attempt to solve all of the problems of maintenance in developing countries. Rather, the Higher International Institute hopes to be part of a chain of similar centres, including that in Nicosia. Although the need for trained maintenance technicians is urgent, the Institute's director does not plan to expand the programme until it is well established and has proved its responsiveness to the needs of developing countries.

The course demands a certain sacrifice on the part of foreign students, many of whom are supporting families at home, like Mayacine N'Diaye. But he thinks it is worth it. "I am glad to be here because I shall be more capable when I go back to the Ministry of Health. I want to pass on my new knowledge, and bring down maintenance costs in Senengal still further. The health budget is very low—we have to do good work with the equipment we have, and we can't do that without a good maintenance service."

Most medical equipment failures in developing countries are due to simple faults such as a blown fuse, a defective electrical connection, or simply the inability of the operator to install the equipment properly.

Therefore, the Lyon training course—unique in France—is designed to be practical. The emphasis is on teaching the student to (1) get the equipment into operating order, (2) perform basic preventive maintenance, (3) carry out common corrective maintenance, and (4) identify the fault in a major breakdown and give correct information to the factory or central repair facility.

However, there is a need of more much training institutions to keep up-to-date all the equipments and help the patients in their diagnosis.

16

CHAPTER

Records Management in a Hospital

Records Management is a programme that involves the functions of creating, administering, retaining, submitting and destroying records. Herbert Hoover has rightly mentioned the advantages of proper records keeping when he says: "A decision is only as good as the facts on which it is based." Records are the memory of the internal and external transactions of an organisation. By external transaction we mean the correspondence between the organization and its patient-beneficiaries. By internal transaction is meant the dealings on external transactions by persons in the organizations at all levels. Records contain a written evidence of the activities of an organization in the form of letters, circulars, reports, contracts, invoices, vouchers, minutes of meeting, books of accounts, etc. Thus, the records management is concerned with the retaining, submitting and destroying of records. The proper maintenance of these records in right quantity and quality is the essence of records management. The success of this record-keeping would be reflected in the timely availability of all the records. In the context of Medical Records, Dr. McGibony had said:

> "A chronicle of the pageantry of medical and scientific progress is found in the hospital records."

Medical record is a clinical, scientific, administrative and legal document relating to patient care in which sufficient data is recorded, written in sequence to justify the diagnosis and warrant the treatment and end results. Whenever a sick individual visits his doctor, either in his private clinic or a hospital, and receives medical treatment, certain amount of documentation is essential. It may be in the form of a very brief note of his symptoms, clinical features, diagnosis and prescription or it may be in the form of detailed case-sheet. Certain amount of documentation is also

CHART 16.1

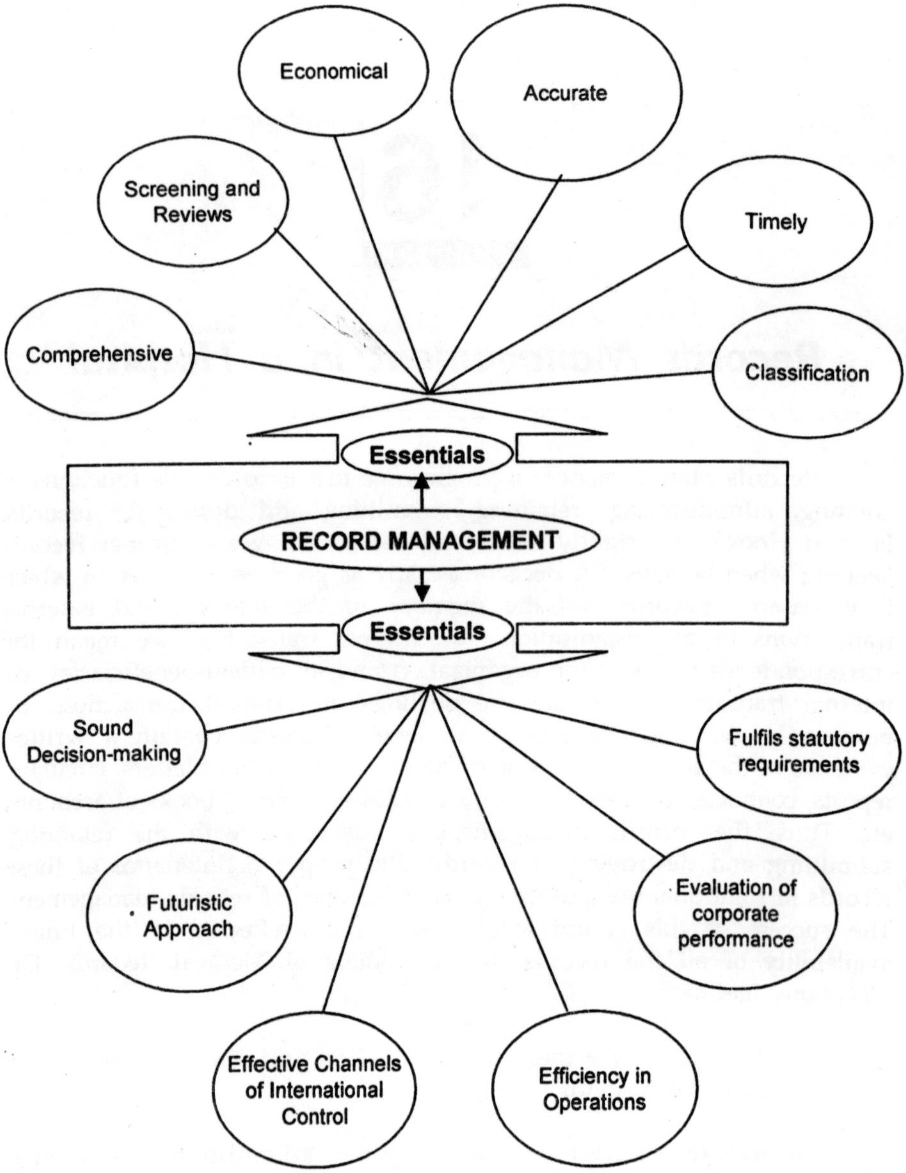

Comprehensive
Screening and Reviews
Economical
Accurate
Timely
Classification
Essentials
RECORD MANAGEMENT
Essentials
Sound Decision-making
Futuristic Approach
Effective Channels of International Control
Efficiency in Operations
Evaluation of corporate performance
Fulfils statutory requirements

done in various registers in OPDs, wards laboratories, X-Ray departments and operation theatre. This documentation is called Medical Record. Documentation about a sick individual is essential for the hospital management in planning, budgeting as well as for medical and epidemiological studies.

According to Huffman Edna, "Medical records provide means of communication between physicians and other professionals contributing to the patient care."

According to Malcolm T. MacEachern: "The medical record, a description of a patient's illness, the treatment administered and the results achieved, goes back into antiquity but its use as an essential tool in the hospital for aiding the patient, the physician and medical research grew out of modern conditions.

Under the Chairmanship of Shri A.P. Jain, a study group on hospitals was convened in 1967 by the Ministry of Health to go into hospital management in India and is popularly known as Jain Committee Report. The Committee has observed that "Medical Records Department is the vital link between the hospitals and public which keeps on record the full details of every patient from the time he enters the hospital to the time of his discharge.

Importance of Medical Records

The medical records serve the patient in the following ways:

- It serves to document the past medical history.
- It helps to avoid omissions and repetitions of investigations and other therapeutic procedures.
- It ensures continuity of patient care.
- It serves as documentary evidence in medico-legal cases.
- It supplies necessary information for insurance and employment purposes.

For the hospital, medical records serve it and its staff by:

- Indicating the type and quantity of work load.
- Furnishing proof of timeliness, type and quality of medical-care.
- Protecting the hospital in legal cases.
- Evaluating proficiency of hospital staff.
- Providing data for future planning by the hospital administration.
- Justifying additional allotment of funds, accommodation and hospital staff.

Moreover, medical records are also beneficial in research as well as for public health:

- It serves as a basis for all clinical research as well as group studies for educational purposes.
- Medical Records are of immense benefit to the Public Health Department at districts/state/central level. These records contain reliable information regarding morbidity and mortality

pattern of the dependent population and thus help to plan preventive measures to provide better health care to the community.

Medical Records serve the medical profession in the following ways:.

- Provide assurance of quality and adequacy of diagnostic and therapeutic measures undertaken.
- Ensure continuity of medical-care.
- Help in evaluation of medical practice.

The data generated by Medical Records is extremely useful for

- Carrying out studies by under/post-graduate students.
- It also aids informal education of the physicians and para-medical staff.

Medico-legal aspects

- Hospital medical records are admissible as documentary evidence in a court of law under the Indian Evidence Act, 1872.
- The information contained in Medical Records can be used for:
  - (i) LIC.
  - (ii) Income Tax purposes.
  - (iii) Execution of wills by patients.
  - (iv) Malpractice suits.
  - (v) Personal injuries suits.
  - (vi) Certification of births and death.

Rights/Ownership/Privileges

Medical Records are primarily a medico-administrative document describing what all has happened to a patient within the hospital. Administratively, they are as important as the records dealing with finance, personnel, or inventory records. Although intimate happenings to the patient during his stay in the hospital are recorded by doctors and nurses in the medical record, yet the record is the property of the hospital and not of the patient or the doctor or any clinical department. The hospital is the owner and custodian of the medical records. As such, it is the responsibility of hospital administration that information contained in the record is not publicly divulged under any circumstances, without consent of the patient, except under due process of law.

The medical record is a clinical, scientific, administrative and legal document relating to patient care in which is recorded sufficient data written in sequence of events to justify the diagnosis and warrant the treatment and end results.

ESSENTIALS OF RECORDS MANAGEMENT

1. Comprehensive

The records should be such as can be easily understood when retrieved back for planning, policy-making and decision-making. The language used should be simple and understandable.

2. Properly Planned

The records be screened at regular intervals of time to weed out the information not required for future. In this way, we can reduce the paper work to twenty-five per cent. This would indirectly help us in locating the desired information quickly.

3. Economical

We should manage the records economically so that we may achieve more with minimum efforts.

4. Accurate

The records should be accurate otherwise its utility would be doubtful.

5. Timely

The time taken in retrieving the information should be as short as possible. Reducing retrieval time is essential for effective materials management.

6. Classification

Records must be classified to be of practical use. The classification be done either on the basis of subject or chronology.

According to Dr. K. Pennathur, records should:

1. Serve specific needs.
2. Have specific objectives and purposes.
3. Be kept to a minimum with respects to number, scope and content.
4. Be designed for least expensive handling.
5. Be up-to-date.
6. Be worth their cost.
7. Be related directly to tabulations and reports that will stem from them.
8. Be available when needed.
9. Be considered valuable by supervisors and lines management.

CONTENTS OF MEDICAL RECORDS

Broadly medical records at lower levels include:

1. The information regarding the characteristics of population collected through baseline survey of villages also provides details about health problems and the health needs in the community. This is useful for preparing a program of health services, education for the area and priorities for health activities.
2. Facts about births and deaths, besides serving as an indicator of population growth, can help to focus attention on target groups for specific health services.
3. The records of pregnant mothers can help to sort out high-risk cases needing institutional delivery, normal pregnancy, cases which can be attended by trained Dai or by female health worker at home for post-natal and infant care at a later stage.
4. Morbidity data about various illnesses occurring in the area can serve as an index of the state of health of the population and prevalent diseases in the area and if any epidemic occurs.
5. Information about reproductive couples, especially together with data on number of living children of each couple, is invaluable for carrying out an effective programme for family planning education and motivation.
6. Records are also most helpful in planning for health education programme.
7. A carefully kept record of stock of drugs, dressings and other equipment received and issued will help in knowing when and how to indent the items required for sub-centre.

The medical record is clear, concise and accurate history of the patient's life and illness, written from the health and medical point of view. The story of the patients illness narrated by the patient, observations made by nurses and the comments and treatment given by the doctors are recorded in the medical record. Thus, the medical record comprises three general sections:

(i) a general section covering administrative and personal data. The socio-economic record of the patient includes: The name of the Patient, Father's or Husband's Name, Age, Sex, Religion, Income, Patient's Address and the Address of nearest relative. Other administrative information which are included are — The data of admission. The in-patient number. The name of the nursing unit and bed number. This sheet is prepared in the Central Admitting Office;

(ii) a nurses section wherein are noted the observations of the trained nurses and the details of treatment administered. This part of the medical record consists of graphic charts relating to Temperature, Pulse, Respiration, Blood Pressure and any other observations maintained, intake output chart and medicine administered;

(iii) a medical section containing statements on the studies, observations, conclusions and activities of the attending doctors or of the intern or the resident working under him. The medical section of the record consists of the entire medical history of the patient. It contains:
- History sheet
- Physical examination sheet
- Provisional diagnosis
- All the investigation reports
- Physicians orders sheet
- Treatment, medical or surgical
- Anesthesia record
- Operation record
- Obstetric record
- Consultancy report
- Progress report
- Final diagnosis
- Discharge summary
- If death—Cause of death
- Autopsy report

CLASSIFICATION

The classification of records would depend upon the nature of organisation. However, it would be useful to classify records into the following four-fold classifications:[1]

(a)	Vital Records	Protected and preserved for a long time.
(b)	Important Records	Not çurrently in use but are of high value to retain.
(c)	Useful Records	Currently used correspondence.
(d)	Transit Records	Useful for only a short period till the subject is alive or active.

MECHANISM OF RECORDS MANAGEMENT

Records are classified and changed into reports.

Reporting

Reports are the information communicated to the higher levels of the health services. They constitute an important management tool to influence future actions. Good management of health services depends on accurate records and reports. Officials at PHC, District, State and Central levels depend on health workers and health assistants for accurate information about health conditions and health services in rural area.[1] They compile the information on routine basis and transmit the same from one level to the next higher level. As the staff at various levels in the health organization have not been able to perceive the utilization of health information either at their level or below for implementation and monitoring of services, it remains unutilized.[2]

There are two basic instruments through which we create and maintain records, i.e. forms and files. Let us discuss in brief about these two mechanisms.

Filing

Filing is the process of classifying, arranging and storing records systematically so that these can be easily retrieved. Neuner and Haynes defined filing as the systematic arrangement for keeping of business correspondence and records so that these may be found and delivered quickly when needed for reference in future; George R. Terry defines, "Filing is the placing of document and papers in acceptable containers according to some pre-determined arrangement so that any of these when required, may be located quickly and conveniently."

Filing Arrangement

The files can be arranged on anyone or more of the following basis depending upon the need of the organization:

1. Alphabetical order
2. Numerical order
3. Geographic order
4. Chronological order
5. Subject-wise

Many variations and innovations in these five general systems of filing have been developed, e.g., the use of colours, sound and special visual devices. In the offices of the Government of India and State Government, filing system is based on subject system. This system has many defects—lack of uniformity, lack of clear-cut demarcation and time-consuming tracing process.

The question of filing system was examined by the Administrative Reforms Commission and they recommended the functional filing system. The proposed system can be elaborated as follows:

(a) The main subjects under the functions, say establishment, common office services, budget, are first listed under functional group headings which are respectively identified by capital letters, 'A', 'B', etc.
(b) Each main subject or main head under each functional group is assigned consecutive Arabic numerals beginning with 'I' which may go upto '99'.
(c) Similarly, the sub-subjects or sub-heads under each main head

are assigned consecutive. Arabic numerals beginning with 'II' which also could go upto '99'.

(d) The identifying subject numerals and sub-subject numerals are separated by '0' the group of numerals to the left of '0' refer the main head while that to the right to its sub-head, topic or aspect.

(e) Files opened under the same subject, etc. are given serial number 1, 2 and 3 and so on and separated from the groups of numerals by an oblique.

(f) The year in which the file is opened is shown separately from the file number by an oblique.

(g) At the end of each file code number is to be indicated with the abbreviated form of a section or a unit.

File Indexing

File indexing is a key to locate the files. Index is a reference list used for locating a particular document in the filing equipment. The following types of indexing may be used for locating:

- Vertical card indexing.
- Visible card indexing.
- Loose leaf book indexing.

Centralized and Decentralized Filing System

Centralized filing system is one, where all the filing equipments and personnel are located in a single area of the office, accessible to all departments by messengers, controlled by a centralized plan or index of the filing. Decentralized filing system, also called departmentalized filing system is one, where each organization makes its own arrangement for filing.

Advantage of Centralized Filing Area

1. It ensures uniformity and standardization of the filing equipment and procedure which can help in easy and quick location of records.
2. It eliminates the need of duplication and distribution to all concerned sections. It encourages completeness of related documents.
3. It enhances economy of time for both file users and file personnel because there is only one place to send material to be filed, and one place to find it.
4. Control is exercised more effectively since one person or group alone is responsible, which minimises oversights and loss of valuable records.
5. It promotes economy of filing equipment and floor space.

To be most effective, a compromise has to be struck between centralized and decentralized filing system. Decentralized filing should be kept to a minimum.

ADVANTAGES OF RECORDS KEEPING

The records help the management in the following ways:

1. Help in Sound Decision-making

Effective decision-making depends to a great extent upon the adequate information provided by the records and availability of these records in time.

2. Effective Channel of Internal Control

Records are very important to ensure internal control. Records can help in minimizing chance of error and prevent occurrence of fraud and completion.

3. Facilitate Evaluation of Health Institutions Performance

The records can help in evaluating the performance of an organization during definite intervals of time and different periods. Besides, records can help in comparing the performance of organization in the same line.

4. Promotes Efficiency of Operations

The effective operation of an organization depend to a great extent upon the speed and accuracy of the records. Records keep the wheels of the organization moving fast.

5. Fulfils Statutory Requirement

Records are also kept in compliance with the provisions of different statutes. Besides, records are needed in the event of litigations, disputes or claims.

6. Futuristic Approach

Analysis of records help in ascertaining future trends which can help in better policy-making and planning. The fundamental reason for promoting maintenance of an adequate medical record is its utility to good patient care, to the doctor, to the hospital and towards medical education and research. Besides, the legal requirements of the hospital medical records are also to be completed.

USE OF HOSPITAL STATISTICS FOR MANAGEMENT

The Medical Records Department in a Hospital is mainly responsible for the collection as well as analysis of the data to ensure utilization of the hospital for patient care. Such data has immense value for the day-to-day management of the hospitals as well as future planning of the hospital services. Let us mention some of the important information which is used by the hospital management to enhance the hospital functioning through hospital records.

1. Death Rates

Hospital deaths include deaths of patients admitted to the hospital. Deaths are generally classified into two categories, i.e. the Gross Deaths and the Net Deaths. Gross deaths includes all the deaths of admitted patients while Net Deaths exclude the patients dying within 48 hours of admission. Net Deaths in a hospital is a reflection on the working of the hospital. Net death rate is calculated as follows:

$$\frac{\text{Number of net deaths during a period of time}}{\text{Total discharges during that period time}} \times 100$$

On an average, net death rates range between 4 to 6 per cent. Any gross variations from the normally expected net death rate indicates an abnormal phenomenon which should be analysed by the hospital management Such deviation can either be due to natural causes or due to failure on the part of one of the service areas of the hospital. In case of later event, correctives need be applied and death rate brought back to the normal expected range.

The use of net death rate for enhancing the efficiency of the hospital services is not only limited to the overall net death rate of the hospital but also can be split into death rates of various departments and units of the hospital. As such. the hospital management can keep a track of the performance of each and every units department of the hospital by keeping a track of their net-death rates. This is being practiced in most of the teaching hospitals, but not in district hospitals.

2. Average Length of Stay

The length of stay of patients is one of the important hospital indices. The day of admission of the patient is always taken into consideration and the date/day of discharge is always ignored. Irrespective of the time of admission or the time of discharge. Through the process of discharge analysis. the average length of stay of patients discharged during a particular period of time is worked out not only for the whole hospital but also department-wise, unit-wise. The aim of this information is to locate the unnecessary length of stay and to discourage it. By reducing the unnecessary length of stay, more patients can be admitted to the hospital and be provided services. This information, therefore, is not only important from the economic point of view but is also important from the community services point of view. Average length of stay is calculated as follows:

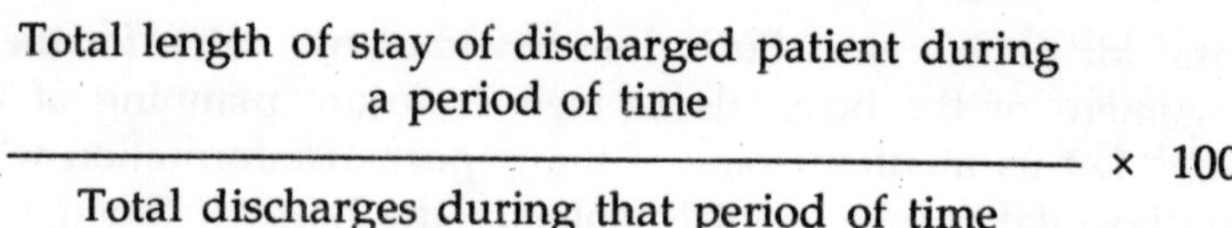

$$\frac{\text{Total length of stay of discharged patient during a period of time}}{\text{Total discharges during that period of time}} \times 100$$

3. Bed Turnover Rate

Bed Turnover Rate indicates the number of patients who have been given services per bed year. It is calculated as follows:

$$\frac{\text{Total number of discharges during a year}}{\text{Total number of authorized beds}} \times 100$$

Bed Turnover Rate is determined by the Average Length of Stay as well as the time interval between one discharge and successive admissions. This time interval is known as T-interval. Also Bed Turnover Rate as well as T -interval are important indicators of the planning/utilization of hospital resources.

4. Bed Occupancy Rate

Bed Occupancy Rate gives the relationship between the availability of facilities and their utilization. Optimum bed occupancy is treated to be between 85-90 percent An occupancy of over 90 per cent means stress is on one or another area of the hospital. When the bed occupancy rate is 100 or more than 100 percent, it is a case of dilution of hospital facilities and lowering of efficiency. Bed Occupancy Rate can be worked out for the whole hospital as well as for each discipline/unit of the hospital. as under:

$$\frac{\text{Average daily census during a period of time}}{\text{Number of authorized beds}} \times 100 = \text{Bed Occupancy Rate}$$

ISSUES AND PROBLEMS OF RECORDS MANAGEMENT IN HOSPITALS

Based upon observations, discussions and analysis, we give here the main problems faced by hospital authorities in Records Management and suggest probable solutions.

(a) Use of Out-dated Forms

At present forms being used in most of the hospitals are not in tune with the improvements in new technology and scientific developments. Some of the columns in the forms are obsolete. While many important columns are not available. It is thus essential that forms must be revised constantly to keep them up-to-date. The ultimate purpose of tabulating the data from forms becomes insignificant as the forms do not convey the desired information. It must be statutory for every organization to get their forms reviewed after every three years either by the internal O & M cells or central O&M organization.

(b) Shortage of Experienced Personnel

The hospital authorities do not attach as much weightage to records management as is done to other resources. This gives less emphasis in terms of resources to this activity. There is generally shortage of trained personnel to handle records. It is suggested that adequate, experienced personnel may be appointed to take care of records management.

(c) Lack of Storage of In-active Records

Storage should be done at a proper place where proper conditions of temperature, circulation of air and humidity are provided. Mostly, we find dirt and dust in this area. After storing the records, indexing is necessary to locate the record for retrieval.

We can reduce congestion and cost through the control of inactive records. This would indirectly help us in finding the relevant record immediately. The Secretariat Training School in its report on Work Study (III) suggested the following improvements to make effective control of the inactive records:

(i) Keep a table of the important contents of a file on the cover or a slip. This will facilitate location of contents which the title of the file or its number may not help to locate speedily.

(ii) Keep documents like records, separately from the files. This will reduce the bulk of the files and assist speedier location and use of documents not related to correspondence and notes.

(iii) Papers containing information may be carried in a third folder separately from notes and correspondence.

(iv) Persons dealing with 'information' should compile the vital elements of information and keep it at hand in cabinets for ready reference. Simple 'Home made' devices can be invented to carry such formation and reduce dependence on records.

(v) Keep a small alphabetical register of important files, cases, reports and other documents in your personal custody for more purposeful follow-up records locations and speedier disposal.

(vi) Need of Effective Handling and Processing of Records: Handling and processing of records should be simple and should consume much time and personnel resources. The expert handling and processing of records would depend upon the design of registry and its place in the office layout, rational and well laid out procedures and the training to the personnel responsible for job.

(d) Evaluation of Records Handling

There is a need to check the records frequently. A random checking can be done with the help of the following two ratios:

$$1.\ \text{Accuracy Ratio} = \frac{\text{No. of references not found}}{\text{No. of references found}}$$

$$2.\ \text{Activity Ratio} = \frac{\text{No. of references not found}}{\text{No. of documents filed}}$$

If the accuracy ratio is half or one per cent, it is thought to be excellent. If it is three per cent or more. it is in a poor state. If the activity ratio is below ten per cent, it exhibits that there is too much inactive material. If it is between ten to twenty per cent, it means that there is a need of improvement while it is more than twenty per cent, it shows that the records are in bad shape. Such evaluations can help in improving the records.

(e) Determination of Records Retention Period

There is no hard and fast rule that specific record should be retained for specific period of time. The decision regarding the retention period should be decided by the organization basing on its needs, requirement and objectives. The records which help in tracing the history of the organization and help in policy-making should be kept for long. The unwanted records should be destroyed to save time and resources.

(f) Transfer of Records

Transfer of records entails two stages, i.e. (i) Dating of unimportant records for destruction and ultimate disposal, (ii) Moving the records from active to incative files and from there to storage area. In a complex organization we can make use of micro-films. Micro-films can help in space saving, safe preservation and clean and easy handling. Besides, these reduce the risk of fire hazards and chances of loosing document.

(g) Poor Quality of Medical Records

Quantitatively, the system of medical records is fairly satisfactory, but qualitatively the medical records need lot of improvements. It is recommended that more efforts should be made by the hospital management. All clinicians as well as medical records officers towards improving the quality of medical records.

Ninth Plan has suggested the need for developing a good HMIS. However, the existing records management is very poor in our CHCs. PHCs and even district hospitals. It is very difficult to locate the records. It is happening at a time when computers with good software are available at cheap cost

HMIS is an essential management tool for effective functioning of the health system. Timely reporting and analysis of data from HMIS could also serve as an early. warning of focal outbreak of disease so that appropriate interventions can be initiated. The Central Bureau of Health Intelligence (CBHI) and the State Bureau of Health Intelligence are nodal agencies for HMIS. During the Eighth Plan Period, an attempt was made to provide a major thrust to HMIS. The CBHI in consultation with the National Informatics Centre (NIC) and State Health departments have developed HMIS version 2.0 for sending information through NICNET on essential health indices. This system is being used by 13 States/UTs for sending district level information. The system is still not fully operational in most States. During the Ninth Plan efforts are being made to ensure that the entire country is covered and all the data pertaining to the Health and Family Welfare Programmes are collected, collated and reported from all the districts through NICNET. The data from HMIS will be utilized not only for improving the efficiency and effectiveness of the health care system but also for effective policy planning.[3] (A separate chapter on HMIS is included in a separate volume)

A Case Study

Medical Record is necessary—

(a) To document to type and quantity of work
(b) To furnish proof of type and quantity of care
(c) To protect hospital in legal medical cases
(d) To evaluate proficiency of medical staff
(e) To assist in future programme planning

The efficiency and working of a hospital can be judged form its record maintenance quality. In order to find the quality of medical records, we selected at random 30 medical sheets of indoor patients, 15 form each sample CHC. We identified 10 points, on the basis of which medical records were to be checked. We tabulated the results of these in Table below in percentage. The table reveals that in 21.1 percent cases, patient name was not available, 22.3 percent had no C.R. number was mentioned and 43.4 percent cases did not have name of attending medical officer. In 6.2 and 6 percent cases there was no month and date of admission written of indoor patient and outdoor patient respectively. In 26 percent cases, no age was mentioned and 43 percent of cases sex of the patient was not mentioned.

In 70 percent cases, no diagnosis was written, in 78 percent cases, no medication was mentioned, while in 80 percent cases, no follow-up details were given. Further, in 87.4 percent cases physical examination and history was complete on 83.4 percent. Even the front sheet has been signed by MO/SMO in only 43.2 percent cases. It was very disheartening to find that there was no certification of time and date of death in 44 percent cases and cause of deaths in 56 percent cases. However, the operation sheet was complete in 71 percent cases.

From the above following inferences can be drawn:

Analysis of "Medical Record Evaluation" in CHC, Haryana

	Percentage	*Percentage*	*Percentage*
1. Are all pages of the case notes correctly identified with:	Yes	No	NA
a. Patient's Name	76.2	21.1	2.7
b. C.R. Number	76.4	22.3	1.3
c. Attending Medical Officer	54.8	43.4	1.8
2. Month and date of admission:			
a. Indoor Patients	92.2	6.2	1.6
b. Outdoor patients	90	6	4
3. Particular of Patients:			
a. Age	71	26	3
b. Sex Male/Female	54	43	3
4. Is the discharge slips contains:			
a. Diagnonsis	22.1	70	7.9
c. Medicaiton	21.8	70	8.2
d. Follow up	10.7	80	9.3
5. Are entries:			
a. Legible	87.4	9.8	2.8
b. Complete	64	28	8
6. Whether physical examination and history of patients completed on admission?	83.4	16.6	–
7. Is the relieved and discharge summary present?	27.6	72.4	–
8. Has the front sheet been correctly filled with signature of MO/SMO?	43.2	55.1	1.7
9. Was death certified in the medical record included	52	44	4
a. time and date	41	56	3/0
b. Cause of death			
10. Whether operation sheet been correctly complete?	71	29	–

(a) Medical record-keeping is good then the future work in time consuming and slow in decision-making.
(b) Decision-making by a doctor, who has not examined him in first instance becomes difficult and irrational.
(c) Medical record-keeping is not good then it is not helpful for future references, comparison and evaluation of past performance.
(d) It causes complications in Medico-legal cases.
(e) Medical record-keeping is not taken seriously, resulting in poor quality of health services.

(f) It avoids the evaluation of medical competence of the OM/SMO concerned.

(g) It is a major hurdle in making referral system and information system a success for which these CHCs have been created.

(h) Poor medical record-keeping leads to poor efficiency, performance, coordination among the doctor and workers and future planning.

Principles of Medical Records Management for future requirement:

- A record must be capable of verification.
- Record-keeping is necessary for policy formulation and decision-making
- Records must be classified to be of use.
- The purpose for which the record kept must be justified.
- The information desired must be available when needed
- Speed and accuracy are of essence for obtaining records for control
- To facilitate the detection of errors.
- Past records are helpful for follow-up action.

CONCLUSION

The success of the use of records depends upon its proper control. Control implies proper designing, printing and economical use in order to do the office work effectively and efficiently. For this purpose, there is a need of setting up a centralized committee with members from all the sections to approve all formats and classifications before they are printed and used. Secondly, a constant study at regular intervals of time of the existing records and record management methodology, etc. must be carried out to examine its relevance *vis-à-vis* the objectives of the organization. This may help in redesigning or eliminating the redundant formats or improving the existing patterns to suit the changed needs. The exercise can result in a great deal of financial saving as well as in efficiency of operations.

Notes and References

1. NIHFW, Management Training Modules for Health Assistants, (Male and. Female), New Delhi, 1987, p. 7.
2. *Ibid.*, p. 149.
3. Ninth Five Year Plan, *op. cit.*, p. 182.

BOOKS BY THE SAME AUTHOR

1. International Administration: WHO South East-Asia Regional Office (New Delhi, 1977), Sterling Publishers
2. Principles, Problems and Prospects of Co-operative Administration (New Delhi, 1979), Sterling Publishers (Co-Author Dr. B.B. Goel)
3. Administration of Personnel in Co-operative (New Delhi, 1979), Sterling Publishers (Co-Author Dr. B.B. Goel)
4. Health Care Administration: Ecology, Principles and Modern Trends (New Delhi, 1980), Sterling Publishers
5. Health Care Administration: Policy-making and Planning (New Delhi, 1980), Sterling Publishers
6. Health Care Administration: Levels and Aspects (New Delhi, 1980), Sterling Publishers
7. International Civil Service: Principles, Problems and Prospects (New Delhi, 1984), Sterling Publishers
8. Public Health Administration (New Delhi, 1984), Sterling Publishers
9. Public Personnel Administration (New Delhi, 1984), Reprint 1987, Sterling Publishers
10. International Civil Services—Principles, Problems and Prospectives (New Delhi, 1984), Sterling Publishers.
11. Social Welfare Administration: Theory and Practice (Vols. I and II) (New Delhi, 1988), Deep & Deep Publications Pvt. Ltd.
12. Hospital Administration and Management (ed.) Co-Author Dr. R. Kumar in 3 volumes (New Delhi, 1989), Deep & Deep Publications Pvt. Ltd.
13. Policy and Administration: Family Planning & Beyond (New Delhi, 1990), Deep & Deep Publications Pvt. Ltd.
14. Modern Management Techniques (Revised and Reprinted) (New Delhi, 1990), Deep & Deep Publications Pvt. Ltd.
15. Development Planning and Administration (ed.) S. Bhatnagar (Co-editor) (New Delhi, 1992), Deep & Deep Publications Pvt. Ltd.
16. Financial Administration and Management (New Delhi, 1993), Sterling Publishers
17. Advanced Public Administration (New Delhi, 1993), Sterling Publishers

18. Personnel Administration and Management
(New Delhi, 1994), Deep & Deep Publications Pvt. Ltd.
19. Educational Policy and Administration
(New Delhi, 1994), Deep & Deep Publications Pvt. Ltd.
20. Slum Improvement Through Participatory Urban Based Community Structures
(New Delhi, 1999), Deep & Deep Publications Pvt. Ltd.
21. Distance Education in 21st Century
(New Delhi, 2000), Deep & Deep Publications Pvt. Ltd.
22. Health Care System and Management: Organization and Structure
(New Delhi, 2000), Deep & Deep Publications Pvt. Ltd.
23. Health Care System and Management: Policies and Programmes
(New Delhi, 2000), Deep & Deep Publications Pvt. Ltd.
24. Health Care System and Management: Management and Administration
(New Delhi, 2000), Deep & Deep Publications Pvt. Ltd.
25. Heath Care System and Management: Primary Health Care Management
(New Delhi, 2000), Deep & Deep Publications Pvt. Ltd.
26. Management Techniques: Principles and Practices
(New Delhi, 2001), Deep & Deep Publications Pvt. Ltd.
27. Encyclopaedia of Disaster Management in 3 Volumes
(New Delhi, 2001), Deep & Deep Publications Pvt. Ltd.
28. Management of Hospitals: Hospital Core Services
(New Delhi, 2002), Deep & Deep Publications Pvt. Ltd.
29. Management of Hospitals: Hospital Supportive Services
(New Delhi, 2002), Deep & Deep Publications Pvt. Ltd.
30. Management of Hospitals: Hospital Preventive and Promotive Services
(New Delhi, 2002), Deep & Deep Publications Pvt. Ltd.
31. Management of Hospitals: Hospital Managerial Services
(New Delhi, 2002), Deep & Deep Publications Pvt. Ltd.
32. Public Personal Administration
(New Delhi, 2002), Deep & Deep Publications Pvt. Ltd.
33. Public Financial Administration
(New Delhi, 2002), Deep & Deep Publications Pvt. Ltd.
34. Urban Development and Management
(New Delhi, 2002), Deep & Deep Publications Pvt. Ltd.
35. Public Administration: Theory and Practices
(New Delhi, 2003), Deep & Deep Publications Pvt. Ltd.
36. Advanced Public Administration (Revised and Enlarged Edition)
(New Delhi, 2003), Deep & Deep Publications Pvt. Ltd.

37. Panchayati Raj in India
(New Delhi, 2003), Deep & Deep Publications Pvt. Ltd.
38. Encyclopedia of Higher Education in 21st Century: Organisation and Structure
(New Delhi, 2004), Deep & Deep Publications Pvt. Ltd.
39. Encyclopaedia of Higher Education in 21st Century: Quality and Excellence
(New Delhi, 2004), Deep & Deep Publications Pvt. Ltd.
40. Encyclopedia of Higher Education in 21st Century, Extension Education Services
(New Delhi, 2004), Deep & Deep Publications Pvt. Ltd.
41. Stress Management and Education: An Indian Perspective
(New Delhi, 2004), Deep & Deep Publications Pvt. Ltd.
42. Human Values and Education:
(New Delhi, 2004), Deep & Deep Publications Pvt. Ltd.
43. Public Health Policy and Administration
(New Delhi, 2004), Deep & Deep Publications Pvt. Ltd.
44. Administration and Management of NGO's: Text and Case Studies
(New Delhi, 2004), Deep & Deep Publications Pvt. Ltd.
45. Nursing Services: Management and Administration
(New Delhi, 2005), Deep & Deep Publications Pvt. Ltd.
46. Population Policy and Family Welfare Administration
(New Delhi, 2005), Deep & Deep Publications Pvt. Ltd.
47. Human Resource Development in 21st Century
(New Delhi, 2005), Deep & Deep Publications Pvt. Ltd.
48. Encyclopaedia of Disaster Management (3 Volumes)
(New Delhi, 2006) Deep & Deep Publications Pvt. Ltd.
49. School Health Education
(New Delhi, 2007), Deep & Deep Publications Pvt. Ltd.
50. Health Education: Theory and Practices
(New Delhi, 2007), Deep & Deep Publications Pvt. Ltd.
51. Good Governance: An Integral Views
(New Delhi, 2007), Deep & Deep Publications Pvt. Ltd.
52. Right to Information and Good Governance
(New Delhi, 2007), Deep & Deep Publications Pvt. Ltd.
53. Disaster Management: Text and Case Studies
(New Delhi, 2007), Deep & Deep Publications Pvt. Ltd.
54. Hospital Administration: Theory and Practices
(New Delhi, 2007), Deep & Deep Publications Pvt. Ltd.
55. Environmental Health Values and Education,
(New Delhi, 2008), Deep & Deep Publications Pvt. Ltd.

56. Administrative and Management Thinkers: Revelvance in New Millennium
(New Delhi, 2008), Deep & Deep Publications Pvt. Ltd.
57. Principles and Practices of Human Values
(New Delhi, 2008), Deep & Deep Publications Pvt. Ltd.
58. Distance Education: Principles, Potentialities and Perspectives
(New Delhi, 2008), Deep & Deep Publications Pvt. Ltd.
59. Educational Administration and Management: An Integral View
(New Delhi, 2008), Deep & Deep Publications Pvt. Ltd.
60. Women Health Education
(New Delhi, 2008), Deep & Deep Publications Pvt. Ltd.
61. Health Care System and Hospital Administration
Vol. 1 (Organizational Structure)
(New Delhi, 2008), Deep & Deep Publications Pvt. Ltd.
62. Health Care System and Hospital Administration
Vol. 2 (Resources: Human, Finance and Material)
(New Delhi, 2008), Deep & Deep Publications Pvt. Ltd.
63. Health Care System and Hospital Administration
Vol. 3 (Policy-making and Programmes)
(New Delhi, 2008), Deep & Deep Publications Pvt. Ltd.
64. Health Care System and Hospital Administration
Vol. 4 (Emerging and Thrust Areas)
(New Delhi, 2008), Deep & Deep Publications Pvt. Ltd.
65. Health Care System and Hospital Administration
Vol. 5 (Primary/Rural Health Care)
(New Delhi, 2008), Deep & Deep Publications Pvt. Ltd.
66. Health Care System and Hospital Administration
Vol. 6 (Secondary and Tertiary Health Care)
(New Delhi, 2008), Deep & Deep Publications Pvt. Ltd.
67. Health Care System and Hospital Administration
Vol. 7 (Management Techniques and Good Governance)
(New Delhi, 2008), Deep & Deep Publications Pvt. Ltd.
68. Education of Lifestyle and Lifetime Diseases
(Deep & Deep Publications Pvt. Ltd.)
69. Health Education Administration—From International Level to Village Level
(Deep & Deep Publications Pvt. Ltd.)
70. Education for Healthy Urban Cities
(Deep & Deep Publications Pvt. Ltd.)
71. Rural Health Education
(Deep & Deep Publications Pvt. Ltd.)

Bibliography

Acton Society Trust, Hospitals and the State: Hospital Organisation and Administration under the National Health Service Series, London: Action Society Trust, 1956, 54p.

Acton Society Trust, Hospitals and the State: Hospital Organisation and Administration under the National Health Service, London: The Trust, 1959, iii, 80p.

Andhra Pradesh, Health and Local Administration Department Panchayats Executive Officers Regulations relating to Recruitment, etc., Hyderabad: The Author, 1956, l6p.

Bannington, B.G., English Public Health Administration, 2nd ed., London: P.S. King, 1929, 325p.

Berkov, Robert, The World Health Organisation: A Study in Decentralized International Administration, Geneva Droz, 1957, 173p.

Better Health by Community Projects Administration, Planning Commission, New Delhi: Community Projects, Planning Commission, n.d., 32p.

Blum, Henrik L., Public Administration: A Public Health Viewpoint, N.Y.: Macmillan, 1963, 532p.

Hugh Flanagan and Peter Spurgeon, Public Sector Managerial Effectiveness: Theory and Practice in the National Health Service, Buckingham: Open Univ. Press, 1996, 128p.

Freeman, Ruth B., Administration of Public Health Services and Edward M. Holmes, Philadelphia: Saunders, 1960, 507p.

Goddard, H.A., Principles of Administration Applied to Nursing Service by H.A. Goddard, Geneva: World Health Organisation, 1958, 106p.

Goel, Rajneesh, Community Health Care, New Delhi: Deep & Deep Publications Pvt. Ltd., 2004, 403p.

Goel, S.L., Health and Care Administration: Policy-making and Planning, Delhi: Sterling, 1980, 288p.

Goel, S.L, Health Care Administration: Ecology, Principles and Modern Trends, Delhi: Sterling, 1980, 233p.

Goel, S.L., Health Care Administration: Levels and Aspects, Delhi: Sterling, 1980, 245p.

Goel, S.L., Health Care System and Management, New Delhi: Deep & Deep Publications Pvt. Ltd., 2004, 4 Vols.

Goel, S.L., International Administration: WHO South-East Asia Regional Office, Delhi: Sterling, 1977, 344p.

Goel, S.L., Population Policy and Family Welfare: Reproductive and Child Health Administration, New Delhi: Deep & Deep Publications Pvt. Ltd., 2005, 526p.

Goel, S.L., Public Health Administration, Delhi: Sterling, 1984, 472p.

Goel, S.L, Public Health Policy and Administration, New Delhi: Deep & Deep Publications Pvt. Ltd., 2005, 651p.

Graduate Study in Public Administration: A Guide to Graduate Programs by Office of Education, Department of Health, Education and Welfare, Washington: United States Government Printing Office, 1961, 158+p.

Greenfield, Margert, State-Local Service for Mental Health, Bureau of Public Administration, Berkeley: The Bureau, 1955, 93p.

Guangde, Sun, Health Care Administration in China, Westport: Greenport, 1993, pp. 53-62.

Handbook on Human Services Administration, edited by Jack Rabin and Marcia B. Steinhauer, New York: Marcel Dekker, 1988, 604p.

Health Policy Research in South Asia: Building Capacity for Reform, edited by Abdo S. Yazbeck and David H. Peters, Washington, D.C.: World Bank, 2003, 428p.

Heaver, Richard, Managing Primary Health Care: Implications of the Health Transition, Washington, D.C.: World Bank, 1995, 41p.

Health Status of the Underprivileged, New Delhi: Centre for Urban Studies, Indian Institute of Public Administration, 1991, 225p.

Indian Institute of Public Administration, Centre for Urban Studies, Urban Health System, edited by P.K. Umashankar and Girish K. Misra, New Delhi: Reliance and IIPA, 1993, 259p.

Institute for Training in Municipal Administration, Administration of Community Health Services, Chicago: ICMA, 1961, 560p.

Johnston, Timothy, Investing in Health: Development Effectiveness in the Health, Nutrition, and Population Sector, Washington, D.C.: World Bank, 1999, 69p.

Khandewale, Shreekant V., Health Administration and the Weaker Sections in an Indian Metropolis, Delhi: Devika, 1996, 231p.

Klinoubol, Kriengkrai, Public Health Development and Administration: A Study of Developing Economy, Delhi: Deep & Deep Publications Pvt. Ltd., 1989. 436p.

Local Self-Government Administration in States of India, 1956, New Delhi: Ministry of Health, 1956, 149p.

Local Self-government Administration in States of India, 1962, Ministry of Health, Delhi: The Manager of Publications, 1962, 161+p.

Legislature Committee on Local Administration by Health, Education and Local Administration Department, Madras, Madras: Health, Education and Local Administration Department, 1958, 5 Parts.

Morden, Margaret Gorsuch, Cooperative Health Administration in Metropolitan, Los Angeles: The Bureau, 1949, 52p.

Panchayat Manual, Madras: Health, Education and Local Administration Department, 1956, 368+p.

Papers in Public Administration, No. 6, Ann Arbor: The Bureau, 1950, 85p.

Public Services M.B.A. Induction Module: India-U.K. context (August-September, 1999: Indian Institute of Public Administration, New Delhi), Gender-related Issues (course material), New Dèlhi: Indian Institute of Public Administration, 1999, vp.

Report of the Regional Training Seminar on Social Security Administration, New Delhi: Regional Office for Asia and Oceania, 1979, 75p.

Rowbottom, R., Hospital Organisation: A Progress Report on the Brunel Health Services Project, London: Heinemann, 1973, 3l4p.

Survey of Research in Public Administration, 1980-90, edited by V.A. Pai Panandiker, Delhi: Konark, 1997, 631p.

Tebow, Hilda P., Staff-Development as an Integral Part of Administration, Washington, D.C.: Department of Health, Education and Welfare, 1959, 33+p.

The Indo-US Symposium on Community Mental Health at National Institute of Mental Health and Neuro Sciences, Bangalore: National Institute of Mental Health and Neuro Sciences, 1992, 520p.

Weaver, Jerry L., Conflict and Control in Health Care Administration, Beverly Hills: n.p., 1975, 197p.

Welfare Administration and Social Welfare Around the World, by Department of Health, Education and Welfare, United States, Washington: Government Printing Office, 1963, 9p.

Wishwakarma, R.K., Health Status of the Underprivileged, New Delhi: Centre for Urban Studies, Indian Institute of Public Administration, 1993, 283p.

Index